Hacker Disassembling Uncovered

HACKER
DISASSEMBLING
UNCOVERED

Kris Kaspersky

alist

A-LIST, LLC
295 East Swedesford Rd.
PMB #285
Wayne, PA 19087
702-977-5377 (FAX)
mail@alistpublishing.com
http://www.alistpublishing.com

This book is printed on acid-free paper.

Hacker Disassembling Uncovered
By Kris Kaspersky

ISBN 1-931769-22-2

Printed in the United States of America

04 7 6 5 4

A-LIST, LLC titles are available for site license or bulk purchase by institutions, user groups, corporations, etc.

Executive Editor: Natalia Tarkova
Book Editor: Julie Laing

Contents

Preface

This book opens the door to the wonderful world of security mechanisms, showing you how protection is created, and then bypassed. It is addressed to anyone who likes captivating puzzles, and to anyone who spends their spare (or office) time rummaging in the depths of programs and operating systems. Lastly, it is for anyone who is engaged constantly or incidentally in writing protections, and who wants to know how to counteract ubiquitous hackers competently and reliably.

This book is devoted to hacking basics — to the skills needed for working with a debugger and a disassembler. The methods of identifying and reconstructing the key structures of the source language — functions (including virtual ones), local and global variables, branches, cycles, objects and their hierarchies, mathematical operators, etc. — are described in detail.

Choosing the tools you will need to use this book is essentially a matter of your personal preferences. Tastes differ. Therefore, don't take everything that I mention below to be carved in stone, but rather as advice. To use this book, you'll need the following:

❑ A *debugger* — **SoftIce**, version 3.25 or higher
❑ A *disassembler* — **IDA** version 3.7*x* (I recommend 3.8; 4.*x* is even better)
❑ A *HEX editor* — any version of **HIEW**
❑ *Development kits* — **SDK** and **DDK** (the last one isn't mandatory, but is really good to have)
❑ An *operating system* — any Windows, but **Windows 2000** or later is strongly recommended
❑ A *compiler* — whichever C/C++ or Pascal compiler you like most (in the book, you'll find a detailed description of the particular features of the Microsoft Visual C++, Borland C++, Watcom C, GNU C, and Free Pascal compilers, although we will mostly work with Microsoft Visual C++ 6.0)

Now, let's talk about all this in more detail:

❑ *SoftIce*. The SoftIce debugger is the hacker's main weapon. There are also free programs — WINDEB from Microsoft, and TRW from LiuTaoTao — but SoftIce is much better, and handier, than all these taken together. Almost any version of Ice will suit our purposes; I use version 3.26 — it's time-tested, maintains its stability, and gets along wonderfully with Windows 2000. The modern 4.*x* version isn't very friendly with my video adapter (Matrox Millennium G450), and in general goes belly up from time to time. Apart from this, among all the new capabilities of the fourth version, only the support of *Frame Point Omission* (FPO) (see the *"Local Stack Variables"* section) is particularly useful for working with the local variables directly addressed through the ESP register. This is an undoubtedly practical feature, but we can do without it if we must. Buy it; you won't regret it. (Hacking isn't the same as piracy, and nobody has yet cancelled honesty.)

❑ *IDA Pro*. The most powerful disassembler in the world is undoubtedly IDA. It's certainly possible to live without it, but it's much better to live with it. IDA provides convenient facilities for navigating the investigated text; automatically recognizes library functions and local variables, including those addressed through ESP; and supports many processors and file formats. In a word, a hacker without IDA isn't a hacker. But I suppose advertising it really isn't necessary. The only problem is, how do you get this IDA? Pirated discs containing it are extremely rare (the latest version I've seen was 3.74, and it was unstable); Internet sites offer it even less often. IDA's developer quickly stops any attempt at unauthorized distribution of the product. The only reliable way to obtain it is to purchase it from the developer (**http//www.idapro.com**) or from an official distributor. Unfortunately, no documentation comes with the disassembler (except for the built-in help, which is very terse and unsystematic).

❑ *HIEW*. HIEW is not only a HEX editor; it is a disassembler, an assembler, and an encrypter all in one. It won't save you from having to buy IDA, but it will more than compensate for IDA in certain cases. (IDA works very slowly, and it's vexing to waste a whole bunch of time if all we need is to take a quick glance at the file under preparation.) However, the main purpose of HIEW isn't disassembling, but *bit hacking* — small surgical interference in a binary file, usually with the aim of cutting off part of the protection mechanism without which it can't function.

☐ *SDK (Software Development Kit — a package for the application developer).* The main thing that we need from the SDK package is documentation on the Win32 API and the DUMPBIN utility for working with PE files. Neither hackers nor developers can do without documentation. At the minimum, you need to know the prototypes and the purpose of the main system functions. This information can be gathered from numerous books on programming, but no book can boast of completeness and depth of presentation. Therefore, sooner or later, you'll have to use an SDK. How can you get an SDK? SDK is a part of MSDN, and MSDN is issued quarterly on compact discs, and is distributed by subscription. (You can learn more about subscription conditions on the official site **http//msdn.microsoft.com**.) MSDN also comes with the Microsoft Visual C++ 6.0 compiler. (It's not a particularly new one, but it will suffice for going through this book.)

☐ *DDK (Driver Development Kit — a package for a developer of drivers).* What is the use of a DDK package for a hacker? It'll help to clear up how the driver is made, how it works, and how can it be cracked. Apart from the basic documentation and plenty of samples, it includes a very valuable file — *NTDDK.h*. This file contains definitions for most of the undocumented structures, and is literally loaded with comments revealing certain curious details of the system's operation. The tools that come with the DDK will also be of use. Among other things, you'll find the WINDEB debugger included in the DDK. This is a rather good debugger, but nowhere near as good as SoftIce; therefore, it is not considered in this book. (If you can't find Ice, WINDEB will do.) The MASM assembler in which drivers are written will be useful, as will certain little programs that make the hacker's life a bit easier. The latest DDK version can be downloaded *for free* from Microsoft's site; just keep in mind that the size of the complete DDK for NT is over 40 MB (packed), and even more space is required on the disk.

☐ *Operating system.* I'm not going to force my own tastes and predilections on the reader; nevertheless, I strongly recommend that you install **Windows 2000** or a later version. My motivation here is that it's a very stable and steadily working operating system, which courageously withstands severe application errors. One thing about a hacker's work is that this surgical interference in the depths of programs quite often makes them go crazy, which results in the unpredictable behavior of the cracked application. Windows 9*x* operating systems, showing their corporative solidarity, frequently "go on strike" alongside the frozen program. Occasionally, the computer will require rebooting dozens of times a day! You should consider yourself lucky if rebooting suffices, and you don't need to restore disks that were destroyed by failure. (This also happens, although seldom.) It's much more difficult to freeze Windows 2000. I "succeed" in doing this no more than twice a month when I haven't had enough sleep, or am negligent. What's more, Windows 2000 allows you to load SoftIce at any moment, without rebooting the system, which is very convenient! Lastly, all the material in this book implies the use of Windows 2000 or a later version, and I rarely mention how it differs from other systems.

I assume that you are already familiar with the assembler. If you don't write programs in this language, you should at least understand what registers, segments, machine instructions, and the like are. Otherwise, this book will likely be too complex and difficult to understand. I suggest that you first find a tutorial on the assembler and thoroughly study it.

Apart from assembler, you should have at least a general notion of the operating system.

And it might be useful if you download all the documentation on processors available from the Intel and AMD sites.

I guess that's enough organizational stuff. Let's get going.

Part I: Getting Acquainted with Basic Hacking Techniques

Introduction

Protection Classifications

Checking *authenticity* is the "heart" of the overwhelming majority of protection mechanisms. In all cases, we have to make sure that the person working with our program is who he or she claims to be, and that this person is authorized to work with the program. The word "person" might mean not only a user, but the user's computer or the medium that stores a licensed copy of the program. Thus, all protection mechanisms can be divided into two main categories:

❏ Protection based on *knowledge* (of a password, serial number, etc.)
❏ Protection based on *possession* (of a key disc, documentation, etc.)

Knowledge-based protection is useless if a legitimate owner isn't interested in keeping the secret. An owner can give the password (and/or serial number) to whomever he or she likes, and thus anyone can use a program with such protection on his or her computer.

Therefore, password protection against illegal copying is not effective. Why, then, do practically all prominent software manufacturers use serial numbers? The answer is simple — to protect their intellectual property with the threat (however unlikely) of brute force. The idea goes approximately as follows: The quiet, work-a-day environment of a certain company is suddenly broken into by a squad of agents dressed in camouflage, comparing the Windows license numbers (Microsoft Office, Microsoft Visual Studio) to license agreements. If they find even one illegal copy, some official pops up seemingly from out of nowhere and starts to joyfully rub his or her hands in anticipation of the expected windfall. At best, they'll force the company to buy all the illegal copies. At worst...

Naturally, nobody is barging in on users in their homes, and nobody is even considering it (yet) — your house is still your castle. Besides, what can you get from a domestic user? A wide distribution of products is good for manufacturers, and who can distribute better than pirates? Even in that case, serial numbers aren't superfluous — unregistered users cannot use technical support, which may push them to purchase legal versions.

Such protection is ideal for giant corporations, but it isn't suitable for small groups of programmers or individual developers, especially if they earn their bread by writing highly specialized programs for a limited market (say, star spectra analysis, or modeling nuclear reactions). Since they cannot apply sufficient pressure, it's unreal for them to ask users to check their licenses, and it's hardly possible to "beat" the payment out of illegal users. All that can be done is through threat and eloquence.

In this case, protection based on the possession of some unique subject that is extremely difficult to copy, or impossible to copy in general (the ideal case), is more appropriate. The first of this kind were key floppies with information written on them in such a manner that copying the floppy disk was impossible. The simplest way (but not the best) to prepare such a floppy was to gently damage the disk with a nail (an awl, a penknife), and then, having determined the sector in which the defect was located (by writing and reading any test information — up until a certain point, reading will proceed normally, followed by "garbage"), register it in the program. Then, each time the program started, it checked whether the defect was located in the same place or not. When floppy disks became less popular, the same technique was used with compact discs. The more affluent cripple their discs with a laser, while ordinary folk still use an awl or nail.

Thus, the program is rigidly bound to a disc, and requires its presence to run. Since copying such a disc is impossible (just try making identical defects on a copy), pirates have to give up.

Other possession-based protection mechanisms frequently modify the subject of possession, limiting the number of program starts or the duration of its use. Such a mechanism is often used in installers. So as to not irritate users, the key is only requested once, when the program is installed, and it's possible to work without the key. If the number of installations is limited, the damage arising from unauthorized installation of one copy on several computers can be slight.

The problem is that all of this deprives a legal user of his or her rights. Who wants to limit the number of installations? (Some people reinstall the operating system and software each month or even several times a day). In addition, key discs are not recognized by all types of drives, and are frequently "invisible" devices on the network. If the protection mechanism accesses the equipment directly, bypassing drivers in order to thwart hackers' attacks more effectively, such a program definitely won't run under Windows NT/2000, and will probably fail under Windows 9*x*. (This is, of course, if it wasn't designed appropriately beforehand. But such a case is even worse, since protection executing with the highest privileges can cause considerable damage to the system.) Apart from that, the key item can be lost, stolen, or just stop working correctly. (Floppy disks are inclined to demagnetize and develop bad clusters, CDs can get scratched, and electronic keys can "burn out".)

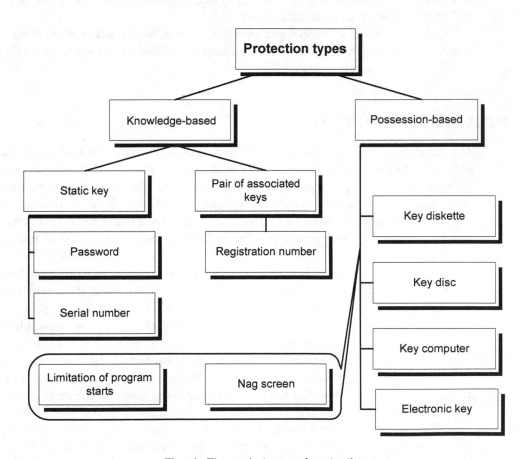

Fig. 1. The main types of protection

Naturally, these considerations concern the effectiveness of keys in thwarting hackers, and not the concept of keys in general. End users are none the better for this! If protection causes inconveniences, users would rather visit the nearest pirate and buy illegal software. Speeches on morals, ethics, respectability, and so on won't have any effect. Shame on you, developers! Why make users' lives even more complicated? Users are human beings too!

That said, protections based on registration numbers have been gaining popularity: Once run for the first time, the program binds itself to the computer, turns on a "counter," and sometimes blocks certain functionalities. To make the program fully functional, you have to enter a password from the developer in exchange for monetary compensation. To prevent pirate copying, the password is often a derivative of key parameters of the user's computer (or a derivative of their user name, in an elementary case).

Certainly, this brief overview of protection types has left many of them out, but a detailed discussion of protection classifications is beyond the scope of this book. We'll leave it for a second volume.

Protection Strength

If protection is based on the assumption that its code won't be investigated and/or changed, it's poor protection. Concealing the source code isn't an insurmountable obstacle to studying and modifying the application. Modern reverse engineering techniques automatically recognize library functions, local variables, stack arguments, data types, branches, loops, etc. And, in the near future, disassemblers will probably be able to generate code similar in appearance to that of high-level languages.

But, even today, analyzing machine code isn't so complex as to stop hackers for long. The overwhelming number of constant cracks is the best testament to this. Ideally, knowing the protection algorithm shouldn't influence the protection's strength, but this is not always possible to achieve. For example, if a server application has a limitation on the number of simultaneous connections in a demo version (which frequently happens), all a hacker needs to do is find the instruction of the process carrying out this check and delete it. Modification of a program can be detected and prevented by testing the checksum regularly; however, the code that calculates the checksum and compares it to a particular value can be found and deleted.

However many protection levels there are — one or one million — the program *can* be cracked! It's only a matter of time and effort. But, when there are no effective laws protecting intellectual property, developers must rely on protection more than law-enforcement bodies. There's a common opinion that if the expense of neutralizing protection isn't lower than the cost of a legal copy, nobody will crack it. This is wrong! Material gain isn't the only motivation for a hacker. Much stronger motivation appears to lie in the *intellectual struggle* (who's more clever: the protection developer or me?), the *competition* (which hacker can crack more programs?), *curiosity* (what makes it tick?), *advancing one's own skills* (to create protections, you first need to learn how to crack them), and simply as an *interesting way to spend one's time.* Many young hackers spend weeks removing the protection from a program that only costs a few dollars, or even one distributed free of charge.

The usefulness of protection is limited to its competition — other things being equal, clients always select unprotected products, even if the protection doesn't restrain the client's rights. Nowadays, the demand for programmers considerably exceeds supply, but, in the distant future, developers should either come to an agreement or completely refuse to offer protection. Thus, protection experts will be forced to look for other work.

This doesn't mean that this book is useless; on the contrary, the knowledge that it provides should be applied as soon as possible, while the need for protection hasn't disappeared yet.

Step One: Warming up

The algorithm of simplest authentication consists of a character-by-character comparison of the password entered by a user to the reference value stored either in the program (which frequently happens), or outside of it — for example, in a configuration file or the registry (which happens less often).

The advantage of such protection is its extremely simple software implementation. Its core is actually only one line of code that, in the C language, could be written as follows: *if (strcmp (password entered, reference password)) {/* Password is incorrect */} else {/* Password is OK*/}.*

Let's supplement this code with procedures to prompt for a password and display the comparison, and then examine the program for its vulnerability to cracking.

Listing 1. The Simplest System of Authentication

```
// Matching the password character by character

#include <stdio.h>
#include <string.h>

#define PASSWORD_SIZE 100
#define PASSWORD        "myGOODpassword\n"
// The CR above is needed
// so as not to cut off
```

```
// the user-entered CR.

int main()
{
// The counter for authentication failures
int count=0;
// The buffer for the user-entered password
char buff[PASSWORD_SIZE];

// The main authentication loop
for(;;)
{
// Prompting the user for a password
// and reading it
printf("Enter password:");
fgets(&buff[0],PASSWORD_SIZE,stdin);

// Matching the entered password against the reference value
if (strcmp(&buff[0],PASSWORD))
// "Scolding" if the passwords don't match;
printf("Wrong password\n");
// otherwise (if the passwords are identical),
// getting out of the authentication loop
else break;

// Incrementing the counter of authentication failures
// and terminating the program if 3 attempts have been used
if (++count>3) return -1;
}

// Once we're here, the user has entered the right password.
printf("Password OK\n");
}
```

In popular movies, cool hackers easily penetrate heavily protected systems by guessing the required password in just a few attempts. Can we do this in the real world?

Passwords can be common words, like "Ferrari," "QWERTY," or names of pet hamsters, geographical locations, etc. However, guessing the password is like looking for a needle in a haystack, and there's no guarantee of success — we can only hope that we get lucky. And lady luck, as we all know, can't be trifled with. Is there a more reliable way to crack this code?

Let's think. If the reference password is stored in the program, and isn't ciphered in some artful manner, it can be found by simply looking at the binary code. Looking at all the text strings, especially those that look like a password, we'll quickly find the required key and easily "open" the program!

The area in which we need to look can be narrowed down using the fact that, in the overwhelming majority of cases, compilers put initialized variables in the data segment (in PE files, in the .data section). The only exception is, perhaps, early Borland compilers, with their maniacal passion for putting text strings in the code segment — directly where they're used. This simplifies the compiler, but creates a lot of problems. Modern operating systems, as opposed to our old friend MS-DOS, prohibit modifying the code segment. Therefore, all variables allocated in it are read-only. Apart from this, on processors with a separate caching system (Pentiums, for example), these string "litter" the code cache, loaded during read ahead and, when they're called for the first time, loaded again from the slow RAM (L2 cache) into the data cache. The result is slower operation and a drop in performance.

So, let's assume it's in the data section. Now, we just need a handy instrument to view the binary file. You can press <F3> in your favorite shell (FAR, DOS Navigator) and, by pressing the <Page Down> key admire the digits scrolling down until it bores you. You can also use a hex-editor (QVIEW, HIEW, etc.) but, in this book, for presentation purposes, I'll use the DUMPBIN utility supplied with Microsoft Visual Studio.

Let's print out the data section (the key is /SECTION:.data) as raw data (the key is /RAWDATA:BYTES), having specified the ">" character for redirecting the output to a file. (The response occupies a lot of space, and only its "tail" would find room on the screen.)

```
> dumpbin /RAWDATA:BYTES /SECTION:.data simple.exe >filename
```

```
RAW DATA #3
00406000: 00 00 00 00 00 00 00 00 00 00 00 00 3B 11 40 00   ............;.@.
00406010: 64 40 40 00 00 00 00 00 00 00 00 00 70 11 40 00   d@@.........p.@.
00406020: 00 00 00 00 00 00 00 00 00 00 00 00 00 00 00 00   ................
00406030: 45 6E 74 65 72 20 70 61 73 73 77 6F 72 64 3A 00   Enter password:.
00406040: 6D 79 47 4F 4F 44 70 61 73 73 77 6F 72 64 0A 00   myGOODpassword..
00406050: 57 72 6F 6E 67 20 70 61 73 73 77 6F 72 64 0A 00   Wrong password..
00406060: 50 61 73 73 77 6F 72 64 20 4F 4B 0A 00 00 00 00   Password OK.....
00406070: 40 6E 40 00 00 00 00 00 40 6E 40 00 01 01 00 00   @n@.....@n@.....
```

Look! In the middle of the other stuff, there's a string that is similar to a reference password (it's printed in bold). Shall we try it? It seems likely we need not even bother: Judging from the source code, it really is the password. The compiler has selected too prominent of a place in which to store it — it wouldn't be such a bad idea to hide the reference password better.

One of the ways to do this is to manually place the reference password value in a section that we choose ourselves. The ability to define the location isn't standard, and, consequently, each compiler (strictly speaking, not actually the compiler, but the linker — but that isn't really important) is free to implement it in any way (or not implement it at all). In Microsoft Visual C++, a special pragma — **data_seg** — is used for this, and indicates in which section the initialized variables following it should be placed. By default, unassigned variables are placed in the **.bbs** section, and are controlled by the **bss_seg** pragma.

Let's add the following lines to Listing 1, and see how they run.

```
int count=0;
// From now on, all the initialized variables will be
// located in the .kpnc section.
#pragma data_seg(."kpnc")
// Note that the period before the name
// isn't mandatory, just customary.
char passwd[]=PASSWORD;
#pragma data_seg()
// Now all the initialized variables will again
// be located in the section by default (i.e., ."data").
char buff[PASSWORD_SIZE]="";
...
if (strcmp(&buff[0],&passwd[0]))


> dumpbin /RAWDATA:BYTES /SECTION:.data simple2.exe >filename

RAW DATA #3
  00406000: 00 00 00 00 00 00 00 00 00 00 00 00 45 11 40 00  ............E.@.
  00406010: 04 41 40 00 00 00 00 00 00 00 00 00 40 12 40 00  .A@.........@.@.
  00406020: 00 00 00 00 00 00 00 00 00 00 00 00 00 00 00 00  ................
  00406030: 45 6E 74 65 72 20 70 61 73 73 77 6F 72 64 3A 00  Enter password:.
  00406040: 57 72 6F 6E 67 20 70 61 73 73 77 6F 72 64 0A 00  Wrong password..
  00406050: 50 61 73 73 77 6F 72 64 20 4F 4B 0A 00 00 00 00  Password OK.....
  00406060: 20 6E 40 00 00 00 00 00 20 6E 40 00 01 01 00 00  n@..... n@.....
  00406070: 00 00 00 00 00 00 00 00 00 00 10 00 00 00 00 00  ................
```

Aha! Now, there's no password in the data section and hackers' attack has been retarded. But don't jump to conclusions. Simply display the list of sections in the file:

```
> dumpbin simple2.exe
```

```
Summary
2000 .data
1000 .kpnc
1000 .rdata
4000 .text
```

The nonstandard section `.kpnc` attracts our attention right away. Well, shall we check to see what's in it?

```
dumpbin /SECTION:.kpnc /RAWDATA simple2.exe
```

```
RAW DATA #4
  00408000: 6D 79 47 4F 4F 44 70 61 73 73 77 6F 72 64 0A 00   myGOODpassword..
```

There's the password! And we thought we hid it. It's certainly possible to put confidential data into a section of noninitialized data (`.bss`), the service RTL section (`.rdata`), or even into the code section (`.text`) — not everyone will look there for the password, and such allocation won't disturb the functioning of the program. But you shouldn't forget about the possibility of an automated search for text strings in a binary file. Wherever the reference password may be, such a filter will easily find it. (The only problem is determining which text string holds the required key; most likely, a dozen or so possible "candidates" will need to be tried.)

If the password is written in Unicode, the search is somewhat more complicated, since not all such utilities support this encoding. But it'd be rather naïve to hope that this obstacle will stop a hacker for long.

Step Two: Getting Acquainted with the Disassembler

In the previous step, we found the password. But how tiresome it is to enter the password each time you start the program! It wouldn't be a bad idea to hack the program so that no password is requested, or so that any password is accepted.

Hack?! It's not difficult. It's tougher to know *what to hack with*. A huge variety of hacker tools exists: disassemblers, debuggers, spyware such as API and message loggers, file (port, registry) call monitors, decompressors, and so on. How can a novice code digger grasp all of these facilities?

Spies, monitors, and decompressors are auxiliary, "Plan B" utilities. The main hacker weapons are the *disassembler* and the *debugger*.

The purpose of a disassembler is clear from its name. Whereas assembling is the translation of assembly instructions into machine code, disassembling is the translation of machine code into assembly instructions.

However, a disassembler can be used to study more than programs written in the assembler. Its range of application is wide, but not boundless. You may wonder where that boundary lies.

All implementations of programming languages can be divided roughly into the following categories:

❑ *Interpreters* execute a program in the order it was typed by the programmer. In other words, interpreters "chew up" the source code, which can be accessed directly, without using additional resources. To start most BASIC and Perl implementations, you need an interpreter in addition to the source code of the program. This is inconvenient both for users (who, to execute a program of 10 KB, need to install an interpreter of 10 MB) and for developers (who likely don't want to give everyone the entire source code of the program). In addition, syntactic parsing takes a lot of time, which means no interpreter can claim great performance.

❏ *Compilers* behave differently. They "grind" the program into machine code that can be executed directly by the processor, without using the source code or an accessory program such as an interpreter. From a user's point of view, a compiled program is a mash of hexadecimal bytes impossible for nonexperts to understand. This facilitates the development of protection mechanisms: You can only crack the simplest algorithms without deciphering them.

Is it possible to obtain the source code of a program from its machine code? No! Compilation is a unidirectional process. Labels and comments aren't included. (However, we can get the gist of the source code without comments — we are hackers, aren't we?) The main stumbling block is *the ambiguous correspondence of machine instructions to constructions in high-level languages.* Moreover, assembling also is a unidirectional process, and automatic disassembling is impossible in principle. However, we will not cram such details into the heads of novice code diggers; we'll leave this problem for later consideration.

❏ Several software development systems lie between compilers and interpreters. The source code is transformed not to machine code, but rather to code in another interpreted language. To execute this code, the "compiled" file needs its own interpreter. FoxPro, Clipper, numerous dialects of BASIC, and certain other languages are examples.

In this last category, program code is still executed via an interpreter, but all extraneous information — labels, variable names, comments — is removed, and meaningful operator names are replaced with digital codes. This "stone" kills two birds: The intermediate language is tweaked for fast interpretation and is optimized for size beforehand, and the program code becomes unavailable for direct investigation (and/or modification).

Disassembling such programs is impossible — disassemblers only work with machine code, and can't "digest" code in an interpreted language (also known as π code) that they don't understand. The processor can't digest π code either. It can only be executed with an interpreter. But the interpreter is just what the disassembler can digest! By investigating how it works, you can "understand" π code and the purpose of its instructions. It's a laborious process! Interpreters can be so complex, and can occupy so many megabytes, that their analysis can take several months or years. Fortunately, there's no need to analyze *each* program. Many interpreters are identical, and π code does not tend to vary significantly from one version to another — at least, the main parts don't change daily. Therefore, it's possible to create a program to translate π code back to source code. It's not possible to restore names of variables; nevertheless, the listing will be readable.

So, disassemblers are used to investigate compiled programs, and can be applied when analyzing "pseudo-compiled" code. If that's the case, they should be suitable for cracking simple.exe. The only question is which disassembler to use.

Not all disassemblers are identical. There are "intellectuals" that automatically recognize constructions (i.e., prologs and epilogs of functions, local variables, cross-references, etc.). There are also "simpletons" that merely translate machine code into assembly instructions.

Intellectual disassemblers are the most helpful, but don't hurry to these: Begin with a manual analysis. Disassembler tools are not always on hand; therefore, it wouldn't be a bad idea to master working "in field conditions" first. Besides, working with a poor disassembler will emphasize "the taste" of good things.

Let's use the familiar DUMPBIN utility — a true "Swiss Army knife" that has plenty of useful functions, including a disassembler. Let's disassemble the code section (bearing the name .text). Redirect the output to a file, since we certainly won't find room for it on the screen.

```
> dumpbin /SECTION:.text /DISASM simple.exe >.code
```

In less than a second, the .code file is created. It has a size of as much as 300 KB. But the source program was shorter by *hundreds of times*! How much time will it take to clear up this "Greek?" The overwhelming bulk of it has no relation to the protection mechanism; it represents the compiler's standard library functions, which are of no use to us. How can we distinguish these from the "useful" code?

Let's think a bit. We don't know where the procedure to match passwords is located, and we don't know how it works. But we can assert with confidence that one of its arguments is a pointer to the reference password. We just need to find where this password is located in memory. Its address will be stored by the pointer.

Let's have a look at the data section once again (or wherever the password is stored).

```
> dumpbin /SECTION:.data /RAWDATA simple.exe >.data
```

```
RAW DATA #3
  00406000: 00 00 00 00 00 00 00 00 00 00 00 00 7B 11 40 00   ............{.@.
```

```
00406010: 6E 40 40 00 00 00 00 00 00 00 00 00 20 12 40 00    n@@......... .@.
00406020: 00 00 00 00 00 00 00 00 00 00 00 00 00 00 00 00    ................
00406030: 45 6E 74 65 72 20 70 61 73 73 77 6F 72 64 3A 00    Enter password:.
00406040: 6D 79 47 4F 4F 44 70 61 73 73 77 6F 72 64 0A 00    myGOODpassword..
00406050: 57 72 6F 6E 67 20 70 61 73 73 77 6F 72 64 0A 00    Wrong password..
00406060: 50 61 73 73 77 6F 72 64 20 4F 4B 0A 00 00 00 00    Password OK.....
```

Aha! The password is located at the offset 0x406040 (the left column of numbers), so the pointer to it also must equal 0x406040. Let's try to find this number in the disassembled listing by searching with any text editor.

Have you found it? Here it is (printed in bold in the text):

```
00401045: 68 40 60 40 00          push        406040h
0040104A: 8D 55 98                lea         edx, [ebp-68h]
0040104D: 52                      push        edx
0040104E: E8 4D 00 00 00          call        004010A0
00401053: 83 C4 08                add         esp, 8
00401056: 85 C0                   test        eax, eax
00401058: 74 0F                   je          00401069
```

This is one of two arguments of the 0x04010A0 function placed on the stack by the push machine instruction. The second argument is a pointer to a local buffer, probably containing the user-entered password.

Here, we have to deviate from our subject to consider passing parameters in detail. The following ways of passing function arguments are the most common: *via registers* and *via the stack*.

Passing parameters via registers is the fastest way, but it's not free from disadvantages: The number of registers is very limited, and it complicates implementing recursion — calling a function from within its own body. Furthermore, before writing new arguments into registers, we need to save the old values in RAM. In this case, isn't it easier to pass arguments through RAM without being tormented by registers?

Most compilers pass arguments via the stack. Compilers have standard way of passing arguments. There are at least two different mechanisms:

❏ The *C convention* pushes arguments onto the stack from right to left (i.e., the first argument of the function is placed on the stack last, and thus appears on top). Deleting arguments from the stack is entrusted not to the function, but to the code calling the function. This is wasteful because each function call makes the program heavier by several bytes. However, it allows us to create functions with a variable number of arguments because the calling code knows the exact number of arguments passed.

The stack usually is cleared by the instruction ADD ESP,xxx, where xxx is the number of bytes to be deleted. Since, in 32-bit mode, each argument as a rule occupies 4 bytes, the number of function arguments is calculated in this way: n_args = $\frac{xxx}{4}$. Optimizing compilers can be more eloquent. To clear a stack of several arguments, they often pop them into unused registers with the POP instruction. Alternatively, an optimizing compiler clears at the time it deems most convenient, rather than immediately after exiting a function.

❑ The *Pascal convention* pushes arguments on the stack from left to right (i.e., the first argument of the function is placed on the stack first, and thus appears on the bottom). The deletion of function arguments is entrusted to the function itself, and is usually performed by the RET xxx instruction (i.e., return from the subroutine and pop xxx bytes from the stack).

The value returned by the function is passed through the EAX register (or EDX:EAX when returning 64-bit variables) in both conventions.

Since our program was written in C, and pushes arguments from right to left, its source code may look like this:

```
(*0x4010A0) (ebp-68, "myGOODpassword")
```

We can be convinced that there are two arguments, not six or ten, by looking at the ADD ESP,8 instruction that immediately follows the CALL:

```
0040104E: E8 4D 00 00 00     call        004010A0
00401053: 83 C4 08           add         esp, 8
```

Now, we only need to understand the goal of the 0x4010A0 function — although, if we used our brains, we'd see this is unnecessary! It's clear that this function checks the password; otherwise, why would the password be passed to it? *How* the function does this is a question of minor importance. What we're really interested in is the return value of the function. So, let's proceed to the following line:

```
00401056: 85 C0              test        eax, eax
00401058: 74 0F              je          00401069
```

What do we see? The TEST EAX,EAX instruction checks if value returned by the function equals zero. If it does, the JE instruction following it jumps to line 0x401096. Otherwise (i.e., if EAX !=0):

```
0040105A: 68 50 60 40 00     push        406050h
```

It seems to be a pointer, doesn't it? Let's verify that assumption by looking at the data segment:

```
00406050: 57 72 6F 6E 67 20 70 61 73 73 77 6F 72 64 0A 00   Wrong password..
```

We are almost there. The pointer has led us to the "Wrong password" string, which the next function outputs to the screen. Therefore, a nonzero EAX value indicates a wrong password, and a zero value indicates a correct one.

OK, let's look at the branch of the program that handles a valid password.

```
0040105F: E8 D0 01 00 00      call        00401234
00401064: 83 C4 04            add         esp, 4
00401067: EB 02               jmp         0040106B
00401069: EB 16               jmp         00401081
...
00401081: 68 60 60 40 00      push        406060h
00401086: E8 A9 01 00 00      call        00401234
```

Well, we see one more pointer. The 0x401234 function was already encountered; it's (presumably) used for string output. We can find the strings in the data segment. This time, "Password OK" is referenced.

The following are some working suggestions: If we replace the JE instruction with JNE, the program will reject the real password as incorrect, and all incorrect passwords will be accepted. If we replace TEST EAX,EAX with XOR EAX,EAX, upon executing this instruction, the EAX register will always contain zero, no matter what password is entered.

Just a trifle remains: to find these bytes in the executable file and correct them.

Step Three: Surgery

Direct modification of an executable file is a serious task. We are restricted by the existing code in that we can't move instructions apart or "push" them together, having thrown away "superfluous parts" of the protection. The offsets of all other instructions would shift, while the values of pointers and jump addresses would remain the same, and thus would point to the wrong spot.

It's rather simple to cope with the elimination of "spare parts." Just stuff the code with NOP instructions (whose opcode is 0x90, not 0x0, as many novice code diggers seem to think), that is, with an empty operation (since, generally, NOP is simply another form of the XCHG EAX,EAX instruction). Things are much more complicated when we move instructions apart! Fortunately, in PE files, "holes" always remain after alignment, which we can fill with our code or data.

But isn't it easier to simply compile the assembled file after we make the required changes? No, it isn't: If an assembler can't recognize pointers passed to a function (as we saw, our disassembler can't distinguish them from constants), it can't correct them properly, and the program won't run.

Therefore, we have to "dissect" the "live" program. The easiest way to do this is to use the HIEW utility that "digests" PE files, and thus simplifies the search for the necessary fragment. Launch it with the executable file name in the command line (hiew simple.exe). Then, press the <Enter> key two times, switch to assembler mode, and press the <F5> key to proceed to the required address. As you may recall, the TEST instruction that checks the string-comparison result returned by the function is located at 0x401056.

```
0040104E: E8 4D 00 00 00      call         004010A0
00401053: 83 C4 08            add          esp, 8
00401056: 85 C0               test         eax, eax
00401058: 74 0F               je           00401069
```

So that HIEW is able to distinguish the address from the offset in the file itself, precede this address with a dot: .401056.

```
00401056: 85C0                test         eax, eax
00401058: 740F                je           00401069    -------- (1)
```

Now, press the <F3> key to switch HIEW to edit mode. Place the cursor at the TEST EAX,EAX instruction, press the <Enter> key, and replace it with XOR EAX,EAX.

```
00001056: 33C0                xor          eax, eax
00001058: 740F                je           00401069
```

Because the new instruction fits exactly in the place of the previous one, press the <F9> key to save the changes to disk, and quit HIEW. Start the program and enter the first password that comes to mind.

```
> simple.exe
Enter password:Hi, blockhead!
Password OK
```

The protection has fallen! But what would we do if HIEW did not know how to "digest" PE files? We'd have to use a context search. Look at the hex dump that the disassembler displays to the left of the assembly instructions. If you try to find the 85 C0 sequence — the TEST EAX,EAX instruction — you won't come up with anything useful: There can be hundreds or more of these TEST instructions in a program. The ADD ESP,8\TEST EAX,EAX combination also is common, since it represents many typical constructions in C: if (func(arg1,arg2))..., if (!func(arg1,arg2))..., while(func(arg1,arg2), etc. The jump address likely will be different at various branches in the program; therefore, the ADD ESP,8/TEST EAX,EAX/JE 00401069 substring has a good chance of being unique. Let's try to find the code that corresponds to it: 83 C4 08 85 C0 74 0F. (To do this, just press the <F7> key in HIEW.)

Yippee! Only one entry is found, and that's just what we need. Now, let's try to modify the file directly in hex mode, without using the assembler. Note that inverting the lower bit of the instruction code results in inverting the condition for branching (i.e., 74 JE → 75 JNE).

It works, doesn't it? (Has the protection gone mad? It doesn't recognize valid passwords, but it welcomes all others.) It's wonderful!

Now, we need to clear up which bytes have changed. For this, we need an original copy of the file we modified (which we prudently saved before editing), and any file "comparer." Today, the most popular ones are **c2u** by *Professor Nimnull* and **MakeCrk** from *Doctor Stein's Labs*. The first is the better of the two; it more precisely meets the most popular "standard," and it knows how to generate the extended XCK format. At worst, we can use the utility that comes with MS-DOS/Windows — fc.exe (an abbreviation of *File Compare*).

Start your favorite comparer, and look at the differences between the original and modified executables.

```
> fc simple.exe simple.ex_ > simple.dif
```
———— differences file
———— hacked file
———— original file

```
> type simple.dif
Comparing files simple.exe and SIMPLE.EX_
00001058: 74 75
```

The left column shows the offset of a byte from the beginning of the file, the second column shows the contents of the byte in the original file, and the third column contains the byte's value after modification. Let's compare that to the report generated by the c2u utility.

```
> c2u simple.exe simple.ex_
```

Corrections are written to the *.crx file, where "*" is the name of the original file. Let's consider the result more closely.

```
>type simple.crx
```

[BeginXCK]————————————————————————
- **Description**   : $) 1996 by Professor Nimnul
- **Crack subject** :
- **Used packer**   : None/UnKn0wN/WWPACK/PKLITE/AINEXE/DIET/EXEPACK/PRO-PACK/LZEXE
- **Used unpacker** : None/UNP/X-TRACT/iNTRUDER/AUT0Hack/CUP/TR0N
- **Comments**   :
- **Target OS**   : D0S/WiN/WNT/W95/0S¤/UNX
- **Protection**   : [████▓▓▓▓▓▓▓▓▓▓▓▓▓▓] %17
- **Type of hack** : Bit hack/JMP Correction
- **Language**   : UnKn0wN/Turbo/Borland/Quick/MS/Visual C/C++/Pascal/Assembler
- **Size**   : 28672
- **Price**   : $000

```
■ Used tools    : TD386 v3.2, HiEW 5.13, C2U/486 v0.10
■ Time for hack : 00:00:00
■ Crack made at : 21-07-2001 12:34:21
■ Under Music   : iRON MAiDEN
[BeginCRA]────────────────────────────────────
Difference(s) between simple.exe & simple.ex_
SIMPLE.EXE
00001058: 74 75
[EndCRA]──────────────────────────────────────
[EndXCK]──────────────────────────────────────
```

The result is the same; there simply is an additional text-file header explaining what kind of a beast this is. The collection of fields differs from one hacker to another. If you want, you can add your own fields or delete someone else's. However, I don't recommend doing that without a good reason. Besides, it's better to adhere to one template. Let's use the one just shown.

Description is simply an explanation. In our case, this may look like this: "Test cracking No. 1."

Crack subject is what we've just cracked. Let's write: "Password protection of simple.exe."

Used packer is the type of packer. In the days of good old MS-DOS, packers were widely used to automatically decompress executable files into memory when they were launched. Thus, disk space was economized (recall the ridiculously small hard disks at the end of the 1980s and the beginning of the 1990s), while protection was strengthened. A packed file cannot be directly investigated nor edited. Before you do anything with the file, you have to unpack it. Both the hacker and users of the CRK file have to do the same. Since our file wasn't packed, we'll leave this field empty or write "None" in it.

Used unpacker is the recommended unpacker. Not all unpackers are identical; many packers provide advanced protection and skillfully resist attempts to remove it. Therefore, unpackers are not simple things. An "intelligent" unpacker easily deals with "tough" packers, but it often has difficulty with simple protection, or vice versa. If an unpacker isn't required, leave this field blank or write "None."

Comments is used to list additional tasks the user should perform before cracking (for example, removing the "system" attribute from the file, or, conversely, setting it). However, additional operations are only required in extreme cases; therefore, this field is usually filled with boasts. (Sometimes you'll even find obscenities concerning the mental abilities of the protection developer.)

Target OS is the operating system for which the cracked product is intended, and *in which the hacker tested it*. The program won't necessarily run under all of the same systems after cracking. For example, Windows 9*x* always ignores the checksum field, but Windows NT doesn't; therefore, if you haven't corrected it, you won't be able to run the cracked program using Windows NT. In our case, the checksum of the PE file header is equal to zero. (This depends on the compiler.) This means the file integrity isn't checked, and the hack will work in Windows NT/9*x*.

Protection is a "respectability level" evaluated as a percentage. Generally, 100% corresponds to the upper limit of the mental abilities of a hacker, but who would ever admit that? It's not surprising that the "respectability level" is usually underestimated, occasionally ten times or more. ("Look everybody! What a cool hacker I am; cracking whatever I like is as easy as A-B-C!")

Type of hack is more useful for other hackers than for users who don't understand protection and hack types. There's no universal classification. The most commonly used term, *bit-hack*, means cracking by changing one or more bits in one or more bytes. A particular case of a bit-hack is the JMP correction — changing the address or condition of a jump (as we've just done). Another term, *NOP-ing*, refers to a bit-hack that replaces certain instructions with the NOP instruction, or inserts insignificant instructions. For example, to erase a two-byte JZ xxx instruction, a combination of two one-byte INC EAX/DEC EAX instructions can be used.

Language or, to be more accurate, the compiler, is the programming environment in which the program was written. In our case, it was Microsoft Visual C++. (We know this because we compiled the program.) How do we know the environment of someone else's program? The first thing that comes to mind is to look in the file for copyrights: They are left by many compilers, including Visual C++. Look for "000053d9:Microsoft Visual C++ Runtime Library." If compilers aren't specified, run the file through IDA. It automatically recognizes most standard libraries, and even indicates particular versions. As a last resort, try to determine the language in which the code was written, taking into account C and Pascal conventions and familiar compiler features. (Each compiler has its own "handwriting." An experienced hacker can figure out how a program was compiled and even discover the optimization key.

Size refers to the size of the cracked program, which is useful for controlling the version. (Different versions of the program often differ in size.) It is determined automatically by the c2u utility; you don't need to specify it manually.

Price refers to the price of a licensed copy of the program. (The user should know how much money the crack has saved him or her.)

Used tools are the instruments used. Not filling in this field is considered bad form — it's interesting to know what instruments were used to hack the program.

This is especially true for users who believe that if they get a hold of these DUMPBIN and HIEW thingies, the protection will fall by itself.

Time for hack is the time spent hacking, including breaks for having a smoke and getting a drink. What percentage of people fills in this field accurately, without trying to look "cool?" It can be given little credence.

Crack made at is the timestamp for the completion of the crack. It's generated automatically, and you don't need to correct it (unless you get up with the sun, want to pretend you are a night owl, and set the time of completion to 3 a.m.).

Under Music is the music that you were listening to when hacking. (It's a pity that there's no field for the name of your pet hamster.) Were you listening to music while hacking? If you were, write it down — let everyone know your inspiration.

Now, we should have the following:

```
[BeginXCK]─────────────────────────────────
■ Description    : Test cracking No. 1
■ Crack subject  : Password protection of simple.exe
■ Used packer    : None
■ Used unpacker  : None
■ Comments       : Hello, sailor! Been at sea a bit too long?
■ Target OS      : WNT/W95
■ Protection     : [▓▓▓▓▓▓▓▓▓▓▓▓▓▓▓▓▓▓▓▓] %1
■ Type of hack   : JMP Correction
■ Language       : Visual C/C++
■ Size           : 28672
■ Price          : $000
■ Used tools     : DUMPBIN, HiEW 6.05, C2U/486 v0.10 & Brain
■ Time for hack  : 00:10:00
■ Crack made at  : 21-07-2001 12:34:21
■ Under Music    : Paul Mauriat L'Ete Indien "Africa"
[BeginCRA]─────────────────────────────────
Difference(s) between simple.exe & simple.ex_
SIMPLE.EXE
00001058: 74 75
[EndCRA]───────────────────────────────────
[EndXCK]───────────────────────────────────
```

To change the same bytes in the original program, we need another utility to do what the CRK (XCRK) file specifies. There are a lot of such utilities nowadays, which adversely affects their compatibility with various CRK formats. The most popular are **cra386** by *Professor Nimnull* and **pcracker** by *Doctor Stein's Labs.*

Of the products for Windows, **Patch Maker** has an advanced user interface (Fig. 2). It includes a file comparer, crk editor, hex editor (for manual corrections?), and crk compiler to generate executable files and save users the trouble of figuring out the crack and how to do it.

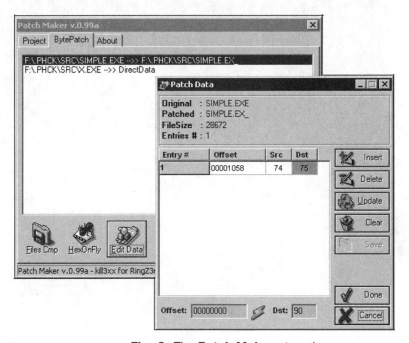

Fig. 2. The **Patch Maker** at work

Some users may find such an interface convenient, but most hackers can't stand the mouse; they prefer console applications and the keyboard.

Step Four: Getting Acquainted with the Debugger

Debugging was initially the step-by-step execution of code, which is also called *tracing*. Today, programs have become so inflated that tracing them is senseless — you'll sink into a whirlpool of nested procedures, and you won't even understand what they do. A debugger isn't the best way to understand a program; an interactive disassembler (IDA, for example) copes better with this task.

We'll defer a detailed consideration of the debugger for a while. (See the section "*Counteracting Debuggers.*") For now, we will focus on the main functions. Using debuggers efficiently is impossible without understanding the following:

❑ Tracing write/read/execute addresses, also called *breakpoints*

❑ Tracing write/read calls to input/output ports (which can no longer be used for protection with modern operating systems because they forbid applications such low-level hardware access — that is now the prerogative of drivers, where protection is seldom implemented)

❑ Tracing the loading of the dynamic link library (DLL) and the calling of certain functions, including system components (which, as we'll see later, is the main weapon of the present-day hacker)

❑ Tracing program/hardware interrupts (which is not particularly relevant, since protection rarely plays with interrupts)

❑ Tracing messages sent to windows and context searches in memory

So far, you don't need to know how the debugger works; you only need to realize that a debugger can do all of these things. However, it is important to know which debugger to use. Turbo Debugger, although widely known, is primitive, and few hackers use it.

The most powerful and universal tool is SoftIce, now available for all Windows platforms. (Some time ago, it only supported Windows 95, not Windows NT.) The fourth version, the latest available when I was writing this, did not work well with my video adapter. Therefore, I had to confine myself to the earlier 3.25 version, which is more reliable.

Method 0: Cracking the Original Password

Using the wldr utility delivered with SoftIce, load the file to be cracked by specifying its name on the command line, for example, as follows:

```
> wldr simple.exe
```

Yes, wldr is a 16-bit loader, and NuMega recommends that you use its 32-bit version, loader32, developed for Windows NT/9x. They have a point, but loader32 often malfunctions. (In particular, it does not always stop at the first line of the program.) However, wldr works with 32-bit applications, and the only disadvantage is that it doesn't support long file names.

If the debugger is configured correctly, a black textbox appears — a surprise to beginners. Command.com in the era of graphical interfaces! Why not? It's faster to type a command than to search for it in a long chain of nested submenus, trying to recollect where you saw it last. Besides, language is the natural means to express thoughts; a menu is best suited for listing dishes at a cafe. As an example, try to print the list of files in a directory using Windows Explorer. Have you succeeded? In MS-DOS, it was simple: dir > PRN.

If you only see INVALID in the text box (this will probably be the case), don't get confused: Windows simply hasn't yet allocated the executable file in memory. You just need to press the <F10> key (an analog of the P command that traces without entering, or stepping over, the function) or the <F8> key (an analog of the T command that traces and enters, or steps into, the function). Everything will fall into place.

```
001B:00401277  INVALID
001B:00401279  INVALID
001B:0040127B  INVALID
```

```
001B:0040127D  INVALID
:P

001b:00401285  push   ebx
001b:00401286  push   esi
001b:00401287  push   edi
001b:00401288  mov    [ebp-18], esp
001B:0040128B  call   [KERNEL32!GetVersion]
001b:00401291  xor    edx, edx
001b:00401293  mov    dl, ah
001b:00401295  mov    [0040692c], edx
```

Pay attention: Unlike the DUMPBIN disassembler, SoftIce recognizes system function names, thus significantly simplifying analysis. However, there's no need to analyze the entire program. Let's quickly try to find the protection mechanism and, without going into detail, chop it off altogether. This is easy to say — and even easier to do! Just recall where the reference password is located in memory. Umm... Is your memory failing? Can you remember the exact address? We'll have to find it!

We'll ask the map32 command for help. It displays the memory map of a selected module. (Our module has the name "simple," the name of the executable file without its extension.)

```
:map32 simple
Owner     Obj Name  Obj#  Address         Size      Type
simple    .text     0001  001B:00401000   00003F66  CODE   RO
simple    .rdata    0002  0023:00405000   0000081E  IDATA  RO
simple    .data     0003  0023:00406000   00001E44  IDATA  RW
```

Here is the address of the beginning of the .data section. (Hopefully you remember that the password is in the .data section.) Now, create the data window using the wc command. Then, issue the d 23:406000 command, and press the <ALT>+<D> key combination to get to the desired window. Scroll using the <↓> key, or put a brick on the <Page Down> key. We won't need to search long.

```
0023:00406040  6D 79 47 4F 4F 44 70 61-73 73 77 6F 72 64 0A 00  myGOODpassword...
0023:00406050  57 72 6F 6E 67 20 70 61-73 73 77 6F 72 64 0A 00  Wrong password..
0023:00406060  50 61 73 73 77 6F 72 64-20 4F 4B 0A 00 00 00 00  Password OK.....
0023:00406070  47 6E 40 00 00 00 00 00-40 6E 40 00 01 01 00 00  Gn@.....@n@.....
0023:00406080  00 00 00 00 00 00 00 00-00 10 00 00 00 00 00 00  ................
0023:00406090  00 00 00 00 00 00 00 00-00 00 00 00 02 00 00 00  ................
```

```
0023:004060A0 01 00 00 00 00 00 00 00-00 00 00 00 00 00 00 00   ................
0023:004060B0 00 00 00 00 00 00 00 00-00 00 00 00 02 00 00 00   ................
```

We've got it! Remember that to be checked, the user-entered password needs to be compared to the model value. By setting a breakpoint at the instruction for reading address 0x406040, we will catch the comparison "by its tail." No sooner said than done.

```
:bpm 406040
```

Now, press the <Ctrl>+<D> key combination (or issue the x command) to exit the debugger. Enter any password that comes to mind — KPNC++, for example. The debugger pops up immediately:

```
001B:004010B0  mov    eax, [edx]
001B:004010B2  cmp    al, [ecx]
001B:004010B4  jnz    004010E4                           (JUMP ↑)
001B:004010B6  or     al, al
001B:004010B8  jz     004010E0
001B:004010BA  cmp    ah, [ECX+01]
001B:004010BD  jnz    004010E4
001B:004010BF  or     ah, ah
Break due to BPMB #0023:00406040 RW DR3   (ET=752.27 milliseconds)
  MSR LastBranchFromIp=0040104E
   MSR LastBranchToIp=004010A0
```

Because of certain architectural features of Intel processors, the break is activated *after* the instruction has been executed (i.e., CS:EIP points to the following executable instruction — to JNZ 004010E4, in our case). Therefore, the memory location with our breakpoint was addressed by the CMP AL, [ECX] instruction. What is in AL? Let's look at the line above: MOV EAX, [EDX]. We can assume that ECX contains a pointer to the string with the reference password (because it caused the break in execution). This means EDX must be a pointer to the password entered by the user. Let's verify our assumption.

```
:d edx
0023:00406040 6D 79 47 4F 4F 44 70 61-73 73 77 6F 72 64 0A 00   myGOODpassword..
:d edx
0023:0012FF18 4B 50 4E 43 2B 2B 0A 00-00 00 00 00 00 00 00 00   KPNC++..........
```

We were right. Now, the only question is how to crack this. We might replace JNZ with JZ, or more elegantly replace EDX with ECX — then the reference password will be compared to itself! Wait a minute... We shouldn't hurry. What if we aren't in the protection routine, but in the library function (actually, in strcmp)? Changing it will result in the program perceiving *any* strings as identical, not just the reference and entered passwords. It won't hurt our example, in which strcmp was only called once, but it would cause normal, fully functional applications to fail. What can be done?

Let's exit strcmp and change the IF that determines whether or not the password is right. For this purpose, P RET is used (to trace until the RET instruction occurs — returning from the function).

```
:P RET
001B:0040104E  call    004010A0
001B:00401053  add     esp, 08
001B:00401056  test    eax, eax
001B:00401058  jz      00401069
001B:0040105A  push    00406050
001B:0040105F  call    00401234
001B:00401064  add     esp, 04
001B:00401067  jmp     0040106B
```

This is familiar. We were previously here with the disassembler. We can take the same steps now: Replace the TEST instruction with XOR, or write the sequence of bytes that identifies... Just a moment. Where are our bytes, the hexadecimal instructions? SoftIce doesn't display them by default, but the CODE ON command forces it to do so.

```
code on
001B:0040104E  E84D000000       call    004010A0
001B:00401053  83C408           add     esp, 08
001B:00401056  85C0             test    eax, eax
001B:00401058  740F             jz      00401069
001B:0040105A  6850604000       push    00406050
001B:0040105F  E8D0010000       call    00401234
001B:00401064  83C404           add     esp, 04
001B:00401067  EB02             jmp     0040106B
```

That's better. But how can we be sure that these bytes will be in the executable file at the same addresses? The question isn't as silly as it may seem. Try to crack the example *crackme0x03* using the method just given. At first, it seems similar to *simple.exe* — even the reference password is located at the same address. Let's set a breakpoint on it, wait for the debugger to pop up, exit the comparing procedure, and look at the code identical to the one we previously came across.

```
001B:0042104E  E87D000000        call    004210D0
001B:00421053  83C408            add     esp, 08
001B:00421056  85C0              test    eax, eax
001B:00421058  740F              jz      00421069
```

Start HIEW, jump to address 0x421053, and... Oops; HIEW is upset with us. It says there's no such address in the file! The last byte ends at 0x407FFF. How can we be at 0x421053 in the debugger but not in the file? Perhaps we're in the body of a Windows system function. But Windows system functions are located much higher — beginning at 0x80000000.

The PE file could be loaded at a different address than the one for which it was created. (This property is called *relocatability*.) The system automatically corrects references to absolute addresses, replacing them with new values. As a result, the file image in memory doesn't correspond to the one written on disk. How can we find the place that needs to be corrected now?

This task is partly facilitated by the system loader, which only can relocate DLLs and always tries to load executable files at their "native" addresses. If this is impossible, loading is interrupted and an error message is sent. Likely, we are dealing with a DLL loaded by the protection we are investigating. Why are DLLs here, and where did they come from?

We'll have to study Listing 2 to find out.

Listing 2. The Source Code of *crackme0x03*

```
#include <stdio.h>
#include <windows.h>


__declspec(dllexport) void Demo()
{
    #define PASSWORD_SIZE 100
    #define PASSWORD        "myGOODpassword\n"

    int count=0;
    char buff[PASSWORD_SIZE]="";

    for(;;)
```

```
    {
    printf("Enter password:");
    fgets(&buff[0], PASSWORD_SIZE-1, stdin);

    if (strcmp(&buff[0], PASSWORD))
    printf("Wrong password\n");
    else break;

    if (++count>2) return -1;
    }
    printf("Password OK\n");
}

main()
{
HMODULE hmod;
void (*zzz)();

if ((hmod=LoadLibrary("crack0~1.exe"))
&& (zzz=(void (*)())GetProcAddress(h,"Demo")))
zzz();

}
```

What a way to call a function! This technique exports it directly from the executable file and loads the same file as a DLL. (Yes, the same file can be both the executable application and the DLL.)

"It doesn't make a difference," a naïve programmer might object. "Everyone knows that Windows isn't so silly as to load the same file twice. LoadLibrary will return the base address of the *crackme0x03* module, but won't allocate memory for it." Nothing of the sort! An artful protection scheme accesses the file by its alternate short name, leaving the system loader in a deep delusion.

The system allocates memory and returns the base address of the loaded module to the hmod variable. The code and data of this module are displaced by the hmod value — the base address of the module with which HIEW and the disassembler work. We can easily figure out the base address: Just call DUMPBIN with the /HEADERS key. (Only a fragment of its response is given.)

```
>dumpbin /HEADERS crack0x03
OPTIONAL HEADER VALUES
        ...
        400000 image base
        ...
```

Hence, the base address is 0x400000 (in bytes). We can determine the load address using the mod -u command in the debugger. (The -u key allows us to display only application modules, not system ones.)

```
:mod -u
hMod Base       PEHeader Module Name    File Name
     00400000 004000D8 crack0x0        \.PHCK\src\crack0x03.exe
     00420000 004200D8 crack0x0        \.PHCK\src\crack0x03.exe
     77E80000 77E800D0 kernel32        \WINNT\system32\kernel32.dll
     77F80000 77F800C0 ntdll           \WINNT\system32\ntdll.dll
```

Two copies of *crack0x03* are loaded at once, and the last one is located at 0x420000 — just what we need! Now, it's easy to calculate that the address 0x421056 (the one we tried to find in the cracked file) "on disk" corresponds to the address 0x421056 - (0x42000 - 0x400000) = 0x421056 - 0x20000 = 0x401056. Let's take a look at that location:

```
00401056: 85C0                         test    eax, eax
00401058: 740F                         je      .000401069   -------- (1)
```

Everything is as expected — see how well it matches the dump produced by the debugger:

```
001B:00421056  85C0                    test    eax, eax
001B:00421058  740F                    jz      00421069
```

This calculation technique is applicable to any DLL, not just to those representing executable files.

If, instead of tracing the addresses, we used the debugger on the program being cracked to look for the sequence of bytes taken from the debugger, including the one in CALL 00422040, would we find the sequence?

```
001B:0042104E  E87D000000              call    004210D0
001B:00421053  83C408                  add     esp, 08
001B:00421056  85C0                    test    eax, eax
001B:00421058  740F                    jz      00421069
:File image in memory
```

```
.0040104E: E87D000000          call     .0004010D0   -------- (1)
.00401053: 83C408             add      esp, 008 ;"□"
.00401056: 85C0               test     eax, eax
.00401058: 740F               je       .000401069   -------- (2)
:File image on disk
```

The same machine code — E8 7D 00 00 00 — corresponds to the CALL 0x4210D0 and CALL 0x4010D0 instructions. How can this be? Here's how: The operand of the 0xE8 processor instruction does not represent the offset of a subroutine; it represents *the difference between the offsets of the subroutine and the instruction next to the CALL instruction*. Therefore, in the first case, 0x421053 (the offset of the instruction next to CALL) + 0x0000007D (don't forget about the reverse byte order in double words) = 0x4210D0 — the required address. Thus, when the load address is changed, we don't need to correct the CALL instruction.

In the *crack0x03* example, the following line is also in another location (which can be found using HIEW):

```
004012C5: 89154C694000                   mov        [00040694C], edx
```

The MOV instruction uses absolute addressing, rather than indirect. What will happen if you change the load address of the module? Will the file image on disk and that in memory be identical in this case?

Looking at the address 0x4212C5 (0x4012C5 + 0x2000) using the debugger, we see that the call does not go to 0x42694C, but to 0x40694C! Our module intrudes in another's domain, modifying it as it likes. This can quickly lead to a system crash! In this case, it doesn't crash, but only because the line being accessed is located in the Startup procedure (in start code), has already been executed (when the application started), and isn't called from the loaded module. It would be another matter altogether if the Demo() function accessed a static variable; the compiler, having substituted its offset, would make the module unrelocatable! It's hard to imagine how DLLs, whose load address isn't known beforehand, manage to work. But there are at least two solutions.

The first is to use indirect addressing instead of direct (for example, [reg+offset_val], where reg is a register containing the base load address, and offset_val is the offset of the memory location from the beginning of the module). This will allow the module to be loaded at any address, but the loss of just one register will appreciably lower the program's performance.

The second is to instruct the loader to correct direct offsets according to a selected base load address. This will slightly slow loading, but it won't affect the speed of the program. This doesn't mean that load time can be neglected; this method simply is preferred by Microsoft.

The problem is distinguishing actual direct offsets from constants that have the same value. It'd be silly to decompile a DLL just to clear up which locations we need to tweak. It's much easier to list the addresses in a special table, bearing the name `Relocation [Fix Up] table`, directly in the loaded file. The linker is responsible for creating it. Each DLL contains such a table.

To get acquainted with the table, compile and study the following listing.

Listing 3. The Source Code of *fixupdemo.c*

```
::fixupdemo.c
__declspec(dllexport) void meme(int x)
{
    static int a=0x666;
    a = x;
}
> cl fixupdemo.c /LD
```

Compile the code, then decompile it right away using "DUMPBIN/DISASM fixupdemo.dll" and "DUMPBIN/SECTION:.data/RAWDATA".

```
10001000: 55                  push      ebp
10001001: 8B EC               mov       ebp, esp
10001003: 8B 45 08            mov       eax, dword ptr [ebp+8]
10001006: A3 30 50 00 10      mov       [10005030], eax
1000100B: 5D                  pop       ebp
1000100C: C3                  ret
```

```
RAW DATA #3
10005000: 00 00 00 00 00 00 00 00 00 00 00 00 33 24 00 10   ............3$..
10005010: 00 00 00 00 00 00 00 00 00 00 00 00 00 00 00 00   ................
10005020: 00 00 00 00 00 00 00 00 00 00 00 00 00 00 00 00   ................
10005030: 66 06 00 00 64 11 00 10 FF FF FF FF 00 00 00 00   f...d..........
```

Judging by the code, the contents of EAX are always written to 0x10005030. Nevertheless, don't jump to conclusions! Try "DUMPBIN/RELOCATIONS fixupdemo.dll".

```
BASE RELOCATIONS #4
        1000 RVA,        154 SizeOfBlock
               7 HIGHLOW
              1C HIGHLOW
```

```
23 HIGHLOW
32 HIGHLOW
3A HIGHLOW
```

The relocation table isn't empty! Its first entry points to the location `0x100001007`, obtained by adding the offset `0x7` with the RVA address `0x1000` and the base load address `0x10000000` (found using DUMPBIN). The location `0x100001007` belongs to the `MOV [0x10005030]`, `EAX` instruction, and it points to the highest byte of the direct offset. This offset is corrected by the loader while linking the DLL (if required).

Want to check? Let's create two copies of one DLL (such as `fixupdemo.dll` and `fixupdemo2.dll`) and load them one by one using the following program:

Listing 4. The Source Code of *fixupload.c*

```
::fixupload.c
#include <windows.h>

main()
{
    void (*demo) (int a);
    HMODULE h;
    if ((h=LoadLibrary("fixupdemo.dll")) &&
        (h=LoadLibrary("fixupdemo2.dll")) &&
        (demo=(void (*) (int a))GetProcAddress(h, "meme")))
        demo(0x777);
}
> cl fixupload
```

Since we can't load two different DLLs at the same address (how will the system know it's the same DLL?), the loader has to relocate one. Let's load the compiled program in the debugger, and set a breakpoint at the `LoadLibraryA` function. This is necessary to skip the startup code and get into the `main` function body. (Program execution doesn't start from the `main` function; instead, it starts from the auxiliary code, in which you can easily "drown.") Where did the `A` character at the end of the function name come from? Its roots are closely related to the introduction of Unicode in Windows. (Unicode encodes each character with

2 bytes. Therefore, $2^{16} = 65,536$ symbols, enough to represent practically all of the alphabets of the world.) The `LoadLibrary` name may be written in any language or in many languages simultaneously — in Russian-French-Chinese, for example. This seems tempting, but doesn't it decrease performance? It certainly does, and substantially. There's a price to be paid for Unicode! ASCII encoding suffices in most cases. Why waste precious processor clock ticks? To save performance, size was disregarded, and separate functions were created for Unicode and ASCII characters. The former received the `W` suffix (*Wide*); the latter received `A` (*ASCII*). This subtlety is hidden from programmers: Which function to call — `W` or `A` — is decided by the compiler. However, when you work with the debugger, you should specify the function name — it cannot determine the suffix independently. The stumbling block is that certain functions, such as `ShowWindows`, have no suffixes; their library names are the same as the canonical one. How do we know?

The simplest way is to look up the import table of the file being analyzed, and find your function there. For example, in our case:

```
> DUMPBIN /IMPORTS fixupload.exe > filename
> type filename
          19D  HeapDestroy
          1C2  LoadLibraryA
           CA  GetCommandLineA
          174  GetVersion
           7D  ExitProcess
          29E  TerminateProcess
...
```

From this fragment, you can see that `LoadLibrary` has the `A` suffix. The `ExitProcess` and `TerminateProcess` functions have no because they don't work with strings.

The other way is to look in the SDK. You won't find library names in it, but the *Quick Info* subsections give brief information on Unicode support (if such support is implemented). If Unicode is supported, the `W` or `A` suffix is indicated; if not, there are no suffixes. Shall we check this?

Here's Quick Info on `LoadLibrary`:

```
QuickInfo
  Windows NT: Requires version 3.1 or later.
  Windows: Requires Windows 95 or later.
  Windows CE: Requires version 1.0 or later.
```

Header: Declared in winbase.h.

Import Library: Use kernel32.lib.

Unicode: Implemented as Unicode and ANSI versions on Windows NT.

We now understand the situation for Windows NT, but what about the one for the more common Windows 95/98? A glance at the KERNEL32.DLL export table shows there is such a function. However, looking more closely, we see something surprising: Its entry point coincides with the entry points of ten other functions!

```
ordinal hint RVA       name
    556  1B3 00039031 LoadLibraryW
```

The third column in the DUMPBIN report is the RVA address — the virtual address of the beginning of the function minus the file-loading base address. A simple search shows that it occurs more than once. Using the srcln program-filter to obtain the list of functions, we get the following:

```
  21:       118   1 00039031 AddAtomW
 116:       217  60 00039031 DeleteFileW
 119:       220  63 00039031 DisconnectNamedPipe
 178:       279  9E 00039031 FindAtomW
 204:       305  B8 00039031 FreeEnvironmentStringsW
 260:       361  F0 00039031 GetDriveTypeW
 297:       398 115 00039031 GetModuleHandleW
 341:       442 141 00039031 GetStartupInfoW
 377:       478 165 00039031 GetVersionExW
 384:       485 16C 00039031 GlobalAddAtomW
 389:       490 171 00039031 GlobalFindAtomW
 413:       514 189 00039031 HeapLock
 417:       518 18D 00039031 HeapUnlock
 440:       541 1A4 00039031 IsProcessorFeaturePresent
 455:       556 1B3 00039031 LoadLibraryW
 508:       611 1E8 00039031 OutputDebugStringW
 547:       648 20F 00039031 RemoveDirectoryW
 590:       691 23A 00039031 SetComputerNameW
 592:       693 23C 00039031 SetConsoleCP
 597:       698 241 00039031 SetConsoleOutputCP
 601:       702 245 00039031 SetConsoleTitleW
 605:       706 249 00039031 SetCurrentDirectoryW
 645:       746 271 00039031 SetThreadLocale
 678:       779 292 00039031 TryEnterCriticalSection
```

What a surprise: All Unicode functions live under the same roof. Since it's hard to believe that LoadLibraryW and, say, DeleteFileW are identical, we have to assume that we are dealing with a "stub," which only returns an error. Therefore, the LoadLibraryW function isn't implemented in Windows 9x.

However, let's get back to the subject at hand. Let's open the debugger, set a breakpoint on LoadLibraryA, then quit the debugger and wait for it to pop up. Fortunately, we won't have to wait long.

```
KERNEL32!LoadLibraryA
001B:77E98023  push     ebp
001B:77E98024  mov      ebp, esp
001B:77E98026  push     ebx
001B:77E98027  push     esi
001B:77E98028  push     edi
001B:77E98029  push     77E98054
001B:77E9802E  push     dword ptr [ebp+08]
```

Let's issue the P RET command to exit LoadLibraryA (we really don't need to analyze it), and return to the easily recognizable main function.

```
001B:0040100B  call     [KERNEL32!LoadLibraryA]
001B:00401011  mov      [ebp-08], eax
001B:00401014  cmp      dword ptr [ebp-08], 00
001B:00401018  jz       00401051
001B:0040101A  push     00405040
001B:0040101F  call     [KERNEL32!LoadLibraryA]
001B:00401025  mov      [ebp-08], eax
001B:00401028  cmp      dword ptr [ebp-08], 00
```

Note the value of the EAX register — the function has returned the load address to it (on my computer, 0x10000000). Continuing to trace (using the <F10> key), wait for the second execution of LoadLibraryA. This time, the load address has changed. (On my computer, it now equals 0x0530000.)

We are getting closer to the demo function call. (In the debugger, it looks like PUSH 00000777\ CALL [EBP-04]. The EBP-04 tells us nothing, but the 0x777 argument definitely reminds us of something in Listing 4.) Don't forget to move your finger from the <F10> key to the <F8> key to enter the function.

```
001B:00531000  55       push     ebp
001B:00531001  8BEC     mov      ebp, esp
001B:00531003  8B4508   mov      eax, [ebp+08]
```

```
001B:00531006   A330505300           mov      [00535030], eax
001B:0053100B   5D                   pop      ebp
001B:0053100C   C3                   ret
```

That's it! The system loader corrected the address according to the base address of loading the DLL itself. This is how it should work. However, there's one problem — neither that location, nor the sequence A3 30 50 53 00, is in the original DLL, which we can easily see via a context search. How can we find this instruction in the original DLL? Perhaps we'd like to replace it with NOPs.

Let's look a little bit higher — at instructions that don't contain relocatable elements: PUSH EBP/MOV EBP, ESP/MOV EAX, [EBP+08]. Why not look for the sequence 55 8B EC xxx A3? In this case, it'll work but, if the relocatable elements were densely packed with "normal" ones, we wouldn't find it. The short sequence would produce many false hits.

A more reliable way to find the contents of relocatable elements is to subtract the difference between the actual and recommended load address from them: 0x535030 (the address modified by the loader) – (0x530000 (the base loading address) – 0x10000000 (the recommended loading address)) = 0x10005030. Taking into account the reverse sequence of bytes, the machine code of the MOV [10005030], EAX instruction should look like this: A3 30 50 00 10. If we search for it using HIEW, miracle of miracles, there it is!

Method 1: Searching Directly for the Entered Password in Memory

Storing a password as plain text in the program's body is more of an exception than rule. Hackers are hardly needed if the password can be seen with the naked eye. Therefore, protection developers try to hide it in every possible way. (We'll discuss how they do this later.) Taking into account the size of modern applications, a programmer may place the password in an unremarkable file stuffed with "dummies" — strings that look like a password, but are not. It's unclear what is fake and what isn't, especially because in a project of average size, there may be several hundreds, or even thousands, of suitable strings.

Let's approach the problem from the opposite side — let's not search for the original password, which is unknown to us, but rather for the string that we've fed to the program as the password. Then, let's set a breakpoint on it, and proceed in the same manner as before. The break will follow the watching call. We'll quit the matching procedure, correct JMP, and…

Let's take another look at the *simple.c* source code that we're cracking.

```
for(;;)
{
    printf("Enter password:");
    fgets(&buff[0], PASSWORD_SIZE, stdin);

    if (strcmp(&buff[0], PASSWORD))
        printf("Wrong password\n");
    else break;
    if (++count>2) return -1;
    }
```

Notice that the user-supplied password is read into buff, and compared to the reference password. If no match is made, the password again is requested from the user — but buff isn't cleared before the next attempt. From this, we can see that, if, upon receiving the message Wrong password, we open the debugger and walk through it with a context search, we may find buff.

So, let's begin. Let's start *simple.exe*, enter any password that comes to mind (KPNC Kaspersky ++, for example), ignore the Wrong cry and press <Ctrl>+<D> — the key combination for calling SoftIce. We needn't search blindly: Windows NT/9x isn't Windows 3.x or MS-DOS, with a common address space for all processes. Now, to keep one process from inadvertently intruding on another, each is allotted address space for its exclusive use. For example, process A may have the number 0x66 written at address 23:0146660, process B may have 0x0 written at the *same address*, 23:0146660, and process C may have a third value. Each process — A, B, or C — won't even suspect the existence of the others (unless it uses special resources for interprocessor communication).

You can find a more detailed consideration of all these issues in books by Helen Custer and Jeffrey Richter. Here, we're more worried about another problem: The debugger called by pressing the <Ctrl>+<D> key combination emerges in another process (most likely in Idle), and a context search over memory gives no results. We need to manually switch the debugger to the necessary address space.

From the documentation that comes with SoftIce, you may know that switching contexts is performed by the **ADDR** command, with either the process name truncated to eight characters or its PID. You can get that with another command — PROC. In cases where the process name is syntactically indistinguishable from a PID — "123," for example — we have to use the PID (the second column of digits in the PROC report).

```
:addr simple
```

Now, let's try the `addr simple` command. Nothing happens. Even the registers remain the same! Don't worry; the word "simple" is in the lower-right corner, identifying the current process. Keeping the same register values is just a bug in SoftIce. It ignores them, and only switches addresses. This is why tracing a switched program is impossible. Searching, however, is another matter.

```
:s 23:0 L -1 "KPNC Kaspersky"
```

The first argument after `s` is the search start address, written as `selector:offset`. In Windows 2000, selector `23` is used address data and the stack. In other operating systems, the selector may differ. We can find it by loading any program, and then read the contents of the `DS` register.

In general, starting a search from a zero offset is silly. According to the memory map, the auxiliary code is located there, and will unlikely contain the required password. However, this will do no harm, and will be much faster than trying to figure out the program load address and where to start the search. The third argument — `L-1` — is the length of the area to search, where `-1` means search until successful. Note that we are not searching for the entire string, but only for part of it (`KPNC Kaspersky`, not `KPNC Kaspersky++`). This allows us to get rid of false results. SoftIce likes to display references to its own buffers containing the search template. They are always located above `0x80000000`, where no normal password ever lives. Nevertheless, it'll be more demonstrative if just the string we need is found using an incomplete substring.

```
Pattern found at 0023:00016E40 (00016E40)
```

We found at least one occurrence. But what if there are more of them in memory? Let's check this by issuing `s` commands until the message `Pattern not found` is received, or until the upper search address of `0x80000000` is exceeded.

```
:s
Pattern found at 0023:0013FF18 (0013FF18)
:s
Pattern found at 0023:0024069C (0024069C)
:s
Pattern found at 0023:80B83F18 (80B83F18)
```

We have *three*! Isn't this too much? It would be silly to set all three breakpoints. In this case, four debug-processor registers will suffice, but even three breakpoints are enough to get us lost! What would we do if we found ten matches?

Let's think: Some matches likely result from reading the input via the keyboard and putting characters into the system buffers. This seems plausible. How can we filter out the "interference?"

The memory map will help: Knowing the owner of an area that possesses a buffer, we can say a lot about that buffer. By typing in `map32 simple`, we obtain approximately the following:

```
:map32 simple
Owner       Obj Name   Obj#   Address        Size       Type
simple      .text      0001   001B:00011000  00003F66   CODE  RO
simple      .rdata     0002   0023:00015000  0000081E   IDATA RO
simple      .data      0003   0023:00016000  00001E44   IDATA RW
```

Hurrah! One of the matches belongs to our process. The buffer at address $0x16E40$ belongs to the data segment and is probably what we need. But we shouldn't be hasty; everything may not be as simple as it seems. Let's look for the address $0x16E40$ in the *simple.exe* file. (Taking into account the reverse sequence of bytes, it'll be `40 6E 01 00`.)

```
> dumpbin /SECTION:.data /RAWDATA simple.exe
RAW DATA #3
  00016030: 45 6E 74 65 72 20 70 61 73 73 77 6F 72 64 3A 00   Enter password:.
  00016040: 6D 79 47 4F 4F 44 70 61 73 73 77 6F 72 64 0A 00   myGOODpassword..
  00016050: 57 72 6F 6E 67 20 70 61 73 73 77 6F 72 64 0A 00   Wrong password..
  00016060: 50 61 73 73 77 6F 72 64 20 4F 4B 0A 00 00 00 00   Password OK.....
  00016070: 40 6E 01 00 00 00 00 00 40 6E 01 00 01 01 00 00   @n......@n......
  00016080: 00 00 00 00 00 00 00 00 00 10 00 00 00 00 00 00   ................
```

We found two of them there. Let's see what references the first one by looking for the substring `16070` in the decompiled code.

```
00011032: 68 70 60 01 00      push      16070h
00011037: 6A 64               push      64h ; Max. Password length (== 100 dec)
00011039: 8D 4D 98            lea       ecx, [ebp-68h]
; The pointer to the buffer
; in which the password should be written
0001103C: 51                  push      ecx
0001103D: E8 E2 00 00 00      call      00011124   ; fgets
00011042: 83 C4 0C            add       esp, 0Ch   ; Popping up three arguments
```

It should be clear where we are in the code, except for a mysterious pointer to $0x16070$. In MSDN, where the prototype of the `fgets` function is described, we'll discover "the mysterious stranger" is a pointer to the `FILE` structure. (According to C convention, arguments are pushed onto the stack from right to left.) The first member of the `FILE` structure is the pointer to the buffer. (In the standard C library, the file input/output is buffered with a size of 4 KB by default.) Thus, the address `0x16E40` is a pointer to an auxiliary buffer, and we can cross it off the list of candidates.

Candidate No. 2 is `0x24069C`. It falls outside the data segment. In general, it's not clear to whom it belongs. Remember the heap? Let's see what's there.

```
:heap 32 simple
    Base     Id  Cmmt/Psnt/Rsvd   Segments  Flags      Process
    00140000  01  0003/0003/00FD          1  00000002   simple
    00240000  02  0004/0003/000C          1  00008000   simple
    00300000  03  0008/0007/0008          1  00001003   simple
```

That's it. We just need to clarify who allocated the memory — the system, or the programmer. The first thing that jumps out is the suspicious and strangely undocumented `0x8000` flag. We can find its definition in WINNT.H, but this won't be helpful unless it shows the system using the flag.

```
#define HEAP_PSEUDO_TAG_FLAG              0x8000
```

To be convinced, load any application into the debugger and give the command `heap 32 proc_name`. The system automatically allocates three areas from the heap — exactly like those in our case. This means that this candidate also has led nowhere.

One address remains: `0x13FF18`. Does it remind you of anything? What was the ESP value while loading? It seems that it was `0x13FFC4`. (Note that in Windows 9*x*, the stack is located in another place. Nevertheless, this reasoning also works for it: Just remember the stack location in your own operating system and know how to recognize it.)

Since the stack grows from the bottom up (i.e., from higher addresses to lower ones), the address `0x13FF18` is located on the stack. That's why it's similar to buffers. In addition, most programmers allocate buffers in local variables that, in turn, are allocated on the stack by the compiler.

Shall we try to set a breakpoint here?

```
:bpm 23:13FF18
:x
Break due to BPMB #0023:0013FF18 RW DR3  (ET = 369.65 microseconds)
  MSR LastBranchFromIp = 0001144F
    MSR LastBranchToIp = 00011156

001B:000110B0  mov     eax, [edx]
001B:000110B2  cmp     al, [ecx]
001B:000110B4  jnz     000110E4
```

```
001B:000110B6   or     al, al
001B:000110B8   jz     000110E0
001B:000110BA   cmp    ah, [ecx+01]
001B:000110BD   jnz    000110E4
001B:000110BF   or     ah, ah
```

We're in the body of the comparing procedure, which should be familiar. Let's display the values of the EDX and ECX pointers to find out what is being compared.

```
:d edx
0023:0013FF18 4B 50 4E 43 2D 2D 0A 00-70 65 72 73 6B 79 2B 2B   KPNC Kaspersky++

:d ecx
0023:00016040 6D 79 47 4F 4F 44 70 61-73 73 77 6F 72 64 0A 00   myGOODpassword..
```

We've already discussed everything else that needs to be done. Let's quit the comparing procedure using the P RET command. Then, we need to find a branch, note its address, and correct the executable file. We're done.

You now are acquainted with one common way of cracking protection based on matching passwords. (Later, you'll see that this method is also suitable for cracking protection based on registration numbers.) Its main advantage is its simplicity. There are at least two drawbacks:

❑ If the programmer clears the buffer after making a comparison, a search for the entered password will give nothing unless the system buffers remain. These are difficult to erase. However, it's also difficult to trace the password from system to local buffers!

❑ With the abundance of auxiliary buffers, it can be difficult to find the "right" one. A programmer may allocate the password buffer in the data segment (a static buffer), on the stack (a local buffer), or on the heap. The programmer may even allocate memory using low-level VirtualAlloc calls. As a result, it sometimes appears necessary to go through all obtained occurrences.

Let's analyze another example: *crackme01*. It's the same as *simple.exe* except for its graphic user interface (GUI). Its key procedure looks like this:

Listing 5. The Source Code of the Key Procedure of *crackme01*

```
void CCrackme_01Dlg::OnOK()
{
char buff[PASSWORD_SIZE];
```

```
m_password.GetWindowText(&buff[0],PASSWORD_SIZE);
if (strcmp(&buff[0],PASSWORD))
{
    MessageBox("Wrong password");
    m_password.SetSel(0,-1,0);
    return;
}
else
{

    MessageBox("Password OK");
}
CDialog::OnOK();
}
```

Everything seems straightforward. Enter the password KPNC Kaspersky++ as usual, but before you press the OK button in response to the wrong password dialog, call the debugger and switch the context.

```
:s 23:0 L -1 'KPNC Kaspersky'
Pattern found at 0023:0012F9FC (0012F9FC)
:s
Pattern found at 0023:00139C78 (00139C78)
```

There are two occurrences, and both are on the stack. Let's begin with the first one. Set a breakpoint and wait for the debugger to emerge. The debugger's window does not make us wait long, but it shows some strange code. Press the <x> key to quit. A cascade of windows follows, each less intelligible than the previous one.

We can speculate that the CCrackme_01Dlg::OnOK function is called directly when the **OK** button is pressed: It's allotted part of the stack for local variables, which is deallocated automatically when the function is exited. Thus, the local buffer with the password that we've entered exists only when it is checked, and then it is erased automatically. Our only bit of luck is the modal dialog, which tells us that we entered the wrong password. While it remains on the screen, the buffer still contains the entered password, which can be found in memory. But this does little to help us trace when this buffer will be accessed. We have to sort through the false windows one by one. At last, we see the string we seek in the data window and some intelligent code in the code window.

```
0023:0012F9FC 4B 50 4E 43 20 4B 61 73-70 65 72 73 6B 79 2B 2B   KPNC
Kaspersky++
0023:0012FA0C 00 01 00 00 0D 00 00 00-01 00 1C C0 A8 AF 47 00
.............G.
0023:0012FA1C 10 9B 13 00 78 01 01 00-F0 3E 2F 00 00 00 00 00
....x....>/.....
0023:0012FA2C 01 01 01 00 83 63 E1 77-F0 AD 47 00 78 01 01 00
.....c.w..G.x...
```

```
001B:004013E3  8A10              mov      dl, [eax]
001B:004013E5  8A1E              mov      bl, [esi]
001B:004013E7  8ACA              mov      cl, dl
001B:004013E9  3AD3              cmp      dl, bl
001B:004013EB  751E              jnz      0040140B
001B:004013ED  84C9              test     cl, cl
001B:004013EF  7416              jz       00401407
001B:004013F1  8A5001            mov      dl, [eax+01]
```

Let's see where ESI points.

```
:d esi
0023:0040303C 4D 79 47 6F 6F 64 50 61-73 73 77 6F 72 64 00 00   MyGoodPassword..
```

All that remains is to patch the executable file. Here, more difficulties are waiting for us. First, the compiler has optimized the code, inserting the strcmp code instead of calling it. Second, it's swarming with conditional jumps! It will take a lot of work to find what we need. Let's approach the problem in a scientific way by viewing the disassembled code, or, to be more exact, its key fragment that compares the passwords:

```
>dumpbin /DISASM crackme_01.exe
  004013DA: BE 3C 30 40 00      mov      esi, 40303Ch
  0040303C: 4D 79 47 6F 6F 64 50 61 73 73 77 6F 72 64 00 MyGoodPassword
```

A pointer to the reference password was placed in the ESI register.

```
  004013DF: 8D 44 24 10         lea      eax, [esp+10h]
```

A pointer to the user-supplied password was placed in the EAX register.

```
  004013E3: 8A 16               mov      dl, byte ptr [esi]
  004013E5: 8A 1E               mov      bl, byte ptr [esi]
  004013E7: 8A CA               mov      cl, dl
  004013E9: 3A D3               cmp      dl, bl
```

A comparison was made to the first character.

```
004013EB: 75 1E              jne        0040140B ←---(3) --->  (1)
```

If the first character didn't match, a jump was made. Further checking would be pointless.

```
004013ED: 84 C9              test       cl, cl
```

Did the first character equal zero?

```
004013EF: 74 16              je         00401407 --->  (2)
```

If so, we reached the end of line and the passwords would be identical.

```
004013F1: 8A 50 01           mov        dl, byte ptr [eax+1]
004013F4: 8A 5E 01           mov        bl, byte ptr [esi+1]
004013F7: 8A CA              mov        cl, dl
004013F9: 3A D3              cmp        dl, bl
```

The next pair of characters were checked.

```
004013FB: 75 0E              jne        0040140B --->  (1)
```

If they were not equal, the check was stopped.

```
004013FD: 83 C0 02           add        eax, 2
00401400: 83 C6 02           add        esi, 2
```

The next two characters were examined

```
00401403: 84 C9              test       cl, cl
```

Did we reach the end of line?

```
00401405: 75 DC              jne        004013E3 ->  (3)
```

No, we didn't. Matching was continued.

```
00401407: 33 C0              xor        eax, eax ←---  (2)
00401409: EB 05              jmp        00401410 --->  (4)
```

This shows EAX was cleared (strcmp returns zero if successful) and quit.

```
0040140B: 1B C0              sbb        eax, eax ←---  (3)
0040140D: 83 D8 FF           sbb        eax, 0FFFFFFFFh
```

This branch is executed when the passwords don't match. EAX was set to a nonzero value. (Guess why.)

```
00401410: 85 C0              test       eax, eax ←---  (4)
```

If EAX equaled zero, a check was made.

```
00401412: 6A 00                    push          0
00401414: 6A 00                    push          0
```

Something was placed on the stack.

```
00401416: 74 38                    je            00401450 <<<< ---→(5)
```

A jump was made somewhere.

```
00401418: 68 2C 30 40 00    push          40302Ch
0040302C: 57 72 6F 6E 67 20 70 61 73 73 77 6F 72 64 00 .Wrong password
```

Aha! "Wrong password." (The code that follows isn't of interest; it's just displaying error messages.)

Now that we understand the algorithm, we can crack it (for example, by replacing the conditional jump in line 0x401416 with an short unconditional jump, such as 0xEB).

Method 2: Setting a Breakpoint at the Password Input Function

We can't call the previous method of directly searching for the entered password elegant or practical. Why should we search for the password, stumbling over irregularly scattered buffers, when we can place a breakpoint directly on the function that reads it? Will it be easier to guess which function the developer used?

The operation can be performed with one of just a few functions. Looking them up won't take a lot of time. In particular, editable field contents often are read with GetWindowTextA or, less frequently, with GetDlgItemTextA.

Since we're talking about windows, let's start our GUI *crackme01* example and set a breakpoint at the GetWindowTextA function ("*bpx GetWindowTextA*"). Since this is a system function, the breakpoint will be global (i.e., it will affect all running applications). Therefore, close all unneeded programs. If you set the breakpoint before starting *crackme01*, you'll get several false windows because the system reads the window contents when displaying the dialog.

Let's enter KPNC Kaspersky++ as usual, then press the <Enter> key. The debugger will show up instantly.

```
USER32!GetWindowTextA
001B:77E1A4E2   55                          push     ebp
001B:77E1A4E3   8BEC                        mov      ebp, esp
```

```
001B:77E1A4E5  6AFF               push    FF
001B:77E1A4E7  6870A5E177         push    77E1A570
001B:77E1A4EC  68491DE677         push    77E61D49
001B:77E1A4F1  64A100000000       mov     eax, fs:[00000000]
001B:77E1A4F7  50                 push    eax
```

Many hacking manuals recommend that we immediately quit the function with P RET, saying there's no need to analyze it. But, we needn't hurry! We should clarify where the entered string is located and set a breakpoint at it. Let's look at the arguments the function accepts and the sequence in which it accepts them. (If you don't remember, view the SDK documentation.)

```
int GetWindowText(
  HWND hWnd,          // Handle to window or control with text
  LPTSTR lpString,    // Address of buffer for text
  int nMaxCount       // Maximum number of characters to copy
);
```

If a program is written in C, it may seem that the arguments are written on the stack according to the C convention. Nothing of the kind! All Windows API functions are called according to the Pascal convention, regardless of the language in which the program is written. Thus, arguments are pushed on the stack from left to right, and the last argument onto the stack is the return address. In 32-bit Windows, all arguments and the return address occupy a double word (4 bytes). Therefore, to reach the pointer to the string, you need to add 8 bytes to the stack's top pointer register, or ESP (one double word for nMaxCount, and another one for lpString). This is represented more clearly in Fig. 3.

In SoftIce, you can display the contents of a specified address using the * operator. (See the debugger documentation for more details.)

```
:d *(esp+8)
0023:0012F9FC 1C FA 12 00 3B 5A E1 77-EC 4D E1 77 06 02 05 00   ....;Z.w.M.w....
0023:0012FA0C 01 01 00 00 10 00 00 00-01 00 2A C0 10 A8 48 00   ..........*...H.
0023:0012FA1C 10 9B 13 00 0A 02 04 00-E8 3E 2F 00 00 00 00 00   .........>/.....
0023:0012FA2C 01 02 04 00 83 63 E1 77-08 DE 48 00 0A 02 04 00   .....c.w..H.....
```

The buffer is filled with garbage because the string hasn't been read yet. Let's quit the function with P RET and see what happens. (Note that it will be impossible to use d *esp+8; after we exit the function, its arguments will be pushed off the stack.)

```
: p ret
:d 0012F9FC
```

```
0023:0012F9FC 4B 50 4E 43 20 4B 61 73-70 65 72 73 6B 79 2B 2B  KPNC Kaspersky++
0023:0012FA0C 00 01 00 00 0D 00 00 00-01 00 1C 80 10 A8 48 00  ..............H.
0023:0012FA1C 10 9B 13 00 0A 02 04 00-E8 3E 2F 00 00 00 00 00  .........>/.....
0023:0012FA2C 01 02 04 00 83 63 E1 77-08 DE 48 00 0A 02 04 00  .....c.w..H.....
```

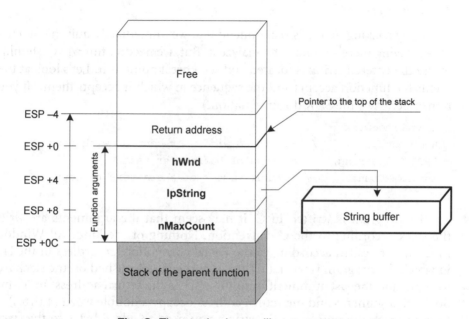

Fig. 3. The stack when calling GetWindowText

This is the buffer we need. Set a breakpoint and wait for the debugger window to show up. Look! (Do you recognize the comparing procedure?) After the first try, we are where we want to be.

```
001B:004013E3   8A10            mov     dl, [eax]
001B:004013E5   8A1E            mov     bl, [esi]
001B:004013E7   8ACA            mov     cl, dl
001B:004013E9   3AD3            cmp     dl, bl
001B:004013EB   751E            jnz     0040140B
001B:004013ED   84C9            test    cl, cl
001B:004013EF   7416            jz      00401407
001B:004013F1   8A5001          mov     dl, [eax+01]
```

This is wonderful! Elegantly, quickly, beautifully — and without any false hits — we defeated the protection.

This method is universal; we'll take advantage of it many times. It simply requires us to determine the key function and set a breakpoint at it. In Windows, all attempts to read a password (calls to a key file, to the registry, etc.) are reduced to calls of API functions. There are many, but the number is finite and known beforehand.

Method 3: Setting a Breakpoint on Messages

Anyone who has had a chance to program in Windows knows that interaction with the operating system is based on *messages*. Practically all Windows API functions are high-level "wrappers" that send messages to Windows. The GetWindowTextA function, an analog of the WM_GETTEXT message, is not an exception.

Consequently, a developer doesn't need to call GetWindowTextA to get the text from an edit window; SendMessageA (hWnd, WM_GETTEXT, (LPARAM) &buff [0]) can be used. *crack02* does just that. Try to load it and set a breakpoint at GetWindow-TextA (GetDlgItemTextA). What happened? It didn't work. Developers use such tricks to lead novice hackers astray.

In this case, you could set a breakpoint at SendMessageA. However, setting a breakpoint at the WM_GETTEXT message is a more universal solution, which works regardless of how the window's contents are read.

In SoftIce, a special command sets a breakpoint on messages: BMSG. But isn't it more interesting to do it yourself?

As you probably know, each window has a special *window procedure* associated with it (i.e., for receiving and processing messages). You could find it and set a breakpoint. The HWND command gives information on the windows of the specified process.

```
<Ctrl-D>
:addr crack02
:hwnd crack02
Handle     Class                         WinProc    TID
Module
 050140    #32770 (Dialog)               6C291B81   2DC
crack02
  05013E   Button                        77E18721   2DC
crack02
  05013C   Edit                          6C291B81   2DC
crack02
  05013A   Static                        77E186D9   2DC
crack02
```

You can locate quickly the edit window with the window procedure address 0x6C291B81. Should you set a breakpoint? No, it's not time yet. Remember that the window procedure is called on more occasions than when the text is read. It would be better to set a breakpoint after you have filtered out all other messages. To begin, study the prototype of this function:

```
LRESULT CALLBACK WindowProc(
    HWND hwnd,          // Handle to window
    UINT uMsg,          // Message identifier
    WPARAM wParam,      // First message parameter
    LPARAM lParam       // Second message parameter
);
```

It's easy to calculate that, when calling the function, the uMsg argument (the message identifier) is offset by 8 bytes relative to the stack-top pointer, ESP. If the value at that position equals WM_GETTEXT (0xD), that is when you want to break!

Here, mention must be made of conditional breaks. Their syntax is considered in detail in the debugger documentation. Programmers familiar with C, however, should find the syntax concise and intuitive.

```
:bpx 6C291B81 IF (esp->8)==WM_GETTEXT
:x
```

Now, quit the debugger. Enter any text as a password, such as Hello, and press the <Enter> key. The debugger will show up right away.

```
Break due to BPX #0008:6C291B81  IF ((ESP->8)==0xD)  (ET=2.52 seconds)
```

You need to determine the address with the read string. The pointer to the buffer is transferred to the buffer through the lParam argument (see SDK for the description of WM_GETTEXT), and lParam itself is placed on the stack at an offset of 0x10 relative to ESP.

```
Return address    ← ESP
hwnd              ← ESP + 0x4
uMsg              ← ESP + 0x8
wParam            ← ESP + 0xC
lParam            ← ESP + 0x10
```

Now, output this buffer to the data window, quit the window procedure with P RET, and... see the text Hello, which you just entered.

```
:d *(esp+10)
:p ret
0023:0012EB28 48 65 6C 6C 6F 00 05 00-0D 00 00 00 FF 03 00 00  Hello...........
0023:0012EB38 1C ED 12 00 01 00 00 00-0D 00 00 00 FD 86 E1 77  ...............w
0023:0012EB48 70 3C 13 00 00 00 00 00-00 00 00 00 00 00 00 00  p<..............
0023:0012EB58 00 00 00 00 00 00 00 00-98 EB 12 00 1E 87 E1 77  ...............w

:bpm 23:12EB28
```

Set the breakpoint given above. The debugger will show up at one "spontaneous" point. (It is obviously "nonuser" code because CS has a value of 0008.) Prepare to press the <x> key to continue tracking the break. You'll suddenly catch sight of the following:

```
0008:A00B017C  8A0A        mov     cl, [edx]
0008:A00B017E  8808        mov     [eax], cl
0008:A00B0180  40          inc     eax
0008:A00B0181  42          inc     edx
0008:A00B0182  84C9        test    cl, cl
0008:A00B0184  7406        jz      A00B018C
0008:A00B0186  FF4C2410    dec     dword ptr [esp+10]
0008:A00B018A  75F0        jnz     A00B017C
```

Aha! The buffer is passed by value, not by reference. The system doesn't allow you to access the buffer directly; it only provides a copy. A character in this buffer, pointed to by the EDX register is copied to CL. (It is clear that EDX contains a pointer to this buffer; it caused the debugger to appear.) Then it's copied from CL to the [EAX] location, where EAX is some pointer (about which we can't yet say anything definite). Both pointers are incremented by one, and CL (the last character read) is checked for equality to zero. If the end of the string isn't reached, the procedure is repeated. If you have to watch two buffers at once, set one more breakpoint.

```
:bpm EAX
:x
```

The debugger soon pops up at the other breakpoint. You should recognize the comparing procedure. The rest is trivial.

```
001B:004013F2  8A1E        mov     bl, [esi]
001B:004013F4  8ACA        mov     cl, dl
001B:004013F6  3AD3        cmp     dl, bl
001B:004013F8  751E        jnz     00401418
001B:004013FA  84C9        test    cl, cl
001B:004013FC  7416        jz      00401414
001B:004013FE  8A5001      mov     dl, [eax+01]
001B:00401401  8A5E01      mov     bl, [esi+01]
```

9x In Windows 9x, messages are processed somewhat differently than in Windows NT. In particular, the window procedure of the edit window is implemented in 16-bit code, with a nasty segment memory model: `segment:offset`. Addresses also are passed differently. What parameter contains the segment? To answer that question, look at SoftIce's breakpoint report:

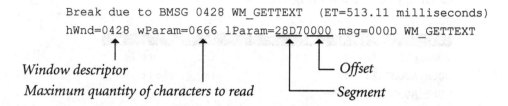

```
Break due to BMSG 0428 WM_GETTEXT  (ET=513.11 milliseconds)
hWnd=0428 wParam=0666 lParam=28D70000 msg=000D WM_GETTEXT
```

Window descriptor

Maximum quantity of characters to read

Offset

Segment

The entire address fits in the `lParam` 32-bit argument — a 16-bit segment and 16-bit offset. Therefore, the breakpoint should look like this: `bpm 28D7:0000`.

Step Five: IDA Emerges onto the Scene

Following Dennis Ritchie's example, it has become typical to begin learning a new programming language by creating the simple "Hello,World!" program. We aren't going to sidestep this tradition. Let's evaluate the capabilities of IDA Pro using the following example. (I recommend that you compile it using Microsoft Visual C++ 6.0. Call "cl.exe first.cpp" from the command line to obtain results consistent with those in this book.)

Listing 6. The Source Code of the *first.cpp* Program

```
#include <iostream.h>
void main()
{
  cout<<"Hello, Sailor!\n";
}
```

The compiler will generate an executable file that is almost 40 KB, the majority of which will be occupied with auxiliary, start, or library code! Attempts to disassemble the code using a disassembler such as W32Dasm won't be successful; the listing will be more than *500 KB*! You can imagine how much time will be eaten up, especially if serious problems occupy dozens of megabytes of disassembled code.

Let's try to disassemble this program using IDA. If the default settings are used, the screen should look as follows upon completion of the analysis (although variations are possible depending on the version):

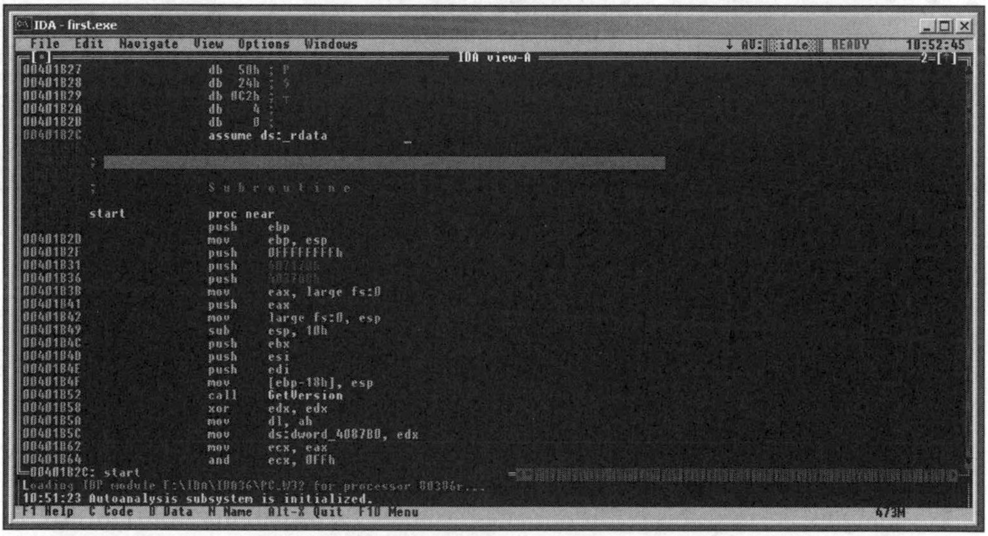

Fig. 4. The IDA Pro 3.6 console interface

Fig. 5. The IDA Pro 4.0 command line interface

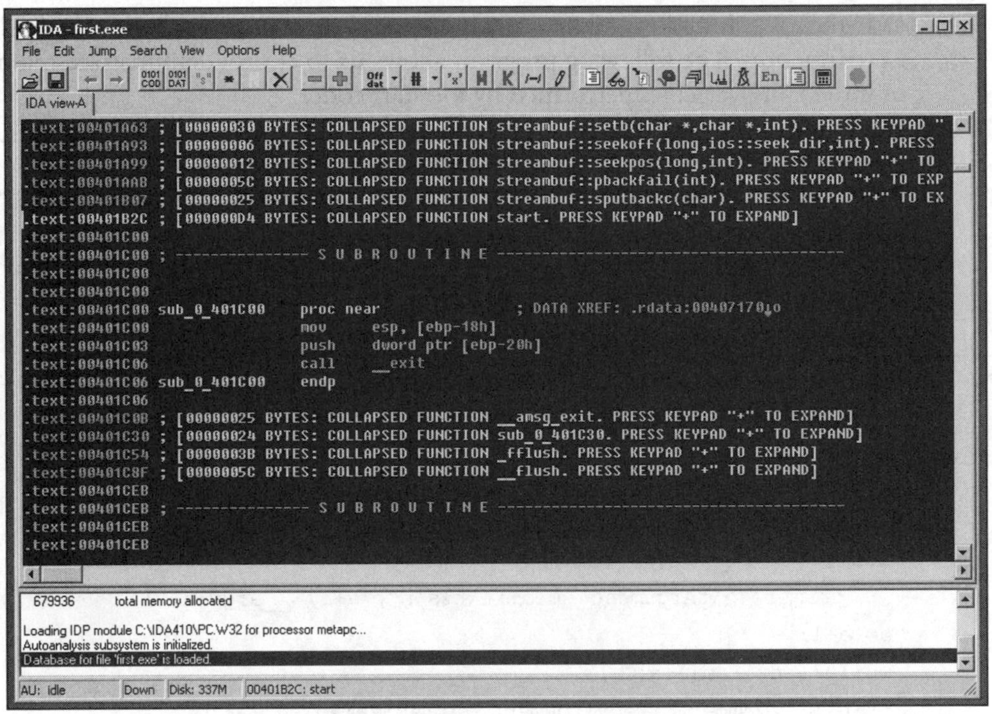

Fig. 6. The IDA Pro 4.0 GUI interface

Beginning with version 3.8*x* (possibly earlier), *collapsing* support appeared in IDA. This feature considerably simplifies code navigation, allowing us to remove lines from screen that aren't of interest at the moment. By default, all library functions are collapsed.

You can expand a function by positioning the cursor on it and pressing the <+> key on the numeric keypad. The <-> key is used to collapse the function.

After finishing analysis of the *first.exe* file, IDA places the cursor on the line .text:00401B2C — the program's entry point. Many novice programmers mistakenly believe that programs written in C start executing from the main function. Actually, immediately after the file is loaded, control is passed to the start function inserted by the compiler. It prepares the following global variables:_osver (the operating system build number), winmajor (the major version number of the operating system), _winminor (the minor version number of the operating system), _winver (the complete version of the operating system incorporating winmajor and winminor),_argc (the number of arguments on the command line), argv (an array of pointers to the argument strings), and environ (an array of pointers to environment variable strings). The start function also initializes the heap and calls the `main` function. After returning control, it completes the process using the `Exit` function. The following program allows us to clearly demonstrate the process of initializing variables performed by the start code:

Listing 7. The Source Code of the *CRt0.demo.c* Program

```
#include <stdio.h>
#include <stdlib.h>
void main()
{
 int a;
 printf(">OS Version:\t\t\t%d.%d\n\
>Build:\t\t\t%d\n\
>Number of arguments:\t%d\n,"\
_winmajor, _winminor, _osver, __argc);
 for (a=0; a<__argc; a++)
    printf(">\tArgument %02d:\t\t%s\n", a+1, __argv[a]);
a=!a-1;
while(_environ[++a]) ;
printf(">Number of environment variables:%d\n", a);
while(a) printf(">\tVariable %d:\t\t%s\n",
    a, _environ[--a]);
}
```

The `main` function looks as though the application doesn't accept any arguments from the command line, but running the program proves the opposite. On my computer, its (abridged) output looks like this:

Listing 8. The Result of Running the *CRt0.demo.c* Program (Abridged)

```
> OS Version:                        5.0
>Build:                              2195
>Number of arguments:                1
>Argument  01:                       CRt0.demo
>Number of environment variables:    30
>Variable  29:                       windir=C:\WINNT
>                  . . .
```

There's no need to analyze the standard start code. The first task is to find where control is passed to the main function. Unfortunately, a guaranteed solution requires the complete analysis of the Start function. Investigators have plenty of tricks, but all of them are based on the implementations of particular compilers[i]; these tricks can't be considered universal.

I recommend that you study the source code of the Start functions of popular compilers, contained in the *CRt0.c* file (Microsoft Visual C++) and in the *c0w.asm* file (Borland C++). This will simplify analysis of the listing obtained from the disassembler. As an illustration, the start code of the *first.exe* program is shown in the following listing as a result of W32Dasm disassembly:

Listing 9. The Start Code of *first.exe* Obtained Using W32Dasm

---

```
//****************** Program Entry Point ********
:00401B2C 55                  push    ebp
:00401B2D 8BEC                mov     ebp, esp
:00401B2F 6AFF                push    FFFFFFFF
:00401B31 6870714000          push    00407170
:00401B36 68A8374000          push    004037A8
:00401B3B 64A100000000        mov     eax, dword ptr fs:[00000000]
:00401B41 50                  push    eax
:00401B42 64892500000000      mov     dword ptr fs:[00000000], esp
:00401B49 83EC10              sub     esp, 00000010
:00401B4C 53                  push    ebx
:00401B4D 56                  push    esi
:00401B4E 57                  push    edi
:00401B4F 8965E8              mov     dword ptr [ebp-18], esp


Reference To: KERNEL32.GetVersion, Ord:0174h


:00401B52 FF1504704000        call    dword ptr [00407004]
:00401B58 33D2                xor     edx, edx
:00401B5A 8AD4                mov     dl, ah
:00401B5C 8915B0874000        mov     dword ptr [004087B0], edx
```

---

[i] For example, Microsoft Visual C, regardless of the main function prototype, always passes three arguments to it: a pointer to the array of pointers to environment variables, a pointer to the array of pointers to command line arguments, and the number of command line arguments. All other functions of the start code take a smaller number of arguments.

```
:00401B62 8BC8              mov      ecx, eax
:00401B64 81E1FF000000      and      ecx, 000000FF
:00401B6A 890DAC874000      mov      dword ptr [004087AC], ecx
:00401B70 C1E108            shl      ecx, 08
:00401B73 03CA              add      ecx, edx
:00401B75 890DA8874000      mov      dword ptr [004087A8], ecx
:00401B7B C1E810            shr      eax, 10
:00401B7E A3A4874000        mov      dword ptr [004087A4], eax
:00401B83 6A00              push     00000000
:00401B85 E8D91B0000        call     00403763
:00401B8A 59                pop      ecx
:00401B8B 85C0              test     eax, eax
:00401B8D 7508              jne      00401B97
:00401B8F 6A1C              push     0000001C
:00401B91 E89A000000        call     00401C30
:00401B96 59                pop      ecx
```

Referenced by a (U)nconditional or (C)onditional Jump at Address:
:00401B8D(C)

```
:00401B97 8365FC00          and      dword ptr [ebp-04], 00000000
:00401B9B E8D70C0000        call     00402877
```

Reference To: KERNEL32.GetCommandLineA, Ord:00CAh

```
:00401BA0 FF1560704000      call     dword ptr [00407060]
:00401BA6 A3E49C4000        mov      dword ptr [00409CE4], eax
:00401BAB E8811A0000        call     00403631
:00401BB0 A388874000        mov      dword ptr [00408788], eax
:00401BB5 E82A180000        call     004033E4
:00401BBA E86C170000        call     0040332B
:00401BBF E8E1140000        call     004030A5
:00401BC4 A1C0874000        mov      eax, dword ptr [004087C0]
:00401BC9 A3C4874000        mov      dword ptr [004087C4], eax
:00401BCE 50                push     eax
:00401BCF FF35B8874000      push     dword ptr [004087B8]
:00401BD5 FF35B4874000      push     dword ptr [004087B4]
:00401BDB E820F4FFFF        call     00401000
:00401BE0 83C40C            add      esp, 0000000C
:00401BE3 8945E4            mov      dword ptr [ebp-1C], eax
```

```
:00401BE6 50              push     eax
:00401BE7 E8E6140000      call     004030D2
:00401BEC 8B45EC          mov      eax, dword ptr [ebp-14]
:00401BEF 8B08            mov      ecx, dword ptr [eax]
:00401BF1 8B09            mov      ecx, dword ptr [ecx]
:00401BF3 894DE0          mov      dword ptr [ebp-20], ecx
:00401BF6 50              push     eax
:00401BF7 51              push     ecx
:00401BF8 E8AA150000      call     004031A7
:00401BFD 59              pop      ecx
:00401BFE 59              pop      ecx
:00401BFF C3              ret
```

IDA knows how to recognize library functions by their signatures. (Almost the same algorithm is used by anti-virus software.) Therefore, disassemblers strongly depend on the version and completeness of the package. Not all IDA Pro versions are capable of working with programs generated by present-day compilers. (See the %*IDA*%/SIG/list file for the list of supported compilers.)

Listing 10. The Start Code of *first.exe* Obtained Using IDA Pro 4.01

```
00401B2C start        proc near
00401B2C
00401B2C var_20       = dword ptr -20h
00401B2C var_1C       = dword ptr -1Ch
00401B2C var_18       = dword ptr -18h
00401B2C var_14       = dword ptr -14h
00401B2C var_4        = dword ptr -4
00401B2C
00401B2C              push     ebp
00401B2D              mov      ebp, esp
00401B2F              push     0FFFFFFFFh
00401B31              push     offset stru_407170
00401B36              push     offset __except_handler3
00401B3B              mov      eax, large fs:0
00401B41              push     eax
00401B42              mov      large fs:0, esp
00401B49              sub      esp, 10h
00401B4C              push     ebx
00401B4D              push     esi
```

```
00401B4E              push     edi
00401B4F              mov      [ebp+var_18], esp
00401B52              call     ds:GetVersion
00401B58              xor      edx, edx
00401B5A              mov      dl, ah
00401B5C              mov      dword_4087B0, edx
00401B62              mov      ecx, eax
00401B64              and      ecx, 0FFh
00401B6A              mov      dword_4087AC, ecx
00401B70              shl      ecx, 8
00401B73              add      ecx, edx
00401B75              mov      dword_4087A8, ecx
00401B7B              shr      eax, 10h
00401B7E              mov      dword_4087A4, eax
00401B83              push     0
00401B85              call     __heap_init
00401B8A              pop      ecx
00401B8B              test     eax, eax
00401B8D              jnz      short loc_401B97
00401B8F              push     1Ch
00401B91              call     sub_401C30        ; _fast_error_exit
00401B96              pop      ecx
00401B97

00401B97 loc_401B97:                                ; CODE XREF: start+61↑j
00401B97              and      [ebp+var_4], 0
00401B9B              call     __ioinit
00401BA0              call     ds:GetCommandLineA
00401BA6              mov      dword_409CE4, eax
00401BAB              call     ___crtGetEnvironmentStringsA
00401BB0              mov      dword_408788, eax
00401BB5              call     __setargv
00401BBA              call     __setenvp
00401BBF              call     __cinit
00401BC4              mov      eax, dword_4087C0
00401BC9              mov      dword_4087C4, eax
00401BCE              push     eax
00401BCF              push     dword_4087B8
00401BD5              push     dword_4087B4
00401BDB              call     sub_401000
00401BE0              add      esp, 0Ch
00401BE3              mov      [ebp+var_1C], eax
00401BE6              push     eax
00401BE7              call     _exit
```

```
00401BEC ; ---------------------------------------------------------------
00401BEC
00401BEC loc_401BEC:                          ; DATA XREF: _rdata:00407170↓o
00401BEC                 mov     eax, [ebp-14h]
00401BEF                 mov     ecx, [eax]
00401BF1                 mov     ecx, [ecx]
00401BF3                 mov     [ebp-20h], ecx
00401BF6                 push    eax
00401BF7                 push    ecx
00401BF8                 call    __XcptFilter
00401BFD                 pop     ecx
00401BFE                 pop     ecx
00401BFF                 retn
00401BFF start           endp ; sp = -34h
```

IDA Pro successfully copes with the above example, acknowledged by the line
"Using FLIRT signature: VC v2.0/4.x/5.0 runtime" in the message box.

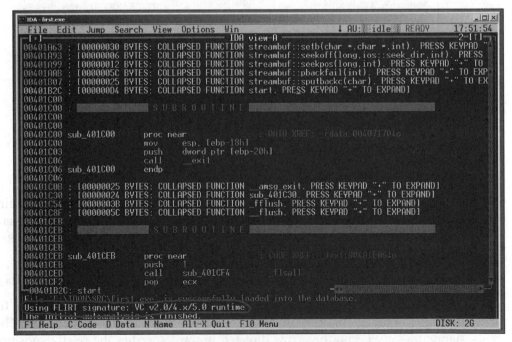

Fig. 7. Loading the signature library

The disassembler has successfully determined the names of all the functions called by the start code, except the one located at the address 0x0401BDB. Knowing that three arguments are passed, and exit is called upon the return from the function, we can assume this exception is main.

There are several ways of getting to the address 0x0401000 to see the main function, including scrolling the screen using the arrows, or pressing the <G> key and entering the required address in the dialog box that appears. However, it's easier and faster to use the navigation system built into IDA Pro. If you place the cursor on a name, constant, or expression and press the <Enter> key, IDA automatically goes to the required address.

In this case, we need to place the cursor on the string sub_401000 (an argument of the call instruction). Press the <Enter> key. The disassembler window should look like this:

```
00401000 ; -------------- S U B R O U T I N E ---------------------
00401000
00401000 ; Attributes: bp-based frame
00401000
00401000 sub_401000 proc near               ; CODE XREF: start+AF↓p
00401000         push    ebp
00401001         mov     ebp, esp
00401003         push    offset aHelloSailor ; "Hello, Sailor!\n"
00401008         mov     ecx, offset dword_408748
0040100D         call    ??6ostream@@QAEAAV0@PBD@Z ;
0040100D                 ;ostream::operator<<(char const *)
00401012         pop     ebp
00401013         retn
00401013 sub_401000 endp
```

The disassembler recognized a string variable and has given it the meaningful name: aHelloSailor. For clarity, in the comment on the right, it has given the original contents: "Hello, Sailor!\n". If you place the cursor on aHelloSailor and press the <Enter> key, IDA will go to the required string:

```
00408040 aHelloSailor db 'Hello, Sailor!',0Ah,0 ; DATA XREF: sub_401000+3↑o
```

The comment DATA XREF: sub_401000+3↑o is known as a *cross-reference*. In the third line of the sub_401000 procedure, a call was made to an offset address. The "o" stands for offset, and the arrow directed upward specifies the relative position of the cross-reference.

If you place the cursor on the `sub_401000+3` expression and press the <Enter> key, IDA Pro will go to the following line:

```
00401003    push    offset aHelloSailor ; "Hello, Sailor!\n"
```

Pressing the <Esc> key cancels the previous move and returns the cursor to its initial position (like the `Back` command in a Web browser). An offset to the string `"Hello, Sailor!\n"` is passed to the procedure `??6ostream@@QAEAAV0@PBD@Z`, the << operator in C++. The strange name comes from the limitation on characters that can be used in names of library functions. Compilers automatically mangle such names, transforming them into gobbledygook suitable only for operation with the linker. Few novice programmers suspect such hidden "machinations."

To facilitate analysis of code, IDA Pro displays the "correct" names in the comments, but it can be forced to show demangled names everywhere. To do this, we need to select the **Demangled names** item from the **Options** menu, then set the **Names** radio button in the dialog box that pops up; after that, the call to the << operator will appear as follows:

```
0040100D    call    ostream::operator<<(char const *)
```

At this point, the analysis of the *first.cpp* application is complete. We only have to rename the `sub_401000` function to `main`. For this, we need to position the cursor on the `0x0401000` string (the function's start address), press the <N> key, and enter "main" in the dialog box that opens. The result should look like this:

```
00401000 ; --------------- S U B R O U T I N E -----------------------
00401000
00401000 ; Attributes: bp-based frame
00401000
00401000 main        proc near              ; CODE XREF: start+AF↓p
00401000             push    ebp
00401001             mov     ebp, esp
00401003             push    offset aHelloSailor ; "Hello, Sailor!\n"
00401008             mov     ecx, offset dword_408748
0040100D             call    ostream::operator<<(char const *)
00401012             pop     ebp
00401013             retn
00401013 main        endp
```

Compare this to W32Dasm. (Only the contents of the `main` function are given.)

```
:00401000 55                    push    ebp
:00401001 8BEC                  mov     ebp, esp

Possible StringData Ref from Data Obj ->"Hello, Sailor!"

:00401003 6840804000           push    00408040
:00401008 B948874000           mov     ecx, 00408748
:0040100D E8AB000000           call    004010BD
:00401012 5D                   pop     ebp
:00401013 C3                   ret
```

Another important advantage of IDA is the ability to disassemble encrypted programs. In the example */SRC/Crypt.com*, a static encryption method, frequently found with "wrapper" protections, was used. This simple trick "dazzles" most disassemblers. For example, processing the *Crypt.com* file using Sourcer results in:

```
Crypt                           proc    far

7E5B:0100                       start:
7E5B:0100  83 C6 06             add     si, 6
7E5B:0103  FF E6                jmp     si ;*
                                ;*No entry point to code
7E5B:0105  B9 14BE              mov     cx, 14BEh
7E5B:0108  01 AD 5691           add     ds:data_1e[di], bp  ; (7E5B:5691=0)
7E5B:010C  80 34 66             xor     byte ptr [si], 66h  ; 'f'
7E5B:010F  46                   inc     si
7E5B:0110  E2 FA                loop    $-4      ; Loop if cx > 0

7E5B:0112  FF E6                jmp     si            ;*
                                ;*No entry point to code
7E5B:114 18 00                  sbb     [bx+si], al
7E5B:116 D2 6F DC               shr     byte ptr [bx-24h],cl ; Shift w/zeros fill
7E5B:119 6E 67 AB 47 A5 2E      db 6Eh, 67h, 0ABh, 47h, 0A5h, 2Eh
7E5B:11F 03 0A 0A 09 4A 35      db 03h, 0Ah, 0Ah, 09h, 4Ah, 35h
7E5B:125 07 0F 0A 09 14 47      db 07h, 0Fh, 0Ah, 09h, 14h, 47h
7E5B:12B 6B 6C 42 E8 00 00      db 6Bh, 6Ch, 42h, E8h, 00h, 00h
7E5B:131 59 5E BF 00 01 57      db 59h, 5Eh, BFh, 00h, 01h, 57h
7E5B:137 2B CE F3 A4 C3         db 2Bh, CEh, F3h, A4h, C3h

Crypt                           endp
```

Sourcer failed to disassemble half of the code, leaving it as a dump, and it incorrectly disassembled the other half! The `JMP SI` instruction at line :0x103 jumps to the address `:0x106`. (When the COM file is loaded, the value in the SI register is equal to `0x100`; therefore, after the `ADD SI, 6` instruction is executed, the SI register contains `0x106`.) However, the instruction following the JMP is at address `0x105`! The source code has a dummy byte inserted in this location, which leads the disassembler astray. That byte is interpreted as the next instruction, leading to a shift in the code to be disassembled.

```
Start:
add  si, 6
jmp  si
db   0B9H     ;
lea  si, _end  ; to the beginning of the encrypted fragment
```

Sourcer is unable to predict register change points. After encountering the JMP SI instruction, it continues disassembling, silently assuming that instructions are sequential. It's possible to create a file of definitions that would indicate a byte of data is located at address `0x105`, but this is inconvenient.

In contrast to Sourcer-like disassemblers, IDA was designed as an interactive, user-friendly environment. IDA doesn't make assumptions; if difficulties arise, it asks the user for help. Therefore, after encountering a register change to an unknown address, it stops further analysis. This means the result of analyzing the *Crypt.com* file looks like this:

```
seg000:0100 start          proc near
seg000:0100                add     si, 6
seg000:0103                jmp     si
seg000:0103 start          endp
seg000:0103
seg000:0103 ; -------------------------------------------------------------
seg000:0105                db  0B9h ;
seg000:0106                db  0Beh ; -
seg000:0107                db   14h ;
seg000:0108                db    1 ;
seg000:0109                db  0Adh ; i
seg000:010A                db   91h ; N
...
```

We can help the disassembler by specifying the `jump` address. In this situation, novice users usually bring the cursor to the corresponding line and press the <C> key, forcing IDA to disassemble the code from that position to the function's end. However, such a solution is erroneous; we still don't know where the branch in line `:0x103` points, or how the code at address `:0x106` receives control.

The correct solution is to add a cross-reference that would link line :0x103 to line :0x106. For this, we need to select **Cross references** from the **View** menu. Then, in the dialog box that opens, we need to fill in the **from** and **to** fields with the values seg000:0103 and seg000:0106, respectively.

As a result, the disassembler output should look as follows. (A bug in IDA 4.01.300 means adding a new cross-reference does not always result in automatic disassembling.)

```
seg000:0100                 public start
seg000:0100 start           proc near
seg000:0100                 add     si, 6
seg000:0103                 jmp     si
seg000:0103 start           endp
seg000:0103
seg000:0103 ; ------------------------------------------------------------
seg000:0105                 db 0B9h
seg000:0106 ; ------------------------------------------------------------
seg000:0106
seg000:0106 loc_0_106:                       ; CODE XREF: start+3↑u
seg000:0106                 mov     si, 114h
seg000:0109                 lodsw
seg000:010A                 xchg    ax, cx
seg000:010B                 push    si
seg000:010C
seg000:010C loc_0_10C:                       ; CODE XREF: seg000:0110↓j
seg000:010C                 xor     byte ptr [si], 66h
seg000:010F                 inc     si
seg000:0110                 loop    loc_0_10C
seg000:0112                 jmp     si
seg000:0112 ; ------------------------------------------------------------
seg000:0114                 db   18h ;
seg000:0115                 db    0 ;
seg000:0116                 db 0D2h ; T
seg000:0117                 db   6Fh ; o
      ...
```

Since IDA Pro doesn't display the target address of the cross-reference, I'd suggest you display it manually. This will improve the code's readability and simplify navigation. Place the cursor on line :0x103, press the <:> key, and enter a comment in the dialog box that opens (for example, "jump to address 0106"). The display will change as follows:

```
seg000:0103          jmp     si      ; Jump to address 0106
```

Such a comment makes it possible to jump to the specified address: Just place the cursor on 0106 and press the <Enter> key. Note that IDA Pro doesn't recognize hexadecimal format in the C style (0x106) or in the MASM\TASM style (0106h).

What does the value 114h represent at line :0x106 — a constant or an offset? To figure this out, we need to analyze the LODSW instruction. Since executing it results in loading the word located at address DS:SI into the AX register, the offset is loaded into the SI register.

```
seg000:0106          mov     si, 114h
seg000:0109          lodsw
```

Pressing the <O> key transforms the constant to an offset. The disassembled code will appear like this:

```
seg000:0106          mov     si, offset unk_0_114
seg000:0109          lodsw
...
seg000:0114 unk_0_114 db  18h     ; DATA XREF: seg000:0106↑o
seg000:0115          db    0     ;
seg000:0116          db  0D2h    ; T
seg000:0117          db  6Fh     ; o
...
```

IDA Pro automatically created a new name — unk_0_114 — that refers to an unknown variable with a size of 1 *byte*. But the LODSW instruction loads a *word* into the AX register; therefore, we need to go to line :0144 and press the <D> key twice to obtain the following code:

```
seg000:0114 word_0_114 dw 18h                    ; DATA XREF: seg000:0106↑o
seg000:0116          db 0D2h ; T
```

What does the word_0_144 location contain? The following code will help us find out:

```
seg000:0106          mov     si, offset word_0_114
seg000:0109          lodsw
```

```
seg000:010A                 xchg    ax, cx
seg000:010B                 push    si
seg000:010C
seg000:010C loc_0_10C:                              ; CODE XREF: seg000:0110↓j
seg000:010C                 xor     byte ptr [si], 66h
seg000:010F                 inc     si
seg000:0110                 loop    loc_0_10C
```

In line :0x10A, the AX register value is moved to the CX register, then used by the LOOP LOC_010C instruction as a loop counter. The loop body is a simple decoder: The XOR instruction decrypts a byte pointed to by the SI register, and the INC SI instruction moves the pointer to the next byte. Therefore, the word_0_144 location contains the number of bytes to be decrypted. Place the cursor on it, press the <N> key, and give it a better name ("BytesToDecrypt," for example).

There's one more unconditional register jump after the decryption loop.

```
seg000:0112                 jmp     si
```

To find out where it transfers control, we need to analyze the code and determine the SI register's contents. For this, the debugger is often used: We set a breakpoint on line 0x112 and, when the debugger window pops up, look for the register value. IDA Pro generates MAP files that contain the debugger information especially for this purpose. In particular, to avoid memorizing the numerical values of all the addresses being tested, each of them can be assigned easily remembered names. For example, if you place the cursor on line seg000:0112, then press the <N> key and enter "BreakHere," the debugger will be able to calculate the return address automatically using its name.

To create a MAP file, click on **Produce output file** in the **File** menu and select **Produce MAP file** from the drop-down submenu, or press the <Shift>+<F10> key combination. In either case, a dialog box will appear, which allows us to specify the data to include in the MAP file: information on segments, names automatically generated by IDA Pro (loc_0_106, sub_0x110, etc.), and demangled names. The contents of the MAP file obtained should be as follows:

```
Start  Stop    Length Name             Class
00100H 0013BH 0003CH seg000            CODE
Address         Publics by Value
0000:0100       start
0000:0112       BreakHere
```

```
0000:0114        BytesToDecrypt
Program entry point at 0000:0100
```

This format is supported by most debuggers, including the most popular one: SoftIce. It includes the `msym` utility, launched by specifying the MAP file on the command line. The SYM file obtained should be placed in the directory where the program being debugged is located, then loaded from the loader *without specifying the extension* (`WLDR Crypt`, for example). Otherwise, the character information won't be loaded.

Then, we need to set a breakpoint using the `bpx BreakHere` command, and quit the debugger with the `x` command. In a second, the debugger window will pop up again, informing us that the processor has reached a breakpoint. Looking at the registers displayed at the top of the screen by default, we can see that `SI` equals 0x12E.

This value can also be calculated mentally, without using the debugger. The `MOV` instruction at line `0x106` loads the offset `0x114` into the `SI` register. From here, the `LODSW` instruction reads the quantity of decrypted bytes — `0x18` — and the `SI` register is increased by the word size (2 bytes). Hence, when the decryption cycle is complete, the `SI` value will be `0x114+0x18+0x2 = 0x12E`.

After calculating the `jump` address in the line `0x112`, let's create a corresponding cross-reference (from `0x122` to `0x12E`) and add a comment to line `0x112` ("Jump to address `012E`"). Creating the cross-reference automatically disassembles the code from the address `seg000:012E` to the end of the file.

```
seg000:012E loc_0_12E:        ; CODE XREF: seg000:0112↑u
seg000:012E              call    $+3
seg000:0131              pop     cx
seg000:0132              pop     si
seg000:0133              mov     di, 100h
seg000:0136              push    di
seg000:0137              sub     cx, si
seg000:0139              repe    movsb
seg000:013B              retn
```

The `CALL $+3` instruction (`$` designates the current value of the `IP` instruction pointer) pushes the `IP` contents to a stack, from which it can be extracted into any general-purpose register. In Intel 80x86 microprocessors, the `IP` register cannot be addressed directly, and only instructions that change the course of execution can read its value, including `call`.

We can supplement lines `0x12E` and `0x131` with a comment — `MOV CX, IP` — or we can calculate and substitute the direct value — `MOV CX, 0x131`.

The POP SI instruction at line 0x132 pops a word off the stack and places it in the SI register. Scrolling the disassembler upward, you will see the PUSH SI instruction at line 0x10B. This is paired with the POP SI instruction, and pushes the offset of the first decrypted byte to the stack. Now, the meaning of the subsequent MOV DI, 0x100\SUB CX, and SI\REPE MOVSB instructions is clear: They move the beginning of the decrypted fragment to the address starting at offset 0x100. Such an operation is characteristic for "wrapper" protections superimposed on a compiled file that should be "reset" to its "native" addresses before it is launched.

Before relocation, the CX register is loaded with the length of the block being copied. (The length is calculated by subtracting the offset of the first decrypted byte from the offset of the second instruction of the code performing relocation.) The true length is 3 bytes shorter; consequently, we need to subtract three from that value. However, the difference has no effect: The contents of memore locations at addresses beyond the end of the decrypted fragment aren't defined, and those locations may contain anything.

The 0x136:PUSH DI and 0x13B:RETN instructions are an analog of the CALL DI instruction: PUSH pushes the return address on the stack, and RETN extracts it and passes control to the corresponding address. Knowing the DI value (0x100), we can add a cross-reference (from :0x13B to :0x100) and a comment to line :0x13B — "Jump to address 0x100." However, after relocation, different code is located at the indicated addresses! Therefore, it's more logical to add the cross-reference from :0x13B to :0x116 and the comment "Jump to address 0x116."

After the new cross–reference is created, IDA will try to disassemble the encrypted code. The following will result:

```
seg000:0116 loc_0_116:    ; CODE XREF: seg000:013B↓u
seg000:0116              shr    byte ptr [bx-24h], cl
seg000:0119              outsb
seg000:011A              stos   word ptr es:[edi]
seg000:011C              inc    di
seg000:011D              movsw
seg000:011E              add    cx, cs:[bp+si]
seg000:0121              or     cl, [bx+di]
seg000:0123              dec    dx
seg000:0124              xor    ax, 0F07h
seg000:0127              or     cl, [bx+di]
seg000:0129              adc    al, 47h
seg000:0129;————————————————————————————————
```

```
seg000:012B        db      6Bh ; k
seg000:012C        db      6Ch ; l
seg000:012D        db      42h ; B
seg000:012E;─────────────────────────────────────
```

Immediate disassembling of the encrypted code is impossible: It must be decrypted first. Most disassemblers aren't able to modify analyzed code on the fly; they require it to be decrypted completely beforehand. In practice, however, things are different. Before decrypting, we need to understand the decryption algorithm by analyzing the accessible part of the file. Then, we can quit the disassembler, decrypt the "secret" fragment, load the file into the disassembler again, and continue analyzing it until the next encrypted fragment occurs. We'll have to repeat the "quit-decrypt-load-analyze" cycle.

IDA allows us to solve the same task with less effort and without quitting the disassembler. This can be achieved because of virtual memory. We can imagine IDA is a "transparent" virtual machine, operating on the physical memory of the computer. To modify memory, we need to know the address. This consists of a pair of numbers: a segment address and an offset.

On the left side, each line's offset and segment name are given (seg000:0116, for example). We can get the base address of a segment from its name: Open the **Segments** window and select the **Segments** item from the **View** menu.

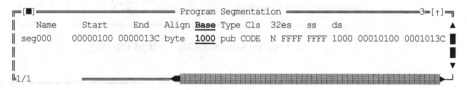

Fig. 8. The **Segments** window

The required address is in the Base column. (It is in bold and underlined in Fig. 8.) Any location of the segment can be addressed using the [segment:offset] construction. Memory cells can be read and modified using the Byte and PatchByte functions, respectively. Calling a=Byte([0x1000,0x100]) reads the cell at 0x100 offset in the segment with the base address of 0x1000; calling PatchByte([0x1000,0x100],0x27) writes the value 0x27 in the memory cell at the 0x100 offset in the segment with the base address of 0x1000. As their names indicate, the functions work one byte at a time.

These two functions and familiarity with the C language are enough to write a decrypting script. The IDA-C implementation doesn't follow completely the ANSI

C standard. In particular, IDA doesn't allow the variable type to be set; the decompiler automatically defines it with the `auto` keyword when it's used for the first time. For example, `auto MyVar, s0` declares two variables: `MyVar` and `s0`.

To create a script, we need to press the <Shift>+<F2> key combination, or select **IDC Command** from the **File** menu. Then, we must enter the source code of the program into the dialog box that pops up.

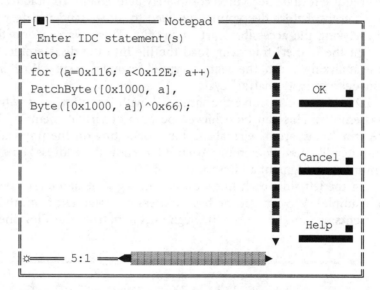

Fig. 9. An embedded script editor

Listing 11. The Source Code of a Decryption Script

```
auto a;
for (a=0x116; a<0x12E; a++)
PatchByte([0x1000, a], Byte([0x1000, a])^0x66);
```

❗ Explanation

As shown, the decryption algorithm sequentially converts the bytes of the encrypted fragment using the `XOR 0x66` operation. (This operation is highlighted in bold.)

```
seg000:010C                 xor     byte ptr [si], 66h
seg000:010F                 inc     si
seg000:0110                 loop    loc_0_10C
```

The encrypted fragment itself starts from address `seg000:0x116` and proceeds to address `seg000:0x12E`. Therefore, decryption in C looks like this: `for (a=0x116; a<0x12E; a ++) PatchByte([0x1000,a], Byte([0x1000,a]^0x66);`

To execute the script, press the <Enter> key (in IDA version 3.8*x* or higher), or the <Ctrl>+<Enter> key combination (in earlier versions). After executing the script, the disassembler window should show the code as it is in Listing 12.

If you encounter an error, you may have used the improper character case (IDA is case sensitive), the wrong syntax, or a base address that does not equal `0x1000`. (Call the **Segments** window again to check its value.) Place the cursor on line `seg000:0116` and press the <U> key to delete the previous disassembling results, then press the <C> key to disassemble the decrypted code anew.

Listing 12. The Output of the Decryption Script

```
seg000:0116 loc_0_116:                          ; CODE XREF: seg000:013B↓u
seg000:0116              mov     ah, 9
seg000:0118              mov     dx, 108h
seg000:011B              int     21h            ; DOS — PRINT STRING
seg000:011B                                     ; DS:DX (string terminated
seg000:011B                                     ; by $)
seg000:011D              retn
seg000:011D ;
    --------------------------------------------------------------
seg000:011E              db  48h ; H
seg000:011F              db  65h ; e
seg000:0120              db  6Ch ; l
seg000:0121              db  6Ch ; l
seg000:0122              db  6Fh ; o
seg000:0123              db  2Ch ; ,
seg000:0124              db  20h ;
seg000:0125              db  53h ; S
seg000:0126              db  61h ; a
seg000:0127              db  69h ; i
seg000:0128              db  6Ch ; l
seg000:0129              db  6Fh ; o
seg000:012A              db  72h ; r
seg000:012B              db  21h ; !
```

```
seg000:012C                 db   0Dh ;
seg000:012D                 db   0Ah ;
seg000:012E                 db   24h ; $
seg000:012F ; ----------------------------------------------------------
```

The chain of characters beginning at address seg000:011E can be converted to a readable string: Place the cursor on it, and press the <A> key. The disassembler window will look like this:

```
seg000:0116 loc_0_116:                          ; CODE XREF: seg000:013B↓u
seg000:0116                 mov      ah, 9
seg000:0118                 mov      dx, 108h
seg000:011B                 int      21h        ; DOS — PRINT STRING
seg000:011B                                     ; DS:DX (string terminated
seg000:011B                                     ; by $)
seg000:011D                 retn
seg000:011D ;
------------------------------------------------------------------
seg000:011E aHelloSailor  db 'Hello, Sailor!', 0Dh, 0Ah, '$'
seg000:012E ;
------------------------------------------------------------------
```

Prior to calling interrupt 0x21, the MOV AH, 9 instruction at line :0116 prepares the AH register: It selects the function that will display the string whose offset is written in the DX register by the next instruction. To successfully assemble the listing, we need to replace the constant 0x108 with a corresponding offset. However, when assembling the code (before relocation), the string that will be displayed is located in another place! To solve this problem, you could create a new segment and copy the decrypted code to it; this would simulate the relocation of the working code.

Explanation

The new segment, MySeg, can have any base address if there's no overlap with the seg000 segment. The initial address of a segment is set equal to a value that the offset makes 0x100 the first byte. The difference between the first and last addresses is the segment length. This can be calculated by subtracting the offset of the beginning of the decrypted fragment from the offset of its end: 0x13B - 0x116 = 0x25.

To create a new segment, select **Segments** from the **View** menu and press the **Insert** button in the dialog box. Another dialog box similar to the following one will appear:

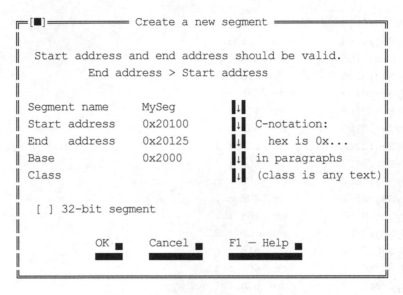

Fig. 10. Creating a new segment

We can use the following script to copy the required fragment to the segment we just created:

Listing 13. The Source Code of the Copying Script

```
auto a;
for (a=0x0; a<0x25; a++) PatchByte([0x2000, a+0x100], Byte([0x1000, a+0x116]));
```

To enter this script, press the <Shift>+<F2> key combination again. The previous script will be lost. (IDA doesn't allow us to work simultaneously with more than one script.) After the operation is complete, the disassembler screen will look like this:

Listing 14. The Result of Executing the Copying Script

```
MySeg:0100 MySeg    segment byte public '' use16
MySeg:0100          assume cs:MySeg
MySeg:0100          ;org 100h
MySeg:0100          assume es:nothing, ss:nothing, ds:nothing, fs:nothing, gs:nothing
MySeg:0100          db 0B4h ;
MySeg:0101          db    9 ;
MySeg:0102          db 0BAh ;
```

```
MySeg:0103          db    8 ;
MySeg:0104          db    1 ;
MySeg:0105          db  0CDh ;
MySeg:0106          db   21h ;
MySeg:0107          db  0C3h ;
MySeg:0108          db   48h ; H
MySeg:0109          db   65h ; e
MySeg:010A          db   6Ch ; l
MySeg:010B          db   6Ch ; l
MySeg:010C          db   6Fh ; o
MySeg:010D          db   2Ch ; ,
MySeg:010E          db   20h ;
MySeg:010F          db   53h ; S
MySeg:0110          db   61h ; a
MySeg:0111          db   69h ; i
MySeg:0112          db   6Ch ; l
MySeg:0113          db   6Fh ; o
MySeg:0114          db   72h ; r
MySeg:0115          db   21h ; !
MySeg:0116          db   0Dh ;
MySeg:0117          db   0Ah ;
MySeg:0118          db   24h ; $
MySeg:0118 MySeg  ends
```

Now, we need to create a cross-reference from :seg000:013B to :MySeg:0x100, converting the chain of characters to a readable string. For this, bring the cursor to line MySeg:0108 and press the <A> key. The disassembler window should change to the following:

Listing 15. The Result of Disassembling the Copied Fragment

```
MySeg:0100 loc_1000_100:                    ; CODE XREF: seg000:013B↑u
MySeg:0100              mov    ah, 9
MySeg:0102              mov    dx, 108h
MySeg:0105              int    21h          ; DOS - PRINT STRING
MySeg:0105                                  ; DS:DX (string terminated by $)
MySeg:0107              retn
MySeg:0107 ; ------------------------------------------------------------
```

```
MySeg:0108 aHelloSailorS    db 'Hello, Sailor!', 0Dh, 0Ah
MySeg:0108                  db '$'
MySeg:0118 MySeg            ends
```

As a result of all these operations, the offsets loaded in the DX register are the same. (In the code, they are in bold.) If we bring the cursor to constant 108h and press the <Ctrl>+<O> key combination, it will change into an offset.

Listing 16. Converting a Constant into an Offset

```
MySeg:0102                  mov    dx, offset aHelloSailorS ; "Hello, Sailor!\r\n$"
MySeg:0105                  int    21h                      ; DOS — PRINT STRING
MySeg:0105                                                  ; DS:DX (string terminated by $)
MySeg:0107                  retn
MySeg:0107 ; --------------------------------------------------------
MySeg:0108 aHelloSailorS    db 'Hello, Sailor!', 0Dh, 0Ah ; DATA XREF: MySeg:0102o
```

The listing obtained is convenient for analysis, but it isn't ready for assembling: No assembler is capable of encrypting the required code. That can be performed manually, but IDA allows us to do the same without using any other tools.

Our demonstration will be more to the point if we make some changes to the file — add waiting for a keystroke, for example. To do this, we can use the assembler integrated into IDA First, however, we should separate the boundaries of MySeg to add some space for new code.

Select **Segments** from the **View** menu. In the window that opens, move the cursor to the MySeg line. Press the <Ctrl>+<E> key combination to open the dialog box for setting segment properties that contain, among other fields, the last address to be changed. We do not need to set an exact value; we can expand the segment with a small surplus over the space required to accommodate the planned changes.

If we try to add the code XOR AX,AX;INT 16h to the program, it would overwrite the beginning of the string "Hello, Sailor!". Therefore, we need to move it downward slightly beforehand (i.e., into higher addresses). We can do so with a script such as:

```
for (a=0x108; a<0x11A; a++) PatchByte([0x2000, a+0x20], Byte([0x2000, a]);
```

Explanation

The declaration of variable a is omitted for brevity. The relocation, as usual, is specified with a surplus to avoid the need for precise calculations. It occurs from left to right because the initial and target fragments do not overlap.

Place the cursor on line :0128 and press the <A> key to transform the chain of characters to a form convenient for reading. Then, bring the cursor to line :0102 and select the **Assembler** from the **Path** program submenu of the **Edit** menu. Enter the instruction MOV DX,128h (where 128h is the new offset of the string) and immediately make it an offset by pressing the <Ctrl>+<O> key combination.

Now, enter the new code. Place the cursor on the ret instruction, call the assembler again, and enter XOR AX,AX <ENTER> INT 16h <Enter> RET <Enter> <Esc>. It wouldn't be a bad idea to clean up a little: Reduce the segment size to the one used, and move the line containing "Hello, Sailor!" upward, closer to the code.

Explanation

The **Disable Address** option in the **Segment Properties** window is called by pressing the <Alt>+<S> key combination. If it is set, you can decrease its size and delete addresses beyond the end of the segment.

If everything is done correctly, the final result should look as follows:

Listing 17. The Final Disassembled Code

```
seg000:0100 ; File Name    : F:\IDAN\SRC\Crypt.com
seg000:0100 ; Format       : MS-DOS COM-file
seg000:0100 ; Base Address: 1000h Range: 10100h-1013Ch Loaded length: 3Ch
seg000:0100
seg000:0100
seg000:0100 ; ================================================
seg000:0100
seg000:0100 ; Segment type: Pure code
seg000:0100 seg000           segment byte public 'CODE' use16
seg000:0100                  assume cs:seg000
seg000:0100                  org 100h
seg000:0100                  assume es:nothing, ss:nothing, ds:seg000
seg000:0100
```

```
seg000:0100 ; --------------- S U B R O U T I N E -----------------------
seg000:0100
seg000:0100
seg000:0100                    public start
seg000:0100 start             proc near
seg000:0100                    add    si, 6
seg000:0103                    jmp    si        ; jump to address 0106
seg000:0103 start             endp
seg000:0103
seg000:0103 ; ------------------------------------------------------------
seg000:0105                    db 0B9h ; ¦
seg000:0106 ; ------------------------------------------------------------
seg000:0106                    mov    si, offset BytesToDecrypt
seg000:0109                    lodsw
seg000:010A                    xchg   ax, cx
seg000:010B                    push   si
seg000:010C
seg000:010C loc_0_10C:                          ; CODE XREF: seg000:0110↓j
seg000:010C                    xor    byte ptr [si], 66h
seg000:010F                    inc    si
seg000:0110                    loop   loc_0_10C
seg000:0112
seg000:0112 BreakHere:                          ; Jump to the 012E address
seg000:0112                    jmp    si
seg000:0112 ; ------------------------------------------------------------
seg000:0114 BytesToDecrypt  dw 18h              ; DATA XREF: seg000:0106↑o
seg000:0116 ; ------------------------------------------------------------
seg000:0116
seg000:0116 loc_0_116:                          ; CODE XREF: seg000:013B↓u
seg000:0116                    mov    ah, 9
seg000:0118                    mov    dx, 108h ; "Hello, Sailor!\r\n$"
seg000:011B                    int    21h      ; DOS — PRINT STRING
seg000:011B                                    ; DS:DX (string terminated
seg000:011B                                    ; by $)
seg000:011D                    retn
seg000:011D ; ------------------------------------------------------------
seg000:011E aHelloSailor    db 'Hello, Sailor!', 0Dh, 0Ah,'$'
seg000:011E                                    ; DATA XREF: seg000:0118↑o
seg000:012E ; ------------------------------------------------------------
seg000:012E
```

```
seg000:012E loc_0_12E:                              ; CODE XREF: seg000:0112↓u
seg000:012E                    call     $+3
seg000:0131                    pop      cx
seg000:0132                    pop      si
seg000:0133                    mov      di, 100h
seg000:0136                    push     di
seg000:0137                    sub      cx, si
seg000:0139                    repe movsb
seg000:013B                    retn
seg000:013B seg000            ends
seg000:013B
MySeg:0100 ; -----------------------------------------------------------
MySeg:0100 ; ===========================================================
MySeg:0100
MySeg:0100 ; Segment type: Regular
MySeg:0100 MySeg             segment byte public '' use16
MySeg:0100                    assume cs:MySeg
MySeg:0100                    ;org 100h
MySeg:0100
MySeg:0100 loc_1000_100:                            ; CODE XREF: seg000:013B↑u
MySeg:0100                    mov      ah, 9
MySeg:0102                    mov      dx, offset aHelloSailor_0
MySeg:0102                             ; "Hello, Sailor!\r\n$"
MySeg:0105                    int      21h          ; DOS — PRINT STRING
MySeg:0105                             ; DS:DX (string terminated by $)
MySeg:0107                    xor      ax, ax
MySeg:0109                    int      16h
MySeg:0109                             ; KEYBOARD — READ CHAR FROM BUFFER,
MySeg:0109                             ; WAIT IF EMPTY
MySeg:0109                             ; Return: AH = scan code, AL = character
MySeg:010B                    retn
MySeg:010B ; -----------------------------------------------------------
MySeg:010C aHelloSailor_0    db 'Hello, Sailor!', 0Dh, 0Ah, '$'
MySeg:010C                             ; DATA XREF: MySeg:0102↑o
MySeg:010C MySeg             ends
MySeg:010C
MySeg:010C                    start
MySeg:010C end
```

Structurally, the program consists of the following parts: *the decoder,* occupying addresses from `seg000:0x100` to `seg000:0x113`; *the one word variable,* containing the number of decrypted bytes that occupies the addresses from `seg000:0x114` to `seg000:0x116`; *the executable code of the program,* occupying the entire `MySeg` segment; and *the loader,* occupying addresses from `seg000:0x12E` to `seg000:0x13B`. All these parts should be copied to the target file in the listed order. Prior to copying, each byte of the executable code should be encrypted using the `XOR` `0x66` operation.

An example of a script that performs these operations is in Listing 18. To load it, just press the <F2> key or select **IDC File** from the **Load File** submenu of the **File** menu.

Listing 18. The Source Code of the Compiler Script

```
// A Compiler for the Crypt file
//
static main()
{
auto a,f;

// The Crtypt2.com file is opened for binary writing.
f = fopen("crypt2.com, ""wb");

// The decoder is copied into the Crypt2 file.
for (a = 0x100; a < 0x114; a++) fputc(Byte([0x1000, a]), f);
// The word that contains the number of bytes to be deciphered is
// found and copied to the file.
fputc( SegEnd([0x2000,0x100]) — SegStart([0x2000,0x100]),f);
fputc(0,f);

// The deciphered fragment is copied and encrypted on the fly.
for(a = SegStart([0x2000, 0x100]); a != SegEnd([0x2000, 0x100]); a++)
    fputc(Byte(a)^0x66,f);
// Code is added to the loader.
for(a = 0x12E; a < 0x13C; a++)
    fputc(Byte([0x1000,a]), f);

// The file is closed.
fclose(f);
}
```

Executing this script will create the *Crypt2.com* file. You can test it by launching it. The program should display a string, wait until a key is pressed, and terminate.

One advantage of such an approach is a "walkthrough" compilation of the file; that is, the disassembled code wasn't assembled! Instead, the original contents, identical to the source file except for the modified lines, were read byte by byte from virtual memory. Repeated assembling practically never gives the results in the original file.

IDA is a convenient tool for modifying files whose source code is unavailable. It's almost the only disassembler capable of analyzing encrypted programs without using additional tools. It has an advanced user interface and a convenient system for navigating code being analyzed. It also can cope with any task.

However, these and many other capabilities can't be used to their full potential without mastery of the script language, which the previous example has confirmed.

Most protection methods can be cracked using standard techniques that don't require you to understand "how it works." A man widely known to investigators for nearly ten years (and with whom I share the same name) once said: "Having the skills to remove protection doesn't imply having the skills to set it." Crackers typically break and destroy. But a hacker's aim isn't breaking (i.e., finding ways to force the program to work at any cost); it's an understanding of the *mechanism*, of "how it works." Breaking is secondary.

Step Six: Using a Disassembler with a Debugger

There are two ways to analyze programs distributed without source code: *disassembling* (a static analysis), and *debugging* (a dynamic analysis). Generally, every debugger has a built-in disassembler; otherwise, we'd have to debug programs directly in machine code!

However, disassemblers included with debuggers usually are primitive and provide few functions. The disassembler built into the popular SoftIce debugger is not much better than DUMPBIN, whose disadvantages we have experienced. The code becomes much more understandable when it's loaded in IDA!

When is the debugger useful? Disassemblers have several limitations because of their static nature.

First, we would have to execute the program on an "emulator" of the processor, "hardwired" into our own heads. In other words, we would need to mentally run the entire program. To do so, we would need to know the purpose of all processor instructions, functions, and structures of the operating system (including undocumented ones).

Second, it's not easy to start analysis at an arbitrary place in the program. We would need to know the contents of registers and memory, but how could we find these? For registers and local variables, we can scroll the disassembler window upward to see the values stored in these locations. But that won't work with global variables, which can be modified by anyone at any time. If only we could set a breakpoint… But what kind of breakpoint works in a disassembler?

Third, disassembling forces us to completely reconstruct the algorithm of each function, whereas debugging allows us to consider a function as a "black box" that only has input and output. Let's assume that we have a function that decrypts the main module of the program. If we're using a disassembler, we have to figure out the decryption algorithm. (This can be a difficult task.) Then, we need to port this function into IDA-C, debug it, and launch a decrypting program. In the debugger, it's possible to execute the function without trying to understand how it works and, after it finishes, to continue the analysis of decrypted code. We could continue the comparison, but it's clear that the debugger doesn't compete with the disassembler; they are partners.

Experienced hackers always use these tools in conjunction. The profram's logic is reconstructed using a disassembler, and details are cleared up on the fly by running the program in a debugger. When doing so, hackers would like to see in the debugger the character names assigned in the disassembler.

Fortunately, IDA Pro allows this to happen! Select the **Produce output file** submenu from the **File** menu, then click **Produce MAP file** (or press the Shift>+<F10> key combination). A dialog box prompting you for a file name will appear. (Enter *simple.map* or similar file name.) Then, a modal dialog box will open, asking which names should be included in the MAP file. Press the <Enter> key, leaving all the default checkboxes. The *simple*.map file will contain all the necessary debug information in Borland's MAP format. The SoftIce debugger doesn't support such a format, however. Therefore, before using the file, we need to convert it to the SYM format using the idasym utility, created for this purpose. It can be downloaded for free from **http://www.idapro.com**, or obtained from the distributor who sold you IDA.

Run `idasym simple.map` on the command line and make sure that *simple.sym* has been created. Then, load the *simple.exe* application in the debugger. Wait until the SoftIce window appears, then give the SYM command to display the contents of the character table. SoftIce's response should look like this (abridged version):

```
:sym
CODE(001B)
    001B:00401000 start
    001B:00401074 __GetExceptDLLinfo
    001B:0040107C _Main
    001B:00401104 _memchr
    001B:00401124 _memcpy
    001B:00401148 _memmove
    001B:00401194 _memset
    001B:004011C4 _strcmp
```

```
     001B:004011F0 _strlen
     001B:0040120C _memcmp
     001B:00401250 _strrchr
     001B:00403C08 _printf
DATA(0023)
     0023:00407000 aBorlandCCopyri
     0023:004070D9 aEnterPassword
     0023:004070E9 aMygoodpassword
     0023:004070F9 aWrongPassword
     0023:00407109 aPasswordOk
     0023:00407210 aNotype
     0023:00407219 aBccxh1
```

It works! It shows the character names that simplify understanding of the code. You also can set a breakpoint at any of them — for example, bpm aMygoodpassword — and the debugger will understand what you want. You no longer need to remember those hexadecimal addresses.

Step Seven: Identifying Key Structures of High-Level Languages

Research of execution algorithms implemented in programs written in high-level languages traditionally starts with the reconstruction of the key structures of the source language — *functions, local* and *global variables, branches, loops,* etc. This makes the disassembler listing more readable and considerably simplifies its analysis.

Present-day disassemblers are rather intelligent, and perform the lion's share of work when recognizing the key structures. In particular, *IDA Pro* successfully copes with the identification of standard library functions, local variables addressed via the ESP register, CASE branches, etc. However, IDA occasionally makes mistakes, thus misleading the code digger. In addition, its high cost sometimes justifies using a different disassembler. For example, people studying an assembler (and the best way to learn about it is to disassemble someone else's programs) can hardly afford IDA Pro.

Certainly, there are more fish in the sea than IDA. *DUMPBIN*, for example, is a part of the regular SDK delivery — why not use it, if it comes down to it? Of course, if there's nothing better on hand, DUMPBIN will do; but in this case, you'll have to forget about the disassembler's intelligence and use your own brain.

We'll first get acquainted with nonoptimizing compilers. The analysis of their code is rather simple and quite comprehensible, even for programming newbies. Then, having mastered the disassembler, we'll proceed to more complex things — to optimizing compilers that generate artful and intricate code.

Functions

The *function* (also called a procedure or a subroutine) is the main structural unit of procedural and object-oriented languages. Therefore, disassembling a code usually starts with identifying functions and the arguments passed to them.

Strictly speaking, the term "function" is not used in all programming languages. Even when it is, its definition varies from one language to another. Without going into detail, we'll take a function to be a separate routine that can be called from various parts of a program. A function either can accept one or more arguments, or it can reject all of them; it can return the result of its execution, or it can return nothing. This isn't important. The key property of the function is returning control to the place from which it was called, and its characteristic feature is it can be called repeatedly from various parts of a program (although some functions are called from only one place).

How does a function know where it should return control? Obviously, the calling code should save a return address and pass it to the called function along with the other arguments. There are plenty of ways to solve this problem: We can, for example, place an instruction for an unconditional jump to the return address at the end of the function before calling it. We also could save the return address in a special variable, then, when the function's execution is complete, make an indirect jump using this variable as an operand of the JUMP instruction. Without going into a discussion of the strong and weak points of each method, I'd like to note that in most cases, compilers use the CALL and RET special machine instructions for calling functions and returning from them.

The CALL instruction pushes the address of the instruction following it on top of the stack, and RET pops it out from there and passes control to it. The address to which the CALL instruction points is the address of the function's beginning. The RET instruction ends the function. (However, be aware that not every RET designates a function's end! See the "*Values Returned by Functions*" section for more details on this issue.)

Thus, we can recognize a function in two ways: by *cross-references* that lead to the CALL machine instruction, or by its *epilog*, which ends with the RET instruction. The cross-references and the epilog allow us to determine the addresses of the function's beginning and end. Jumping a bit ahead (see the section "*Local Stack Variables*"), I'd like to note that at the beginning of many functions, there is a special sequence of instructions, called a *prolog*, which is also suitable for identifying functions.

Cross-references. Looking up the disassembled code, let's find all CALL instructions; the contents of their operands are simply the required addresses of the function's beginning. The addresses of the nonvirtual functions called by name are calculated during compilation, and the operand of the CALL instruction in such cases represents an immediate value. Thanks to this, the address of the function's beginning can be discovered by simple analysis: Using a context search, we find all CALL substrings and remember (or write down) immediate operands.

Let's consider the following example:

Listing 19. A Direct Function Call

```
func();

main()
{
        int a;
        func();
        a=0x666;
        func();
}

func()
{
        int a;
        a++;
}
```

The result of its compilation should look approximately like this:

Listing 20. The Disassembled Code for the Direct Function Call

```
.text:00401000 push    ebp
.text:00401001 mov     ebp, esp
.text:00401003 push    ecx
.text:00401004 call    401019
.text:00401004    ; Here we've caught the CALL instruction
.text:00401004    ; in which the immediate operand
.text:00401004    ; is an address of the function's beginning or,
.text:00401004    ; to be more exact, its offset in the code segment
.text:00401004    ; (.text, in this case). Now we can jump to the
.text:00401004    ; .text:00401019 line, and, having named the function,
.text:00401004    ; replace the operand of the CALL instruction with
```

```
.text:00401004    ; the call offset Function_name construction.
.text:00401009 mov   dword ptr [ebp-4], 666h
.text:00401010 call  401019
.text:00401010    ; Here is yet another function call! Having looked at
.text:00401010    ; the .text:401019 line, we see that this combination
.text:00401010    ; of instructions is already defined as a function,
.text:00401010    ; and all we have to do is to replace call 401019 with
.text:00401010    ; call offset Function_name.
.text:00401015 mov     esp, ebp
.text:00401017 pop     ebp
.text:00401018 retn
.text:00401018    ; Here we've encountered an instruction for returning from
.text:00401018    ; the function; however, this is not necessarily
.text:00401018    ; the function's end — a function can have several exits.
.text:00401018    ; However, next to this ret is the beginning of
.text:00401018    ; My function, identifiable by the operand of
.text:00401018    ; the call instruction. Since the functions can't overlap,
.text:00401018    ; it seems likely that this ret is the function's end!
.text:00401019 push    ebp
.text:00401019    ; The operands of several call instructions
.text:00401019    ; have references to this line.
.text:00401019    ; Hence, this is an address of a function's beginning.
.text:00401019    ; Every function should have its own name.
.text:00401019    ; How should we name it? Let's name it My function. :-)
.text:0040101A mov   ebp, esp
.text:0040101C push   ecx
.text:0040101D mov   eax, [ebp-4]
.text:00401020 add   eax, 1        ; This is the body of My function.
.text:00401023 mov   [ebp-4],eax
.text:00401026 mov   esp, ebp
.text:00401028 pop   ebp
.text:00401029 retn
.text:00401029; This is the end of My function.
```

As you can see, everything is pretty simple. However, the task becomes much more complicated if the programmer (or the compiler) uses indirect function calls, passing their addresses via the register and dynamically calculating the address while executing the program. In particular, an operation with virtual functions is implemented just in this way. (See the section "*Virtual Functions.*")

In any case, the compiler should somehow save the function address in code, which allows us to find and calculate it. It's even easier to load the analyzed application in the debugger, set a breakpoint on the CALL instruction "under investigation," and, after waiting for the debugger to pop up, see to which address it will pass control.

Let's consider the following example:

Listing 21. Calling a Function Using a Pointer

```
func();
main()
{
        int (a*)();
        a=func;
        a();
}
```

Generally, the result of its compilation should be this:

Listing 22. The Disassembled Code for Calling a Function Using a Pointer

```
.text:00401000     push      ebp
.text:00401001     mov       ebp, esp
.text:00401003     push      ecx
.text:00401004     mov       dword ptr [ebp-4], 401012
.text:0040100B     call      dword ptr [ebp-4]
.text:0040100B ; Here is the CALL instruction that implements
.text:0040100B ; an indirect call of the function
.text:0040100B ; at the address contained in the [EBP-4] cell.
.text:0040100B ; How can we know what is contained there?
.text:0040100B ; Let's scroll the disassembler screen up a little
.text:0040100B ; until we encounter the mov dword ptr [ebp-4],401012 line.
.text:0040100B ; Aha! Then control is passed to the .text:401012 address.
.text:0040100B ; This is exactly the address of the function's beginning.
.text:0040100B ; Let's name the function and replace
.text:0040100B ; mov dword ptr [ebp-4], 401012 with
.text:0040100B ; mov dword ptr [ebp-4], offset Function_name.
.text:0040100E     mov       esp, ebp
.text:00401010     pop       ebp
.text:00401011     retn
```

Some quite rare programs use indirect calls of functions that involve a complex calculation of their addresses. Let's consider the following example:

Listing 23. Calling a Function Using a Pointer and a Complex Calculation of the Target Address

---

```
func_1();
func_2();
func_3();

main()
{
        int x;
        int a[3]={(int) func_1,(int) func_2, (int) func_3};
        int (*f)();

        for (x=0; x<3; x++)
        {
                f=(int (*)()) a[x];
                f();
        }
}
```

Generally, the result of disassembling should look like this:

Listing 24. The Disassembled Code for Calling a Function Using a Pointer and a Complex Calculation of the Target Address

---

```
.text:00401000  push   ebp
.text:00401001  mov    ebp, esp
.text:00401003  sub    esp, 14h
.text:00401006  mov    [ebp+0xC], offset sub_401046
.text:0040100D  mov    [ebp+0x8], offset sub_401058
.text:00401014  mov    [ebp+0x4], offset sub_40106A
.text:0040101B  mov    [ebp+0x14], 0
.text:00401022  jmp    short loc_40102D
.text:00401024  mov    eax, [ebp+0x14]
.text:00401027  add    eax, 1
.text:0040102A  mov    [ebp+0x14], eax
.text:0040102D  cmp    [ebp+0x14], 3
.text:00401031  jge    short loc_401042
```

```
.text:00401033 mov    ecx, [ebp+0x14]
.text:00401036 mov    edx, [ebp+ecx*4+0xC]
.text:0040103A mov    [ebp+0x10], edx
.text:0040103D call   [ebp+0x10]
.text:0040103D ; This is the indirect function call. And what's
.text:0040103D ; in [EBP+0x10]? Having looked at the previous line,
.text:0040103D ; we see that we have the EDX value in [EBP+0x10].
.text:0040103D ; And what is the EDX value? Scrolling up for one line,
.text:0040103D ; we see that EDX is the same as the contents of
.text:0040103D ; the [EBP+ECX*4+0xC] location.
.text:0040103D ; What a mess! Besides the fact that we have
.text:0040103D ; to learn the contents of this cell, we also have
.text:0040103D ; to calculate its address! What is ECX equal to?
.text:0040103D ; The contents of [EBP+0x14], it seems.
.text:0040103D ; And what is the value of [EBP+0x14]?
.text:0040103D ; "Just a moment," we murmur, scrolling up the
.text:0040103D ; disassembler window. Got it! In line 0x40102A,
.text:0040103D ; EAX's contents are loaded into it.
.text:0040103D ; It's certainly possible to waste a lot of time
.text:0040103D ; and effort reconstructing the entire key algorithm
.text:0040103D ; (especially now that we've come to the end of the analysis),
.text:0040103D ; but are there any guarantees that there will be no
.text:0040103D ; mistakes? It's much faster and more reliable to load
.text:0040103D ; the program being investigated into the debugger, set
.text:0040103D ; a breakpoint on line text:0040103D, and then, wait
.text:0040103D ; until the debugger window pops up and see what is there
.text:0040103D ; in the [EBP+0x10] cell. The debugger will pop up three
.text:0040103D ; times, and it will show a new address each time! Bear in
.text:0040103D ; mind that you will only notice this in the disassembler after
.text:0040103D ; you have completed the entire reconstruction of the
.text:0040103D ; algorithm. However, you shouldn't cherish any illusions
.text:0040103D ; about the power of the debugger. A program can
.text:0040103D ; call the same function one thousand times, and can
.text:0040103D ; call a different function the one thousand first time!
.text:0040103D ; The debugger cannot reveal this. The fact is that
.text:0040103D ; such a function call can occur at any moment — when
.text:0040103D ; a certain combination of the current time, the phase of the
.text:0040103D ; moon, and the data processed by the program occurs, for
```

```
.text:0040103D  ; example. Certainly, we aren't going to run the program
.text:0040103D  ; under the debugger for ages. The disassembler is
.text:0040103D  ; quite another matter. A complete reconstruction
.text:0040103D  ; of the algorithm will allow us to unequivocally
.text:0040103D  ; and reliably trace all addresses of indirect calls.
.text:0040103D  ; That's why the disassembler and the debugger
.text:0040103D  ; should be galloping in one harness.
.text:00401040  jmp     short loc_401024
.text:00401042
.text:00401042  mov     esp, ebp
.text:00401044  pop     ebp
.text:00401045  retn
```

The most difficult cases are "manual" function calls that use a JMP instruction that preliminarily pushes the return address on the stack. In general, a call using JMP looks like this: PUSH ret_addrr/JMP func_addr, where ret_addrr and func_addr are a direct or an indirect return address and the function's beginning address, respectively. (By the way, keep in mind that the PUSH and JMP instructions don't always follow one after the other; occasionally, they are separated by other instructions.)

You might ask: What is so bad about CALL, and why do we use JMP at all? The function called by the CALL instruction always passes control to the instruction next to CALL after returning control to the parent function. In some cases (for example, when performing structured exception handling), the execution returns from the function and continues from a completely different branch of the program, rather than from the instruction next to CALL. If this is the case, we have to manually specify the required return address and call the child function using JMP.

It can be very difficult to identify such functions (especially if they have no prolog); a context search gives no result because the body of any program contains plenty of JMP instructions used for near jumps. How, then, can we analyze all of them? If we don't identify the functions, two of them will drop out of sight — the called function and the function to which control is passed just upon returning. Unfortunately, there is no quick and easy solution to this problem; the only hook here is that the calling JMP practically always goes beyond the boundaries of the function in whose body it's located. We can determine the boundaries of a function by using an epilog.

Let's consider the following example:

Listing 25. A "Manual" Function Call Using JMP

```
funct();

main()
{
        __asm
        {
                LEA  ESI, return_addr
                PUSH ESI
                JMP  funct
        return_addr:
        }


}
```

Generally, the result of its compilation should look like this:

Listing 26. The Disassembled Code for a "Manual" Function Call Using JMP

```
.text:00401000 push  ebp
.text:00401001 mov   ebp, esp
.text:00401003 push  ebx
.text:00401004 push  esi
.text:00401005 push  edi
.text:00401006 lea   esi, [401012h]
.text:0040100C push  esi
.text:0040100D jmp   401017
.text:0040100D ; This would seem to be a simple branch —
.text:0040100D ; what could possibly be unusual in it? However, it's not
.text:0040100D ; a simple branch, but a masked function call. How
.text:0040100D ; do we know this? Let's go to address 0x401017 and see.
.text:0040100D ; .text:00401017    push  ebp
.text:0040100D ; .text:00401018    mov   ebp,  esp
.text:0040100D ; .text:0040101A    pop   ebp
.text:0040100D ; .text:0040101B    retn
```

```
.text:0040100D ; What do you think — where does this ret return control?
.text:0040100D ; Naturally, to the address that lies on the top of the
.text:0040100D ; stack. And what do we have there? PUSH EBP from line
.text:0040100D ; 401017 is popped back by the POP from line 40101B.
.text:0040100D ; Well... let's return back to the JMP instruction
.text:0040100D ; and begin slowly scrolling the disassembler window up,
.text:0040100D ; tracing all calls to the stack. Here it is!
.text:0040100D ; The PUSH ESI instruction from line 401000C throws the
.text:0040100D ; contents of the SI register onto the top of the stack,
.text:0040100D ; and the register takes the value of 0x401012,
.text:0040100D ; which is simply the address of the beginning
.text:0040100D ; of the function called by the JMP instruction.
.text:0040100D ; (To be more exact, it's not an address but an offset.
.text:0040100D ; But this isn't of great importance.)
.text:00401012 pop    edi
.text:00401013 pop    esi
.text:00401014 pop    ebx
.text:00401015 pop    ebp
.text:00401016 retn
```

Automatically identifying functions using IDA Pro. The IDA Pro disassembler is capable of analyzing operands of the CALL instructions, which allows it to divide the program into functions automatically. Besides which, IDA quite successfully copes with most indirect calls. However, it can't yet master complex calls and manual function calls that use the JMP instruction. This shouldn't cause much distress, since constructions of this kind are extremely rare; they make up less than one percent of "normal" function calls, which are easily recognized by IDA.

Prolog. Most nonoptimizing compilers place the following code, called a *prolog*, at the beginning of the function.

Listing 27. The Generalized Code of a Function Prolog

```
push   ebp
mov    ebp, esp
sub    esp, xx
```

Generally, the purpose of a prolog comes down to the following: if the EBP register is used for addressing local variables (as is often the case), it must be saved in the stack before using it. (Otherwise, the called function will make the parent function "go crazy".) Then, the current value of the stack pointer register (ESP) is copied into EBP — *the stack frame is opened*, and the ESP value is decreased by the size of the memory block allocated for local variables.

The PUSH EBP/MOV EBP, ESP/SUB ESP, xx sequence can be used to find all functions in the file being investigated, including those that have no direct references to them. In particular, IDA Pro uses this technique. However, optimizing compilers know how to address local variables through the ESP register and use EBP, as well as any other general-purpose register. The prolog of the optimized functions consists of only one SUB ESP,xxx instruction. Unfortunately, this sequence is too short to be used as a signature of the function. A more detailed story about function epilogs is ahead. (See the "*Local Stack Variables*" section.) Therefore, to avoid unnecessary repetition, I don't cover this topic in much detail here.

Epilog. At the end of its "life," the function closes the stack frame, moving the stack pointer downward, and then restores the former value of EBP (only if the optimizing compiler didn't address local variables via ESP using EBP as a general-purpose register). The function's *epilog* can work in one of two ways: Either ESP is increased by the proper value using the ADD instruction, or the EBP value that points to the bottom of the stack frame is copied into it.

Listing 28. The Generalized Code of a Function Epilog

Epilog 1		Epilog 2	
pop	ebp	mov	esp, ebp
add	esp, 64h	pop	ebp
retn		retn	

▶ *Note*

The POP EBP/ADD ESP, xxx and MOV ESP, EBP/POP EBP instructions needn't follow one after another; they can be separated by other instructions. Therefore, a context search is unsuitable for finding epilogs — we will have to use a search *on a mask*.

If the function was written taking into account the Pascal convention, it should clear the stack of arguments itself. In the overwhelming majority of cases, this is done by the RET n instruction, where n is the number of bytes popped from the stack upon returning. Functions obeying the C convention leave clearing the stack to the code that called them and always terminate with the RET instruction. Windows API functions obey a combination of the C and Pascal conventions — arguments are placed on the stack from right to left, but clearing the stack is done by the function itself. (See the "*Function Arguments*" section for more details on this.)

Thus, RET can be a sufficient indication of the function's epilog, but not just any epilog is the function's end. If the function has several RET operators in its body (as is often the case), the compiler usually generates an epilog for each of them. Check whether there's a new prolog after the end of the epilog, or if the code of the old function continues. Don't forget that compilers usually don't place a code that never receives control into an executable file. In other words, the function will have only one epilog, and everything after the first RET will be thrown out as unnecessary.

Listing 29. Eliminating Code after the Unconditional RET Operators

```
int func(int a)        push    ebp
{                      mov     ebp, esp
                       mov     eax, [ebp+arg_0]
    return a++;        mov     ecx, [ebp+arg_0]
    a=1/a;             add     ecx, 1
    return a;          mov     [ebp+arg_0], ecx
                       pop     ebp
}                      retn
```

On the other hand, if an unplanned exit from the function occurs when some condition becomes true, such a RET will be preserved by the compiler and "embraced" with a branch jumping over the epilog.

Listing 30. A Function with Several Epilogs

```
int func(int a)
{
    if (!a) return a++;
    return  1/a;
}
```

Listing 31. The Disassembled Code for the Compiled Function with Several Epilogs

```
        push    ebp
        mov     ebp, esp
        cmp     [ebp+arg_0], 0
        jnz     short loc_0_401017
```

```
mov     eax, [ebp+arg_0]
mov     ecx, [ebp+arg_0]
add     ecx, 1
mov     [ebp+arg_0], ecx
pop     ebp
retn
; Yes, this is obviously the function's epilog;
; but it's followed by a code continuing the function,
; not a new prolog at all!
```

loc_0_401017:   ; CODE XREF: sub_0_401000+7↑j

```
; This cross-reference that leads us to a branch indicates that this code
; is a continuation of the former function, and not the beginning
; of a new one, since "normal" functions are called using not JMP,
; but CALL! And what if it's an "abnormal" function? Well, that's
; easy to check. Just figure out whether the return address is
; on the top of the stack or not. It isn't there;
; hence, our assumption about the function code's continuation
; is true.
     mov     eax, 1
     cdq
     Idiv    [ebp+arg_0]

     loc_0_401020:          ; CODE XREF: sub_0_401000+15↑j
     pop     ebp
     retn
```

A special remark

Starting with the 80286 processor, two instructions — ENTER and LEAVE — have appeared in the instruction set. They are specifically intended for opening and closing the stack frame. However, they are practically never used by present-day compilers. Why? The reason is that ENTER and LEAVE are very sluggish, much slower than PUSH EBP/MOV EBP, ESP/SUB ESB,xxx, and MOV ESP,EBP/POP EBP. So, on a Pentium, ENTER takes ten clock cycles to execute; this sequence normally takes only seven cycles. Similarly, LEAVE requires five clock cycles, although the same operation can be executed in two cycles (or even fewer if you separate MOV ESP,EBP/POP EBP with an instruction. Therefore, the contemporary reader will likely never come across either ENTER or LEAVE. However, it shouldn't be too much trouble to remember their purpose. (You suddenly may want to disassemble ancient programs or programs written in assembler. It's no secret that many of those who write in assembler don't know the subtleties of the processor's operation very well, and their manual optimization is appreciably worse than the compiler's when it comes to performance.)

Naked functions. The Microsoft Visual C++ compiler supports the non-standard attribute *naked*, which allows programmers to create functions without a prolog and an epilog. Yes, without a prolog and an epilog *at all!* The compiler doesn't even place RET at the end of the function; you have to do it manually using an assembly insert __asm{ret}. (Using return alone doesn't produce the desired result.)

Generally, support for naked functions was planned only for writing drivers in pure C (well, almost pure — with small assembly inserts), but it has gained unexpected recognition among developers of protection mechanisms, too. It's really pleasant to have the possibility of manually creating functions without worrying that the compiler will cripple them in an unpredictable way.

For us code diggers, this means that one or more functions that contain neither a prolog nor an epilog can occur in the program. Well, what's so scary about this? Optimizing compilers also throw out the prolog and leave only the RET from the epilog, but functions are easily identified by their CALL instructions.

Identifying inline functions. The most effective way to avoid the overhead inflicted by calling functions is to not call them. Really, why can't we insert the function's code directly in the calling function? Certainly, this will appreciably increase the size (especially as the function is called from more places), but it will also considerably increase the program's performance (if the inline function is called frequently).

Do inline functions hinder the analysis of a program? Well, inlining increases size of the parent function and makes its code less readable. Instead of CALL\TEST AX,EAX\JZ xxx containing an evident branch, we see a heap of instructions reminiscent of nothing and whose operation logic has yet to be figured out.

Recall that we already came across such a technique when analyzing *crackme02*:

Listing 32. The Disassembled Code for an Inline Function

```
mov     ebp, ds:SendMessageA
push    esi
push    edi
mov     edi, ecx
push    eax
push    666h
```

```
          mov     ecx, [edi+80h]
          push    0Dh
          push    ecx
          call    ebp ; SendMessageA
          lea     esi, [esp+678h+var_668]
          mov     eax, offset aMygoodpassword ; "MyGoodPassword"

loc_0_4013F0:                            ; CODE XREF: sub_0_4013C0+52↑j
          mov     dl, [eax]
          mov     bl, [esi]
          mov     cl, dl
          cmp     dl, bl
          jnz     short loc_0_401418
          test    cl, cl
          jz      short loc_0_401414
          mov     dl, [eax+1]
          mov     bl, [esi+1]
          mov     cl, dl
          cmp     dl, bl
          jnz     short loc_0_401418
          add     eax, 2
          add     esi, 2
          test    cl, cl
          jnz     short loc_0_4013F0

loc_0_401414:                            ; CODE XREF: sub_0_4013C0+3C↑j
          xor     eax, eax
          jmp     short loc_0_40141D

loc_0_401418:                            ; CODE XREF: sub_0_4013C0+38↑j
          sbb     eax, eax
          sbb     eax, 0FFFFFFFFh

loc_0_40141D:                            ; CODE XREF: sub_0_4013C0+56↑j
          test    eax, eax
          push    0
          push    0
          jz      short loc_0_401460
```

To summarize, inline functions have neither their own prolog nor epilog. Their code and local variables (if any) are completely inlined in a calling function — the resulting compilation looks exactly as if there were no function call at all. The only catch is that inlining the function inevitably results in doubling its code in all places where it's used. This can be revealed (although with difficulty), because the inline function, when it becomes a part of a calling function, undergoes optimization in the context of the parent function, which results in significant variations in the code. Let's consider this example:

Listing 33. The Pass-Through Optimization of an Inline Function

```
#include <stdio.h>
__inline int max(int a, int b)
{
        if(a>b) return a;
        return b;
}

int main(int argc, char **argv)
{
        printf("%x\n", max(0x666, 0x777));
        printf("%x\n", max(0x666, argc));
        printf("%x\n", max(0x666, argc));

        return 0;
}
```

Generally, the result of its compilation will look like this:

Listing 34. The Disassembled Code for the Pass-Through Optimization of an Inline Function

```
    push    esi
    push    edi
    push    777h        ; This is the code of the first call of max.
    ; The compiler has already calculated the value
    ; that the max function returns and inserted it in the program,
    ; thus getting rid of an extra function call.

    push    offset aProc  ; "%x\n"
```

```
        call    printf
        mov     esi, [esp+8+arg_0]
        add     esp, 8

        cmp     esi, 666h       ; The code of the second call of max
        mov     edi, 666h       ; The code of the second call of max
        jl      short loc_0_401027   ; The code of the second call of max
        mov     edi, esi        ; The code of the second call of max

loc_0_401027:                   ; CODE XREF: sub_0_401000+23↑j
        push    edi
        push    offset aProc    ; "%x\n"
        call    printf
        add     esp, 8

        cmp     esi, 666h        ; The code of the third call of max
        jge     short loc_0_401042   ; The code of the second call of max
        mov     esi, 666h        ; The code of the second call of max

        ; See how the code of the function has changed! First, the sequence
        ; of executing instructions has changed: It was CMP -> MOV -> Jx, and
        ; has become CMP -> Jx-> MOV. Second, the JL branch has mysteriously
        ; turned into JGE! However, there's nothing really mysterious in this —
        ; it's just that a pass-through optimization has occurred! Since after
        ; the third call of the max function, the argc variable that the compiler
        ; placed in the ESI register isn't used anymore. The compiler can use
        ; the possibility of directly modifying this register instead of using
        ; a temporary variable and allocating the EDI register to it.
        ; (See the "Register and Temporary Variables" section.)

loc_0_401042:                   ; CODE XREF: sub_0_401000+3B↑j
        push    esi
        push    offset aProc    ; "%x\n"
        call    printf
        add     esp, 8
        mov     eax, edi
        pop     edi
        pop     esi
        retn
```

When calling the function for the first time, the compiler throws out all of its code, having calculated the result of its operation at compile time. (Really, 0x777 is always greater than 0x666; there's no need to waste processor time comparing them.) The second call is only slightly similar to the third one, although the same arguments were passed to both functions. Here, a mask search will not help (nor a context search). Even a skilled expert will fail to understand whether the same function is called or not!

DOS **Memory models and 16-bit compilers.** Up until now, the address of a function was understood as its *offset* in a code segment. The *flat* memory model of 32-bit Windows NT/9*x* packs all three segments — the code segment, the stack segment, and the data segment — in a uniform 4-gigabyte address space, allowing us to forget about the existence of segments in general.

The 16-bit applications for MS-DOS and Windows 3.*x* are another matter. In these, the maximum segment size is only 64 KB, which is not enough for most applications. In *tiny* memory models, the code, stack, and data segments are also located in the single address space. In contrast to the *flat* model, this address space is extremely limited in size, and serious applications should be stuffed in several different segments.

In this case, it's not enough to know the function's offset to call a function — you also must specify the segment in which it's located. However, today we can forget about this old-fashioned rule with a clear conscience. In view of the forthcoming 64-bit Windows version, describing 16-bit code in detail would simply be ridiculous.

Order of translating functions. Most compilers allocate functions in an executable file in the order they were declared in the program.

Start-up Functions

If we were to ask the first programmer who comes along: "With what function does the execution of a Windows program start?" We would most likely hear the answer: "With WinMain" — which is a mistake. Actually, the first to receive control is the *start-up code*, which is imperceptibly inserted by the compiler. Having executed the necessary initialization procedures, at some point the start-up code calls WinMain. After the completion of WinMain, the start-up code receives control again and performs a thorough deinitialization.

In most cases, the start-up code isn't of any interest to us; finding the WinMain function becomes the first task for the code digger. If IDA Pro recognizes the compiler, it identifies WinMain automatically; otherwise, we have to use our own brains and hands. The standard compiler usually contains the source codes of its libraries, including the start-up code procedures. For example, in the Microsoft Visual C++ package, the start-up code is located in the *CRT\SRC\crto.c* file in the version for static linking, in the *CRT\SRC\crtexe.c* file in the version for dynamic linking (i.e., the library code isn't linked to the file, but is called from a DLL), and in the *CRT\SRC\wincmdln.c* file in the version for console applications. In the Borland C++ package, all files containing the start-up code are stored in a separate directory (Startup). In particular, the start-up code for Windows applications is contained in the *c0w.asm* file. Now that I have explained source codes a bit, it'll be much easier to understand the disassembler listing.

But what should you do if a compiler that is unknown or unavailable to you was used for the investigated program? Before we begin a tiresome manual analysis, let's see what kind of prototype the WinMain function has:

```
int WINAPI WinMain(
  HINSTANCE hInstance,        // Handle to current instance
  HINSTANCE hPrevInstance,    // Handle to previous instance
  LPSTR lpCmdLine,            // Pointer to command line
  int nCmdShow                // Show state of window
);
```

First, four arguments (see the "*Function Arguments*" section) are quite enough. In most cases, WinMain appears to be the function of the start-up code that is richest in arguments. Second, the last argument placed in the stack — hInstance — is most often calculated on the fly by calling the GetModuleHandleA function. For example, having met a construction of the type CALL GetModuleHandleA, we can assert with a high degree of confidence that the following function is nothing else than WinMain. Finally, the call to WinMain is usually located near the end of the code of the start-up function. It's usually followed by no more than two or three functions such as exit or XcptFilter.

Let's consider the following code fragment. Our attention is arrested by the multitude of PUSH instructions pushing the arguments into the stack, the last one of which passes the result of executing GetModuleHandleA. This means we are dealing with nothing else than the call to WinMain (and IDA confirms that this is indeed the case).

Listing 35. Identifying the WinMain Function by the Arguments Passed to It

```
.text:00401804  push   eax
.text:00401805  push   esi
.text:00401806  push   ebx
```

```
.text:00401807  push   ebx
.text:00401808  call   ds:GetModuleHandleA
.text:0040180E  push   eax
.text:0040180F  call   _WinMain@16
.text:00401814  mov    [ebp+var_68], eax
.text:00401817  push   eax
.text:00401818  call   ds:exit
```

However, things are not always that simple. Many developers modify the source start-up code, sometimes considerably, when it is available. As a result, executing a program may start not with WinMain, but with any other function. In addition, the start-up code can contain an operation critical for understanding the algorithm (a decryptor of the main code, for example). Therefore, it's *always* necessary to skim through the start-up code to figure out if it contains something unusual.

Matters are similar with dynamic link libraries (.dll). Their execution doesn't start with the DllMain function (if there's one in the DLL at all), but rather with __DllMainCRTStartup by default. However, developers sometimes change the defaults, specifying the start-up function they need using the /ENTRY key of the linker. Strictly speaking, DllMain is not a *start-up* function — it's called not only when loading DLL, but also when unloading and when the process that has linked the function creates/terminates a new thread. Having received messages about these events, the developer can undertake some actions (for example, prepare code for working in a multithreaded environment). But is this significant for the analysis of the program? Most often, the dynamic link library must not be analyzed as a whole; rather, the operation of some functions exported by it must be investigated. If DllMain performs any operations — say, initializes variables — then other functions somehow related to these variables should contain direct references to them that lead straight to DllMain. Thus, we don't need to manually search for DllMain — it'll come to light by itself. It would be nice if this were *always* the case! But life is more complicated than any rules. What if there is a certain destructive code in DllMain, or if the library, besides its main activity, spies on threads to trace their appearance? Then, we can't do without a direct analysis of its code.

It's more difficult to reveal DllMain than WinMain; if IDA doesn't find it, the situation is hopeless. First, the prototype of DllMain is relatively unsophisticated and doesn't contain anything special:

```
BOOL WINAPI DllMain(
   HINSTANCE hinstDLL,   // Handle to DLL module
```

```
    DWORD fdwReason,       // Reason for calling function
    LPVOID lpvReserved     // Reserved
);
```

Second, its call comes from the depth of a rather impressive function, __DllMainCRTStartup, and there's no way to easily make sure that it's exactly that CALL we need. There are some catches, however. When the initialization fails, DllMain returns FALSE. The code of __DllMainCRTStartup checks this value, and jumps are possible even to the end of the function. The body of the start-up function contains few of such branches, and only one of them is usually connected to the function accepting three arguments.

Listing 36. Identifying DllMain by the Failed Initialization Code

```
.text:1000121C          push      edi
.text:1000121D          push      esi
.text:1000121E          push      ebx
.text:1000121F          call      _DllMain@12
.text:10001224          cmp       esi, 1
.text:10001227          mov       [ebp+arg_4], eax
.text:1000122A          jnz       short loc_0_10001238
.text:1000122C          test      eax, eax
.text:1000122E          jnz       short loc_0_10001267
```

Having scrolled the window a bit upward, it's easy to make sure that the EDI, ESI, and EBX registers contain lpvReserved, fdwReason, and hinstDLL, respectively. Hence, we're dealing with the DllMain function. (The source code of __DllMainCRTStartup is contained in the *dllcrt0.c* file, which I strongly recommend that you study.)

At last, we've reached the main function of console Windows applications. As always, the execution of the program does not start with it, but rather with the mainCRTStartup function that passes control to main only after initializing the *heap*, and the input/output system that prepares the command line arguments. The main function accepts only two arguments: int main(int argc, char **argv). This is not enough to distinguish it from other functions. However, there is one fact that proves to be helpful — that the keys of the command line are accessible not only through arguments, but also through global variables — `__argc` and `__argv`. Therefore, the call to `main` usually looks like this:

Listing 37. Identifying the `main` Function

```
.text:00401293        push     dword_0_407D14
.text:00401299        push     dword_0_407D10
.text:0040129F        call     _main
.text:0040129F ; Both arguments of the function are
.text:0040129F ; pointers — .text:0040129F points to global variables.
.text:0040129F ; (See the "Global Variables" section.)
.text:004012A4        add      esp, 0Ch
.text:004012A7        mov      [ebp+var_1C], eax
.text:004012AA        push     eax
.text:004012AA ; The value returned by the function is passed
.text:004012AA ; to the exit function as the code of the process' completion
.text:004012AA ; Hence, this is main.
.text:004012AA
.text:004012AB        call     _exit
```

Note that the result of completing `main` is passed to the function next to it. (As a rule, this is the `exit` library function.)

Thus, you should have an understanding of how to identify the main types of start-up functions. Certainly, in life, things don't happen as simply as they do in theory. In any case, the techniques described above will appreciably simplify the analysis.

Virtual Functions

By definition, a virtual function is *defined at the run time of a program*. When a virtual function is called, the executable code should correspond to the dynamic type of the object from which the function is called. The address of a virtual function can't be determined at compile time — we have to do this just before we call it. Therefore, a virtual function always answers an *indirect* call. (The only exception is a virtual function of a static object.)

While nonvirtual C++ functions are called in exactly the same way as normal C functions, virtual functions are called in a substantially different way. The method of calling isn't standardized; it depends on the implementation of a particular compiler. But the references to all virtual functions are usually placed into a special array — a *virtual table* (*VTBL*). The *virtual table pointer* (*VPTR*) is placed in each instance of the object that uses at least one virtual function. Nonderived objects, or objects with a single inheritance, have no more than one VPTR, while objects with multiple inheritance can have several VPTRs.

Virtual functions usually are called indirectly through the pointer to the virtual table — for example, CALL [EBX+0x10], where EBX is the register containing the offset of the virtual table in memory, and 0x10 is the offset of the pointer to the virtual function inside the virtual table. The only exception is a virtual function of a static object.

The analysis of virtual function calls involves a number of complications, the most unpleasant of which is the necessity of backtracing the code to keep track of the value of the register used for indirect addressing. It's good to initialize this by an immediate value of the type MOV EBX, offset VTBL near the place where it's used. However, the pointer to VTBL is most often passed to a function as an implicit argument, or, even worse, the same register pointer is used for calling several different virtual functions. Then an uncertainty arises: Exactly which value (values) does it have in the given location of the program?

Let's analyze the following example (first recalling that the virtual function of the derived class is invoked for objects of the derived class, even if it is called using a pointer or reference to the base class):

Listing 38. Calling a Virtual Function

```
#include <stdio.h>

class Base{
 public:
      virtual void demo(void)
      {
            printf("BASE\n");
       };

      virtual void demo_2(void)
      {
            printf("BASE DEMO 2\n");
       };
```

```
        void demo_3(void)
        {
                printf("Nonvirtual BASE DEMO 3\n");
        };

};

class Derived: public Base{
 public:
        virtual void demo(void)
        {
                printf("DERIVED\n");
        };

        virtual void demo_2(void)
        {
                printf("DERIVED DEMO 2\n");
        };

        void demo_3(void)
        {
                printf("Nonvirtual DERIVED DEMO 3\n");
        };
};

main()
{
        Base *p = new Base;
        p->demo();
        p->demo_2();
        p->demo_3();

        p = new Derived;
        p->demo();
        p->demo_2();
        p->demo_3();
}
```

In general, the disassembled code of its compiled version should look like this:

Listing 39. The Disassembled Code for Calling a Virtual Function

```
main  proc near          ; CODE XREF: start+AF↓p
      push   esi
      push   4
      call ??2@YAPAXI@Z  ; operator new(uint)
      ; EAX c is a pointer to the allocated memory block.
      ; Four bytes of memory are allocated for the instance of a new
      ; object. The object consists of only one pointer to VTBL.

      add    esp, 4
      test   eax, eax
      jz  short loc_0_401019 ; --> Memory allocation error
      ; Checking whether memory allocation is successful

      mov dword ptr [eax], offset BASE_VTBL
      ; Here the pointer to the virtual table of the BASE class
      ; is written in the instance of the object just created.
      ; We can make sure that this is a virtual table of the BASE class
      ; by analyzing the table's elements. They point to members
      ; of the BASE class, and therefore, the table itself is
      ; a virtual table of the BASE class.

      mov    esi, eax             ; ESI = **BASE_VTBL

      ; The compiler then writes the pointer to the object instance
      ; (the pointer to the pointer to BASE_VTBL) in ESI. Why?
      ; The pointer is written to the instance
      ; of the object in ESI (see the section "Objects,
      ; Structures, and Arrays"), but all these details are of no use
      ; at this point. Therefore, we'll simply say that ESI
      ; contains the pointer to the pointer to the virtual table
      ; of the BASE class, without going into why this double pointer
      ; is necessary.

      jmp short loc_0_40101B

loc_0_401019:                      ; CODE XREF: sub_0_401000+D↑j
```

```
        xor esi, esi
        ; This overwrites the pointer to the object instance with NULL.
        ; (This branch receives control only if there is a failure
        ; in allocating memory for the object.)
        ; The null pointer will evoke the structural exception handler
        ; at the first attempt of calling.

loc_0_40101B:              ; CODE XREF: sub_0_401000+17↑j
        mov eax, [esi]     ; EAX = *BASE_VTBL == *BASE_DEMO

        ; Here, the pointer to the virtual table of the BASE class is
        ; placed in EAX, keeping in mind that the pointer to the virtual,
        ; table also is the pointer to the first element of this table.
        ; The first element of the virtual table, in turn, contains
        ; the pointer to the first virtual function
        ; (in the declaration order) of the class.


        mov ecx, esi        ; ECX = this

        ; Now, the pointer to the instance of the object is written into
        ; ECX, passing an implicit argument — the this pointer —
        ; to the called function.
        ; (See the "Function Arguments" section.)

        call dword ptr [eax] ; CALL BASE_DEMO

        ; This is what we came for — the call of
        ; the virtual function! To understand which function is called,
        ; we should know the value of the EAX register.
        ; Scrolling the disassembler window upward, we see that EAX points
        ; to BASE_VTBL, and the first element of BASE_VTBL (see below)
        ; points to the BASE_DEMO function.
        ; Therefore,
        ; this code calls the BASE_DEMO function, and
        ; the BASE_DEMO function is a virtual function.

        mov    edx, [esi]           ; EDX = *BASE_DEMO
        ; The pointer to the first element of the virtual table
        ; of the BASE class is placed into EDX.
```

```
mov     ecx, esi            ; ECX = this
; The pointer to the object instance is placed into ECX.
; This is an implicit argument of the function — the this
; pointer. (See "The this Pointer" section.)

call    dword ptr [edx+4]   ; CALL [BASE_VTBL+4] (BASE_DEMO_2)
; Here's one more call of a virtual function! To understand
; which function is called, we should know the contents of the
; EDX register. Scrolling the screen window upward, we see that
; it points to BASE_VTBL; thus, EDX+4 points to the second
; element of the virtual table of the BASE class, which, in turn,
; points to the BASE_DEMO_2 function.

push    offset aNonVirtualBase ; "Nonvirtual BASE DEMO  3\n"
call    printf
; Here's a call of a nonvirtual function. Pay attention — it's
; implemented in the same way as the call of a regular C function.
; Note that this is an inlined function; that is, it's declared
; directly in the class, and instead of calling it,
; code is inserted.

push 4
call    ??2@YAPAXI@Z          ; operator new(uint)
; The calls of DERIVED class functions continue.
; In general, we only needed the DERIVED class here
; to show how virtual tables are arranged.

add     esp, 8          ; Clearing the stack after printf and new
test    eax, eax
jz      short loc_0_40104A   ; Memory allocation error
mov     dword ptr [eax], offset DERIVED_VTBL
mov     esi, eax             ; ESI == **DERIVED_VTBL
jmp     short loc_0_40104C

loc_0_40104A:                          ; CODE XREF: sub_0_401000+3E↑j
    xor     esi, esi

loc_0_40104C:                          ; CODE XREF: sub_0_401000+48↑j
```

```
mov     eax, [esi]          ; EAX = *DERIVED_VTBL
mov     ecx, esi            ; ECX = this
call    dword ptr [eax]     ; CALL [DERIVED_VTBL] (DERIVED_DEMO)
mov     edx, [esi]          ; EDX = *DERIVED_VTBL
mov     ecx, esi            ; ECX=this
call    dword ptr [edx+4]   ; CALL [DERIVED_VTBL+4] (DERIVED_DEMO_2)

push    offset aNonVirtualBase ; "Nonvirtual BASE DEMO 3\n"
call    printf
; Note that the called BASE_DEMO function is of the base class,
; not of the derived one!

add     esp, 4
pop     esi
retn
main    endp


BASE_DEMO    proc near      ; DATA XREF: .rdata:004050B0↓o
push    offset aBase            ; "BASE\n"
call    printf
pop     ecx
retn
BASE_DEMO       endp


BASE_DEMO_2 proc near       ; DATA XREF: .rdata:004050B4↓o
push    offset aBaseDemo2   ; "BASE DEMO 2\n"
call    printf
pop     ecx
retn
BASE_DEMO_2                 endp


DERIVED_DEMO  proc near     ; DATA XREF: .rdata:004050A8↓o
push    offset aDerived     ; "DERIVED\n"
call    printf
pop     ecx
retn
DERIVED_DEMO                endp


DERIVED_DEMO_2  proc near   ; DATA XREF: .rdata:004050AC↓o
push    offset aDerivedDemo2 ; "DERIVED    DEMO 2\n"
```

```
        call    printf
        pop     ecx
        retn
DERIVED_DEMO_2 endp


DERIVED_VTBL    dd offset DERIVED_DEMO   ; DATA XREF: sub_0_401000+40↑o
                dd offset DERIVED_DEMO_2
BASE_VTBL       dd offset BASE_DEMO      ; DATA XREF: sub_0_401000+F↑o
                dd offset BASE_DEMO_2
; Note that the virtual tables "grow" from the bottom up
; in the order classes were declared in the program, and the elements
; of the virtual tables "grow" from top down in the order virtual
; functions were declared in the class. This is not always the case.
; The order of allocating tables and their elements isn't standardized
; and depends entirely on the developer of the compiler;
; however, in practice, most of compilers behave in this manner.
; Virtual functions are allocated close to each other
; in the order that they were declared.
```

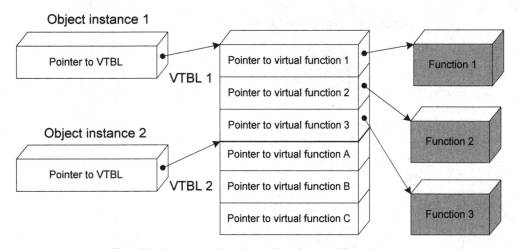

Fig. 11. Implementing the calls of virtual functions

Identifying a pure virtual function. If a function is declared in the base class and implemented in the derived class, such a function is called a *pure virtual function.* A class containing at least one such function is considered an *abstract class.*

The C++ language prohibits the creation of instances of an abstract class. How can they be created anyway, if at least one of the functions of a class is undefined?

Note

At first glance, it's not defined — and that's OK. A pure virtual function in a virtual table is replaced with a pointer to the library function __purecall. What is this function for? At the compile time, it's impossible to catch all attempts of calling pure virtual functions. But if such a call occurs, the control will be passed to __purecall, substituted here beforehand. It will then yell at you about the prohibition on calling pure virtual functions and will terminate the application.

Thus, the presence of the pointer to __purecall in the virtual table indicates that we're dealing with an abstract class. Let's consider the following example:

Listing 40. Calling a Pure Virtual Function

```
#include <stdio.h>

class Base{
public:
        virtual void demo(void)=0;

};

class Derived:public Base {
public:
        virtual void demo(void)
        {
        printf("DERIVED\n");
        };
};

main()
{

        Base *p = new Derived;
        p->demo();
}
```

In general, the result of compiling it should look like this:

Listing 41. The Disassembled Code for Calling a Pure Virtual Function

---

```
Main    proc    near                ; CODE XREF: start+AF↓p
        push    4
        call    ??2@YAPAXI@Z
        add     esp, 4
        ; Memory is allocated for the new instance of the object.

        test    eax, eax
        ; This checks whether allocating memory is successful.

        jz      short loc_0_401017
        mov     ecx, eax
        ; ECX = this

        call    GetDERIVED_VTBL
        ; The pointer to the virtual table of the DERIVED class
        ; is placed in the instance of the object.

        jmp     short loc_0_401019

loc_0_401017:                       ; CODE XREF: main+C↑j
        xor     eax, eax
        ; EAX is set to null.

loc_0_401019:                       ; CODE XREF: main+15↑j
        mov     edx, [eax]
        ; Here, an exception is thrown on calling to a null pointer.

        mov     ecx, eax
        jmp     dword ptr [edx]
        main    endp

GetDERIVED_VTBL proc near           ; CODE XREF: main+10↑p
        push    esi
        mov     esi, ecx
        ; The implicit argument this is passed to the function
        ; through the ECX register.

        call    SetPointToPure
```

```
        ; The function places the pointer to __purecall
        ; in the object instance. This function is a stub for the case
        ; of an unplanned call of a pure virtual function.

        mov     dword ptr [esi], offset DERIVED_VTBL
        ; The pointer to the virtual table of the DERIVED class is placed
        ; in the object instance, overwriting the previous value
        ; of the pointer to __purecall).

        mov     eax, esi
        pop     esi
        retn
GetDERIVED_VTBL                 endp


DERIVED_DEMO  proc near         ; DATA XREF: .rdata:004050A8↓o
        push    offset aDerived ; "DERIVED\n"
        call    printf
        pop     ecx
        retn
DERIVED_DEMO  endp


SetPointToPureproc near         ; CODE XREF: GetDERIVED_VTBL+3↓p
        mov     eax, ecx
        mov     dword ptr [eax], offset PureFunc
        ; The pointer to the special function __purecall is written
        ; at the [EAX] address (in the instance of the new object).
        ; The purpose of this function is to catch attempts of calling
        ; pure virtual functions in the course of executing the program.
        ; If such an attempt occurs, __purecall will scold you again,
        ; saying that you shouldn't call a pure virtual function,
        ; and will terminate the operation.

        retn
SetPointToPureendp

DERIVED_VTBL  dd offset DERIVED_DEMO  ; DATA XREF: GetDERIVED_VTBL+8↑o
PureFunc      dd offset __purecall   ; DATA XREF: SetPointToPure+2↑o
        ; Here is a pointer to the stub-function __purecall.
        ; Hence, we're dealing with a pure virtual function.
```

Sharing a virtual table between several instances of an object. However many instances of an object might exist, all of them use the same virtual table. The virtual table belongs to the object, not to the instance of this object. Exceptions to this rule are further on in this section.

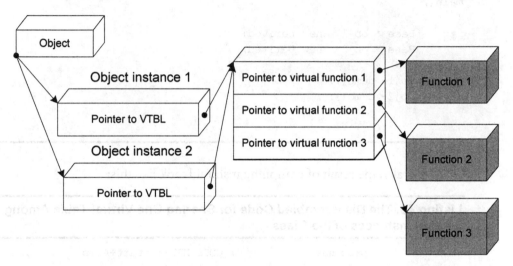

Fig. 12. Sharing one virtual table among several instances of the object

To confirm this, let's consider the following example:

Listing 42. Sharing One Virtual Table Among Several Instances of the Class

---

```
#include <stdio.h>

class Base{
 public:
        virtual demo ()
        {
                printf   ("Base\n");
        }
};

class Derived:public Base{
 public:
        virtual demo()
```

```
        {
                printf("Derived\n");
        }
};

main()
{
        Base * obj1 = new Derived;
        Base * obj2 = new Derived;

        obj1->demo();
        obj2->demo();

}
```

Generally, the result of compiling it should look like this:

Listing 43. The Disassembled Code for Sharing One Virtual Table Among Several Instances of the Class

```
main            proc near           ; CODE XREF: start+AF↓p
        push    esi
        push    edi
        push    4
        call    ??2@YAPAXI@Z        ; operator new(uint)
        add     esp, 4
        ; Memory is allocated for the first instance of the object.

        test    eax, eax
        jz      short loc_0_40101B
        mov     ecx, eax
        ; EAX points to the first instance of the object.

        call    GetDERIVED_VTBL
        ; EAX contains the pointer to the virtual table of the DERIVED class.

        mov     edi, eax            ; EDI = *DERIVED_VTBL
        jmp     short loc_0_40101D

loc_0_40101B:                       ; CODE XREF: main+E↑j
        xor     edi, edi
```

```
loc_0_40101D:                        ; CODE XREF: main+19↑j
    push    4
    call    ??2@YAPAXI@Z             ; operator new(uint)
    add     esp, 4
    ; Memory is allocated for the second instance of the object.

    test    eax, eax
    jz      short loc_0_401043
    mov     ecx, eax                 ; ECX is this

    call    GetDERIVED_VTBL
    ; Note that the second object instance
    ; uses the same virtual table.

DERIVED_VTBL  dd offset DERIVED_DEMO  ; DATA XREF: GetDERIVED_VTBL+8↑o
BASE_VTBL     dd offset BASE_DEMO     ; DATA XREF: GetBASE_VTBL+2↑o
; Note that the virtual table is common for all instances of the class.
```

Copies of virtual tables. Well, it's obvious that a single virtual table is quite enough for working successfully. However, in practice, we often face a situation in which the file being investigated is swarmed by copies of these virtual tables. What kind of invasion is this, where is it from, and how can we counteract it?

If a program consists of several files compiled into separate object modules (such an approach is used in practically all more or less serious projects), the compiler, obviously, should place its own virtual table in each object module for each class used by that module. Really, how can the compiler know about the existence of other object modules, and about the presence of virtual tables in them? This leads to unnecessary duplication of virtual tables, which consumes memory and complicates the analysis. However, at link time, the linker can detect copies and delete them, and compilers use various heuristic algorithms to increase the efficiency of the generated code. The following algorithm has gained the greatest popularity: The virtual table is placed in the module that contains the first non-inline, non-virtual implementation of a function of the class. Each class is usually implemented in one module, and in most cases such heuristics works. Things are worse if a class consists of only virtual or inline functions — in this case, the compiler "breaks down" and starts pushing virtual tables into all modules where this class is used. The last hope for deleting the "garbage" copies is pinned on the linker — but don't think the linker is a panacea. Actually, these problems should worry the developers of compilers and linkers (if they're worried about the volume of memory occupied by the program); for analysis, the superfluous copies are only an annoyance, not a hindrance.

A linked list. In most cases, a virtual table is an ordinary array. Certain compilers, however, present it as a linked list. Each element of the virtual table contains a pointer to the following element. Elements are not close to each other, but rather are scattered over the entire executable file.

In practice, however, linked lists are rarely used, so we won't consider this case here — just know that it sometimes occurs. If you come across linked lists, you can figure it out according to the circumstances.

Calling through a thunk. When looking through a virtual table in the case of multiple inheritance, be ready to encounter a pointer not to a virtual function, but to a code that modifies the this pointer so that it points to an instance of the object from which the "replacing function" has been taken. This technique was offered by C++ language developer Bjarne Stroustrup, who borrowed it from early implementations of *Algol-60*. In Algol, the code that corrects the this pointer is known as a *thunk,* and the call itself is known as a *call through the thunk.* This terminology is applicable in C++ as well.

Although calling through the thunk provides a more compact storage of virtual tables, modifying the pointer results in an excessive overhead when processors with a pipeline architecture are used. (Pentium — the most commonly used processor — has an architecture of just this kind.) Therefore, using thunk calls is justified only in programs that are critical to the size, not to the speed.

A complex example that places nonvirtual functions in virtual tables. Until now, we have considered only the simplest examples of using virtual functions. Life, however, is more complex, and you may occasionally be in for a big surprise with these virtual tables. Let's consider a complex case of inheritance that involves a name conflict:

Listing 44. Placing Nonvirtual Functions in Virtual Tables

```
#include <stdio.h>

class A{
public:
        virtual void f() { printf("A_F\n");};
```

```
};

class B{
public:
        virtual void f() { printf("B_F\n");};
        virtual void g() { printf("B_G\n");};
};

class C: public A, public B {
public:
        void f(){ printf("C_F\n");}
}

main()
{
        A *a = new A;
        B *b = new B;
        C *c = new C;
        a->f();
        b->f();
        b->g();
        c->f();
}
```

What will the virtual table of class C look like? Well, let's think. Since class C is derived from classes A and B, it inherits the functions of both of them. However, the virtual function f() from class B overloads the virtual function of the same name from class A; therefore, it is not inherited from class A. Furthermore, since the nonvirtual function f() is also present in the derived C class, it overloads the virtual function of the derived class. (If a function is declared virtual in the base class, it will be virtual in the derived class by default.) Thus, a virtual table of class C should contain only one element — the pointer to the virtual function g(), inherited from B. The virtual function f() is called as a regular C function. Is this right? No, it's not!

This is the case when *a function that isn't explicitly declared virtual is called through the pointer — as a virtual function.* Moreover, the virtual table of the class will contain three, not two, elements! The third element is a reference to the virtual function f() inherited from B, but this element is immediately replaced by the compiler with a thunk to C::f(). Phew! Tough, huh? Maybe it'll become more understandable after studying the disassembled listing.

Listing 45. The Disassembled Code for Placing Nonvirtual Functions in Virtual Tables

---

```
main        proc near               ; CODE XREF: start+AF↓p
       push    ebx
       push    esi
       push    edi
       push    4
       call    ??2@YAPAXI@Z         ; operator new(uint)
       add     esp, 4
       ; Memory is allocated for an instance of object A.


       test    eax, eax
       jz      short loc_0_40101C
       mov     ecx, eax            ; ECX =   this
       call    Get_A_VTBL          ; a[0]=*A_VTBL
       ; The pointer to the virtual table of the object
       ; is placed in its instance.


       mov     ebx, eax            ; EBX =   *a
       jmp     short loc_0_40101E


loc_0_40101C:                      ; CODE XREF: main+F↑j
       xor     ebx, ebx


loc_0_40101E:                      ; CODE XREF: main+1A↑j
       push    4
       call    ??2@YAPAXI@Z        ; operator new(uint)
       add     esp, 4
       ; Memory is allocated for the instance of object B.


       test    eax, eax
       jz      short loc_0_401037
       mov     ecx, eax            ; ECX = this
       call    Get_B_VTBL          ; b[0] = *B_VTBL
       ; The pointer to the virtual table of the object
       ; is placed in its instance.
```

```
        mov     esi, eax                ; ESI = *b
        jmp     short loc_0_401039


loc_0_401037:                           ; CODE XREF: main+2A↑j
        xor     esi, esi


loc_0_401039:                           ; CODE XREF: main+35↑j
        push    8
        call    ??2@YAPAXI@Z            ; operator new(uint)
        add     esp, 4
        ; Memory is allocated for the instance of object C.
        test    eax, eax
        jz      short loc_0_401052
        mov     ecx, eax                ; ECX = this
        call    GET_C_VTBLs             ; ret: EAX=*c
        ; The pointer to the virtual table of the object
        ; is placed in its instance.
        ; Attention: Look into the GET_C_VTBLs function.

        mov     edi, eax                ; EDI =   *c
        jmp     short loc_0_401054


loc_0_401052:                   ; CODE XREF: main+45↑j
        xor     edi, edi


loc_0_401054:                   ; CODE XREF: main+50↑j
        mov     eax, [ebx]              ; EAX =   a[0] = *A_VTBL
        mov     ecx, ebx                ; ECX =   *a
        call    dword ptr [eax]         ; CALL [A_VTBL] (A_F)
        mov     edx, [esi]              ; EDX =   b[0]
        mov     ecx, esi                ; ECX =   *b
        call    dword ptr [edx]         ; CALL [B_VTBL] (B_F)
        mov     eax, [esi]              ; EAX =   b[0] = B_VTBL
        mov     ecx, esi                ; ECX =   *b
        call    dword ptr [eax+4]       ; CALL [B_VTBL+4] (B_G)
        mov     edx, [edi]              ; EDX =   c[0] = C_VTBL
        mov     ecx, edi                ; ECX =   *c
        call    dword ptr [edx]         ; CALL [C_VTBL] (C_F)
        ; Attention: The nonvirtual function is called as a virtual one!
```

```
        pop     edi
        pop     esi
        pop     ebx
        retn
main            endp

GET_C_VTBLs     proc near           ; CODE XREF: main+49↑p
        push    esi                 ; ESI = *b
        push    edi                 ; ECX = *c
        mov     esi, ecx            ; ESI = *c
        call    Get_A_VTBL          ; c[0]=*A_VTBL
        ; The pointer to the virtual table of the A class
        ; is placed in the instance of object C.

        lea     edi, [esi+4]        ; EDI = *c[4]
        mov     ecx, edi            ; ECX = **_C_F
        call    Get_B_VTBL          ; c[4]=*B_VTBL
        ; The pointer to the virtual table of class B is added
        ; in the instance of object C — that is, object C now contains
        ; two pointers to two virtual tables of the base class.
        ; Let's see how the compiler will cope with the name conflict.

        mov     dword ptr [edi], offset C_VTBL_FORM_B ; c[4]=*_C_VTBL
        ; The pointer to the virtual table of class B is replaced
        ; with the pointer to the virtual table of class C.
        ; (See the comments directly in the table.)

        mov     dword ptr [esi], offset C_VTBL ; c[0]=C_VTBL
        ; Once more — now the pointer to the virtual table of class A
        ; is replaced with the pointer to the virtual table of class C.
        ; What a poorly written code!
        ; It could easily have been cut down at compile time!

        mov     eax, esi            ; EAX = *c
        pop     edi
        pop     esi
        retn
GET_C_VTBLs     endp

Get_A_VTBL      proc near               ; CODE XREF: main+13↑p GET_C_VTBLs+4↑p
        mov     eax, ecx
```

```
        mov     dword ptr [eax], offset A_VTBL
        ; The pointer to the virtual table of class B
        ; is placed in the instance of the object.

        retn
Get_A_VTBL      endp



A_F             proc near           ; DATA XREF: .rdata:004050A8↑o
        ; This is the virtual function f() of class A.

        push    offset aA_f         ; "A_F\n"
        call    printf
        pop     ecx
        retn
A_F                                 endp



Get_B_VTBL      proc near           ; CODE XREF: main+2E↑p GET_C_VTBLs+E↑p
        mov     eax, ecx
        mov     dword ptr [eax], offset B_VTBL
        ; The pointer to the virtual table of class B
        ; is placed in the instance of the object.

        retn
Get_B_VTBL      endp


B_F             proc near           ; DATA XREF: .rdata:004050AC↑o
        ; This is the virtual function f() of class B.
        push    offset aB_f         ; "B_F\n"
        call    printf
        pop     ecx
        retn
B_F                                 endp


B_G             proc near           ; DATA XREF: .rdata:004050B0↑o
        ; This is the virtual function g() of class B.

        push    offset aB_g         ; "B_G\n"
        call    printf
```

```
        pop     ecx
        retn
B_G             endp


C_F             proc near           ; CODE XREF: _C_F+3↑j
        ; The nonvirtual function f() of class C looks like and is called
        ; as a virtual one!

        push    offset aC_f         ; "C_F\n"
        call    printf
        pop     ecx
        retn
C_F             endp


_C_F            proc near           ; DATA XREF: .rdata:004050B8↑o
        sub     ecx, 4
        jmp     C_F
        ; Look what a strange function this is! This is exactly the same
        ; thunk of which we were speaking a moment ago. First, it's never
        ; called (although it would have been called if we had decided
        ; to address the replaced virtual function, and if
        ; the this pointer pointed "right past" this function).
        ; Second, it's a thunk to the C_F function.
        ; What is ECX decreased for? The compiler has placed the this pointer,
        ; which, before decreasing, tried to point to the entire object
        ; inherited from class B. Upon decreasing, it started pointing
        ; to the previous sub-object — that is, to the contents
        ; of the f() function called by JMP.

_C_F                            endp

A_VTBL          dd offset A_F       ; DATA XREF: Get_A_VTBL+2↑o
; This is the virtual table of the A class.

B_VTBL          dd offset B_F       ; DATA XREF: Get_B_VTBL+2↑o
                dd offset B_G
; This is the virtual table of class B, which contains the pointers
; to two virtual functions.

C_VTBL          dd offset C_F       ; DATA XREF: GET_C_VTBLs+19↑o
```

```
; The virtual table of class C contains the pointer
; to the function f() which isn't explicitly declared
; virtual, but is virtual by default.

C_VTBL_FORM_B dd offset _C_F        ; DATA XREF: GET_C_VTBLs+13↑o
              dd offset B_G
; The virtual table of class C is copied by the compiler from
; class B. It originally consisted of two pointers to the f() and g()
; functions, but the compiler resolved the conflict of names
; at compile time, and replaced the pointer to B::f()
; with the pointer to the adapter for C::f().
```

Thus, the virtual table of a derived class actually includes virtual tables of all base classes (at least, of those classes from which it inherits virtual functions). In this case, the virtual table of class C contains the pointer to the C function, which isn't explicitly declared virtual but is virtual by default, and the virtual table of class B. The problem is how to figure out that the C::f() function isn't explicitly declared virtual, but is virtual by default, and how to find all base classes of class C.

Let's begin with the latter. The virtual table of class C doesn't contain any hint as to its relation to class A, but let's look at the contents of the GET_C_VTBLs function. There is an attempt to embed the pointer to the virtual table in the instance of class C, and, therefore, class C is derived from A. (This is really only an attempt, because the embedded pointer to the virtual table of class A is immediately overwritten by the new pointer to the "corrected" virtual table of class A, which contains the corrected addresses of the virtual functions of class C.) Someone might raise the objection that this isn't a reliable approach — the compiler might optimize the code by throwing out the call to the virtual table of class A, since it's not needed anyway. This is true, it *might* do so indeed. But in practice, however, most compilers don't do this. If they do, they leave enough redundant information allowing us to determine the base classes, even in a mode of aggressive optimization. Another question is: Do we really need to determine "parents" from whom not a single function is inherited? (If at least one function is inherited, no complexities arise in the analysis.) In general, it isn't a crucial point for the analysis. Still, the more accurately the original code of the program is reconstructed, the more readable and comprehensible it will be.

Now let's proceed to the function f(), which isn't explicitly declared virtual, but is virtual by default. Let's speculate about what would happen if it actually was explicitly declared virtual. It would overlap the same function of the base classes, and we would encounter no absurdity in the compiled program (like we did in those thunks). The function isn't virtual, although it tends to look like it. Theoretically, the smart compiler could throw out a thunk and a duplicated element of the virtual table of the c class, but such intelligence isn't exhibited in practice. Functions explicitly declared virtual and functions that are virtual by default are absolutely identical; therefore, they can't be distinguished in the disassembled code.

Static binding. Is there any difference between the instance of an object created as MyClass zzz, or MyClass *zzz=new MyClass? Certainly. In the first case, the compiler can determine the addresses of virtual functions at compile time, whereas the addresses have to be calculated at run time in the second case. One more distinction: Static objects are allocated on the stack (in the data segment), and dynamic ones on the heap. The table of virtual functions is persistently created by compilers in both cases. When each function is called (including a nonvirtual one), the this pointer containing an address of the instance of an object is prepared. (As a rule, the pointer is placed in one of the general-purpose registers. See the "*Function Arguments*" section for more details.)

Thus, if we encounter a function called directly by its offset, but at the same time listed in the virtual table of a class, we can be sure that it's a virtual function of a static instance of an object.

Let's consider the following example:

Listing 46. Calling a Static Virtual Function

```
#include <stdio.h>

class Base{
 public:
        virtual void demo(void)
        {
         printf("BASE DEMO\n");
        };

        virtual void demo_2(void)
        {
         printf("BASE DEMO 2\n");
        };

        void demo_3(void)
```

```
        {
         printf("Nonvirtual BASE DEMO 3\n");
        };

    };


        class Derived: public Base{
         public:
         virtual void demo(void)
         {
         printf("DERIVED DEMO\n");
          };

        virtual void demo_2(void)
        {
         printf("DERIVED DEMO 2\n");
        };

        void demo_3(void)
        {
         printf("Nonvirtual DERIVED DEMO 3\n");
        };
    };


main()
{
        Base p;
        p.demo();
        p.demo_2();
        p.demo_3();

        Derived d;
        d.demo();
        d.demo_2();
        d.demo_3();
}
```

Generally, the disassembled listing of the compiled version of this program should look like this:

Listing 47. The Disassembled Code for Calling a Static Virtual Function

---

```
main            proc near               ; CODE XREF: start+AF↓p

var_8           = byte ptr -8           ; derived
var_4           = byte ptr -4           ; base
        ; The instances of objects are often (but not always) allocated
        ; on the stack from the bottom up, that is, in the order opposite
        ; from which you declared them in the program.

        push    ebp
        mov     ebp, esp
        sub     esp, 8

        lea     ecx, [ebp+var_4]        ; base
        call    GetBASE_VTBL            ; p[0]=*BASE_VTBL
        ; Notice that the instance of the object is located on the stack,
        ; not on the heap! This, of course, doesn't yet prove the static
        ; nature of the instance of the object (dynamic objects can be allocated
        ; on the stack, too), but nevertheless hints at the "statics."

        lea     ecx, [ebp+var_4]        ; base
        ; The this pointer is prepared
        ; (in case it will be needed for the function).

        call    BASE_DEMO
        ; A direct call of the function! Along with its presence
        ; in the virtual table, this is the evidence of the static
        ; character of the declaration of the object instance.

        lea     ecx, [ebp+var_4]        ; base
        ; A new this pointer is prepared to the base instance.

        call    BASE_DEMO_2
        ; A direct call of the function. Is it there in the virtual table?
        ; Yes, it is! This means that it's a virtual function,
```

```
        ; and the instance of the object is declared static.

        lea    ecx, [ebp+var_4]    ; base
        ; The this pointer is prepared for the nonvirtual function demo_3.

        call   BASE_DEMO_3
        ; This function isn't present in the virtual table
        ; (see the virtual table), hence, it's not a virtual one.

        lea    ecx, [ebp+var_8]    ; derived
        call   GetDERIVED_VTBL     ; d[0]=*DERIVED_VTBL

        lea    ecx, [ebp+var_8]    ; derived
        call   DERIVED_DEMO
        ; same as above...

        lea    ecx, [ebp+var_8]    ; derived
        call   DERIVED_DEMO_2
        ; same as above...

        lea    ecx, [ebp+var_8]    ; derived
        call   BASE_DEMO_3_
        ; Attention: The this pointer points to the DERIVED object
        ; when the function of the BASE object is called!
        ; Hence, the BASE function is a derived one.

        mov    esp, ebp
        pop    ebp
        retn
main    endp

BASE_DEMO     proc near           ; CODE XREF: main+11↑p
; This is the demo function of the BASE class.

        push   offset aBase       ; "BASE\n"
        call   printf
        pop    ecx
        retn
BASE_DEMO     endp

BASE_DEMO_2   proc near           ; CODE XREF: main+19↑p
```

```
; This is the demo_2 function of the BASE class.

        push    offset aBaseDemo2   ; "BASE DEMO 2\n"
        call    printf
        pop     ecx
        retn
BASE_DEMO_2   endp


BASE_DEMO_3   proc near             ; CODE XREF: main+21↑p
; This is the demo_3 function of the BASE class.

        push    offset aNonVirtualBase ; "Nonvirtual BASE DEMO  3\n"
        call    printf
        pop     ecx
        retn
BASE_DEMO_3   endp


DERIVED_DEMO  proc near             ; CODE XREF: main+31↑p
; This is the demo function of the DERIVED class.

        push    offset aDerived     ; "DERIVED\n"
        call    printf
        pop     ecx
        retn
DERIVED_DEMO  endp


DERIVED_DEMO_2proc near             ; CODE XREF: main+39↑p
; This is the demo_2 function of the DERIVED class.

        push    offset aDerivedDemo2 ; "DERIVED    DEMO 2\n"
        call    printf
        pop     ecx
        retn
DERIVED_DEMO_2endp


BASE_DEMO_3_  proc near             ; CODE XREF: main+41↑p
; This is the demo_3 function of the DERIVED class.
; Attention: The demo_3 function occurs in the program twice.
; The first time, it appeared in the object of the BASE class,
; and the second time, it appeared in the DERIVED object.
```

```
; The DERIVED object inherited it from the BASE class,
; and has made a copy of it.
; This is kind of silly, isn't it?
; It'd be better off using the original…
; But you see, this simplifies the analysis
; of the program!

            push    offset aNonVirtualDeri ; "Nonvirtual DERIVED DEMO 3\n"
            call    printf
            pop     ecx
            retn
BASE_DEMO_3_ endp

GetBASE_VTBL  proc near            ; CODE XREF: main+9↑p
; In the instance of the BASE object,
; the offset of its virtual table is written.

            mov     eax, ecx
            mov     dword ptr [eax], offset BASE_VTBL
            retn
GetBASE_VTBL  endp

GetDERIVED_VTBL proc near          ; CODE XREF: main+29↑p
; In the instance of the DERIVED object,
; the offset of its virtual table is written.

            push    esi
            mov     esi, ecx
            call    GetBASE_VTBL
            ; Aha! Our object is derived from BASE.

            mov     dword ptr [esi], offset DERIVED_VTBL
            ; The pointer is written to the DERIVED virtual table.

            mov     eax, esi
            pop     esi
            retn
GetDERIVED_VTBL                    endp


BASE_VTBL     dd offset BASE_DEMO  ; DATA XREF: GetBASE_VTBL+2↑o
```

```
                dd offset BASE_DEMO_2
DERIVED_VTBL   dd offset DERIVED_DEMO   ; DATA XREF: GetDERIVED_VTBL+8↑o
                dd offset DERIVED_DEMO_2
; Note that the virtual table occurs even where it's not needed!
```

Identifying derived functions. Identifying derived nonvirtual functions is a rather subtle problem. At first you might think that if they're called like regular C functions, it's impossible to recognize in what class the function was declared. The compiler destroys this information at compile time — but not all of it. Before it calls each function (it doesn't matter whether it's a derived one or not), the `this` pointer must be created in case it is required by the function pointing to the object from which this function is called. For derived functions, the `this` pointer stores the offset of the derived object, not the base one. That's all! If the function is called with various `this` pointers, it's a derived function.

It's more difficult to figure out from which object the function has been derived. There are no universal solutions to this. Still, if we've singled out the A object that uses the `f1()`, `f2()`... functions and the B object that uses the `f1()`, `f3()`, `f4()`... functions, then we can safely assert that the `f1()` function is derived from class A. However, if the `f1()` function has never been called from the instance of the class, we won't be able to determine whether it's a derived one or not.

Let's consider all this in the following example:

Listing 48. Identifying Derived Functions

```c
#include <stdio.h>

class Base{
 public:
    void base_demo(void)
    {
        printf("BASE DEMO\n");
    };

    void base_demo_2(void)
    {
        printf("BASE DEMO 2\n");
    };
};

class Derived: public Base{
```

```
public:
     void derived_demo(void)
     {
          printf("DERIVED DEMO\n");
     };

     void derived_demo_2(void)
     {
          printf("DERIVED DEMO 2\n");
     };
};
```

Generally, the disassembled listing of the compiled version of this program should look like this:

Listing 49. The Disassembled Code for Identifying Derived Functions

```
main          proc near            ; CODE XREF: start+AF↓p
       push   esi
       push   1
       call   ??2@YAPAXI@Z         ; operator new(uint)
       ; A new instance of some object is created.
       ; We don't yet know of which one. Let's say, it is the a object.

       mov    esi, eax             ; ESI = *a
       add    esp, 4
       mov    ecx, esi             ; ECX = *a (this)
       call   BASE_DEMO
       ; Now we're calling BASE_DEMO, taking into account the fact
       ; that this points to a.

       mov    ecx, esi             ; ECX = *a (this)
       call   BASE_DEMO_2
       ; Now we're calling BASE_DEMO_2, taking into account the fact
       ; that this points to a.

       push   1
       call   ??2@YAPAXI@Z         ; operator new(uint)
       ; One more instance of some object is created; let's call it b.

       mov    esi, eax             ; ESI = *b
```

```
        add     esp, 4
        mov     ecx, esi                ; ECX = *b (this)
        call    BASE_DEMO
        ; Aha! We're calling BASE_DEMO, but now this points to b.
        ; Hence, BASE_DEMO is related to both a and b.

        mov     ecx, esi
        call    BASE_DEMO_2
        ; Here we're calling BASE_DEMO_2, but now this points to b.
        ; Hence, BASE_DEMO_2 is related to both a and b.

        mov     ecx, esi
        call    DERIVED_DEMO
        ; Now we're calling DERIVED_DEMO. The this pointer points to b,
        ; and we can't see any relation between DERIVED_DEMO and a.
        ; When calling, this has never pointed to a.

        mov     ecx, esi
        call    DERIVED_DEMO_2
        ; the same...

        pop     esi
        retn
main            endp
```

So you see, you can identify nonvirtual derived functions. The only difficulty is how to distinguish the instances of two different objects from instances of the same object.

We've already discussed identifying derived virtual functions. They are called in two stages — the offset of the virtual table of the base class is written in the object instance, then it's replaced with the offset of the virtual table of the derived class. Even though the compiler optimizes the code, the redundancy remainder will be greater than necessary for distinguishing derived functions from other ones.

Identifying virtual tables. Now, having thoroughly mastered virtual tables and functions, we'll consider a very insidious question: Is any array of pointers to functions a virtual table? Certainly not! Indirectly calling a function through a pointer is often used by programmers in practice. An array of pointers to functions... hmm. Well, it's certainly not typical, but it happens, too!

Let's consider the following example — it's a somewhat ugly and artificial, but to show a situation where a pointer array is vitally necessary, we'd have to write hundreds of lines of code.

Listing 50. An Imitation of a Virtual Table

```
#include <stdio.h>

void demo_1(void)
{
        printf("Demo 1\n");
}

void demo_2(void)
{
        printf("Demo 2\n");
}

void call_demo(void **x)
{
        ((void (*)(void)) x[0])();
        ((void (*)(void)) x[1])();
}

main()
{
        static void* x[2] =
        { (void*) demo_1,(void*) demo_2};
        // Attention: If you initialize an array
        // in the course of the program (i.e.,
        // x[0]=(void *) demo_1, ...), the compiler will generate
        // an adequate code that writes the functions' offsets
        // at run time, which is absolutely unlike a virtual table!
        // On the contrary, initializing an array when it's declared
        // causes ready pointers to be placed in the data segment,
        // which resembles a true virtual table.
        // (By the way, this also helps save CPU clocks ticks.)

        call_demo(&x[0]);
}
```

Now, see if you can distinguish a handmade table from a true one.

Listing 51. Distinguishing an Imitation from a True Virtual Table

```
main            proc near               ; CODE XREF: start+AF↓p
        push    offset Like_VTBL
        call    demo_call
        ; A pointer to something very similar to a virtual table is passed
        ; to the function. But having grown wise with experience, we easily
        ; discover this crude falsification. First, the pointers to VBTL aren't
        ; passed so simply. (The code used for this isn't that basic.)
        ; Second,
        ; they're passed via the register, not via the stack.
        ; Third, no existing compiler uses the pointer to a virtual table
        ; directly, but places it in an object. But here, there's neither
        ; an object nor a this pointer. Therefore, this isn't a virtual table,
        ; although to the untrained eye, it looks very similar.

        pop     ecx
        retn
main            endp

demo_call       proc near               ; CODE XREF: sub_0_401030+5↑p

arg_0                                   = dword ptr  8
        ; That's it! The argument is a pointer,
        ; and virtual tables are addressed through the register.

        push    ebp
        mov     ebp, esp
        push    esi
        mov     esi, [ebp+arg_0]
        call    dword ptr [esi]
        ; Here's a two-level function call — through the pointer
        ; to the array of pointers to the function, which is typical for
        ; calling virtual functions. But again, the code is too simple —
        ; calling virtual functions involves a lot of redundancy,
        ; and in addition, the this pointer is absent.

        call    dword ptr [esi+4]
```

```
        ; The same thing here. This is too simple
        ; for calling a virtual function.

        pop    esi
        pop    ebp
        retn
demo_call    endp


Like_VTBL    dd offset demo_1    ; DATA XREF:main
             dd offset demo_2
        ; The pointer array externally looks like a virtual table,
        ; but does not reside where virtual tables usually reside.
```

Let's recap the main signs of a falsification:

☐ The code is too simple — a minimum number of registers are used, and there is no redundancy. Calling virtual tables is much more intricate.

☐ The pointer to a virtual function is placed in the instance of an object, and is passed via the register, not via the stack. (See "*The* this *Pointer*" section.)

☐ There is no `this` pointer, which is always created before calling a virtual function.

☐ Virtual functions and static variables are located in various places of the data segment — therefore, we can distinguish them at once.

Is it possible to organize the function call by reference so the compilation of the program produces a code identical to the call of a virtual function? Theoretically, yes. But in practice, it's hardly possible to do so (especially without intending to). Because of its high redundancy, the code that calls virtual functions is very specific and can be recognized on sight. It's easy to imitate a common technique of working with virtual tables, but it's impossible to exactly reproduce it without assembly inserts.

Conclusion. In general, working with virtual functions involves many redundancies and "brakes," and the analysis of them is very labor-consuming. We permanently have to keep many pointers in mind and remember where each of them points. Still, code diggers seldom face insoluble problems.

Constructors and Destructors

Why is it difficult to identify the *constructor*? First, in most cases, the constructor is called automatically when a new instance of the object is created. This makes it the first function to be called — but only *if* it is called. The constructor is *optional*; it may be present in an object, or it may not. Therefore, the function called first isn't always a constructor!

Second, by looking at the description of the C++ language, we learn that the constructor doesn't return a value. This is unusual in regular functions, but this feature isn't unique and can't be used to reliably identify the constructor. What should we do then?

According to the standard, the constructor shouldn't throw exceptions automatically, even if the memory allocation for the object fails. Most compilers implement this requirement by placing a check for a null pointer before evoking the constructor. The control is passed to the constructor *only* if memory for the object has been allocated successfully.

In contrast, the other functions of the object are always called, even if the attempt to allocate memory was unsuccessful. To be precise, the other functions *try to be called*. If a memory allocation error occurs, a null pointer is returned. This causes an exception to be thrown when the first call is attempted for these functions. The control is then passed to the handler of the corresponding exception.

Thus, the function enclosed only by checks for a null pointer is a constructor. Theoretically, a similar check can be used when other functions are called, but I have not come across such functions yet.

The *destructor*, like the constructor, is optional; the object's function called last must not necessarily be a destructor. Nevertheless, it's simple to distinguish a destructor from any other function — it's called only if memory has been successfully allocated and the object has been created. This is a documented property of the language; it must be implemented by all compilers. Just as with the constructor, a "ring" of null pointers is placed in the code, but no confusion arises because the constructor is called first, and the destructor last.

An object consisting entirely of one constructor or one destructor is a special case. How can we figure out what we're dealing with? The call of a constructor is practically always followed by a code that resets `this` to zero if memory allocation was unsuccessful; there's nothing of the kind for a destructor. What's more, the destructor is rarely called directly from the parent procedure. Instead, the destructor is called from a function wrapper, along with the `delete` operator that releases the memory acquired by the object. So, it's quite possible to distinguish a constructor from a destructor!

To better understand these distinctions, let's consider the following example:

Listing 52. An Example of a Constructor and a Destructor

```
#include <stdio.h>

class MyClass{
 public:
        MyClass(void);
        void demo(void);
        ~MyClass(void);

};

MyClass::MyClass()
{
        printf("Constructor\n");
}

MyClass::~MyClass()
{
        printf("Destructor\n");
}

void MyClass::demo(void)
{
        printf("MyClass\n");
}

main()
{
        MyClass *zzz = new MyClass;
        zzz->demo();
        delete zzz;

}
```

In general, the disassembled code of the compiled version of this example should look like this:

Listing 53. The Disassembled Code for a Constructor and a Destructor

---

```
Constructor proc near              ; CODE XREF: main+11↓p
; This is a constructor function. We can make sure that this is
; a constructor by looking at an implementation of its call.
; (See the main function below.)

        push    esi
        mov     esi, ecx
        push    offset aConstructor ; "Constructor\n"
        call    printf
        add     esp, 4
        mov     eax, esi
        pop     esi
        retn
Constructor     endp


Destructor      proc near          ; CODE XREF: __destructor+6↓p
; This is a destructor function. We can make sure that this is
; a destructor by looking at the implementation of its call.
; (See the main function below.)

        push    offset aDestructor ; "Destructor\n"
        call    printf
        pop     ecx
        retn
Destructor      endp


demo            proc near          ; CODE XREF: main+1E↓p
; This is an ordinary demo function.
        push    offset aMyclass    ; "MyClass\n"
        call    printf
        pop     ecx
        retn
demo            endp




main            proc near          ; CODE XREF: start+AF↓p
```

```
        push    esi
        push    1
        call    ??2@YAPAXI@Z            ; operator new(uint)
        add     esp, 4
        ; Memory is allocated for a new object,
        ; or, rather, an attempt is made to do so.

        test    eax, eax
        jz      short loc_0_40105A
        ; A check for whether the allocation of memory for the object
        ; is successful. Pay attention to the jump destination.
        ; The destination is XOR ESI, ESI, which resets the poiner to the object.
        ; Attempting to use the null pointer causes an exception
        ; to be thrown, but the constructor should not throw an exception,
        ; even though allocating memory for the object is unsuccessful.
        ; Therefore, the constructor gets control
        ; only if the memory allocation is a success.
        ; Hence, the function preceding XOR ESI, ESI is just a constructor!

        mov     ecx, eax
        ; The this pointer is prepared.

        call    Constructor
        ; This function is a constructor, since it's called
        ; only if the memory allocation is a success.

        mov     esi, eax
        jmp     short loc_0_40105C

loc_0_40105A:                           ; CODE XREF: main+D↑j
        xor     esi, esi
        ; The pointer to the object is reset
        ; to cause an exception when attempting to use the pointer.
        ; Attention: The constructor never throws an exception,
        ; therefore, the function below definitely isn't a constructor.

loc_0_40105C:                           ; CODE XREF: main+18↑j
        mov     ecx, esi
```

```
        ; The this pointer is prepared.

        call    demo
        ; An ordinary function of the object is called.

        test    esi, esi
        jz      short loc_0_401070
        ; Checking the this pointer for NULL. The destructor is called
        ; only if memory for the object has been allocated.
        ; (If not, we likely have nothing to release.)
        ; Thus, the following function is a destructor and nothing else.

        push    1
        ; The number of bytes to release. (This is necessary for delete.)

        mov     ecx, esi
        ; Preparing the this pointer.

        call    __destructor
        ; The destructor is called.

loc_0_401070:                         ; CODE XREF: main+25↑j
        pop     esi
        retn
main            endp


__destructor  proc near               ; CODE XREF: main+2B↑p
; This is a destructor function. Notice that the destructor
; is usually called from the same function as delete.
; (This is not always the case.)

arg_0                           = byte ptr  8
        push    ebp
        mov     ebp, esp
        push    esi
        mov     esi, ecx
        call    Destructor
        ; A user-defined destructor function is called.

        test    [ebp+arg_0], 1
```

```
        jz      short loc_0_40109A
        push    esi
        call    ??3@YAXPAX@Z         ; operator delete(void *)
        add     esp, 4
        ; Memory is released, previously allocated for the object.

loc_0_40109A:                        ; CODE XREF: __destructor+F↑j
        mov     eax, esi
        pop     esi
        pop     ebp
        retn    4
__destructor endp
```

For objects in automatic memory, the constructor/destructor can't be identified. If an object is placed on the stack (in automatic memory), no checks are performed for the success of its allocation. In this case, the call of the constructor becomes indistinguishable from the calls of other functions. The situation is similar with the destructor: The stack memory is released automatically upon the function's completion, and the object ceases without evoking `delete` (only used for deleting objects from the heap).

To make sure of this, let's modify the `main` function of our previous example as follows.

Listing 54. A Constructor/Destructor for an Object on the Stack

```
main()
{
      MyClass zzz;
      zzz.demo();
}
```

In general, the result of compiling this code should look like this:

Listing 55. The Compilation of a Constructor/Destructor for an Object on the Stack

```
main            proc near            ; CODE XREF: start+AF↓p

var_4           = byte ptr -4
; The zzz local variable is an instance of the MyClass object.

        push    ebp
```

```
mov     ebp, esp
push    ecx
lea     ecx, [ebp+var_4]
; The this pointer is prepared.

call    constructor
; The constructor is invoked just like an ordinary function!
; We can guess, although not with complete certainty,
; that this is a constructor judging from its contents alone.
; (The constructor usually initializes an object.)

lea     ecx, [ebp+var_4]
call    demo
; Notice that calling the demo function
; doesn't differ from calling the constructor!

lea     ecx, [ebp+var_4]
call    destructor
; Calling the destructor, as we already understand,
; has no specific peculiarities.

mov     esp, ebp
pop     ebp
retn
main            endp
```

Identifying the constructor/destructor in global objects. Global objects (also known as static objects) are allocated in the data segment at compile time. Hence, memory allocation errors are basically impossible. Does this mean that, as with stack objects, we can't reliably identify the constructor/destructor? Not quite.

A global object is accessible from many places in the program, but its constructor should be called only *once*. How is this done? Most compilers simply use a global variable-flag initially equal to zero, then incremented by one before the first call of the constructor (set to TRUE, in a more general case). We just have to find out whether the flag is equal to zero when the program iterates. If it's not, we must skip calling the constructor. Once again, the constructor is encircled with a branch that allows us to reliably distinguish it from all other functions.

Things are easier still with the destructor: If the object is global, it's deleted only when the program is completed. And what can trace it, besides run time type information (RTTI)? A special function, such as _atexit, receives the pointer to the destructor, saves it, and then invokes it when it becomes necessary. The special function should be called only once. To avoid using yet another flag, it's called just after the constructor is invoked. At first, the object may seem to consist of the constructor/destructor only, but this is not the case! Don't forget that _atexit doesn't immediately pass control to the destructor code; it only remembers the pointer to it for later use.

Thus, it's simple to identify the constructor/destructor of the global object, as the following example proves:

Listing 56. A Constructor/Destructor for a Global Object

```
main()
{
      static MyClass zzz;
      zzz.demo();


}
```

Generally, the result of compiling this code should look like this:

Listing 57. The Compilation of a Constructor/Destructor for a Global Object

---

```
main        proc near          ; CODE XREF: start+AF↓p
      mov    cl, byte_0_4078E0   ; This is a flag for initializing
                                 ; the instance of the object.

      mov    al, 1
      test   al, cl
      ; Is the object initialized?

      jnz    short loc_0_40106D
      ; Yes, it's initialized; the constructor shouldn't be called.

      mov    dl, cl
      mov    ecx, offset unk_0_4078E1 ; This is an instance of the object.
      ; The this pointer is prepared.

      or     dl, al
```

```
        ; The initialization flag is set,
        ; and the constructor called.

        mov    byte_0_4078E0, dl    ; This is a flag for initializing
                                    ; the instance of the object.
        call   constructor
        ; Notice that the instance of the object
        ; is already initialized (see the check above),
        ; and the constructor isn't called.
        ; Thus, it can be easily identified!

        push   offset thunk_destructo
        call   _atexit
        add    esp, 4
        ; This is passing pointer to the destructor to the _atexit function.
        ; The destructor should be called upon completion of the program.


loc_0_40106D:                       ; CODE XREF: main+A↑j
        mov   ecx, offset unk_0_4078E1 ; This is an instance of the object.
        ; The this pointer is prepared.


        jmp   demo
        ; Calling demo


main           endp


thunk_destructo:                    ; DATA XREF: main+20↑o
        ; This is a thunk to the destructor function.

        mov   ecx, offset unk_0_4078E1 ; This is an instance of the object.
        jmp   destructor

byte_0_4078E0 db 0                  ; DATA XREF: mainr main+15↑w
                                    ; This is a flag for initializing
                                    ; the instance of the object.
unk_0_4078E1  db 0                  ; DATA XREF: main+Eo main+2D↑o...
                                    ; This is an instance of the object.
```

Similar code is generated by Borland C++; the only difference is Borland creates artful calls of all destructors. These calls are placed in a special procedure that usually resides before or near library functions, and so they're easy to identify. Take a look:

Listing 58. A Constructor/Destructor for a Global Object Using Borland C++

```
_main           proc near           ; DATA XREF: DATA:00407044↓o
        push    ebp
        mov     ebp, esp
        cmp     ds:byte_0_407074, 0 ; A flag for initializing the object
        jnz     short loc_0_4010EC
        ; If the object is already initialized, the constructor isn't called.


        mov     eax, offset unk_0_4080B4 ; An instance of the object
        call    constructor
        inc     ds:byte_0_407074    ; A flag for initializing the object
        ; The flag is incremented by one
        ; (to set the TRUE value).


loc_0_4010EC:                       ; CODE XREF: _main+A↑j
        mov     eax, offset unk_0_4080B4 ; An instance of the object
        call    demo


        xor     eax, eax
        pop     ebp
        retn
_main           endp


call_destruct proc near             ; DATA XREF: DATA:004080A4↓o
; This function contains the calls of all the destructors of global
; objects. Since the call of each destructor is encircled by the check
; for the initialization flag, this function can be easily identified —
; only this function contains such encircling code. (Calls of
; constructors are usually scattered over the entire program.)


        push    ebp
        mov     ebp, esp
        cmp     ds:byte_0_407074, 0 ; A flag for initializing the object
        jz      short loc_0_401117
```

```
        ; Is the object initialized?

    mov    eax, offset unk_0_4080B4 ; An instance of the object
        ; The this pointer is prepared.

    mov    edx, 2
    call   destructor


loc_0_401117:                      ; CODE XREF: call_destruct+A↑j
    pop    ebp
    retn
call_destruct endp
```

Virtual destructor. A destructor can be virtual, too! It's useful if the instance of a derived class is deleted using the pointer to the base object. Since virtual functions belong to the class of an object, not the class of a pointer, a virtual destructor is invoked according to the object type, not the pointer type. However, these subtleties concern programming. Code diggers are interested in how to identify the virtual destructor. It's easy — a virtual destructor combines the properties of a typical destructor and of a virtual function. (See the "*Virtual Functions*" section.)

Virtual constructor. Is there such a thing? Standard C++ doesn't support anything of the kind. That is, it doesn't *directly* support a virtual constructor; programmers seldom need one. Still, if they do, they could write some emulating code. The code is placed in a virtual function (not the constructor!) specially chosen for this purpose. It looks approximately like this: `return new (class_name) (*this)`. This trick is not pretty, but it works.

Certainly, there are other solutions. A detailed discussion of them is beyond the scope of this book. It would require a profound knowledge of C++, would occupy too much space, and would hardly interest most readers.

So, the identification of a virtual constructor is basically impossible because it lacks a concept. Its emulation can be performed using any of dozens of solutions — go ahead; try and count them all. However, in most cases, virtual constructors are virtual functions that take the `this` pointer as an argument and return the pointer to a new object. This isn't a reliable identification criterion, but it's better than nothing.

One constructor, two constructor... There may be more than one object constructor. This doesn't influence the analysis in any way. Only one constructor is chosen by the compiler, depending on the declaration of the object, and it is invoked for each object instance. One essential detail: Various object instances may invoke various constructors — be on guard!

More than one way to skin a cat, or, **Attention: the empty constructor.** Certain limitations of a constructor (no returned value, in particular) have resulted in the *empty-constructor* programming style. The constructor is deliberately left empty, and all initializing code is placed in a special member function called `Init`. The strong and weak points of such a style could be the subject of a separate discussion. It's enough for code diggers to know that such a style exists, and is actively used — not only by individual programmers, but also by giant companies such as Microsoft. Therefore, don't be surprised if you encounter a call of an empty constructor; just look for the initializing function among the ordinary members.

Objects, Structures, and Arrays

The internal representation of objects is similar to the representation of structures in the C language. (After all, objects are structures, too.) We'll look at how to identify both of them.

Structures are popular among programmers. They allow programmers to unite related data under one roof, making the program listing more readable and understandable. Accordingly, identifying structures during disassembling facilitates the analysis of code. To the great regret of code diggers, structures exist only in the source code of a program. They almost completely "dissolve" at compile time and become indistinguishable from ordinary variables that are not related to one another in any way.

Let's consider the following example:

Listing 59. Eliminating Structures at Compile Time

```
#include <stdio.h>
#include <string.h>

struct zzz
{
        char s0[16];
        int a;
        float f;
```

```
};

func(struct zzz y)
// Clearly, it's better to avoid passing a structure by value.
// Here, this is done deliberately to demonstrate
// the hidden creation of a local variable.

{
        printf("%s %x %f\n", &y.s0[0], y.a, y.f);
}
main()
{
        struct zzz y;
        strcpy(&y.s0[0], "Hello, Sailor!");
        y.a = 0x666;
        y.f = 6.6;
        func(y);
}
```

In general, the disassembled listing of the compiled version of this program should look like this:

Listing 60. The Disassembled Code Eliminating Structures at Compile Time

```
main            proc near              ; CODE XREF: start+AF↓p

var_18          = byte ptr -18h
var_8           = dword ptr -8
var_4           = dword ptr -4
; The members of the structure are indistinguishable
; from ordinary local variables.

        push    ebp
        mov     ebp, esp
        sub     esp, 18h
        ; A place is allocated on the stack.

        push    esi
        push    edi
        push    offset aHelloSailor ; "Hello, Sailor!"

        lea     eax, [ebp+var_18]
```

```
; This is the pointer to the local variable var_18.
; The variable next to it is located at offset 8,
; hence, 0x18-0x8=0x10 — 16 bytes — this is just how much
; var_18 occupies, which hints to us that it's a string.
; (See the "Literals and Strings" section.)

push    eax
call    strcpy
; The string is copied from the data segment to the local variable —
; a member of the structure.
add     esp, 8
mov     [ebp+var_8], 666h
; The value of 0x666 is assigned to a variabe of DWORD type.

mov     [ebp+var_4], 40D33333h
; This value is equal to 6.6 in the float format.
; (See the "Function Arguments" section.)

sub     esp, 18h
; Memory is allocated for the hidden local variable
; used by the compiler for passing a member of the structure
; to the function by value.
; (See the "Register and Temporary Variables" section.)

mov     ecx, 6
; Six double words (or 24 bytes) will be copied: 16 bytes to the
; string variable, and 4 bytes each to the float and int variables.

lea     esi, [ebp+var_18]
; A pointer is obtained to the structure to be copied.

mov     edi, esp
; A pointer is obtained to the hidden local variable just created.

repe movsd
; Copying!

call    func
; The pointer to the hidden local variable
; isn't passed,
; since it already lies on the top of the stack.

add     esp, 18h
```

```
        pop     edi
        pop     esi
        mov     esp, ebp
        pop     ebp
        retn
main            endp
```

Now, we'll replace the structure with a sequential declaration of the same variables:

Listing 61. The Resemblance between Structures and Ordinary Variables

```
main()
{
        char s0[16];
        int a;
        float f;

        strcpy(&s0[0], "Hello, Sailor!");
        a=0x666;
        f=6.6;
}
```

Now, let's compare the disassembled listing of the compiled version of this example with the previous code:

Listing 62. Comparing Structures with Ordinary Variables

```
main            proc near              ; CODE XREF: start+AF↓p

var_18          = dword ptr -18h
var_14          = byte ptr -14h
var_4           = dword ptr -4
; There is likely to be some difference here! The local variables
; are placed on the stack in the order that the compiler prefers,
; and not in the order in which they were declared in the program.
; The members of the structure, on the other hand,
; need to be placed in the order in which they were declared.
; However, when disassembling, the initial order of variables is unknown,
```

```
; and we can't determine whether they are ordered
; "correctly" or not.

        push    ebp
        mov     ebp, esp
        sub     esp, 18h
        ; 0x18 bytes of the stack space are allocated (as in the previous example).

        push    offset aHelloSailor ; "Hello, Sailor!"
        lea     eax, [ebp+var_14]
        push    eax
        call    strcpy
        add     esp, 8
        mov     [ebp+var_4], 666h
        mov     [ebp+var_18], 40D33333h
        ; The code coincides byte for byte!
        ; Hence, it's impossible
        ; to distinguish a structure
        ; from a simple collection of local variables.

        mov     esp, ebp
        pop     ebp
        retn
main                            endp

func            proc near       ; CODE XREF: main+36↑p

var_8           = qword ptr -8
arg_0           = byte  ptr  8
arg_10          = dword ptr  18h
arg_14          = dword ptr  1Ch
        ; Although only one argument — an instance of the structure —
        ; is passed to the function, in the disassembled code, we can't
        ; distinguish it from a sequential transfer of several local variables
        ; on the stack. Therefore, we can't reconstruct
        ; the original prototype of the function!

        push    ebp
        mov     ebp, esp
        fld     [ebp+arg_14]
        ; The floating-point number is loaded, which is located
```

```
; at the offset 0x14, relative to the EAX pointer, on the FPU stack.

sub    esp, 8
; Eight bytes are allocated for a local variable.

fstp   [esp+8+var_8]
; The floating-point number value (which we've just read)
; is stored in the local variable.

mov    eax, [ebp+arg_10]
push   eax
; The previously stored real variable is read
; and pushed to the stack.

lea    ecx, [ebp+arg_0]
; A pointer to the first argument is obtained.

push   ecx
push   offset aSXF        ; "%s %x %f\n"
call   printf

add    esp, 14h
pop    ebp
retn
func           endp
```

It seems likely that we won't be able to distinguish structures from ordinary variables. Will an individual code digger really have to recognize the "relationship" of data and bind the data with "conjugal ties," occasionally making mistakes and inexactly reconstructing the source code of the program? Well, yes and no. Yes, because the instance of a structure declared and used in the same translation unit is "unwrapped" at compile time in independent variables. These are addressed individually by their actual, possibly indirect, addresses. No, because *in this case*, the scope has only one pointer to the instance of a structure. Therefore, all structure members are called through the pointer to a corresponding instance of this structure. (Since the structure is out of the scope — for example, passed to another function by reference — then calculating the actual addresses of its members is impossible at compile time.)

Just a moment. You probably know that array elements are addressed in exactly the same way: The base pointer points to the beginning of an array. The offset of a required element relative to the beginning of an array is added (an index of the element multiplied by its size). The result of calculations will be the actual pointer to the required element.

The fundamental difference between arrays and structures is that arrays are *homogeneous* (consisting of elements of an identical type), and structures may be either homogeneous or *heterogeneous* (consisting of elements of various types). Therefore, structures and arrays can be easily identified by determining the memory locations addressed through a common base pointer, then determining the variable type. If we find more than one type, we're probably dealing with a structure. If we find only one type, a structure or an array are equally probable. We have to judge by the circumstances and the program.

Let's suppose a programmer takes it into his or her head to determine the dependence of the amount of coffee he or she drinks each day of the week. The programmer may either use the array `day[7]` or start the structure `struct week{int Monday; int Tuesday;…}` to keep record. In either case, the codes generated by the compiler will be identical — and not only the codes, but the meanings as well! In this context, a structure is indistinguishable physically and logically from an array. The programmer's choice is a matter of personal preference.

Keep in mind that arrays, as a rule, are long; when their elements are addressed, they frequently are accompanied by various mathematical operations on the pointer. In addition, array elements typically are processed in a loop, whereas the members of a structure are usually "picked out" individually.

What's even more unpleasant is that the C and C++ languages allow (if not provoke) the explicit conversion of types, and… oh, wait. During disassembling, it seems unlikely that we can figure out whether we're dealing with data of different types united under one roof (a structure), or with a handmade conversion applied to an array. Strictly speaking, such conversions turn an array into a structure. (An array is homogeneous by definition; it can't store data of different types.)

Let's modify the previous example so the pointer is passed to a function, not to the structure, and see what kind of code the compiler generates:

Listing 63. Passing a Structure Pointer to a Function

```
funct          proc near           ; CODE XREF: sub_0_401029+29↓p

var_8          = qword ptr -8
```

```
arg_0           = dword ptr  8
; The function takes only one argument!

        push    ebp
        mov     ebp, esp
        mov     eax, [ebp+arg_0]
        ; This is loading the argument passed to the function in EAX.
        fld     dword ptr [eax+14h]
        ; The floating-point value, located at the offset 0x14
        ; relative to the EAX pointer, is loaded to the FPU stack.
        ; Therefore, first of all, EAX (the argument passed to the
        ; function) is the pointer. Second, it's not a simple pointer,
        ; but a base one that is used for accessing elements
        ; of a structure or an array. Let's recall the type
        ; of the first element (a floating-point value),
        ; and continue our analysis.

        sub     esp, 8
        ; Eight bytes are allocated for local variables.

        fstp    [esp+8+var_8]
        ; This is storing the real value that we've just read
        ; in a local variable — var_8.

        mov     ecx, [ebp+arg_0]
        ; The value of the pointer passed to the function is loaded in ECX.

        mov     edx, [ecx+10h]
        ; The value located at the offset 0x10 is loaded in EDX.
        ; Aha! It's certainly not a floating-point value.
        ; Hence, we're dealing with a structure.

        push    edx
        ; The previously read value is pushed to the stack.

        mov     eax, [ebp+arg_0]
        push    eax
        ; We obtain a pointer to the structure (that is, to its first member)
        ; and push it to the stack. Since the nearest element is located
        ; at the offset 0x10, the first element of the structure is likely
```

```
; to occupy all 0x10 of these bytes, although this isn't necessarily
; the case. Possibly, the rest members of the structure simply are
; not used. We can figure out how matters actually do stand
; by having a look at the calling (parent) function that
; initialized this structure. We can, however, approximately
; reconstruct its view even without doing this.

; struct xxx{
; char x[0x10] || int x[4] || __int16[8] || __int64[2];
; int y;
; float z;
; }

push    offset aSXF         ; "%s %x %f\n"
; The format specification string allows us
; to ascertain the data types.
; The first element is undoubtedly char x[x010],
; since it's output as a string.
; Hence, our preliminary assumption that this is a structure is correct!

call    printf
add     esp, 14h
pop     ebp
retn
funct           endp

main            proc near          ; CODE XREF: start+AF↓p

var_18          = byte ptr -18h
var_8           = dword ptr -8
var_4           = dword ptr -4
; At first glance, we seem to be dealing
; with several local variables.

push    ebp
mov     ebp, esp
sub     esp, 18h
; The frame of the stack is open.
```

```
push    offset aHelloSailor ; "Hello, Sailor!"
lea     eax, [ebp+var_18]
push    eax
call    unknown_libname_1
; unknown_libname_1 is a strcpy, and we can figure this out without
; even analyzing its code. The function takes two arguments —
; the pointer of 0x10 bytes to the local buffer (the size of 0x10
; is obtained by subtracting the offset of the nearest variable
; from the offset of this variable relative to the frame of the stack).
; strcmp has exactly the same prototype, but this can't be strcmp,
; since the local buffer isn't initialized.
; It can only be a receiving buffer.

add     esp, 8
; The arguments are popped off the stack.

mov     [ebp+var_8], 666h
; Initializing a local variable var_8 of DWORD type.

mov     [ebp+var_4], 40D33333h
; This is initializing a local variable var_4 of type... no,
; not of DWORD type (despite the fact that it looks like DWORD).
; Having analyzed how this variable is used
; in the func function to which it's passed, we recognize
; a floating-point value with a size of 4 bytes in it.
; Therefore, it's a floating-point number.
; (See the "Function Arguments" section
; for more details.)

lea     ecx, [ebp+var_18]
push    ecx
; Now we've gotten to the essentials!
; The function receives the pointer to the local variable
; var_18 — a string buffer with a size of 0x10 bytes,
; but analysis of the called function allows us to figure out
; that it addresses not only the first 0x10 bytes of the stack
; of the parent function, but all 0x18 bytes!
; Therefore, the pointer to the structure — not the pointer
```

```
;  to the string buffer — is passed to the function.

;  struct x{
;          char var_18[10];
;          int var_8;
;          float var_4
;  }
;
;  Since data types are different, this is a structure,
;  not an array.

call     funct
add      esp, 4
mov      esp, ebp
pop      ebp
retn
sub_0_401029   endp
```

Identifying objects. Objects of the C++ language are actually structures that include data, processing methods (functions), and protection attributes (of the types public, friend...).

The data elements of an object are processed by the compiler as if they were ordinary members of a structure. Nonvirtual functions are called by the offset; they aren't contained in the object. Virtual functions are called through a special pointer to the virtual table contained in an object, and protection attributes are deleted at compile time. We can distinguish a public function from a protected one by remembering that a protected function is called only from its own object; a public one can be called from other objects.

So, what exactly is an object (or object instance)? Let's assume that we have the following object:

Listing 64. The Structure of an Object

```
class MyClass{
      void demo_1(void);
      int a;
      int b;

public:
```

```
        virtual void demo_2(void);
        int c;
};


MyClass zzz;
```

The object instance will be "grinded" by the compiler into the following structure (Fig. 13):

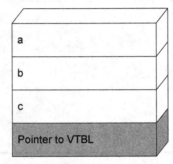

Fig. 13. A representation of an object in memory

The code digger has to solve several problems: How can we distinguish objects from simple structures? How can we find the size of objects? How can we determine which function belongs to which object? Let's answer the questions in the order they are posed.

In general, it's impossible to distinguish an object from a structure; an object is just a structure that has private members by default. To declare objects, we can use the struct or the class keyword. For classes with unprotected members, it's preferable to use struct because members of a structure are public by default. Compare these two examples:

Listing 65. Declaring Objects Using the struct or the class Keyword

```
struct MyClass{                       class MyClass{
        void demo(void);                      void demo_private(void);
        int x;                                int y;
private:                              public:
        void demo_private(void);        void demo(void);
        int y;                                int x;
};                                    };
```

The listings differ in their syntax, but the code generated by the compiler will be identical. Therefore, it's best to learn to distinguish objects from structures as soon as possible.

Let's regard structures that contain at least one function as objects. How can we determine which function belongs to which object? This is relatively simple with virtual functions: They're called indirectly through the pointer to the virtual table. The compiler places this pointer in each object instance pertaining to that virtual function. Nonvirtual functions are called using their actual addresses, just like normal functions that don't belong to any object. Is the situation hopeless? By no means. Each function of an object is passed an implicit argument — the `this` pointer, which refers to the object instance pertaining to that function. The object instance isn't the object, but something related to it. Therefore, reconstructing the initial structure of objects in a disassembled program seems feasible.

The *size of objects* is determined using the same `this` pointers — as the difference between adjacent pointers (for objects located on the stack or in the data segment). If object instances are created using the `new` operator, the code contains the call for the `new` function that takes as an argument the number of bytes to be allocated. This number is exactly the size of the object.

Well, that's pretty much all. We just need to add that when many compilers create an object instance that contains neither data nor virtual functions, they allocate a minimum amount of memory (usually, 1 byte) for the object instance, even though they don't use it. Why do they do this? Memory isn't made of rubber, and you can't allocate 1 byte on the heap — the granulation causes a considerable piece, the size of which varies from 4 bytes to 4 KB depending on the heap implementation, to be eaten off!

The memory is allocated because the compiler vitally needs to define the `this` pointer. Alas, `this` can't be a null pointer, since an exception would be thrown during the first attempt of calling. In addition, the `delete` operator should delete something, but first, this "something" should be allocated…

Arrrgh! Although C++ developers tell us over and over that their language is no less efficient than pure C, all implementations of C++ compilers that I know generate very buggy and sluggish code. Well, all this is just talk; let's proceed to the consideration of particular examples:

Listing 66. Identifying an Object and Its Structure

```
#include <stdio.h>

class MyClass{
```

```
public:
        void demo(void);
        int x;
private:
        demo_private(void);
        int y;
};

void MyClass::demo_private(void)
{
        printf("Private\n");
}

void MyClass::demo(void)
{
        printf("MyClass\n");
        this->demo_private();
        this->y=0x666;
}

main()
{
        MyClass *zzz = new MyClass;
        zzz->demo();
        zzz->x=0x777;
}
```

In general, the disassembled code of the compiled version of this program should look like this:

Listing 67. The Disassembled Code for Identifying an Object and Its Structure

```
main            proc near               ; CODE XREF: start+AF↓p
        push    esi
        push    8
        call    ??2@YAPAXI@Z            ; operator new(uint)
        ; Using the new operator, we allocate 8 bytes for the instance of
        ; some object. Generally, it's not very certain at all that memory
        ; is allocated for an object (there might be something like
        ; char *x = new char[8]), so let's not consider this assertion
        ; as dogma, and accept it as a working hypothesis.
```

```
; Further analysis will show how matters actually stand.

mov     esi, eax
add     esp, 4

mov     ecx, esi
; A this pointer is prepared and passed
; to the function through the register. Hence, ECX is
; a pointer to the instance of an object! (See
; "The this Pointer" section for more detail.)

call    demo
; We've at last gotten to the call of the demo function!
; It's not yet clear what this function does (for clarity,
; a character name is assigned to it), but we know that it belongs
; to the object instance to which ECX points. Let's name
; this instance a. Furthermore, since the function that calls
; demo (that is, the function we're in now) doesn't belong to a
; (a was created by this very function — the instance of
; the object couldn't just "pull itself out by the hair"),
; the demo function is a public one. A good start, isn't it?

mov     dword ptr [esi], 777h
; Well, well... we remember that ESI points to the object instance,
; and then we find out that there's one more public member
; in the object - a variable of type int.
; According to preliminary conclusions, the object looked like this:
; class myclass{
;  public:
;  void demo(void); // Note that void is used because the function
;                   // neither receives nor returns anything.
; int x;
;}

pop     esi
retn
main        endp


demo        proc near       ; CODE XREF: main+F↑p
```

```
; now we're in the demo function, which is a member of object A.

        push    esi
        mov     esi, ecx
        ; The this pointer passed to the function is loaded in ECX.

        push    offset aMyclass     ; "MyClass\n"
        call    printf
        add     esp, 4
        ; A line is displayed. This isn't interesting, but later...

        mov     ecx, esi
        call    demo_private
        ; Oops! That's it! One more function is called!
        ; Judging from this, this is a function of our object,
        ; and it probably has the private attribute,
        ; since it's only called from the function of the very object.

        mov     dword ptr [esi+4], 666h
        ; Well, there's one more variable in the object, and it's probably
        ; private. Then, according to our-current understanding,
        ; the object should look like this:
        ; class myclass{
        ; void demo_provate(void);
        ; int y;
        ; public:
        ; void demo(void); // Note that void is used because the function
        ;                  // neither receives nor returns anything.

        ;   int x;
        ; }
        ;
        ; So, we've not only identified the object, but also figured out
        ; its structure! We can't guarantee that it's free from errors.
        ; (For example, the assumption about the privacy of demo_private
        ; and y is based only on the fact that they've never been called
        ; from outside the object.)
        ; Nevertheless, OOP isn't as terrible as it's made out to be,
        ; and it's possible to reconstruct the code of a program,
```

```
        ; at least approximately.

        pop     esi
        retn
demo            endp


demo_private    proc near               ; CODE XREF: demo+12↑p
; This is the private demo function - nothing interesting.
        push    offset aPrivate     ; "Private\n"
        call    printf
        pop     ecx
        retn
demo_private    endp
```

Objects and instances. There are no objects in the code generated by the compiler. There are only *object instances*. This would seem to make no difference. The instance of an object is the object itself, right? No, it isn't. There's a basic difference between an object and an instance: An object is a representation of the class (i.e., the *structure* in memory); an object instance (in a generated code) is a substructure of this. Suppose we have class A, which contains the functions a1 and a2. Then, suppose two of its instances have been created — we'll call function a1 from one of them and a2 from the other. Using the this pointer, we can only clarify that one instance possesses the function a1 and the other one possesses a2. It's impossible to figure out whether these instances are spawned by one or two objects! Inheritable functions aggravate the situation: They aren't duplicated in derived classes. An ambiguity arises: Suppose the a1 and a2 functions are connected with one instance. The a1, a2, and a third function, which we'll call a3, are connected with another instance. In this case, the instances may belong to one class (the a3 function simply isn't called from the first instance), or the second instance may be derived from the first class. The code generated by the compiler will be identical in either case. We'd have to restore the hierarchy of classes based on the sense and purpose of the functions that belong to those classes. Only a psychic could approximate the original code.

In summary, never confuse an object instance with the object itself. Also, remember that objects only exist in the source code and are deleted at compile time.

On the street where you live... And where do structures, arrays, and objects live? In the memory, of course! There are three types of allocation: on the *stack* (automatic memory), in the *data segment* (static memory), and on the *heap* (dynamic memory). Each type has its own "personality." Let's take the stack as an example: Memory allocation is automatic and occurs at compile time. Only the total amount of memory allocated for all local variables is determined definitely; it's basically impossible to determine how much memory each of them occupies individually. Suppose we have the code `char a1[13]; char a2[17]; char a3[23]`. If the compiler aligns arrays to multiple addresses, the difference in the offsets of the neighboring arrays may not equal the sizes. The only hope for determining the original size is to find checks for going beyond the array boundaries. (However, these are rarely done.) One more unpleasant point: If one of the arrays is declared but never used, nonoptimizing compilers (and even some optimizing ones) may, nevertheless, allocate space on the stack for it. It will adjoin the previous array. We'll have to guess whether this is the array size, or if the unused array is "stuffed" in its end! Well, we can cope with arrays somehow, but matters are worse with structures and objects. Nobody provides a program with a code that traces violations of the structure (object) boundaries. Such violations are impossible, unless the programmer works with pointers too carelessly.

Let's leave the size alone and move on to problems of allocating and finding pointers. As mentioned above, if the array (object, structure) is declared in the direct scope of a translation unit, it's "ripped open" at compile time. In this case, its members are addressed using an actual offset, not the base pointer. Objects can be identified by the pointers to the virtual tables contained in them, but not all tables of pointers to functions are virtual tables! They may simply be pointer arrays to functions defined by the programmer. An experienced code digger can easily recognize such situations (see the "*Virtual Functions*" section); nevertheless, they're rather unpleasant.

Objects located in static memory are easier to handle; because of their global nature, they have a special flag preventing a repeated call of the constructor. (See the "*Constructors and Destructors*" section for more details.) Therefore, it's easy to distinguish an object instance located in the data segment from a structure or an array. However, we come across the same difficulties when defining the size.

Finally, objects (structures, arrays) located on the heap are incredibly easy to analyze! Memory is allocated by a function that explicitly takes the number of bytes to be allocated as an argument. It then returns a pointer to the beginning of the instance of an object (structure, array). In addition, instances are always called through the base pointer, although the declaration is done within the scope. (This can't be done any other way, since the actual addresses of the dynamic memory blocks being allocated are unknown at compile time.)

The *this* Pointer

The `this` pointer is a true "life buoy" that saves us from drowning in the stormy ocean of OOP. Using just `this`, we can determine to which object instance the called function belongs. Since all nonvirtual functions of an object are called directly using the actual address, the object appears to be split at compile time into the functions that compose it. If there were no `this` pointers, it would be impossible to reconstruct the hierarchy of functions!

Thus, correct identification of `this` is very important. The only problem is how to distinguish it from pointers to arrays and structures. We identify an object instance using the `this` pointer; if `this` points to allocated memory, we are dealing with an object instance. However, by definition, `this` is a pointer that refers to an object instance. We have a never-ending loop! Fortunately, there is a loophole — a specific code handles the `this` pointer, allowing us to distinguish it from all other pointers.

Generally, each compiler has its own specifics; I strongly recommend that you study them by disassembling your own C ++ programs. However, there are some commonly accepted guidelines for most implementations. Since `this` is an implicit argument of each member function of a class, it seems reasonable to defer further discussion of its identification until the "*Function Arguments*" section. Here we'll just give a brief table summarizing the mechanisms of passing `this` in various compilers:

Table 1. The Mechanisms of Passing the `this` Pointer

Compiler	Function type				
	default	fastcall	cdecl	stdcall	Pascal
Microsoft Visual C++	The `this` pointer is passed through the `ECX` register.		The `this` pointer is passed through the stack as the last argument.		The `this` pointer is passed through the stack as the last argument of a function.
Borland C++	The `this` pointer is passed through the `EAX` register.				
Watcom C++					

The *new* and *delete* Operators

The compiler translates the new and delete operators into calls of library functions that can be precisely recognized like ordinary library functions. (See the "*Library Functions*" section.) IDA Pro, in particular, can recognize library functions automatically, removing this concern from the user's mind. However, not everyone has IDA Pro. In addition, it doesn't know all library functions and doesn't always recognize new and delete among those it knows. Thus, there are lots of reasons for identifying these functions manually.

The new and delete operators can have any implementation, but Windows compilers rarely implement functions for working independently with the heap — there's no need for them. It's easier to use the operating system services. However, it's naive to expect the call of HeapAlloc instead of new, or HeapFree instead of delete. The compiler isn't that simple! The new operator is translated into the new function, which calls malloc for memory allocation; malloc, in turn, calls *heap_alloc* (or a similar function, depending on the implementation of the memory management library). This function acts as a "wrapper" for the Win32 API procedure of the same name. Releasing memory is performed in a similar way.

It's too tedious to go deep into the jungle of nested calls. But it's possible to identify new and delete in a less laborious way. Let's recall all we know about the new operator:

The new operator takes only one argument — the number of memory bytes to be allocated. This argument is calculated at compile time in the majority of cases, making it a constant.

- ❏ If the object contains neither data nor virtual functions, its size is one memory unit (the minimum memory allocation, giving this something to point to). Therefore, a lot of calls will be of the PUSH 01\CALL xxx type, where xxx is simply the new address. The typical size of objects is less than 100 bytes. So look for a frequently called function that has a constant smaller than 100 bytes as an argument.
- ❏ The new function is one of the most popular library functions, so look for a function that has a "crowd" of cross-references.
- ❏ Impressively, new returns the this pointer, and this is easily identified, even when you are glancing over the code. (See "*The* this *Pointer*" section.)
- ❏ The result returned by new is always checked for equality to zero. If it equals zero, the constructor (if there is one — see the "*Constructors and Destructors*" section) isn't called.

The new operator has more "birthmarks" than necessary to quickly and reliably identify it, so there's no need to waste time analyzing its code. Still, keep in mind that new is used not only to create new object instances, but also to allocate memory for arrays, structures, and, occasionally, single variables (of the sort int *x = new int; it's usually pretty stupid, but some people do it). Fortunately, it's simple to distinguish the creation of a new object instance from the allocation of memory — neither arrays, nor structures, nor single variables have the this pointer!

To sum up, let's consider a code fragment generated by the Watcom compiler (IDA Pro doesn't recognize its "native" new operator):

Listing 68. Identifying the new Operator

```
main_           proc near           ; CODE XREF: __CMain+40↓p
        push    10h
        call    __CHK
        push    ebx
        push    edx
        mov     eax, 4
        call    W?$nwn_ui_pnv
; This is, as we'll find out later, the new function.
; By the way, IDA has recognized it,
; but you'd have to be a psychic to recognize the memory
; allocation operator in this gobbledygook! For now, notice
; that the new function accepts one argument — a constant of a very
; small value. That is, it's certainly not an offset.
; (See the "Constants and Offsets" section.)
; Passing the argument via the register tells us nothing —
; Watcom treats many library functions in such a manner.
; Other compilers, on the other hand,
; always push an argument to the stack.


        mov     edx, eax
        test    eax, eax
```

```
; The result returned by the function is checked for null
; (this is typical for new).

jz      short loc_41002A
mov     dword ptr [eax], offset BASE_VTBL
; Aha! The function has returned a pointer to the location where
; the pointer to the virtual table (or at least to an array
; of functions) is written. EAX suspiciously resembles this,
; but to be sure of this, we need more signs.

loc_41002A:                         ; CODE XREF: main_+1A↑j
    mov     ebx, [edx]
    mov     eax, edx
    call    dword ptr [ebx]
; There is no longer any doubt that EAX is the this pointer,
; and this code is
; just the call of a virtual function!
; Hence, the W?$nwm_ui_pnv function is new
; (what else could have returned this?)
```

It's more difficult to identify delete. This function has no specific features. It takes only one argument: a pointer to the memory area to be released. In the most cases, the pointer is this. But, the this pointer is accepted by dozens, if not hundreds, of other functions! There's one, tiny distinction between delete and other functions — in most cases, delete receives the this pointer via the stack, whereas the other functions receive it via the register. Unfortunately, certain compilers (for example, Watcom) pass arguments via registers to many library functions, hiding all distinctions. What's more, delete returns nothing, but there are lots of functions that behave in the same way. The call of delete follows the call of the destructor (if there is one), but the destructor is identified as the function preceding delete. Now we're in a vicious circle!

All we can do is analyze the contents of the function — sooner or later, delete calls HeapFree. Other variants are possible; Borland C++, for example, contains libraries that work with the heap at the low level, so memory is released by calling VirtualFree. Fortunately, IDA Pro identifies delete in most cases, and you needn't strain yourself.

Approaches to implementing the heap. In many programming manuals on C++ ("*Advanced Windows*" by Jeffrey Richter, for example), you will be urged to allocate memory using new, not malloc. This is because new employs the effective memory management tools of the operating system, whereas `malloc` uses its own (rather sluggish) heap manager. But this is a rather strained argument! The standard says nothing about heap implementation, and we don't know beforehand which function will appear more effective. Everything depends on the specific libraries of a specific compiler.

Let's consider memory management in the standard libraries of three popular compilers: *Microsoft Visual C ++*, *Borland C ++*, and *Watcom C ++*.

In Microsoft Visual C++, both `malloc` and `new` represent a thunk to the same `__nh_malloc` function. Therefore, either function can be used successfully. `__nh_malloc` calls `__heap_alloc`, which, in turn, calls the Windows API function `__heapAlloc`. (It's worth noting that `__heap_alloc` can call its own heap manager if the system's manager is unavailable. In Microsoft Visual C++ 6.0, however, only one wrapper of the hook remains; its own heap manager was excluded.)

Things are quite different in Borland C++. First, it works directly with the Windows virtual memory and implements its own heap manager based on `VirtualAlloc/VirtualFree` functions. Testing shows that it performs poorly on Windows 2000. (I didn't test other systems.) It also places superfluous code in the program that increases its size. In addition, `new` calls the `malloc` function — not directly, but through several layers of "wrapping" code! Therefore, contrary to all guidelines, in Borland C++, calling `malloc` is more effective than calling `new`.

Watcom C++ (its eleventh version, in any case — the latest one I could find) implements `new` and `malloc` in practically identical ways: Both of them refer to `_nmalloc`, a "thick" wrapper of `LocalAlloc`, the 16-bit Windows function that itself is a thunk to `HeapAlloc`!

Library Functions

Reading code of a program written in a high-level language, we can only analyze the implementation of standard library functions (such as `printf`) in exceptional cases. But there's really no need to do so! We already know the purpose of such functions. If there are some uncertainties, we can consult the documentation.

Analyzing a disassembled listing is another matter. Function names are rarely present, so it's impossible to determine visually whether we're dealing with `printf` or another function. We have to delve into the algorithm, which is easier said than done! The `printf` is a complex interpreter of the format specification string; it's difficult to make it out right away. Of course, there are more monstrous functions, whose operation algorithms have no relation to the analysis of the program under investigation. The same `new` can allocate memory from the Windows heap or use its own manager. It's enough to know that it's `new`, a function for memory allocation, and not `free` or `open`.

On average, library functions constitute 50 percent to 90 percent of a program. This is especially true of programs composed in visual development environments that employ automatic code generation (*Microsoft Visual C++* and *Delphi*, for example). Library functions are sometimes more intricate and difficult to understand than the simple program code. It's almost insulting — the lion's share of effort needed to perform the analysis appears to be a waste. Is it possible to optimize this process?

The ability of *IDA Pro* to recognize standard library functions of numerous compilers favorably distinguishes it from most other disassemblers. Unfortunately, IDA (like everything created by man) is far from ideal — the list of supported libraries may be extensive, but particular versions from specific suppliers or certain memory models may be lacking. Moreover, not all functions, even those from libraries known to IDA, are recognized. (The reasons for this will be given later.)

An unrecognized function is half the trouble. A function recognized incorrectly is much worse, since this results in errors (sometimes hard to find) in the analysis of the program, or leads a code digger to a dead end. For example, `fopen` is called, and the result it returns is transferred to `free`. Then, `fopen` returns a pointer to the `FILE` structure, and `free` deletes it. However, what if `free` isn't `free` at all? What if it's `fseek`? Having skipped the operation of positioning, we won't be able to figure out the correct structure of the file with which the program works.

It's easier to recognize IDA errors if we understand how the disassembler performs recognition. For some reason, many people assume a trivial CRC (Cyclic Redundancy Check) is involved. It is tempting to perform a CRC, but this would be unsuitable for solving this task. The main obstacles are variable fragments, namely, *relocatable elements*. (See "*Step Four: Getting Acquainted with the Debugger*" for more details.) Relocatable elements can be ignored when you perform a CRC — if you remember to perform the same operation in the function being identified. Nevertheless, the developer of IDA has chosen another way. It's more intricate and artful, but more efficient.

The key idea is that there's no need to waste time performing a CRC — a trivial character-by-character matching, ignoring relocatable elements, will do for preliminary identification of the function. Truthfully, matching is not performed; instead, a search is made for a particular sequence of bytes in the standard base, organized as a binary tree. The time a binary search takes is proportional to the log of the number of records in the base. Common sense tells us that the length of a template (a signature, or the sequence being matched) should be sufficient to clearly identify the function. However, IDA's developer decided to limit us to the first 32 bytes. (This is rather few, especially allowing for the prolog, which is practically identical for all functions.)

And rightly so! Many functions end up on the same leaf of the tree, causing a *collision*, or ambiguity in the identification. To resolve the situation, CRC16 is calculated from the thirty-second byte to the first relocatable element for all the functions that can collide, then compared to CRC16 for standard functions. As a rule, this works. But if the first relocatable element is too close to the thirty-second byte, the sequence for counting CRC16 appears too short or even of zero length. (The thirty-second byte can be a relocatable element.) For a repeated collision, we find the byte in the functions by which they differ and remember its offset in the base.

With IDA, we match character-by-character not to the end, but only for 32 bytes; we calculate CRC not for the entire function, but depending on the case; and we consider the last byte as the "key" one, but not always. Many functions coincide byte-to-byte but completely differ in their names and purpose. You don't believe me? Then look at the following:

Listing 69. The Difficulty in Identifying Library Functions

```
read:                        write:
    push ebp                     push ebp
    mov ebp, esp                 mov ebp, esp
    call _read                   call _write
    pop ebp                      pop ebp
    ret                          ret
```

Here we must analyze relocatable elements! This is not a far-fetched example; there are lots of similar functions. The libraries from Borland, in particular, teem with them. It's no wonder that IDA frequently "stumbles" over them and runs into gross errors. Let's take the following function as an example:

```
void demo(void)
{
print("DERIVED\n");
};
```

Even IDA 4.17, the latest version available while I was writing this book, makes a mistake, calling it __pure error:

```
CODE:004010F3  __pure_error_  proc near        ; DATA XREF: DATA:004080BC↑o
CODE:004010F3                 push    ebp
CODE:004010F4                 mov     ebp, esp
CODE:004010F6                 push    offset aDerived ; format
CODE:004010FB                 call    _printf
CODE:00401100                 pop     ecx
CODE:00401101                 pop     ebp
CODE:00401102                 retn
CODE:00401102  __pure_error_  endp
```

Is it worth talking about the unpleasant consequences this error can have for analysis? You could be sitting, stupidly staring at the disassembler listing, and for the life of you be unable to understand what a fragment does. It's only later that you figure out one or more functions were identified incorrectly!

To decrease the number of errors, IDA tries to recognize the compiler by the startup code. It then loads only the library of that compiler's signatures. Therefore, it's easy to "dazzle" IDA by slightly modifying the start code. This code usually is delivered with the source texts of the compiler, so alterations can be made easily. Changing one byte at the beginning of the startup function will suffice. And that's all — the hacker has to give up! Fortunately, IDA provides the possibility of manually loading the base of signatures (*FILE\Load file\FLIRT signature file*), but how can we determine which library versions' signatures must be loaded? Guessing takes too much time. It helps if you visually identify the compiler. (Experienced code diggers usually succeed in doing so, since each compiler has a unique "handwriting.") Instead, you could simply use libraries from the delivery of one compiler in a program compiled by another compiler.

Be prepared to identify library functions by yourself. This task consists of three stages: deciding if the function is a library one, determining the origin of the library, and identifying the function according to this library.

The linker usually allocates functions in the order of the listing of OBJ modules and libraries. Most programmers specify their own OBJ modules, then libraries. (Compilers independently calling the linker upon termination of their operation also behave in this way.) Therefore, we can conclude that library functions are located at the end of the program, and the code of the function is at the beginning. There are exceptions to this rule, but it often works.

Fig. 14. The structure of pkzip.exe, showing all library functions
in one place — at the end of the code segment, but before
the beginning of the data segment

Let's consider, for example, the structure of the well-known program pkzip.exe (Fig. 14). The diagram constructed by IDA 4.17 shows all library functions concentrated in one place — at the end of the code segment. They closely adjoin the data segment. In most cases, the start-up function is located at or close to the beginning of the library functions. Finding start-up isn't a problem; it coincides with the entry point into the file!

Thus, we can take it almost for granted that all functions located "below" start-up (that is, at higher addresses) are library ones. Has IDA recognized them, or has it shifted this problem to you? Two situations are possible: No functions are recognized, or only some functions are recognized.

If no functions are recognized, it is likely that IDA failed to identify the compiler or encountered unknown versions of libraries. Recognizing compilers is a matter for a special consideration. For now, we'll focus on recognizing library versions.

First, many libraries contain copyrights that include the name of the manufacturer and the library version — simply look for the corresponding text strings in the binary file. If they aren't there, it doesn't matter. We'll perform a simple context search to find other text strings (as a rule, error messages) in all the libraries we can reach. (Code digger should have many compilers and big libraries on their hard disks.) Possible options are: There are no other text strings; there are strings, but they are found in many libraries; or the fragment being searched for isn't found. In the first two cases, we need to single out a distinctive byte sequence, which doesn't contain relocatable elements, from one or several library functions. Then we must search for it again in all accessible libraries. If this doesn't help, then you don't have the required library.

Such a situation is bad, but not hopeless! Without the required library, we wouldn't be able to restore the function names automatically, but we could find the purpose of the functions. The names of the Windows API functions called from the libraries allow us to identify at least the category of the library (for example, for working with files, memory, graphics, etc.). Mathematical functions are typically rich with coprocessor instructions.

Disassembling is similar to solving a crossword puzzle: Unknown words are guessed using known ones. In some contexts, the name of a function follows from its purpose. For example, we could ask the user for a password, then pass it to the X function along with the standard password. If the completion result is zero, we write "password OK;" we also write something appropriate for the opposite situation. Your intuition suggests that the X function is `strcmp`, doesn't it? This is a simple case. But if you encounter an unfamiliar subroutine, don't despair over its "monstrosity." Look at all of its entries, paying attention to *who* calls it, *when*, and *how many times*.

A statistical analysis clarifies many things. Each function, like each letter in an alphabet, occurs at a specific rate. The dependence on context also gives us food for thought. For example, a function for reading from the file can't precede a function for opening it!

Other catches include arguments and constants. For arguments, everything is more or less clear. If a function receives a string, it obviously is from the library for working with strings; if a function receives a floating-point value, it possibly belongs to the mathematical library. The number and type of arguments (if we take them into account) substantially narrow the range of possible candidates. Things are even easier with constants — many functions accept a flag that can have a limited number of values as an argument. Except for bit flags, which are as alike as peas in a pod, unique values are frequently encountered. Although they do not positively identify the function, they do narrow the range of "suspects." Besides which, functions may contain characteristic constants. For example, if you encounter a standard polynomial for calculating the CRC, you can be sure that the "suspect" calculates the checksum. An objection can be raised here: All these are details. Perhaps there's a point to this. Having identified some of the functions, the rest of them can be identified using the rule of the contraries. But at least it's possible to know the kind of library and where to search for it.

Finally, the identification of algorithms (that is, the purposes of functions) is greatly facilitated by knowledge of these algorithms. In particular, a code that performs LZ packing (unpacking) is so distinctive that it can be recognized at a glance — you just need to know this packing mechanism. If you don't know the mechanism, however, analysis of a program will be extremely difficult! Some people may assume that we wouldn't obtain such information. However, despite a common opinion that a hacker is a hacker, first, and a programmer, second, everything in life is contradictory. The programmer who doesn't know how to program can make a living — there are many libraries; just use them and earn! A hacker can break off a serial number without higher mathematics, but will get on better knowing computer science.

Libraries were created to relieve developers from having to penetrate into those areas of learning that they deem unnecessary. Alas, code diggers don't get off as easy. They have to use their hands, their heads, and even their spinal cords. This is the only way to disassemble serious programs. Sometimes a solution comes while you're on a train, or even asleep.

The analysis of library functions is a difficult aspect of disassembling. It's simply wonderful that you have the option of identifying their names by the signatures.

Function Arguments

Identifying function arguments is a key part of the analysis of disassembled programs. So prepare yourself: This section may seem long and boring. Unfortunately, there's no way around it — knowing the basics of hacking has its price!

There are three ways to pass arguments to a function: via the *stack*, via *registers*, and via the stack and registers *simultaneously*. The transfer of implicit arguments through global variables comes close to joining this list, but this is covered in another section ("*Global Variables*").

Arguments can be transferred *by value* or *by reference*. In the first case, a *copy* of the corresponding variable is passed to the function; in the second case, a *pointer* is passed.

Conventions on passing arguments. To work successfully, the calling function should not only know the prototype of the called function, but also should "agree" upon the method of passing arguments with it: by reference or by value, via registers or via the stack. If arguments are passed via registers, it shows which argument is placed in which register. If arguments are passed via the stack, it must define the order in which arguments are placed. It also must ascertain who is "responsible" for clearing up the stack of arguments after the called function is executed.

The ambiguity of the mechanism for passing arguments is one of the reasons for incompatibility between various compilers. Why not force all compiler manufacturers to follow one method? Alas, this solution would pose more problems than it would solve.

Each mechanism has its own merits and drawbacks, and each is interrelated with the language. In particular, C's looseness concerning the observance of function prototypes is possible because the arguments are pushed out from the stack not by the called function (child), but by the calling one (parent), which re-members what it has passed. For example, two arguments are passed to the `main` function: the count of command-line arguments, and the pointer to an array that contains them. However, if a program doesn't work with the command line (or receives the argument in another way), a prototype of `main` can be declared in the following manner: `main()`.

In *Pascal*, such a trick would result either in a compilation error or in the program crash. In this language, the stack is cleared by the child function. If the function fails to do this (or does this incorrectly, popping out a number of words different from the number passed to it), the stack will be unbalanced, and everything will come crashing down. (More specifically, all addressing of the local variables of the parent function will be impaired, and a random value will appear on the stack instead of the return address.)

The drawback of C's solution is the insignificant increase in the size of the generated code. We need to insert a processor instruction (and occasionally more than one) to pop arguments from the stack after each function call. In Pascal, this instruction is used in the function directly, and consequently, occurs only once in the program.

Having failed to find a suitable middle ground, compiler developers have decided to use all possible data-transfer mechanisms. To cope with compatibility problems, they have standardized each mechanism by adopting a number of conventions:

❏ *The C convention* (designated as `__cdecl`) directs you to send arguments to the stack from right to left in the order in which they are declared. It charges the called function with clearing the stack. The names of the functions that observe the C convention are preceded with the "_" character, automatically inserted by the compiler. The `this` pointer (in C++ programs) is transferred via the stack last.

❏ *The Pascal convention* (designated as `PASCAL`[i]) directs you to send arguments to the stack from left to right in the order in which they are declared. It charges the calling function with clearing the stack.

---

[i] Nowadays the `PASCAL` keyword is regarded to be out-of-date, and has gone out of use; the similar WinAPI convention can be used instead of it.

❐ *The standard convention* (designated as `__stdcall`) is a hybrid of the C and Pascal conventions. Arguments are sent to the stack from right to left, but clearing the stack is performed by the calling function. The names of functions that adhere to the standard convention are preceded with the "_" character and end with the "@" suffix. This is followed by the number of bytes being transferred to the function. The `this` pointer (in C++ programs) is transferred via the stack last.

❐ *The fastcall convention* dictates that you transfer arguments via registers. Compilers from Microsoft and Borland support the `__fastcall` keyword, but they interpret it differently. Watcom C++ doesn't understand the `__fastcall` keyword, but it has a special `pragma` — "`aux`" — in its pocket that allows you to manually choose the registers for transferring arguments (see the "*Fastcall Conventions*" explanation further on for more details). The names of the functions that adhere to the `__fastcall` convention are preceded by the "@" character, which is automatically inserted by the compiler.

❐ *The default convention.* If there's no explicit declaration of the call type, the compiler usually uses its own conventions and chooses them at its own discretion. The `this` pointer is the most influenced — by default, most compilers transfer it via a register. For Microsoft, this is `ECX`, for Borland it is `EAX`, and for Watcom it is `EAX`, `EDX`, or both of them. Other arguments can be transferred via registers if the optimizer considers this a better way. The mechanism of transferring arguments and the logic of sampling them is different in different compilers. It is also unpredictable — we have to figure it out from the situation.

Goals and tasks. When analyzing a function, a code digger faces the following task: He or she must determine *what type of convention is used for calling*, count the *number of arguments* being transferred to the function (and/or being used by the function), and clarify the *type* and *purpose* of arguments. Shall we begin?

The convention type is roughly identified by the way the stack is cleared. If it's cleared by the called function, we're dealing with `cdecl`; otherwise, we are dealing with `stdcall` or `PASCAL`. This uncertainty occurs because, if the original prototype of the function is unknown, the order for placing arguments onto the stack can't be determined. But if the compiler is known and the programmer has used the default types of calls, it's possible to determine the type of function call. In programs for Windows, both `PASCAL` and `stdcall` calls are widely used, so the uncertainty remains. However, nothing changes the order of transferring arguments: If both calling and called functions are available, we can always establish a correspondence between transferred and received arguments. In other words, if the actual order of passing arguments is known (and it should be known —

see the calling function), we don't even need to know the sequence of arguments in the function prototype.

Another matter is presented by library functions whose prototypes are known. If you know the order in which arguments are placed into the stack, it's possible to figure out their type and purpose from the prototype!

Determining the number of arguments and the way they are passed. As we mentioned above, arguments can be passed via the stack, via registers, or via both the stack and registers simultaneously. Implicit arguments can also be transferred via global variables.

If the stack was only used for passing arguments, it'd be easy to count them. Alas, the stack is actively used for temporary storage of the data from registers, too. Therefore, if you encounter the PUSH instruction, don't rush to identify it as an argument. It's impossible to determine the number of bytes passed to the function as arguments, but we can easily determine the number of bytes that are popped from the stack after the function is completed!

If the function obeys the standard or Pascal convention, it clears the stack using the RET n instruction (n is simply the required value in bytes). Things are not as simple with cdecl functions. In general, their call is followed by the instruction ADD ESP,n (again, n is the required value in bytes). But variations are possible; there could be a *delay in clearing the stack,* or arguments could be popped into any free register. However, we'll defer optimizing riddles, being content with non-optimizing compilers.

We can assume that the number of bytes placed onto the stack equals the number of those popped out; otherwise, after the function is executed, the stack will become unbalanced, and the program will crash. (Optimizing compilers allow a misbalance of the stack in some parts, but we'll save this discussion for later.) Hence, the number of arguments equals the number of transferred bytes divided by the word size[i]. Is this correct? No, it isn't! Few arguments occupy exactly one element of the stack. The type double, for example, consumes 8 bytes; a character string transferred by value, not by reference, will "eat" as many bytes as it needs. In addition, a string, data structure, array, or object can be pushed onto the stack using the MOVS instruction instead of PUSH. (By the way, the use of MOVS is strong evidence that the argument was passed by value.)

Let's try to sort out the mess I've created in our heads. It's impossible to determine the number of arguments passed via the stack by analyzing the code

---

[i] The word is understood not only as 2 bytes, but also as the size of operands by default; in 32-bit mode, the word equals 4 bytes.

of the calling function. Even the number of passed bytes cannot be determined definitively. The type of transfer is also veiled in obscurity. In the "*Constants and Offsets*" section, we'll return to this question. For now, we'll give the following example: `PUSH 0x40404040/CALL MyFuct:0x404040`. What is this: an argument passed by value (the constant `0x404040`), or a pointer to something located at the offset `0x404040` (passed by reference)? This problem can't be resolved, can it?

Don't worry; the curtain hasn't fallen yet, and we'll continue the fight. The majority of problems can be solved by an analysis of the called function. Having clarified how it treats the arguments passed to it, we'll determine both their type and quantity. For this, we'll have to become acquainted with addressing arguments on the stack. For an easy warm-up, let's consider the following example:

Listing 70. A Mechanism of Passing Arguments

```
#include <stdio.h>
#include <string.h>


struct XT{
        char s0[20];
        int x;
};


void MyFunc(double a, struct XT xt)
{
        printf("%f, %x, %s\n", a, xt.x, &xt.s0[0]);
}


main()
{
        struct XT xt;
        strcpy(&xt.s0[0], "Hello, World!");
        xt.x = 0x777;
MyFunc(6.66, xt);
}
```

The disassembled listing of this program compiled using the Microsoft Visual C++ compiler with its default configuration looks like this:

Listing 71. The Disassembled Code for Passing Arguments Using Visual C++

```
main            proc near                ; CODE XREF: start+AF↓p

var_18          = byte ptr -18h
var_4           = dword ptr -4

        push    ebp
        mov     ebp, esp
        sub     esp, 18h
        ; The first PUSH relates to the function prolog,
        ; not the arguments being passed.

        push    esi
        push    edi
        ; The lack of explicit initialization of registers indicates
        ; that they probably are saved on the stack, not passed as
        ; arguments. However, if arguments passed to this function
        ; not only via the stack, but also via the ESI
        ; and EDI registers, placing them onto the stack might indicate
        ; that the arguments will be passed to the next function.

        push    offset aHelloWorld ; "Hello, World!"
        ; Aha! Here is the passing of the argument — a pointer to the
        ; string. (Strictly speaking, passing probably occurs. See the
        ; "Constants and Offsets" section for an explanation.)
        ; Theoretically, it's possible to save a constant temporarily on
        ; the stack, then pop it out into any of available registers.
        ; It's also possible to directly address it in the stack.
        ; However, I know no compilers capable of these
        ; cunning maneuvers. Placing a constant onto the stack
        ; is always an indication of passing an argument.

        lea     eax, [ebp+var_18]
        ; The pointer to a local buffer is placed in EAX.

        push    eax
```

```
; EAX is saved on the stack.
; The series of arguments is indissolvable. Having recognized
; the first argument, we can be sure that everything pushed
; onto the stack is an argument, too.
```

```
call    strcpy
; The prototype of the strcpy (char*, char*) function doesn't allow
; us to determine the order in which arguments are placed. However,
; since all library C functions obey the cdecl convention, the
; arguments are placed from right to left. Thus, the code initially
; looked like this: strcpy(&buff[0],"Hello, World!"). Could the
; programmer instead use a conversion such as stdcall? This is
; extremely unlikely, since the strcpy itself would have to be
; recompiled; otherwise, where it would learn that the order
; in which arguments are placed has changed? Although standard
; libraries are, as a rule, delivered with the source codes
; included, practically nobody ever recompiles them.
```

```
add     esp, 8
; Since 8 bytes are popped out of the stack, we can conclude that
; two words of arguments were passed to the function. Consequently,
; PUSH ESI and PUSH EDI were not arguments of the function!
```

```
mov     [ebp+var_4], 777h
; The constant 0x777 is placed in a local variable.
; It's certainly a constant, not a pointer, because in Windows
; no user data can be stored in this memory area.
```

```
sub     esp, 18h
; Memory is allocated for a temporary variable. Temporary variables
; are created when arguments are passed by value. Therefore, let's
; prepare ourselves for the next "candidate" to be an argument.
; (See the "Register and Temporary Variables" section.)
```

```
mov     ecx, 6
; The constant 0x6 is placed in ECX. We don't yet know the purpose.
```

```
lea     esi, [ebp+var_18]
; The pointer to the local buffer, which contains the copied
; string "Hello, World!", is placed in ESI.
```

```
mov     edi, esp
; The pointer is copied to the top of the stack in EDI.

repe movsd
; Here it is — passing the string by value. The entire string is
; copied on the stack, swallowing 6*4 bytes of it (where 6 is the value
; of the ECX counter, and 4 is the size of the double word — movsd).
; Hence, this argument occupies 20 (0x14) bytes of stack space. We'll
; use this value to determine the number of arguments according to
; the number of bytes being popped out. The data from [ebp+var_18]
; to [ebp+var_18-0x14] (that is, from var_18 to var_4) is copied
; to the stack. But var_4 contains the constant 0x777!
; Therefore, it will be passed to the function together with the string.
; This will allow us to reconstruct the initial structure:
; struct x{
;       char s0[20]
;        int x
; }
; It turns out that a structure is passed to the function,
; not a single string!
push    401AA3D7h
push    0A3D70A4h
; Two more arguments are placed onto the stack. Why two?
; This may be a single argument of type int64, or a double one.
; It's not really possible to determine from the code which type it is.

call    MyFunc
; MyFunc is called. Unfortunately, we can't figure out the
; function's prototype. It's only clear that the first argument
; (from the left, or from the right?) is a structure, and it's followed
; either by two int, or by one int64, also known as double.
; We can clear up this situation by analyzing the called function,
; but we'll defer this until after we've mastered addressing
; arguments to the stack.

add     esp, 20h
; This popped out 0x20 bytes. Since 20 bytes (0x14) account for one
; structure, and 8 bytes for the following two arguments,
; we obtain 0x14+0x8=0x20, which is what we wanted to prove.
```

```
        pop     edi
        pop     esi
        mov     esp, ebp
        pop     ebp
        retn
sub_401022      endp


aHelloWorld     db 'Hello,World!',0      ; DATA XREF: sub_401022+8↑o
align 4
```

The disassembled listing of this program compiled using Borland C ++ will be somewhat different. Let's look at it as well:

Listing 72. The Disassembled Code of Passing Arguments Using Borland C++

```
_main           proc near               ; DATA XREF: DATA:00407044↓o

var_18          = byte ptr -18h
var_4           = dword         ptr -4

        push    ebp
        mov     ebp, esp
        add     esp, 0FFFFFFE8h
        ; This is addition with a minus sign.
        ; Having pressed <-> in IDA, we obtain ADD ESP, -18h.

        push    esi
        push    edi
        ; For now, everything is happening just as in the previous example.

        mov     esi, offset aHelloWorld ; "Hello, World!"
        ; Here, we see some differences.
        ; The strcpy call has vanished. The compiler didn't even expand
        ; the function by replacing it where the call takes place —
        ; it simply excluded the call!

        lea     edi, [ebp+var_18]
        ; The pointer to the local buffer is placed in EDI.
```

```
mov     eax, edi
; The same pointer is placed in EAX.

mov     ecx, 3
repe movsd
movsb
; Note: 4*3+1=13 bytes are copied — 13, not 20 as we would expect
; judging from the structure declaration.
; This is how the compiler has optimized the code:
; It has copied only the string into the buffer,
; ignoring its uninitialized "tail."

mov     [ebp+var_4], 777h
; The value of the constant 0x777 is assigned to a local variable.

push    401AA3D7h
push    0A3D70A4h
; Same here. We can't determine whether these two numbers
; are one or two arguments.

lea     ecx, [ebp+var_18]
; The pointer to the string's beginning is placed in ECX.

mov     edx, 5
; The constant 5 is placed in EDX. (The purpose isn't yet clear.)

loc_4010D3:                         ; CODE XREF: _main+37↓j
push    dword ptr [ecx+edx*4]
; What kind of awful code is this? Let's try to figure it out
; starting from its end. First of all, what does ECX+EDX*4 make?
; ECX is the pointer to the buffer,
; and we understand that pretty clearly, but EDX*4 == 5*4 == 20.
; Aha! So we obtained a pointer to the end of the string,
; not to its beginning. Actually it's a pointer not to the end,
; but to the variable ebp+var_4 (0x18-0x14=0x4). If this is
; the pointer to var_4, then why is it calculated in such an
; intricate manner? We're probably dealing with a structure.
; And look: The push instruction sends a double word onto the stack
; that is stored at the address according to this pointer.
```

```
        dec    edx
        ; Now we decrement EDX... Do you get the feeling
        ; that we're dealing with a loop?

        jns    short loc_4010D3
        ; This jump works until EDX is a negative number,
        ; which confirms our assumption about the loop. Yes, this
        ; unnatural construction is used by Borland to pass the argument —
        ; a structure — to the function by value!

        call   MyFunc
        ; Look: The stack isn't cleared! This is
        ; the last function called, and stack doesn't need
        ; to be cleared — so Borland doesn't bother.

        xor    eax, eax
        ; The result returned by the function is zeroed.
        ; In Borland,void functions always return zero.
        ; Actually, the code placed after their call zeroes EAX.

        pop    edi
        pop    esi
        ; The EDI and ESI registers that were stored previously are restored.

        mov    esp, ebp
        ; ESI is restored, which is why the stack wasn't cleared
        ; upon calling the last function!

        pop    ebp
        retn
_main           endp
```

Note that, by default, Microsoft C ++ transfers arguments from right to left, and Borland C++ transfers them from left to right! There's no standard call type that, while passing arguments from left to right, would make the calling function clear the stack. Borland C++ uses its own call type, which isn't compatible with anything.

Addressing arguments in the stack. The basic concept of the stack includes two operations: pushing elements onto the stack, and popping the last element off it. Accessing an arbitrary element is something new! However, such a deviation from the rules significantly increases the operating speed. If we need, say, the third element, why can't we pull it from the stack directly, without removing the first two elements? The stack is not only a "pile," as popular tutorials on programming teach us, but also an array. Therefore, knowing the position of the stack pointer (as we must — otherwise, where would we put the next element?) and the size of the elements, we can calculate the offset of any element, then easily read it.

The stack, like any other homogeneous array, has a drawback: It can store only one type of data (double words, for example). If we need to place 1 byte (such as an argument of the `char` type), we must expand it to a double word and place it as a whole. If an argument occupies four words (`double`, `int64`), we need two stack elements to pass it.

Besides passing arguments, the stack also saves the return address of the function. This requires one or two stack elements, depending on the type of the function call (`near` or `far`). The `near` call operates within one segment; we need to save only the offset of the instruction that follows the `CALL` instruction. If the calling function is in one segment and the called one is in another segment, we need to remember both the segment and the offset to know where to return to. The return address is placed after the arguments; therefore, the arguments appear behind it relative to the top of the stack. Their offset varies depending on how many stack elements the return address occupies — one or two. Fortunately, the flat memory model of Windows NT/9x allows us to forget about segmented memory model just as we would forget a bad dream; we can use only `near` calls everywhere.

Nonoptimizing compilers use a special register (usually, `EBP`) for addressing arguments that copies the value of the stack pointer register to the beginning of the function. Since the stack grows from higher addresses to lower ones, the offsets of all arguments (including the return address) are positive. The offset of the Nth argument is calculated using the following formula:

```
arg_offset = N*size_element+size_return_address
```

The argument number N counts from the top of the stack beginning from zero; the size of one stack element is `size_element`, generally equal to the bit capacity of the segment element (4 bytes in Windows NT/9x); and the space taken up by the return address in bytes is `size_return_address` (usually 4 bytes in Windows NT/9x). In addition, we often have to solve the opposite task: using a known offset of an element to determine the number of the argument being addressed. The following formula, easily derived from the previous one, is helpful for this:

$$N = \frac{\text{arg\_offset} - \text{size\_return\_address}}{\text{size\_element}}.$$

However, since the old EBP value should be saved in the same stack before copying the current ESP value to EBP, we must correct this formula, adding the EBP register capacity (BP in 16-bit mode) to the size of the return address.

From the hacker's point of view, there's a key advantage of such addressing of arguments: Having seen an instruction like MOV EAX, [EBP+0x10] somewhere in the middle of the code, we can instantly calculate which argument is being addressed. However, to save the EBP register, the optimizing compilers address arguments directly via ESP. The difference is basic! The ESP value changes during the function's execution; it changes every time data is pushed onto or popped off the stack. Thus, the offset of arguments relative to ESP doesn't remain constant either. To determine exactly which argument is addressed, we need to know the value of ESP at a given point of the program. For this, we have to trace all of its changes from the beginning of the function. We'll discuss this "artful" addressing in greater detail later. (See the "*Local Stack Variables*" section.) For now, let's return to the previous example (it's time to complete it) and analyze the called function:

Listing 73. The Disassembled Code of a Function Receiving Arguments

```
MyFunc          proc near           ; CODE XREF: main+39↑p

arg_0           = dword   ptr  8
arg_4           = dword   ptr  0Ch
arg_8           = byte ptr  10h
arg_1C          = dword   ptr  24h
     ; IDA recognized four arguments passed to the function.
     ; However,we shouldn't blindly trust IDA. If one argument
     ; (int64, for example)is passed as several words, IDA will accept it
     ; as several arguments, not as one! Therefore, the result produced
     ; by IDA should be interpreted as follows: no less than four arguments
     ; were passed to the function. However, again, everything is not that easy!
     ; Nothing prevents the called function from accessing
     ; the stack of the parent function as deeply as it wants.
     ; Perhaps nobody passed us any arguments,
     ; and we've rushed into the stack and stolen something from it.
     ; This mainly results from programming errors
     ; that occur because of confusion over prototypes. However, we need
     ; to take into account such a possibility. (In any case, you'll
     ; encounter it sometimes, so be informed). The number next to 'arg'
     ; represents the offset of the argument relative to the beginning
```

```
; of the stack frame. Note: the stack frame is shifted
; by 8 bytes relative to EBP — 4 bytes hold the saved
; return address, and an additional 4 bytes are used
; for saving the EBP register.
```

```
push      ebp
mov       ebp, esp
lea       eax, [ebp+arg_8]
; A pointer to an argument is obtained. Attention: a pointer to
; an argument, not an argument pointer! Now, let's figure out
; for which argument we're obtaining this pointer. IDA has already
; calculated that this argument is displaced by 8 bytes relative to
; the beginning of the stack frame. In the original code,
; the bracketed expression looked like ebp+0x10 — just as it is shown
; by most disassemblers. If IDA were not so clever, we would have had
; to manually and permanently subtract 8 bytes from each
; address expression. We'll still have a chance to practice this.
; What we pushed onto the stack last is on top.
; Let's look at the calling function to find what we pushed (see the
; variant compiled by Microsoft Visual C++). Aha! The last items
; were the two unclear arguments. Before them, a structure
; consisting of a string and a variable of the int type was placed
; onto the stack. Thus, EBP+ARG_8 points to a string.
```

```
push      eax
; The obtained pointer is pushed onto the stack.
; The pointer likely will be passed to the next function.
```

```
mov       ecx, [ebp+arg_1C]
; The contents of the EBP+ARG_1C argument are placed in ECX.
; What does it point to?
; You may recall that the int type is in the structure at an offset
; of 0x14 bytes from the beginning, and ARG_8 is simply
; its beginning.Consequently, 0x8+0x14 == 0x1C. That is,
; the value of the variable of the int type is a member
; of the structure, and is placed in ECX.
```

```
push      ecx
```

```
; The obtained variable is placed onto the stack. It was passed
; by value, because ECX stores the value, not the pointer.

mov        edx, [ebp+arg_4]
; Now, we take one of the two unclear arguments
; that were placed last onto the stack...

push       edx
; ... and push them onto the stack again to pass
; the argument to the next function.

mov        eax, [ebp+arg_0]
push       eax
; The second unclear argument is pushed onto the stack.

push       offset aFXS    ; "%f,%x,%s\n"
call       _printf
; Oops! Here we have the call of printf, passing a format
; specification string! The printf function, as you probably know,
; has a variable number of arguments, the type and quantity
; of which are specified by this string. Remember
; that we first placed the pointer to the string on the stack.
; The rightmost specifier %s indicates the output
; of a string. Then, a variable of the int type was placed onto the
; stack. The second specifier is %x — the output of an integer
; in hexadecimal representation. Then comes the last specifier —
; %f — which corresponds to placing two arguments onto the stack.
; If we look into the programmer's guide for Microsoft Visual C++,
; we'll see that the %f specifier outputs a floating-point value,
; which, depending on the type, can occupy 4 bytes (float)
; or 8 bytes (double). In this case, it obviously occupies
; 8 bytes, making it a double. Thus, we've reconstructed
; the prototype of our function. Here it is:
; cdecl MyFunc (double a, struct B b)
; The call type is cdecl — that is, the stack was cleared by
; the calling function. Alas, the original order of
; passing arguments can't be figured out. Remember that
; Borland C++ cleared the stack using the calling function,
; but changed the order of passing parameters.
```

```
; It seems likely that if a program was compiled by Borland C++,
; we can simply reverse the order of arguments. Unfortunately,
; it's not so easy. If there was an explicit conversion
; of the function type to cdecl, Borland C++
; would follow its orders. Then, reversing the
; order of arguments would give an incorrect result! However, the
; original order of arguments in the function prototype doesn't play
; a role. It's only important to establish a correspondence between
; the passed and accepted arguments, which we have done.
; Note: This was possible only with the combined analysis
; of the called and calling functions.
; Analysis of just one of them wouldn't give us any results.
; Note: Never completely rely on the format specification string.
; Since the specifiers are formed manually by the programmer,
; errors sometimes are hard to detect
; and give an extremely mysterious code after compilation!

add        esp, 14h
pop        ebp
retn
MyFunc     endp
```

We've made some progress; we successfully reconstructed the prototype of our first function. However, we have many miles to go before we reach the end of the section. If you're tired, take a rest and clear your head. We're going to move on to an important, but boring subject — the comparative analysis of various types of function calls and their implementation in popular compilers.

Let's begin by learning the standard convention on calls — stdcall. Take a look at the following example:

Listing 74. A Demonstration of the stdcall Call

```c
#include <stdio.h>
#include <string.h>


__stdcall MyFunc(int a, int b, char *c)
{
        return a+b+strlen(c);
}
```

```
main()
{
        printf("%x\n", MyFunc(0x666, 0x777, "Hello, World!"));
}
```

The disassembled listing of this example compiled with Microsoft Visual C++ using the default settings should look like this:

Listing 75. The Disassembled Code for the `stdcall` Call

```
main        proc near           ; CODE XREF: start+AF↓p
    push    ebp
    mov     ebp, esp

    push    offset aHelloWorld ; const char *
    ; The pointer to the aHelloWorld string is placed onto the stack.
    ; By examining the source code (fortunately, we have it),
    ; we'll find this is the rightmost argument passed
    ; to the function. Therefore, we have a call of stdcall
    ; or cdecl type, not Pascal. Notice that the string is passed
    ; by reference, not by value.

    push    777h ; int
    ; One more argument is placed onto the stack — a constant of type int.
    ; (IDA, from version 4.17, automatically determines its type.)

    push    666h ; int
    ; The last, leftmost argument is passed to the function —
    ; a constant of type int.

    call    MyFunc
    ; Note that the function call isn't followed by any instructions
    ; for clearing the stack from the arguments placed into it.
    ; If the compiler hasn't decided on
    ; a delayed cleanup, it is likely that the stack is cleared
    ; by the called function. Consequently, the type of call
```

```
                  ; is stdcall, which was what we wanted to prove.


                  push    eax
                  ; The value returned by the function is passed
                  ; to the following function as an argument.


                  push    offset asc_406040 ; "%x\n"
                  call    _printf
                  ; OK, this is the next printf function. The format string shows
                  ; that the passed argument has the int type.


                  add     esp, 8
                  ; This popped 8 bytes from the stack. Of these, 4 bytes relate
                  ; to the argument of type int, and 4 bytes to the pointer
                  ; to the format string.


                  pop     ebp
                  retn
main              endp

                  ; int __cdecl MyFunc(int,int,const char *)
MyFunc            proc near           ; CODE XREF: sub_40101D+12↑p
                  ; Beginning with version 4.17, IDA automatically reconstructs the
                  ; function prototypes. However, it does not always do this correctly.
                  ; In this case, IDA has made a gross error — the call type cannot
                  ; be cdecl, since the stack is cleared up by the called function!
                  ; It seems likely that IDA doesn't even attempt
                  ; to analyze the call type. Instead, it probably takes
                  ; the call type from the default settings
                  ; of the compiler that it has recognized. In general, the results
                  ; of IDA's work should be cautiously interpreted.


arg_0             = dword ptr  8
arg_4             = dword ptr  0Ch
arg_8             = dword ptr  10h
```

```
push    ebp
mov     ebp, esp
push    esi
; This, apparently, is saving the register on the stack.
; It's not passing it to the function because the register hasn't
; been explicitly initialized, neither by the calling function,
; nor by the called one.

mov     esi, [ebp+arg_0]
; The last argument pushed onto the stack is placed into
; the ESI register.

add     esi, [ebp+arg_4]
; The contents of ESI are added to the last argument placed
; onto the stack.

mov     eax, [ebp+arg_8]
; The next-to-last argument is written into EAX...

push    eax                     ; const    char *
; ... and pushed onto the stack.

call    _strlen
; Since strlen expects a pointer to a string, we can conclude
; that the next-to-last argument is a string passed by reference.

add     esp, 4
; The last argument is popped from the stack.

add     eax, esi
; As you'll remember, ESI stores the first two arguments, and EAX
; contains the returned string length. Thus, the function
; sums up two of its arguments with the string length.

pop     esi
pop     ebp
```

```
retn    0Ch
; The stack is cleared by the called function; therefore,
; the call type is stdcall or Pascal. Let's assume it's stdcall.
; Then, the function prototype should look like this:
; int MyFunc (int a, int b, char *c)
;
; Two variables of the int type, followed by a string, are on the top
; of the stack. Since the top of the stack always contains what
; was placed on it last, and, according to stdcall, the arguments are
; pushed from right to left, we obtain exactly this order of arguments.

MyFunc          endp
```

Now let's examine how the cdecl function is called. Let's replace the stdcall keyword in the previous example with cdecl:

Listing 76. A Demonstration of the cdecl Call

```
#include <stdio.h>
#include <string.h>

__cdecl MyFunc(int a, int b, char *c)
{
        return a+b+strlen(c);
}

main()
{
        printf("%x\n", MyFunc(0x666, 0x777, "Hello, World!"));
}
```

The disassembled listing of the compiled example should look like this:

Listing 77. The Disassembled Code for the cdecl Call

```
main            proc near               ; CODE XREF: start+AF↓p
        push    ebp
        mov     ebp, esp

        push    offset aHelloWorld ; const char *
```

```
        push    777h                    ; int
        push    666h                    ; int
        ; The arguments are passed to the function via the stack.

        call    MyFunc
        add     esp, 0Ch
        ; The stack is cleared by the calling function.
        ; This means that the call type is cdecl, since the other two
        ; conventions charge the called function with clearing the stack.

        push    eax
        push    offset asc_406040    ; "%x\n"
        call    _printf
        add     esp, 8
        pop     ebp
        retn
main            endp

        ; int __cdecl MyFunc(int,int,const char *)
        ; This time, IDA has correctly determined the call type.
        ; However, as previously shown, it could have made a mistake.
        ; So we still shouldn't rely on it.

MyFunc          proc near               ; CODE XREF: main+12↑p

arg_0           = dword ptr  8
arg_4           = dword ptr  0Ch
arg_8           = dword ptr  10h
; Since the function has the cdecl type,
; arguments are passed from right to left. Its prototype looks
; like this: MyFunc (int arg_0, int arg_4, char *arg_8).

        push    ebp
        mov     ebp, esp
        push    esi
        ; ESI is saved on the stack.

        mov     esi, [ebp+arg_0]
        ; The arg_0 argument of the int type is placed into ESI.

        add     esi, [ebp+arg_4]
        ; It's added to arg_4.
```

```
        mov     eax, [ebp+arg_8]
        ; The pointer to the string is placed into EAX.

        push    eax                 ; const char *
        ; It's passed to the strlen function via the stack.

        call    _strlen
        add     esp, 4

        add     eax, esi
        ; The string length arg_8 is added to the sum of arg_0 and arg_4.

        pop     esi
        pop     ebp
        retn
MyFunc          endp
```

Before we proceed to the really serious things, let's consider the last standard type — PASCAL:

Listing 78. A Demonstration of the PASCAL Call

```
#include <stdio.h>
#include <string.h>

// Attention! Microsoft Visual C++ no longer supports the PASCAL call
// type. Instead, it uses the similar WINAPI call type
// defined in the windows.h file.

#if defined(_MSC_VER)
#include <windows.h>
// We include windows.h only when we compile using Microsoft
// Visual C++; a more effective solution for other compilers is
// using the PASCAL keyword — if they support it (as Borland does).

#endif

// This kind of programming trick makes the listing less readable,
// but it allows us to compile the code with more than one compiler.
```

```
#if defined(_MSC_VER)
WINAPI
#else
__pascal
#endif

MyFunc(int a, int b, char *c)
{
        return a+b+strlen(c);
}

main()
{
        printf("%x\n", MyFunc(0x666, 0x777, "Hello, World!"));
}
```

The disassembled listing of this program compiled with Borland C++ should look like this:

Listing 79. The Disassembled Code for the PASCAL Call Using Borland C++

```
; int __cdecl main(int argc,const char **argv,const char *envp)
_main          proc near            ; DATA XREF: DATA:00407044↓o


        push    ebp
        mov     ebp, esp

        push    666h                     ; int
        push    777h                     ; int
        push    offset aHelloWorld ; s
        ; The arguments are passed to the function. Reviewing
        ; the source code, we notice that the arguments are passed
        ; from left to right. However, if the source code isn't available,
        ; it's impossible to establish this! Fortunately, the original
        ; function prototype is not of much importance.


        call    MyFunc
```

```
; The function doesn't clear the stack!
; If this is not the result of optimization, the call type is
; PASCAL or stdcall. Since PASCAL is already out of the question,
; we'll assume we're dealing with stdcall.

        push    eax
        push    offset unk_407074   ; format
        call    _printf
        add     esp, 8

        xor     eax, eax
        pop     ebp
        retn
_main           endp


; int __cdecl MyFunc(const char *s,int,int)
; IDA has given an incorrect result again!
; The call type is obviously not cdecl!
; Although the order of arguments is the reverse,
; everything else about the function prototype
; is suitable for use.

MyFunc          proc near           ; CODE XREF: _main+12↑p

s               = dword ptr  8
arg_4           = dword ptr  0Ch
arg_8           = dword ptr  10h

        push    ebp
        mov     ebp, esp
; The stack frame is opened.

        mov     eax, [ebp+s]
; The pointer to the string is placed into EAX.

        push    eax
        call    _strlen
; It's passed to the strlen function.

        pop     ecx
; One argument is deleted by popping it from the stack
; into any available register.
```

```
        mov     edx, [ebp+arg_8]
        ; The arg_8 argument of type int is placed in EDX.

        add     edx, [ebp+arg_4]
        ; It's added to the arg_4 argument.

        add     eax, edx
        ; The string length is added to the sum of arg_8 and arg_4.

        pop     ebp
        retn    0Ch
        ; The stack is cleared by the called function.
        ; This means that its type is PASCAL or stdcall.

MyFunc          endp
```

As you can see, the identification of basic call types and the reconstruction of the function prototypes are rather simple. The only thing that might spoil the mood is confusion between PASCAL and stdcall. However, the order of placing arguments onto the stack is of no importance, except in special cases. We'll give one here:

Listing 80. Distinguishing PASCAL from stdcall

```
#include <stdio.h>
#include <windows.h>
#include <winuser.h>

// CALLBACK procedure for receiving timer messages
VOID CALLBACK TimerProc(
  HWND hwnd,      // Handle of the window for timer messages
  UINT uMsg,      // WM_TIMER message
  UINT idEvent,   // Timer identifier
  DWORD dwTime    // Current system time
)
{
            // All beeps
 MessageBeep((dwTime % 5)*0x10);    // The time elapsed, in seconds,
                                    // is displayed from the moment
```

```
                                             // the system starts.
printf("\r:=%d", dwTime/1000);
}



main()
// This is a console application, but it also can have
// a message loop and can set the timer!
{
        int a;
        MSG msg;


        // The timer is set by passing the address of the TimerProc
        // procedure to it.


        SetTimer(0,0,1000,TimerProc);


        // This is the message loop. When you're fed up with it,
        // press <Ctrl>+<Break> to break the loop.


        while (GetMessage(&msg, (HWND) NULL, 0, 0))
        {
                                TranslateMessage(&msg);
                                DispatchMessage(&msg);
        }
}
```

Let's compile an example like this — `cl pascal.callback.c USER32.lib` — and see what results:

Listing 81. The Disassembled Code for Distinguishing PASCAL from stdcall

```
main          proc near              ; CODE XREF: start+AF↓p
; This time, IDA hasn't determined the function prototype.


Msg           = MSG ptr -20h
; IDA recognized one local variable and even determined
```

```
; its type.

        push    ebp
        mov     ebp, esp
        sub     esp, 20h

        push    offset TimerProc    ; lpTimerFunc
        ; The pointer is passed to the TimerProc function.

        push    1000                ; uElapse
        ; The timer time delay is passed.

        push    0                   ; nIDEvent
        ; The nIDEvent argument is always ignored in console applications.

        push    0                   ; hWnd
        ; There are no windows, so we're passing NULL.

        call    ds:SetTimer
        ; The Win32 API functions are called according to the stdcall
        ; convention. Knowing their prototype (described in the SDK),
        ; we can determine the type and purpose of arguments.
        ; In this case, the source code looked like this:

        ; SetTimer(NULL, BULL, 1000, TimerProc);

loc_401051:                         ; CODE XREF: main+42↓j
        push    0                   ; wMsgFilterMax
        ; NULL — no filter

        push    0                   ; wMsgFilterMin
        ; NULL — no filter

        push    0                   ; hWnd
        ; NULL — no windows in the console application

        lea     eax, [ebp+Msg]
        ; Get the pointer to the msg local variable.
        ; The type of this variable is determined only
        ; on the basis of the prototype of the GetMessageA function.
```

```
        push    eax                     ; lpMsg
        ; Pass the pointer to msg.

        call    ds:GetMessageA
        ; The GetMessageA(&msg, NULL, NULL, NULL) function is called.

        test    eax, eax
        jz      short loc_40107B
        ; This is the check for WM_QUIT.

        lea     ecx, [ebp+Msg]
        ; ECX contains the pointer to the filled MSG structure...

        push    ecx                     ; lpMsg
        ; ... and passes it to the TranslateMessage function.

        call    ds:TranslateMessage
        ; The TranslateMessage(&msg) function is called.

        lea     edx, [ebp+Msg]
        ; EDX contains the pointer to msg...

        push    edx                     ; lpMsg
        ; ... and passes it to the DispatchMessageA function.

        call    ds:DispatchMessageA
        ; The DispatchMessageA function is called.

        jmp     short loc_401051
        ; This is the message handling loop...

loc_40107B:                             ; CODE XREF: main+2C↑j
        ; ... and the output.

        mov     esp, ebp
        pop     ebp
        retn
main            endp
```

```
TimerProc      proc near              ; DATA XREF: main+6↑o
; IDA hasn't automatically reconstructed the prototype of TimerProc as
; a consequence of the implicit call of this function by the operating
; system — we'll have to do this ourselves. We know TimerProc is
; passed to the SetTimer function. Looking into the description
; of SetTimer (SDK should always be near at hand!), we'll find
; its prototype:
;
;   VOID CALLBACK TimerProc(
;   HWND hwnd,      // Handle of window for timer messages
;   UINT uMsg,      // WM_TIMER message
;   UINT idEvent,   // Timer identifier
;   DWORD dwTime    // Current system time
;   )
;
; Now we just have to clarify the call type. This time, it's important.
; Since we don't have the code of the calling function
; (it's located deep under the hood of the operating system),
; we'll be able to find out the argument types
; only if we know the order in which they are passed.
; We already mentioned above that all CALLBACK functions obey the
; Pascal convention. Don't confuse CALLBACK functions with Win32 API
; functions! The former are called by the operating system,
; the latter by an application.
;
; OK, the call type of this function is PASCAL. This means that arguments
; will be pushed from left to right, and the stack is cleared by the
; called function. (You should make sure that this is really the case.)

arg_C          = dword          ptr 14h
; IDA has revealed only one argument — although, judging by the prototype,
; four of them are passed. Why? It's simple: The function used
; only one argument. It didn't even address the rest of them.
; It appears that IDA was not able to determine them!
; By the way, what kind of argument is this?
; Let's see: Its offset is 0xC. On the top of the stack, we find
; what was pushed onto it last. On the bottom, we should see
; the opposite. But it turns out
; that dwTime was placed onto the stack first! (Since we have the source code,
```

```
; we know for certain that arg_C is dwTime.) The Pascal convention
; requires pushing arguments in the reverse order. Something is wrong
; here... The program works, however (launch it to check). The SDK
; says CALLBACK is an analog of FAR PASCAL. So everything is clear
; with FAR — all calls are near in WinNT/9x . But how can we explain
; the inversion of pushing arguments? Let's look into <windef.h>
; and see how the PASCAL type is defined there:
;
; #elif (_MSC_VER >= 800) || defined(_STDCALL_SUPPORTED)
; #define CALLBACK     __stdcall
; #define WINAPI       __stdcall
; #define WINAPIV      __cdecl
; #define APIENTRY     WINAPI
; #define APIPRIVATE   __stdcall
; #define PASCAL       __stdcall
;
; Well, who would have thought it! The call declared
; as PASCAL is actually stdcall! And CALLBACK is also defined
; as stdcall. At last, everything is clear. (Now, if someone tells you
; that CALLBACK is PASCAL, you can smile and say that a hedgehog is
; a bird, although a proud one — it won't fly until you kick it!)
; It seems likely that rummaging in the jungle of include files may
; be beneficial. By the way, perversions with overlapping types
; create a big problem when adding modules written in an environment
; that supports call conventions of the PASCAL function to a C project.
; Since PASCAL in Windows is stdcall, nothing will work!
; However, there's still the PASCAL keyword.
; It isn't overlapping, but it also isn't supported by the
; most recent versions of Microsoft Visual C++. The way out is to use
; the assembly inserts or Borland C++, which, like many other
; compilers, continues to support the Pascal convention.
;
; So, we've clarified that arguments
; are passed to the CALLBACK functions from right to left,
; but the stack is cleared by the called function,
; as must be done according to the stdcall convention.

        push    ebp
        mov     ebp, esp
```

```
mov     eax, [ebp+arg_C]
; The dwTime argument is placed into EAX. How did we get this?
; There are three arguments before it on the stack.
; Each has a size of 4 bytes. Consequently, 4*3=0xC.

xor     edx, edx
; EDX is zeroed.

mov     ecx, 5
; A value of 5 is placed in ECX.
div     ecx
; dwTime (in EAX) is divided by 5.

shl     edx, 4
; EDX contains the remainder from division; using the cyclic shift
; instruction, we multiply it by 0x10 (or 4th degree of 2).

push    edx                  ; uType
; The obtained result is passed to the MessageBeep function.
; In the SDK, we'll find that MessageBeep accepts
; the constants such as NB_OK, MB_ICONASTERISK, MB_ICONHAND, etc.,
; but nothing is said about the immediate values
; of each constant. However, the SDK informs us that MessageBeep
; is described in the WINUSER.h file. Let's open it and search
; for MB_OK using the context search:

;
; #define MB_OK                        0x00000000L
; #define MB_OKCANCEL                  0x00000001L
; #define MB_ABORTRETRYIGNORE          0x00000002L
; #define MB_YESNOCANCEL               0x00000003L
; #define MB_YESNO                     0x00000004L
; #define MB_RETRYCANCEL               0x00000005L
;
; #define MB_ICONHAND                  0x00000010L
; #define MB_ICONQUESTION              0x00000020L
; #define MB_ICONEXCLAMATION           0x00000030L
; #define MB_ICONASTERISK              0x00000040L
```

```
; All the constants that we're interested in
; have values of 0x0, 0x10, 0x20, 0x30, and 0x40. Now we can
; get a sense of the program. We divide by 5 the time elapsed
; from the system startup (in milliseconds). The remainder
; is a number belonging to the interval from 0 to 4. This number
; is multiplyed by 0x10, — 0x0, 0x0x10 — 0x40.

call    ds:MessageBeep
; All possible types of beeps.

mov     eax, [ebp+arg_C]
; dwTime is placed into EAX.

xor     edx, edx
; EDX is zeroed.

mov     ecx, 3E8h
; The decimal equivalent of 0x3E8 is 1000.

div     ecx
; dwTime is divided by 1000;
; that is, milliseconds are converted into seconds and...

push    eax
; ... the result passed to the printf function.

push    offset aD          ; "\r:=%d"
call    _printf
add     esp, 8
; printf("\r:=%d")

pop     ebp
retn    10h
; Please turn the lights off when you leave — i.e.,
; clear the stack yourself!


TimerProc       endp
```

An important remark on the types defined in <WINDOWS.H>! We spoke about this in the comments on the previous listing, but repetition is justified; after all, not all readers grasp the analysis of disassembled listings.

The CALLBACK and WINAPI functions obey the Pascal calling convention, but PASCAL is defined in <WINDEF.H> as stdcall (and as cdecl on some platforms). Thus, on the INTEL platform, Windows functions follow the same convention: Arguments are pushed onto the stack from right to left, and the stack is cleared by the called function.

To make ourselves familiar with the Pascal convention, let's create a simple Pascal program and disassemble it (PASCAL calls occur in other programs, but it makes sense to study PASCAL calls in Pascal programs):

Listing 82. A Demonstration of the PASCAL Call

```
USES WINCRT;
Procedure MyProc(a:Word; b:Byte; c:String);
begin
        WriteLn(a+b,' ',c);
end;


BEGIN
        MyProc($666,$77,'Hello, Sailor!');
END.
```

The disassembled code of this program compiled using Turbo Pascal for Windows should look like this:

Listing 83. The Disassembled Code for the PASCAL Call Compiled Using Turbo Pascal for Windows

```
PROGRAM         proc near
        call    INITTASK
        ; INITTASK is called from KRNL386.EXE to initialize a 16-bit task.

        call    @__SystemInit$qv ; __SystemInit(void)
        ; The SYSTEM module is initialized.

        call    @__WINCRTInit$qv ; __WINCRTInit(void)
```

```
        ; The WinCRT module is initialized.

        push    bp
        mov     bp, sp
        ; The function prolog is in the middle of the function.
        ; This is Turbo Pascal!

        xor     ax, ax
        call    @__StackCheck$q4Word ; Stack overflow check (AX)

        push    666h
        ; Note that the arguments are passed from left to right.

        push    77h ; 'w'
        mov     di, offset aHelloSailor ; "Hello, Sailor!"
        ; DI contains a pointer to the string "Hello, Sailor!"

        push    ds
        push    di
        ; The FAR pointer is passed, not NEAR —
        ; that is, both segment and offset of the string.

        call    MyProc
        ; The stack is cleared by the called function.

        leave
        ; The function's epilog closes the stack frame.

        xor     ax, ax
        call    @Halt$q4Word          ; Halt(Word)
        ; The program ends!

PROGRAM         endp

MyProc          proc near             ; CODE XREF: PROGRAM+23↑p
; IDA hasn't determined the function prototype.
; We'll just have to do this ourselves!

var_100         = byte ptr -100h
```

```
; This is a local variable. Since it's located at 0x100 bytes
; above the stack frame, it seems to be an array of 0x100 bytes
; (the maximum string length in Pascal is 0xFF bytes).
; It's likely to be the buffer allocated for the string.

arg_0          = dword ptr  4
arg_4          = byte ptr  8
arg_6          = word ptr  0Ah
; The function accepted three arguments.


        push   bp
        mov    bp, sp
        ; The stack frame is opened.


        mov    ax, 100h
        call   @__StackCheck$q4Word ; Stack overflow check (AX)
        ; Here, we find out if there are 100 bytes available on the stack,
        ; which we need for local variables.


        sub    sp, 100h
        ; Space is allocated for local variables.


        les    di, [bp+arg_0]
        ; The pointer to the rightmost argument is obtained.


        push   es
        push   di
        ; We passed the far pointer to the arg_0 argument,
        ; with its segment address not even popped from the stack!


        lea    di, [bp+var_100]
        ; The pointer to the local buffer is obtained.


        push   ss
        ; Its segment address is pushed onto the stack.


        push   di
        ; The buffer offset is pushed onto the stack.


        push   0FFh
```

```
; The maximum string length is pushed.

call    @$basg$qm6Stringt14Byte ; Store string
; The string is copied into the local buffer (consequently,
; arg_0 is a string). This way of achieving the goal, however,
; seems a little strange. Why not use a reference?
; Turbo Pascal won't let us —
; the strings are passed by value in Pascal.
; :-(


mov     di, offset unk_1E18
; A pointer is obtained to the output buffer.
; Here, we need to become acquainted with the output system
; of Pascal — it is strikingly different from the C output
; system. First, the left-side order of pushing arguments
; onto the stack doesn't allow us (without using additional
; tricks) to organize support for procedures that have
; a variable number of arguments.
; But WriteLn is just a procedure with a variable number
; of parameters, isn't it?
; No, it's not a procedure! It's an operator.
; At compile time, the compiler divides it into several
; procedure calls to output each argument separately.
; Therefore, in the compiled code, each procedure takes a fixed
; number of arguments. There will be three of them in our case:
; The first one will be used to output the sum of two numbers
; (accepted by the WriteLongint procedure), the second one
; to output the blank space as a character (WriteChar),
; and the last one to output the string (WriteString).
; In Windows, it's impossible
; to output the string directly into the window and forget about it,
; because the window may require redrawing.
; The operating system doesn't save its contents — this would
; require a big memory space in a graphic environment with a high
; resolution. The code that outputs the string should know how
; to repeat the output on request. If you have ever programmed
; in Windows, you likely remember that all output should be placed
; into the WM_PAINT message handler. Turbo Pascal allows us to treat
; the window under Windows as a console. In this case,
```

```
; everything displayed earlier should be stored somewhere.
; Since local variables cease to exist as soon as their procedures
; are executed, they are not suitable for storing the buffer.
; Either the heap or the data segment remains. Pascal uses the latter —
; we've just received the pointer to such a buffer. In addition,
; to boost the output performance,
; Turbo Pascal creates a simple cache. The WriteLingint, WriteChar,
; and WriteString functions merge the results of their activity,
; represented by characters in this buffer. In the end, the call
; of WriteLn follows, which outputs the buffer contents into the window.
; The run-time system track the redrawing of the window,
; and, if necessary, repeats the output
; without involving the programmer.


push    ds
push    di
; The buffer address is pushed onto the stack.


mov     al, [bp+arg_4]
; The type of the arg_4 argument is byte.


xor     ah, ah
; The higher byte of the AH register is zeroed.


add     ax, [bp+arg_6]
; This summed up arg_4 and arg_6. Since al was previously extended
; to AX, arg_6 has the Word type. (When summing two numbers of different
; types, Pascal extends the smaller number to the size of the larger
; one.) Apart from this, the calling procedure passes the value 0x666
; with this argument, which would not fit in 1 byte.


xor     dx, dx
; DX is zeroed...


push    dx
; ... and pushed onto the stack.


push    ax
; The sum of two left arguments is pushed onto the stack.
```

```
push    0
; One more zero!

call    @Write$qm4Text7Longint4Word ; Write(varf; v: Longint; width: Word)
; The WriteLongint function has the following prototype:
; WriteLongint(Text far &, a: Longint, count: Word).
; Text far & — the pointer to the output buffer
; a — the long integer being output
; count — how many variables should be output
; (if zero — one variable)
;
; Consequently, in our case, we output one variable — the sum of two
; arguments. A small addition — the WriteLongint function doesn't
; follow the Pascal convention, since it doesn't clear the stack
; completely, but leaves the pointer to the buffer on the stack.
; The compiler developers have accepted this solution to achieve
; better performance: If other functions need the pointer to the
; buffer (at least one of them does — WriteLn), why should we pop it,
; then push it back again each time? If you look into the end
; of the WriteLongint function, you'll see RET 6. The function
; pops two arguments from the stack — two words for Longint,
; and one word for count. Such a lovely technical detail! It's
; small, but it can lead to great confusion, especially if a code
; digger is not familiar with the Pascal input\output system!


push    20h ; ' '
; The next argument is pushed onto the stack for passing it to
; the WriteLn function. The pointer to the buffer is still on the stack.

push    0
; We need to output only one character.

call @Write$qm4Text4Char4Word ; Write(var f; c: Char; width: Word)

lea     di, [bp+var_100]
; A pointer is obtained to the local copy of the string
; passed to the function.
```

```
        push    ss
        push    di
        ; Its address is pushed onto the stack.

        push    0
        ; This is the output of only one string!

        call @Write$qm4Textm6String4Word ; Write(var f; s: String; width: Word)

        call    @WriteLn$qm4Text ; WriteLn(var f: Text)
        ; It seems likely that no parameters are passed to the functions.
        ; Actually, the pointer to the buffer lays on the top of the stack
        ; and waits for its "hour of triumph."
        ; Upon completion of WriteLn, it will be removed from the stack.


        call    @__IOCheck$qv        ; Exit if error.
        ; Check if the output is successful.

        leave
        ; The stack frame is closed.


        retn    8
        ; Since 8 bytes are popped from the stack, we now have everything
        ; we need to reconstruct the prototype of our procedure.
        ; It looks like this:
        ; MyProc(a: Byte, b: Word, c: String)

MyProc          endp
```

Turbo Pascal turned out to be very artful! This analysis has taught us a good lesson: We can never be sure that the function will pop all arguments passed to it from the stack. In addition, it's impossible to determine the number of arguments by the number of machine words popped from the stack!

Fastcall conventions. However unproductive the transfer of arguments via the stack might be, the stdcall and cdecl call types are standardized, and they should be observed. Otherwise, the modules compiled by one compiler (libraries, for example) will be incompatible with modules compiled by other compilers. However, if the called function is compiled by the same compiler as the calling one, we don't need to follow the standard conventions. Instead, we can take advantage of the more effective passing of arguments via registers.

Beginners may wonder: Why hasn't the passing of arguments via registers been standardized? Is anyone planning to do so? The response is: Who would standardize it? Committees on the standardization of C and C++? Certainly not! All platform-dependent solutions are left to compiler developers — each developer is free to implement them as desired, or not to implement them. Readers still may ask: What prevents the compiler developers for one specific platform from reaching common agreements?

Developers have agreed to pass the value returned by the function through [E]AX:[[E]DX], although the standard doesn't discuss specific registers. At least, they have a partial agreement: Most manufacturers of 16-bit compilers have observed conventions without making compatibility claims. But the fastcall is so named because it is aimed at providing maximum performance. The optimization technique doesn't stand still, and introducing a standard is equivalent to anchoring a ball and chain to your leg. On the other hand, the average gain from passing arguments via registers is slight, and many compiler developers forsake speed for simplicity of implementation. If performance is crucial, we can use the inline functions.

This reasoning likely will interest programmers, but code diggers are worried about the reconstruction of function prototypes, not about performance. Is it possible to find out what arguments the fastcall function receives without analyzing its code (that is, looking only at the calling function)? The popular answer, "No, because the compiler passes arguments via the most 'convenient' registers," is wrong, and the speaker clearly shows his or her ignorance of the compilation procedure.

In compiler development, there is a *translation unit*: Depending on the implementation, the compiler may translate the program code in its entirety, or it may translate each function separately. The first type incurs substantial overhead, since we need to store the entire parse tree in memory. The second type saves in the memory only each function's name and reference to the code generated for it. Compilers of the first type are rare; I've never come across (although I have heard about) such a C\C++ compiler for Windows. Compilers of the second type are more efficient, require less memory, and are easier to implement; they are good in all respects except for their intrinsic inability to perform pass-through optimization. Each function is optimized individually and independently. Therefore, the compiler can't choose the optimal registers for passing arguments, since it doesn't know how they're handled by the called function. Functions translated independently should follow conventions, even if this isn't advantageous.

Thus, knowing the "handwriting" of the particular compiler, we can reconstruct the function prototype with minimal effort.

Borland C ++ 3.x passes arguments via the AX(AL), DX(DL), and BX(BL) registers. When no free registers remain, arguments are pushed onto the stack from left to right. Then they're popped by the called function (stdcall).

The method of passing arguments is rather interesting. The compiler doesn't assign each argument its "own" registers; instead, it provides each argument easy access to the "pile" of candidates stacked in order of preference. Each argument takes as many registers from the pile as it needs, and when the pile is exhausted, the stack is used. The only exception is arguments of the long int type, which are always passed via DX:AX (the higher word is passed via DX) or, if that's impossible, via the stack.

If each argument occupies no more than 16 bits (as is often the case), the first argument from the left is placed into AX(AL), the second one into DX(DL), and the third one into BX(BL). If the first argument from the left is of the long int type, it takes two registers from the pile at once: DX:AX. The second argument gets the BX(BL) register. Nothing remains for the third argument, so it is passed via the stack. When long int is passed as the second argument, it is sent to the stack, since the AX register it needs is already occupied by the first argument. In this case, the third argument is passed via DX. Finally, if long int is the third argument from the left, it goes onto the stack. The first two arguments are passed via AX(AL) and DX(DL), respectively.

Floating-point values and far pointers are always passed via the main stack (not via the stack of the coprocessor, as common sense would tell us).

Table 2. The Fastcall Preferences of Borland C++ 3.x for Passing Arguments

Argument type	Preferences		
	1st argument	2nd argument	3rd argument
Char	AL	DL	BL
Int	AX	DX	BX
Long int	DX:AX	DX:AX	DX:AX
Near pointer	AX	DX	BX
Far pointer	Stack	Stack	Stack
Float	Stack	Stack	Stack
Double	Stack	Stack	Stack

Microsoft C++ 6.0 also behaves much like the Borland C++ 3.x compiler, except that it changes the order of preferences of the candidates for passing pointers — namely, the BX register has priority. This is logical because the early 80x86 microprocessors didn't support indirect addressing via AX or DX. In those microprocessors, the value passed to the function had to be moved to BX, SI, or DI.

Table 3. The Fastcall Preferences of Microsoft C++ 6.0 for Passing Arguments

Argument type	Preferences		
	1st argument	2nd argument	3rd argument
Char	AL	DL	BL
Int	AX	DX	BX
Long int	DX:AX	DX:AX	DX:AX
Near pointer	BX	AX	DX
Far pointer	Stack	Stack	Stack
Float	Stack	Stack	Stack
Double	Stack	Stack	Stack

Borland C++ 5.x is similar to its predecessor, Borland C++ 3.x. However, it prefers the CX register to BX and places arguments of int and long int types in any suitable 32-bit registers, not in DX:AX. This is the result of converting the compiler from 16-bit to 32-bit mode.

Table 4. The Fastcall Preferences of Borland C++ 5.x for Passing Arguments

Argument type	Preferences		
	1st argument	2nd argument	3rd argument
Char	AL	DL	CL
Int	EAX	EDX	ECX
Long int	EAX	EDX	ECX
Near pointer	EAX	EDX	ECX
Far pointer	Stack	Stack	Stack
Float	Stack	Stack	Stack
Double	Stack	Stack	Stack

Microsoft Visual C++ 4.x–6.x, when possible, passes the first argument from the left via the ECX register, the second one via the EDX register, and the rest via the stack. Floating-point values and far pointers are always transferred via the stack. The argument of the __int64 type (a nonstandard, 64-bit integer introduced by Microsoft) is always passed via the stack.

If __int64 is the first argument from the left, the second argument is passed via ECX, and the third one via EDX. If __int64 is the second argument, the first one is passed via ECX, and the third one via EDX.

Table 5. The Fastcall Preferences of Microsoft C++ 4.x–6x for Passing Arguments

Argument type	Preferences		
	1st argument	2nd argument	3rd argument
Char	CL	DL	Not used
Int	ECX	EDX	Not used
__int64	Stack	Stack	Stack
Long int	ECX	ECX	Not used
Near pointer	ECX	EDX	Not used
Far pointer	Stack	Stack	Not used
Float	Stack	Stack	Not used
Double	Stack	Stack	Not used

Watcom C greatly differs from compilers from Borland and Microsoft. In particular, it doesn't support the fastcall keyword. (This results in serious compatibility problems.) By default, Watcom always passes arguments via registers. Instead of the commonly used "pile of preferences," Watcom strictly assigns a certain register to each argument: The EAX register is assigned to the first argument, EDX to the second one, EBX to the third one, and ECX to the fourth one. If it is impossible to place an argument into the specified register, this argument, and *all other arguments to the right of it*, are pushed onto the stack! In particular, by default, the float and double types are pushed onto the stack of the main processor, which spoils the whole thing.

Table 6. The Default Method Used by Watcom for Passing Arguments

Argument type	Assignment			
	1st argument	2nd argument	3rd argument	4th argument
Char	AL	DL	BL	CL
Int	EAX	EDX	EBX	ECX
Long int	EAX	EDX	EBX	ECX
Near pointer	ECX	EDX	EBX	ECX
Far pointer	Stack	Stack	Stack	Stack
Float	CPU stack	CPU stack	CPU stack	CPU stack
	FPU stack	FPU stack	FPU stack	FPU stack
Double	CPU stack	CPU stack	CPU stack	CPU stack
	FPU stack	FPU stack	FPU stack	FPU stack

The programmer may arbitrarily set his or her own order for passing arguments using the aux pragma, which has the following format: *pragma aux *function_name* parm [*the list of registers*]. The list of registers allowable for each type of argument is given in the following table.

Table 7. The Registers for Passing Arguments in Watcom C

Argument type	Permitted registers					
Char	EAX	EBX	ECX	EDX	ESI	EDI
Int	EAX	EBX	ECX	EDX	ESI	EDI
Long int	EAX	EBX	ECX	EDX	ESI	EDI
Near pointer	EAX	EBX	ECX	EDX	ESI	EDI
Far pointer	DX:EAX	CX:EBX	CX:EAX	CX:ESI	DX:EBX	DI:EAX
	CX:EDI	DX:ESI	DI:EBX	SI:EAX	CX:EDX	DX:EDI
	DI:ESI	SI:EBX	BX:EAX	FS:ECX	FS:EDX	FS:EDI
	FS:ESI	FS:EBX	FS:EAX	GS:ECX	GS:EDX	GS:EDI
	GS:ESI	GS:EBX	GS:EAX	DS:ECX	DS:EDX	DS:EDI
	DS:ESI	DS:EBX	DS:EAX	ES:ECX	ES:EDX	ES:EDI
	ES:ESI	ES:EBX	ES:EAX			

continues

Table 7 Continued

Argument type	Permitted registers					
Float	8087	???	???	???	???	???
Double	8087	EDX:EAX	ECX:EBX	ECX:EAX	ECX:ESI	EDX:EBX
	EDI:EAX	ECX:EDI	EDX:ESI	EDI:EBX	ESI:EAX	ECX:EDX
	EDX:EDI	EDI:ESI	ESI:EBX	EBX:EAX		

I'll give a few explanations. First, arguments of the char type are passed via 32-bit registers, not via 8-bit ones. Second, the unexpectedly large number of possible pairs of registers for passing far pointers is striking. Third, the segment address may be passed not only via segment registers, but also via 16-bit, general-purpose registers.

Floating-point arguments can be passed via the stack of the coprocessor — just specify 8087 instead of the register name and compile the program using the -7 key (or -fpi, or -fpu87) to inform the compiler that the coprocessor's instructions are allowed. The documentation on Watcom says that arguments of the double type can also be passed via pairs of 32-bit, general-purpose registers, but I have failed to force the compiler to generate such a code. Maybe I don't know Watcom well enough, or perhaps an error occurred. I also have never encountered any program in which floating-point values have been passed via general-purpose registers. However, these are subtleties.

Thus, when analyzing programs compiled using Watcom, remember that arguments can be passed via practically any register.

Identifying arguments sent to and received from registers. Both the called and calling functions must follow conventions when passing arguments via registers. The compiler should place arguments into the registers where the called function expects them to be, rather than into those "convenient" for the compiler. As a result, before each function that follows the fastcall convention, a code appears that "shuffles" the contents of registers in a strictly determined manner. The manner depends on the specific compiler. The most popular methods of passing arguments were considered above. If your compiler isn't in the list (which is quite probable — compilers spring up like mushrooms after a rain), experiment to figure out its "nature" yourself or consult its documentation. Developers rarely disclose such subtleties — not because of the desire to keep it secret, but because the documentation for each byte of the compiler wouldn't fit into a freight train.

Analyzing the code of the calling function does not help us recognize passing arguments via registers unless their initialization is evident. Therefore, we need to analyze the called function. In most cases, the registers saved on the stack just after the function receives control did not pass arguments, and we can strike them off the list of "candidates." Among the remaining registers, we need to find the ones whose contents are used without obvious initialization. At first, the function appears to receive arguments via just these registers. Upon closer examination, however, several issues emerge. First, implicit arguments of the function (the this pointer, pointers to the object virtual tables, etc.) often are passed via registers. Second, an unskilled programmer might believe the value should be equal to zero upon its declaration. If he or she forgets about initialization, the compiler places the value into the register. During program analysis, this value might be mistaken for the function argument passed via the register. Interestingly, this register accidentally may be explicitly initialized by the calling function. The programmer, for example, could call some function before this one, whose return value (placed into EAX by the compiler) wasn't used. The compiler could place the uninitialized variable into EAX. When, upon the normal completion of the execution, the function returns zero, everything may work. To catch such a bug, the code digger should analyze the algorithm and figure out whether the code of the successful function's completion is really placed into EAX, or if the variables were overwritten.

If we discard "clinical" cases, passing arguments via registers doesn't strongly complicate the analysis.

A practical investigation of the mechanism of passing arguments via registers. Let's consider the following example. Note the conditional compilation directives used for compatibility with various compilers:

Listing 84. Passing Arguments via Registers

```
#include <stdio.h>
#include <string>

#if defined(__BORLANDC__) || defined (_MSC_VER)
// This branch of the program should be compiled only by Borland C++
// or Microsoft C++ compilers that support the fastcall keyword.

__fastcall
#endif

// Next is the MyFunc function, which has various types of arguments
// for demonstrating the mechanism of passing them.
```

```
MyFunc(char a, int b, long int c, int d)
{

#if defined(__WATCOMC__)
// This branch is specially intended for Watcom C.
// The aux pragma forcefully sets the order of passing arguments
// via the following registers: EAX, ESI, EDI, EBX.
#pragma aux MyFunc parm [EAX] [ESI] [EDI] [EBX];
#endif
        return a+b+c+d;
}

main()
{

        printf("%x\n", MyFunc(0x1, 0x2, 0x3, 0x4));
        return 0;
}
```

The disassembled code of this example compiled using the Microsoft Visual C++ 6.0 compiler should look like this:

Listing 85. The Disassembled Code for Passing Arguments Compiled Using Microsoft Visual C++

```
main          proc near            ; CODE XREF: start+AF↓p
        push    ebp
        mov     ebp, esp

        push    4
        push    3
        ; If you run out of registers, the arguments are pushed onto the stack
        ; from right to left, passed to the calling function,
        ; then cleared from the stack by the called function (that is,
        ; everything is done just as if the stdcall convention were observed).

        mov     edx, 2
        ; EDX is used for passing the argument second from the left.
        ; It's easy to determine its type — this is int.
        ; It's certainly not char, and it's not a pointer.
        ; (A value of 2 is strange for a pointer.)
```

```
        mov     cl, 1
        ; The CL register is used for passing the argument
        ; first from the left (that is, of the char type —
        ; only variables of the char type have a size of 8 bits).

        call    MyFunc
        ; Already, we can reconstruct the prototype of the function:
        ; MyFunc(char, int, int, int).
        ; We've made a mistake by taking the long int type for int,
        ; but these types are identical
        ; in the Microsoft Visual C++ compiler.


        push    eax
        ; The result just obtained is passed to the printf function.

        push    offset asc_406030 ; "%x\n"
        call    _printf
        add     esp, 8

        xor     eax, eax
        pop     ebp
        retn
main            endp



MyFunc          proc near               ; CODE XREF: main+E↑p

var_8           = dword ptr -8
var_4           = byte ptr -4

arg_0           = dword ptr  8
arg_4           = dword ptr  0Ch
; Only two arguments are passed to the function
; via the stack, and IDA successfully recognized them.

        push    ebp
        mov     ebp, esp
        sub     esp, 8
```

```
; This allocates 8 bytes for local variables.

mov    [ebp+var_8], edx
; The EDX register was not explicitly initialized before its
; contents were loaded into the var_8 local variable.
; Therefore, it is used for passing arguments!
; This program was compiled by Microsoft Visual C++,
; and, as you probably know, it passes arguments via
; the ECX:EDX registers. Therefore, we can infer that we're
; dealing with the second-from-the-left argument
; of the function. Somewhere below, we'll probably come across
; a reference to ECX — to the first-from-the-left argument
; of the function (although not necessarily —
; the first argument might not be used by the function).

mov    [ebp+var_4], cl
; Actually, the reference to CL kept us from waiting long for it.
; Since the argument of the char type is passed via CL,
; the first function argument is probably char.
; However, the function simply may be accessing
; the lower byte of the argument (for example, of the int type).
; However, looking at the code of the calling function, we can
; make sure that only char, not int, is passed to the function.
; Incidentally, note the stupidity of the compiler — was it really
; necessary to pass arguments via registers to send them
; immediately into local variables? After all, addressing
; the memory negates all the benefits of the fastcall convention!
; It's even hard to describe such a call as "fast."

movsx  eax, [ebp+var_4]
; EAX is loaded with the first-from-the-left argument passed
; via CL, which is of the char type with a signed extension to
; a double word. Hence, it's signed char (that is, char,
; by default, for Microsoft Visual C++).

add    eax, [ebp+var_8]
; The contents of EAX are added with the argument second from the left.

add    eax, [ebp+arg_0]
; The argument third from the left, passed via the stack,
; is added to the previous sum...
```

```
add     eax, [ebp+arg_4]
; ... and all this is added to the fourth argument,
; also passed via the stack.

mov     esp, ebp
pop     ebp
; The stack frame is closed.

retn    8
; We cleared up the stack,
; as required by the fastcall convention.
MyFunc                          endp
```

Now, let's compare this with the result of disassembling the code generated by the Borland C++ compiler.

Listing 86. The Disassembled Code for Passing Arguments Compiled Using Borland C++

```
; int __cdecl main(int argc, const char **argv, const char *envp)
_main           proc near         ; DATA XREF: DATA:00407044↓o

argc            = dword ptr  8
argv            = dword ptr  0Ch
envp            = dword ptr  10h

        push    ebp
        mov     ebp, esp

        push    4
        ; Arguments are passed via the stack. Glancing downward,
        ; we discover explicit initialization of the ECX, EDX,
        ; and AL registers. There were no registers left for the fourth
        ; argument, so it had to be passed via the stack.
        ; Hence, the argument fourth from the left of the function is 0x4.

        mov     ecx, 3
        mov     edx, 2
        mov     al, 1
        ; All this code can do is pass arguments via registers.
```

```
        call    MyFunc

        push    eax
        push    offset unk_407074 ; format
        call    _printf
        add     esp, 8

        xor     eax, eax

        pop     ebp
        retn
_main           endp


MyFunc          proc near           ; CODE XREF: _main+11↑p

arg_0           = dword             ptr 8
; Only one argument has been passed to the function
; via the stack.

        push    ebp
        mov     ebp, esp
        ; The stack frame is opened.

        movsx   eax, al
        ; Borland has generated a code that is more optimized than
        ; the one generated by Microsoft. Borland saved memory
        ; by not sending the local variable into the register.
        ; However, Microsoft Visual C++ is also capable of doing so,
        ; provided that the optimization key is specified.
        ; Also, note that Borland handles arguments in expressions
        ; from left to right as they are listed in the function prototype,
        ; whereas Microsoft Visual C++ acts in the opposite manner.

        add     edx, eax
        add     ecx, edx
        ; The EDX and CX registers haven't been initialized.
        ; Hence, the arguments were passed to the function via them.
```

```
mov     edx, [ebp+arg_0]
; EDX is loaded with the last function argument
; passed via the stack...

add     ecx, edx
; ... summed again,

mov     eax, ecx
; ... and passed to EAX. (EAX is the register in which
; the function places the result of its execution.)

pop     ebp
retn    4
; The stack is cleared.


MyFunc                            endp
```

And last, the result of disassembling the same example compiled with Watcom C should look like this.

Listing 87. The Disassembled Code for Passing Arguments via Registers Compiled Using Watcom C

```
main_           proc near           ; CODE XREF: __CMain+40↓p
       push    18h
       call    __CHK
; Checking for stack overflow.

       push    ebx
       push    esi
       push    edi
; The registers are pushed onto the stack.

       mov     ebx, 4
       mov     edi, 3
       mov     esi, 2
       mov     eax, 1
; The arguments are passed via the registers we specified!
; Note that the first argument of the char type
; is passed via the 32-bit EAX register.
; Watcom's behavior significantly complicates
; the reconstruction of function prototypes. In this case,
```

```
        ; the values are placed into the registers in the order
        ; in which the arguments were declared in the function prototype,
        ; beginning from the right. Alas, this happens relatively rarely.

        call    MyFunc

        push    eax
        push    offset unk_420004
        call    printf_

        add     esp, 8
        xor     eax, eax
        pop     edi
        pop     esi
        pop     ebx
        retn
main_           endp


MyFunc          proc near           ; CODE XREF: main_+21↑p
; The function doesn't receive even a single argument from the stack.

        push    4
        call    __CHK

        and     eax, 0FFh
        ; Zeroing the higher 24 bits and referencing the register before
        ; initializing it suggests that the char type is passed via EAX.
        ; Unfortunately, we can't say what kind of argument it is.


        add     esi, eax
        ; The ESI register has not been initialized by our function.
        ; Therefore, an argument of the int type is transferred via it.
        ; We can assume it's the argument second from the left
        ; in the function prototype, since the registers in the calling
        ; function are initialized in the order in which they are listed
        ; in the prototype (if nothing hinders this beginning from
        ; the right), and expressions are calculated from left to right.
        ; The original order of arguments is not crucial, but,
        ; it's nice if we succeed in determining it.
```

```
        lea     eax, [esi+edi]
        ; Oops! Do you believe that
        ; the pointer is being loaded into EAX? And that ESI and EDI,
        ; passed to the function, are also pointers? EAX with its char
        ; type becomes similar to an index. Alas! The Watcom compiler
        ; is too artful, and it's easy to run into gross errors when
        ; analyzing programs compiled using it. Yes, EAX is a pointer in
        ; the sense that LEA is used to calculate the sum of ESI and EDI.
        ; But neither the calling function nor the called one access
        ; the memory by this pointer. Therefore, the function
        ; arguments are constants, rather than pointers!

        add     eax, ebx
        ; Similarly, EDX contains the argument that was passed
        ; to the function.
        ; The function prototype should look like this:

        ; MyFunc(char a, int b, int c, int d)
        ; However, the order of arguments might differ.

        retn
MyFunc          endp
```

As you can see, passing arguments via registers isn't especially complex; it's even possible to reconstruct the original prototype of the called function. However, we've considered a rather idealized situation. In real programs, passing immediate values only is rarely done. Now, having mastered `fastcall`, let's disassemble a more difficult example.

Listing 88. A Difficult `fastcall` Example

```
#if defined(__BORLANDC__) || defined (_MSC_VER)
__fastcall
#endif
MyFunc(char a, int *b, int c)
{
#if defined(__WATCOMC__)
#pragma aux MyFunc parm [EAX] [EBX] [ECX];
```

```
#endif
return a+b[0]+c;
}


main()
{
        int a=2;
        printf("%x\n", MyFunc(strlen("1"), &a, strlen("333")));
}
```

The result of disassembling the compiled code of this example should look like this:

Listing 89. The Disassembled Code of the Difficult `factcall` Example

```
main            proc near             ; CODE XREF: start+AF↓p

var_4           = dword         ptr -4

        push    ebp
        mov     ebp, esp
        ; The stack frame is opened.

        push    ecx
        push    esi
        ; The registers are pushed onto the stack.

        mov     [ebp+var_4], 2
        ; A value of 2 is placed into the var_4 local variable.
        ; The type is determined from the fact that the variable occupies
        ; 4 bytes. (See the "Local Stack Variables" section
        ; for more details.)

        push    offset a333           ; const char *
        ; A pointer to the "333" string is passed to the strlen function.
        ; The arguments of MyFunc are passed from right to left as required.

        call    _strlen
        add     esp, 4
```

```
push    eax
; Here, the value returned by the function is either saved
; onto the stack or passed to the next function.

lea     esi, [ebp+var_4]
; The pointer to the var_4 local variable is placed into ESI.

push    offset a1           ; const char *
; The pointer to the a1 string is passed to the strlen function.

call    _strlen
add     esp, 4

mov     cl, al
; The returned value is copied to the CL register, and EDX is
; initialized. Since ECX:EDX are used for passing arguments to
; fastcall functions, the initialization of these two registers
; prior to calling the function is not accidental!
; We can assume that the leftmost argument of the char type
; is transferred via CL.

mov     edx, esi
; ESI containes the pointer to var_4. Therefore, the second
; argument of the int type, placed into EDX, is passed by reference.

call    MyFunc
; The preliminary function prototype looks like this:
; MyFunc(char *a, int *b, int c)
; Where did the c argument come from? Do you remember the code
; in which EAX was pushed onto the stack? Neither before nor after
; the function call was it popped out! To be sure of this,
; we need to see how many bytes the called function removes
; from the stack. Another interesting fact is that the values
; returned by the strlen function were not assigned to
; local variables, but were directly passed to MyFunc.
; This suggests that the source code of the
; program looked like this:
; MyFunc(strlen("1"),&var_4,strlen("333"));
```

```
        ; This is not necessarily the case — the compiler might optimize the
        ; code, throwing out the local variable if it isn't used anymore.
        ; However, judging from the code of the called function, the
        ; compiler works without optimization. In addition, if the values
        ; returned by the strlen functions are used only once as arguments
        ; of MyFunc, assigning them to local variables simply
        ; obscures the essence of the program. Moreover, for a code digger,
        ; it's more important to understand the algorithm of a program
        ; than to restore its source code.

        push    eax
        push    offset asc_406038 ; "%x\n"
        call    _printf
        add     esp, 8

        pop     esi

        mov     esp, ebp
        pop     ebp
        ; The stack frame is closed.

        retn
main            endp


MyFunc          proc near           ; CODE XREF: main+2E↑p

var_8           = dword ptr -8
var_4           = byte ptr -4
arg_0           = dword ptr  8
; The function accepts one argument.
; Hence, EAX has been pushed onto the stack.


        push    ebp
        mov     ebp, esp
        ; The stack frame is opened.

        sub     esp, 8
```

```
; This allocated 8 bytes for local variables.

mov    [ebp+var_8], edx
; Since EDX is used without explicit initialization,
; the function argument second from the left is passed
; via it (according to the fastcall convention of the Microsoft
; Visual C++ compiler). Having analyzed the code of the calling
; function, we know that EDX contains the pointer to var_4.
; Therefore, var_8 contains the pointer to var_4.

mov    [ebp+var_4], cl
; The leftmost argument of the function is passed via CL,
; and then immediately placed into the var_4 local variable.

movsx  eax, [ebp+var_4]
; var_4 is extended to signed int.

mov    ecx, [ebp+var_8]
; ECX is loaded with the contents of the var_8 pointer passed
; via EDX. As you may remember, the pointer was passed
; to the function via EDX.

add    eax, [ecx]
; EAX, which stores the first-from-the-left argument of the function,
; is added with the contents of the memory location referenced
; by the ECX pointer.

add    eax, [ebp+arg_0]
; Here is a reference to the function argument
; that was passed via the stack.

mov    esp, ebp
pop    ebp
; The stack frame is closed.

retn   4
; One argument was passed to the function via the stack.
MyFunc     endp
```

Simple? Yes, it is! Then let's consider the result of creative work with Borland C++, which should look like this:

Listing 90. The Disassembled Code for `fastcall` Compiled Using Borland C++

```
; int __cdecl main(int argc, const char **argv, const char *envp)
_main           proc near            ; DATA XREF: DATA:00407044↓o

var_4           = dword ptr -4
argc            = dword ptr  8
argv            = dword ptr  0Ch
envp            = dword ptr  10h


        push    ebp
        mov     ebp, esp
        ; The stack frame is opened.

        push    ecx
        ; ECX is saved... Just a moment! This is something new! In previous
        ; examples, Borland never saved ECX when entering a function.
        ; It seems likely that some argument has been passed to the
        ; function via ECX, and this function is passing it
        ; to other functions via the stack. However convincing
        ; such a solution might look, it's incorrect! The compiler simply
        ; allocates 4 bytes for local variables. Why? How did we determine this?
        ; Look: IDA recognized one local variable — var_4. But memory
        ; for it was not explicitly allocated. In any case, there was
        ; no SUB ESP, 4 instruction. But wait: PUSH ECX results in a decrease
        ; of the ESP register by four! Oh, this optimization...

        mov     [ebp+var_4], 2
        ; A value of 2 is placed into a local variable.

        push    offset a333         ; s
        ; A pointer to the "333" string is passed to the function.

        call    _strlen
        pop     ecx
```

```
; The argument is popped from the stack.

push    eax
; Here we are either passing the value
; returned by the strlen function
; to the following function as the stack argument,
; or we are temporarily saving EAX onto the stack.
; (Later, it will become clear that the latter assumption is true.)

push    offset a1            ; s
; The pointer to the AL string is passed to the strlen function.

call    _strlen
pop     ecx
; The argument is popped from the stack.

lea     edx, [ebp+var_4]
; The offset of the var_4 local variable is loaded into EDX.

pop     ecx
; Something is popped from the stack, but what exactly? Scrolling
; the screen of the disassembler upward, we find that EAX was pushed
; last onto the stack and contained the value returned by the strlen
; ("333") function. It is now located in the ECX register.
; (Borland passes the argument second from the left via it.)
; Incidentally, a note for fastcall fans: fastcall
; doesn't always provide the anticipated call acceleration —
; Intel 80x86 doesn't have enough registers, and they continually
; need to be saved onto the stack. Passing an argument via
; the stack would require only one reference to memory: PUSH EAX.
; Here we have two — PUSH EAX and POP ECX!

call    MyFunc
; When reconstructing the function prototype, don't forget about
; the EAX register — it's not initialized explicitly,
; but it stores the value returned by the last call of strlen.
; Since the Borland C++ 5.x compiler
; uses the preferences EAX, EDX, and ECX, we can conclude
; that the function argument first from the left is passed to EAX,
; and the other two arguments — to EDX and ECX, respectively.
```

```
; Note that Borland C++, unlike Microsoft Visual C++,
; doesn't handle arguments in the order in which they appear in the list.
; Instead, it computes the values of all functions, "pulling" them
; out from right to left, then proceeds to variables and constants.
; This stands to reason: Functions change the values of many
; general-purpose registers. Until the last function is called,
; the passing of arguments via registers should not begin.

push    eax
push    offset asc_407074 ; format
call    _printf
add     esp, 8

xor     eax, eax
; The zero value is returned.

pop     ecx
pop     ebp
; The stack frame is closed.

retn
_main                     endp


MyFunc        proc near         ; CODE XREF: _main+26↑p
push    ebp
mov     ebp, esp
; The stack frame is opened.

movsx   eax, al
; EAX is extended to the signed double word.

mov     edx, [edx]
; EDX is loaded with the contents of the memory location
; referenced by the EDX pointer.

add     eax, edx
; The first argument of the function is added to the variable
; of the int type, passed by reference as the second argument.

add     ecx, eax
```

```
; The third argument of the int type is added to the previous sum.

mov    eax, ecx
; The result is placed back into EAX.
; What a stupid compiler this is! Wouldn't it be simpler
; to swap the arguments in the previous instruction?

pop    ebp
; The stack frame is closed.

       retn
MyFunc                             endp
```

Now let's consider the disassembled code of the same example compiled using Watcom C, which always has something new to teach us.

Listing 91. The Disassembled Code for `fastcall` Compiled Using Watcom C

```
main_          proc near        ; CODE XREF: __CMain+40↓p

var_C          = dword          ptr -0Ch

       push   18h
       call   __CHK
; The stack overflow is checked.

       push   ebx
       push   ecx
; The registers being modified are saved —
; or maybe memory is allocated for local variables?

       sub    esp, 4
; This is certainly the allocation of memory for one local variable.
; Therefore, the two PUSH instructions we saw above
; save the registers.

       mov    [esp+0Ch+var_C], 2
; A value of 2 is placed into the local variable.
```

```
        mov     eax, offset a333 ; "333"
        call    strlen_
        ; Note that Watcom passes the pointer to the string
        ; to the strlen function via the register!

        mov     ecx, eax
        ; The value returned by the function is copied into the ECX register.
        ; Watcom knows that the next call of strlen won't spoil this register!

        mov     eax, offset a1      ; "1"
        call    strlen_

        and     eax, 0FFh
        ; Since strlen returns the int type, here we have
        ; an explicit type conversion: int -> char.

        mov     ebx, esp
        ; EBX is loaded with the pointer to the var_C variable.

        call    MyFunc
        ; Which arguments were passed to the function?
        ; EAX (probably the leftmost argument), EBX (explicitly
        ; initialized prior to calling the function), and probably ECX
        ; (although this is not necessarily the case).
        ; ECX might contain a register variable, but in that case
        ; the called function should not access it.

        push    eax
        push    offset asc_42000A ; "%x\n"

        call    printf_

        add     esp, 8
        add     esp, 4
        ; And they say Watcom is an optimizing compiler!
        ; It can't even unite two instructions into one!
        pop     ecx
        pop     ebx

        retn
main_           endp
```

```
MyFunc          proc near          ; CODE XREF: main_+33↑p
        push    4
        call    __CHK
; The stack is checked.

        and     eax, 0FFh
; The 24 higher bits are zeroed repeatedly. It would not be bad
; if Watcom were more certain about where to perform this
; operation — in the called function or in the calling one.
; However, such doubling simplifies the reconstruction
; of the function prototypes.


        add     eax, [ebx]
; EAX of type char, now extended to int, is added with the
; variable of the int type passed by reference via the EBX register.

        add     eax, ecx
; Aha! Here is the reference to ECX. We now know
; that this register was used for passing arguments.

        retn
; The function prototype should look as this:
; MyFunc(char EAX, int *EBX, int ECX)
; Notice that it was possible to reconstruct it
; only by performing the combined analysis
; of the called and calling functions!

MyFunc                                  endp
```

Passing floating-point values. Most code breakers don't know the particulars of floating-point arithmetic and avoid it like the plague. There's nothing terribly complex about it, and mastering the coprocessor takes only a couple of days. However, it's much more difficult to master the mathematical libraries that emulate floating-point calculations (especially if IDA doesn't recognize the names of the library functions). But what contemporary compiler makes use of such libraries? The microprocessor and coprocessor are integrated within the same chip. Therefore, the coprocessor, starting from 80486DX (if my memory doesn't fail me), is always available; there's no need to programmatically emulate it.

Until the end of the 1990s, many hackers thought it possible to live their entire lives without coming across floating-point arithmetic. Indeed, in the good old days, processors were as slow as turtles, few people had coprocessors, and the tasks computers had to solve allowed hackers to use tricks and solutions that employed integer arithmetic.

Today, everything has changed. Floating-point calculations performed by the coprocessor at the same time as the execution of the main program are completed even faster than the integer calculations processed by the main processor. Programmers, inspired by such prospects, began to use floating-point data types even where integer ones had been more than sufficient. Contemporary code diggers can hardly do without knowledge of coprocessor instructions.

80x87 coprocessors support three types of floating-point data: short 32-bit, long 64-bit, and extended 80-bit. These correspond to the following types of the C language: float, double, and long double[i] (see Table 8).

Table 8. Basic Information on Floating-Point Types of the 80x87 Coprocessors

Type	Size	Value range	Preferred types of transfer
Float	4 bytes	$10^{-38}...10^{38}$	CPU registers, CPU stack, FPU stack
Double	8 bytes	$10^{-308}...10^{308}$	CPU registers, CPU stack, FPU stack
Long double	10 bytes	$10^{-4932}...10^{4932}$	CPU stack, FPU stack
Real[ii]	6 bytes	$2.9*10^{-39}...1.7*10^{38}$	CPU registers, CPU stack, FPU stack

Arguments of the float and double types can be passed to the function in three ways: via *general-purpose registers of the main processor,* via the *stack of the main processor,* or via the *stack of the coprocessor.* Arguments of the long double type require too many general-purpose registers to be passed using this method. In most cases, they are pushed onto the stack of the main processor or that of the coprocessor.

The first two ways are already familiar to us, but the third one is something new! The 80x87 coprocessor has eight 80-bit registers (designated as ST(0), ST(1),

---

[i] Attention: The ANSI C standard doesn't require a precise representation of the types mentioned above. This statement is valid only for some implementations of the PC platform.
[ii] The Turbo Pascal type.

ST(2), ST(3), ST(4), ST(5), ST(6), and ST(7)) organized as a wraparound stack. This means that most of the coprocessor instructions don't operate with the register indexes; their destination is the top of the stack. For example, to add two floating-point numbers, we need to push them onto the stack of the coprocessor. Then we must call the addition instruction that adds the two numbers lying on the top of the stack and returns the result via the stack again. We have the option of adding the number that lies on the stack of the coprocessor to the number located in the RAM, but it's impossible to directly add two numbers located in the RAM!

Thus, the first stage of floating-point operations is pushing the operands onto the coprocessor stack. This operation is performed by the instructions of the FLDxx series (listed with brief explanations in Table 9). In most cases, we use the FLD source instruction, which pushes a floating-point number from the RAM or the coprocessor register onto the coprocessor stack. Strictly speaking, this is not one instruction; it's four instructions in one package, which have the opcodes 0xD9 0x0?, 0xDD 0x0?, 0xDB 0x0?, and 0xD9 0xCi for loading the *short, long,* and *extended-real* values and the *FPU register*, respectively. The ? character is an address field that specifies whether the operand is in the register or in memory, and the i character is an index of the FPU register.

The impossibility of loading floating-point numbers from CPU registers makes it senseless to use them for passing float, double, or long double arguments. In any case, to push these arguments onto the coprocessor stack, the called function would have to copy the contents of registers to the RAM. No matter what you do, there's no way to get rid of memory calls. Therefore, passing floating-point types via registers is rarely done. They are passed predominantly via the CPU stack or via the coprocessor stack along with the usual arguments. (This can be done only by advanced compilers — Watcom, in particular — and not by Microsoft Visual C++ or Borland C++.)

However, certain "peculiar" values can be loaded without addressing the memory; in particular, there are instructions for pushing numbers (zero, one, π, and certain others — the complete list is given in Table 9) onto the coprocessor stack.

An interesting feature of the coprocessor is support for integer calculations. I don't know of any compiler that uses this capability, but sometimes it's used in assembly inserts; therefore, it's unwise to neglect learning the integer coprocessor instructions.

Table 9. The Coprocessor Instructions for Sending/Receiving Arguments

Instruction	Purpose
FLD *source*	Pushes a floating-point number from the *source* onto the top of the coprocessor stack
FSTP *destination*	Pops a floating-point number from the top of the coprocessor stack into the *destination*
FST *destination*	Copies a floating-point number from the top of the coprocessor stack into the *destination*
FLDZ	Pushes 0 onto the top of the coprocessor stack
FLD1	Pushes 1 onto the top of the coprocessor stack
FLDPI	Pushes π onto the top of the coprocessor stack
FLDL2T	Pushes the binary logarithm of ten onto the top of the coprocessor stack
FLDL2E	Pushes the binary logarithm of the number *e* onto the top of the coprocessor stack
FLDLG2	Pushes the decimal logarithm of two onto the top of the coprocessor stack
FLDLN2	Pushes the natural logarithm of two onto the top of the coprocessor stack
FILD *source*	Pushes an integer from the *source* onto the top of the coprocessor stack
FIST *destination*	Copies an integer from the top of the coprocessor stack into the *destination*
FISTP *destination*	Pops an integer from the top of the coprocessor stack into the *destination*
FBLD *source*	Pushes a decimal number from the *source* onto the top of the coprocessor stack
FBSTP *destination*	Copies a decimal number from the top of the coprocessor stack into the *destination*
FXCHST (*index*)	Exchanges values between the top of the coprocessor stack and the ST register (*index*)

The double and long double types occupy more than one word, and transferring them via the CPU stack takes several iterations. As a result, we can't always determine the type and number of arguments passed to the called function by analyzing the code of the calling function. Instead, investigate the algorithm of the called function. Since the coprocessor can't determine the type of the operand located in the memory (that is, the coprocessor doesn't know how many bytes it occupies), a separate instruction is assigned to each type. The assembler syntax hides these distinctions, allowing the programmer to ignore the subtleties of implementation. (Nevertheless, some people say that the assembler is a low-level language.) Few people know that FADD [float] and FADD [double] are *different* machine instructions having the opcodes 0xD8 ??000??? and 0xDC ??000???, respectively. Analyzing the disassembled listing doesn't give us any information on the floating-point types; to obtain this information, we need to get down to the machine level and sink our teeth into hexadecimal dumps of instructions.

Table 10 presents the opcodes of the main coprocessor instructions that work with memory. Note that performing arithmetic operations directly over floating-point values of the long double type is impossible; they must first be loaded onto the coprocessor stack.

Table 10. The Opcodes of the Main Coprocessor Instructions

Instruction	Type		
	Float	Double	Long double
FLD	0xD9 ??000???	0xDD ??000???	0xDB ??101???
FSTP	0xD9 ??011???	0xDD ??011???	0xDB ??111???
FST	0xD9 ??010???	0xDD ??010???	None
FADD	0xD8 ??000???	0xDC ??000???	None
FADDP	0xDE ??000???	0xDA ??000???	None
FSUB	0xD8 ??100???	0xDC ??100???	None
FDIV	0xD8 ??110???	0xDC ??110???	None
FMUL	0xD* ??001???	0xDC ??001???	None
FCOM	0xD8 ??010???	0xDC ??010???	None
FCOMP	0xD8 ??011???	0xDC ??011???	None

(The second byte of the opcode is presented in binary form. The ? character denotes any bit.)

A note on floating-point types of the Turbo Pascal language. Since the C language is machine-oriented, its floating-point types coincide with the coprocessor floating-point types. The main floating-point type of Turbo Pascal is Real; it occupies 6 bytes, which is not "native" to the computer. Therefore, for calculations carried out using the coprocessor, `Real` is programmatically converted to the `Extended` type (`long double` in terms of C). This takes up the lion's share of the performance. Unfortunately, the built-in mathematical library, intended to replace the coprocessor, does not support other types. When a "live" coprocessor is available, pure coprocessor types — `Single`, `Double`, `Extended`, and `Comp` — appear that correspond to `float`, `double`, `long double`, and `__int64`.

The mathematical library functions that provide support for floating-point calculations receive floating-point arguments from the registers. The first argument from the left is placed into `AX`, `BX`, `DX`; the second argument, if there is one, is placed into `CX`, `SI`, `DI`. The system functions that implement the interface to the processor (in particular, the functions for converting the `Real` type into the `Extended` type) receive arguments from registers and return the result via the coprocessor stack. Finally, the application functions and procedures receive floating-point arguments from the CPU stack.

Depending on the settings of the compiler, the program may be compiled either using the built-in mathematical library (the default), or by employing direct calls of the coprocessor instructions. (This is the `/N$+` key.) In the first case, the program doesn't use the coprocessor's capabilities, even though it's installed in the computer. In the second case, if the coprocessor is available, the compiler uses its computational capabilities; if the coprocessor isn't available, any attempt to call a coprocessor instruction results in the generation of the `int 0x7` exception by the main processor. This will be caught by the software coprocessor emulator, the same thing as the built-in library supporting floating-point calculations.

Now that you have a general outline of how floating-point arguments are passed, you are burning with the desire to see it "live," right? To begin with, let's consider a simple example.

Listing 92. Passing Floating-Point Arguments to a Function

```
#include <stdio.h>

float MyFunc(float a, double b)
{
#if defined(__WATCOMC__)
#pragma aux MyFunc parm [8087];
// To be compiled using the -7 key
#endif
    return a+b;
}
```

```
main()
{
        printf("%f\n", MyFunc(6.66, 7.77));
}
```

The disassembled listing of this code, compiled with Microsoft Visual C++, should look as follows:

Listing 93. The Disassembled Code for Passing Floating-Point Arguments

```
main            proc near               ; CODE XREF: start+AF↓p

var_8           = qword                 ptr -8
; A local variable, this is likely to occupy 8 bytes.

        push    ebp
        mov     ebp, esp
        ; The stack frame is opened.

        push    401F147Ah
        ; Unfortunately, IDA can't represent an operand as a floating-point
        ; number. Besides which, we can't determine
        ; whether or not this number is floating-point.
        ; It can be of any type: either int or a pointer.

        push    0E147AE14h
        push    40D51EB8h
        ; A draft of the prototype looks like this:
        ; MyFunc(int a, int b, int c)

        call    MyFunc
        add     esp, 4
        ; Here we go! Only one machine word is taken from the stack,
        ; whereas three words are pushed there!

        fstp    [esp+8+var_8]
        ; A floating-point number is pulled from the coprocessor stack.
        ; To find out which one, we need to press <ALT>+<O>,
        ; select Text representation from the pop-up menu,
```

```
; choose the Number of opcode bytes item, and enter
; the number of characters for opcode instructions (4, for example).
; To the left of FSTP, its machine representation —
; DD 1C 24 — appears. Using Table 10, we can determine the data
; type with which this instruction works. It's double.
; Therefore, the function has returned a floating-point value
; via the coprocessor stack.
; Since the function returns floating-point values, it's possible
; that it receives them as arguments. We can't confirm this
; assumption without carrying out an analysis of MyFunc.

        push    offset aF          ; "%f\n"
; A pointer is passed to the format specification string,
; which orders the printf function to output one floating-point number.
; But we're not placing it in the stack!
; How can this be? Let's scroll the disassembler window
; upward while thinking over the ways of solving the problem.
; Closely examining the FSTP [ESP+8+var_8] instruction,
; let's figure out where it places the result of its work.
; IDA has determined var_8 as qword ptr-8. Therefore, [ES+8-8] is
; the equivalent of [ESP] — that is, the floating-point variable
; is pushed directly onto the top of the stack.
; And what's on the top? Two arguments that were passed
; to MyFunc and not popped off the stack.
; What an artful compiler! It hasn't bothered to create
; a local variable, and it used the function arguments
; to temporarily store data!

        call    _printf
        add     esp, 0Ch
; Three machine words are popped off the stack.

        pop     ebp
        retn
main            endp


MyFunc          proc near          ; CODE XREF: sub_401011+12↑p

var_4           = dword ptr -4
```

```
arg_0           = dword ptr  8
arg_4           = qword ptr  0Ch
; IDA detected only two arguments, while three machine words
; were passed to the function! One of the arguments is likely to
; occupy 8 bytes.

        push    ebp
        mov     ebp, esp
        ; The stack frame is opened.

        push    ecx
        ; No, this is not saving ECX — it's allocating memory for
        ; a local variable, since the var_4 variable is
        ; where the saved ECX is located.

        fld     [ebp+arg_0]
        ; The floating-point variable at the [ebp+8] address
        ; (the leftmost argument),
        ; is pushed onto the coprocessor stack.
        ; To learn the type of this variable, let's look at opcode
        ; of the instructions FLD — D9 45 08. Aha! D9 — hence, float.
        ; It turns out that the argument first from the left is float.

        fadd    [ebp+arg_4]
        ; The float type arg_0 is added to the argument
        ; second from the left of the type...
        ; If the first argument is float, should the second one
        ; also be float? Not necessarily! Let's peep into the opcode —
        ; it's DC 45 0C. Hence, the second argument is double, not float!

        fst     [ebp+var_4]
        ; The value from the top of the coprocessor stack (where the result
        ; of addition is located) is copied into the var_4 local
        ; variable. Why? We suddenly might need it.
        ; The value is not popped off, but copied! It still remains
        ; in the stack. Thus, the prototype of MyFunc looked like
        ; this: double MyFunc (float a, double b);

        mov     esp, ebp
```

```
    pop     ebp
    ; The stack frame is closed.


    retn


MyFunc                                 endp
```

The result of compiling with Borland C++ 5.x is almost identical to that of the example we just considered using Microsoft Visual C++ 6.x. Therefore, we'll proceed to the analysis of an example compiled using Watcom C (as always, Watcom is highly instructive).

Listing 94. The Disassembled Code for Passing Floating-Point Arguments Compiled Using Watcom

```
main_           proc near           ; CODE XREF: __CMain+40↓p


var_8           = qword             ptr -8
; A local variable, this is likely to occupy 8 bytes.


    push    10h
    call    __CHK
    ; Checking for stack overflow


    fld     ds:dbl_420008
    ; A variable of the double type taken from the data segment
    ; is loaded onto the top of the coprocessor stack. IDA has
    ; successfully determined the variable type,
    ; having added the dbl prefix to it.
    ; If IDA hadn't determined the type, we would have to examine
    ; the opcode of the FLD instruction.


    fld     ds:flt_420010
    ; A variable of the float type is loaded onto the top of the
    ; stack.


    call    MyFunc
    ; MyFunc is called, and two arguments are passed via
```

```
        ; the coprocessor stack. The prototype looks like this:
        ; MyFunc(float a, double b).

        sub     esp, 8
        ; Memory is allocated for a local variable of 8 bytes.

        fstp    [esp+8+var_8]
        ; A floating-point variable of the double type is popped off the top
        ; of the stack. The type is determined by the variable's size.

        push    offset unk_420004
        call    printf_
        ; This is a trick we already know — passing var_8
        ; to the printf function!

        add     esp, 0Ch
        retn
main_           endp


MyFunc          proc near            ; CODE XREF: main_+16↑p

var_C           = qword ptr -0Ch
var_4           = dword ptr -4
; IDA has found two local variables.

        push    10h
        call    __CHK

        sub     esp, 0Ch
        ; Space is allocated for local variables.

        fstp    [esp+0Ch+var_4]
        ; A floating-point variable of the float type
        ; is popped off the top of the coprocessor stack.
        ; (As you may recall, it was placed there last.)
        ; Let's make sure of this by peeping into the opcode
        ; of the FSTP instruction. It is D9 5C 24 08.
        ; If 0xD9 is there, then it's float.

        fstp    [esp+0Ch+var_C]
```

```
        ; A floating-point variable of the double type
        ; is popped off the top of the coprocessor stack.
        ; (As you may remember, it was placed there before float.)
        ; To be on the safe side,
        ; check the opcode of the FSTP instruction. It is DD 1C 24.
        ; If 0xDD is there, it must be double.

        fld     [esp+0Ch+var_4]
        ; The float is pushed back onto the top of the stack...

        fadd    [esp+0Ch+var_C]
        ; ... and added to double. They dare to say that Watcom C
        ; is an optimizing compiler! It's difficult to agree with this
        ; when the compiler doesn't know that swapping the terms
        ; doesn't change the sum!


        add     esp, 0Ch
        ; Memory that was allocated for local variables is released.

        retn
MyFunc                                  endp

dbl_420008      dq 7.77                 ; DATA XREF: main_+A↑r
flt_420010      dd 6.6599998            ; DATA XREF: main_+10↑r
```

Now comes Turbo Pascal for Windows 1.0. Let's enter the following example in the text editor:

Listing 95. Passing Floating-Point Values Using Turbo Pascal

```
USES WINCRT;

Procedure MyProc(a:Real);
begin
        WriteLn(a);
end;

VAR
        a: Real;
        b: Real;
```

```
BEGIN
        a:=6.66;
        b:=7.77;
        MyProc(a+b);
END.
```

Now, we'll compile it without coprocessor support. (This is the default.)

Listing 96. The Disassembled Code for Passing Floating-Point Values

```
PROGRAM        proc near

        call    INITTASK
        call    @__SystemInit$qv ; __SystemInit(void)
        ; The System unit is initialized.

        call    @__WINCRTInit$qv ; __WINCRTInit(void)
        ; The WINCRT unit is initialized.

        push    bp
        mov     bp, sp
        ; The stack frame is opened.

        xor     ax, ax
        call    @__StackCheck$q4Word ; Stack overflow check (AX)
        ; This checks if there are at least 0 free bytes in the stack.

        mov     word_2030, 0EC83h
        mov     word_2032, 0B851h
        mov     word_2034, 551Eh
        ; A variable of the Real type is initialized.
        ; We know that it's Real
        ; only from the source code of the program.
        ; It's impossible to visually distinguish this series
        ; of instructions from three variables of the Word type.

        mov     word_2036, 3D83h
        mov     word_2038, 0D70Ah
        mov     word_203A, 78A3h
        ; Another variable of the Real type is initialized.
```

```
        mov     ax, word_2030
        mov     bx, word_2032
        mov     dx, word_2034
        mov     cx, word_2036
        mov     si, word_2038
        mov     di, word_203A
        ; Two variables of the Real type are passed via registers.

        call    @$brplu$q4Realt1 ; Real(AX:BX:DX)+= Real(CX:SI:DI)
        ; Fortunately, IDA recognized the addition operator
        ; in this function. It has even prompted us as to its prototype.
        ; If IDA hadn't helped us, it would be difficult to understand
        ; what this long and intricate function does.

        push    dx
        push    bx
        push    ax
        ; The returned value is passed to the MyProc procedure via
        ; the stack. Consequently, the MyProc prototype looks like this:
        ; MyProc(a:Real).

        call    MyProc

        pop     bp
        ; The stack frame is closed.

        xor     ax, ax
        call    @Halt$q4Word         ; Halt(Word)
        ; The program's execution is halted.

PROGRAM         endp

MyProc          proc near            ; CODE XREF: PROGRAM+5C↑p

arg_0           = word ptr 4
arg_2           = word ptr 6
arg_4           = word ptr 8
; The three arguments passed to the procedure,
; as we have already clarified, represent three "sections"
; of one argument of the Real type.
```

```
        push    bp
        mov     bp, sp
        ; The stack frame is opened.

        xor     ax, ax
        call    @__StackCheck$q4Word ; Stack overflow check (AX)
        ; Are there 0 bytes in the stack?

        mov     di, offset unk_2206
        push    ds
        push    di
        ; The pointer to the string output buffer is pushed onto the stack.

        push    [bp+arg_4]
        push    [bp+arg_2]
        push    [bp+arg_0]
        ; All three received arguments are pushed onto the stack.

        mov     ax, 11h
        push    ax
        ; The output width is 17 characters.

        mov     ax, 0FFFFh
        push    ax
        ; The number of digits after the point is maximal.

        call    @Write$qm4Text4Real4Wordt3
        ; Write(var f; v: Real; width, decimals: Word)
        ; The floating-point number is output into the unk_2206 buffer.

        call    @WriteLn$qm4Text ; WriteLn(var f: Text)
        ; The string is sent from the buffer to the display.

        call    @__IOCheck$qv          ; Exit if error
        pop     bp
        retn    6
MyProc                                 endp
```

Now, using the /$N+ key, let's put the coprocessor instructions into action, and see how this will affect the code.

**Listing 97. The Disassembled Code for Passing Floating-Point Values
Compiled to Use Coprocessor Instructions**

```
PROGRAM                        proc near

    call   INITTASK
    call   @__SystemInit$qv ; __SystemInit(void)
; The System module is initialized.

    call   @__InitEM86$qv ; Initialize software emulator
; The coprocessor emulator is turned on.

    call   @__WINCRTInit$qv ; __WINCRTInit(void)
; The WINCRT module is initialized.

    push   bp
    mov    bp, sp
; The stack frame is opened.

    xor    ax, ax
    call   @__StackCheck$q4Word ; Stack overflow check (AX)
; Checking for stack overflow

    mov    word_21C0, 0EC83h
    mov    word_21C2, 0B851h
    mov    word_21C4, 551Eh
    mov    word_21C6, 3D83h
    mov    word_21C8, 0D70Ah
    mov    word_21CA, 78A3h
; We're not yet able to determine the type of initialized
; variables. They could be Word or Real.

    mov    ax, word_21C0
    mov    bx, word_21C2
    mov    dx, word_21C4
    call   @Extended$q4Real ; Convert Real to Extended
; Now we transfer word_21C0, word_21C2, and word_21C4
; to the function that converts Real to Extended,
; loading the latter to the coprocessor stack. Therefore,
; word_21C0 through word_21C4 is a variable of the Real type.

    mov    ax, word_21C6
```

```
        mov     bx, word_21C8
        mov     dx, word_21CA
        call    @Extended$q4Real ; Convert Real to Extended
        ; Similarly, the word_21C6 through word_21CA variable is of the Real type.

        wait
        ; Now we wait for the coprocessor to finish its work.

        faddp   st(1), st
        ; Two numbers of the Extended type that are located on the top
        ; of the coprocessor stack are added;
        ; the result is saved on the same stack.

        call    @Real$q8Extended
        ; Extended is converted to Real.
        ; The argument is passed via the coprocessor stack
        ; and returned into the AX, BX, and DX registers.

        push    dx
        push    bx
        push    ax
        ; The AX, BX, and DX registers contain a value of the Real type.
        ; Therefore, the procedure prototype looks like this:
        ; MyProc(a:Real);

        call    MyProc

        pop     bp
        xor     ax, ax
        call    @Halt$q4Word ; Halt(Word)
PROGRAM endp


MyProc          proc near           ; CODE XREF: PROGRAM+6D↑p

arg_0           = word ptr  4
arg_2           = word ptr  6
arg_4           = word ptr  8
; As we already know, these three arguments are actually
; one argument of the Real type.
```

```
        push    bp
        mov     bp, sp
        ; The stack frame is opened.

        xor     ax, ax
        call    @__StackCheck$q4Word ; Stack overflow check (AX)
        ; Checking for stack overflow

        mov     di, offset unk_2396
        push    ds
        push    di
        ; The pointer to the string output buffer is pushed onto the stack.

        mov     ax, [bp+arg_0]
        mov     bx, [bp+arg_2]
        mov     dx, [bp+arg_4]
        call    @Extended$q4Real
        ; Real is converted to Extended.

        mov     ax, 17h
        push    ax
        ; The output width is 0x17 characters.

        mov     ax, 0FFFFh
        push    ax
        ; This is for the number of digits after the decimal point.
        ; Everything we have is to be outputted.

        call    @Write$qm4Text8Extended4Wordt3
        ; Write(var f; v: Extended{st(0)
        ; width decimals: Word)
        ; The floating-point number from the coprocessor stack
        ; is outputted into the buffer.

        call    @WriteLn$qm4Text ; WriteLn(var f: Text)
        ; The string from the buffer is printed.

        call    @__IOCheck$qv         ; Exit if error
        pop     bp
        retn    6
MyProc                              endp
```

The conventions on `thiscall` usage, and the conventions on default calling. In C++ programs, each function of the object implicitly accepts the `this` argument — a pointer to the object instance from which the function was called. We already discussed this topic in detail in the section "*The* this *Pointer.*"

As far as I know, all C++ compilers use the combined calling convention by default, passing explicit arguments via the stack (if the function isn't declared as `fastcall`). The `this` pointer is passed via the register that has the greatest preference. (See Tables 2–7.)

In contrast, the `cdecl` and `stdcall` conventions require that you transfer all arguments via the stack — including the `this` implicit argument, placed on the stack after all explicit arguments. (In other words, `this` is the leftmost argument.)

Let's consider the following example:

Listing 98. Passing the `this` Implicit Argument

```
#include <stdio.h>

class MyClass{
public:
        void            demo(int a);
        // The prototype of demo actually looks like this:
        // demo(this, int a)

        void __stdcall demo_2(int a, int b);
        // The prototype of demo_2 looks like this:
        // demo_2(this, int a,  int b)

        void __cdecl   demo_3(int a, int b, int c);
        // The prototype of demo_3 looks like this:
        // demo_3(this, int a, int b, int c)

};


// To save space, the implementation of the demo, demo_2,
// and demo_3 functions is not given here.

main()
{
```

```
        MyClass *zzz = new MyClass;
        zzz->demo();
        zzz->demo_2();
        zzz->demo_3();
}
```

The disassembled code of this example, compiled using Microsoft Visual C++ 6.0, is given in the following listing. (I show only the main function; the rest of the program isn't of interest now.)

Listing 99. The Disassembled Code for Passing the this Implicit Argument

```
main            proc near              ; CODE XREF: start+AF↓p
        push    esi
        ; ESI is saved in the stack.


        push    1
        call    ??2@YAPAXI@Z          ; operator new(uint)
        ; This allocates 1 byte for the object instance.


        mov     esi, eax
        ; ESI contains the pointer to the object instance.


        add     esp, 4
        ; An argument is popped off the stack.


        mov     ecx, esi
        ; Via ECX, the this pointer is passed to the demo function.
        ; As you may remember, the Microsoft Visual C++ compiler uses
        ; the ECX register to pass the first argument of the function.
        ; In this case, the this pointer is just that argument.
        ; The Borland C++ 5.x compiler would pass this via
        ; the EAX register, since this compiler gives it
        ; the greatest preference. (See Table 4.)


        push    1
        ; The explicit argument of the function is pushed onto the stack.
        ; If this was the fastcall function, this argument
        ; would have been placed into the EDX register.
        ; It turns out that we are dealing with the type of the default
```

```
                   ; calling convention.

           call    Demo

           push    2
           ; The rightmost argument is pushed onto the stack.

           push    1
           ; The argument second from the right is pushed onto the stack.

           push    esi
           ; The this implicit argument is pushed onto the stack.
           ; Such a method of passing arguments indicates that an explicit
           ; conversion of the function type to stdcall or cdecl
           ; has taken place. Scrolling the disassembler screen downward,
           ; we can see that the stack is cleared by the called function.
           ; Therefore, it complies with the stdcall convention.

           call    demo_2

           push    3
           push    2
           push    1
           push    esi
           call    sub_401020
           add     esp, 10h
           ; If a function clears the stack up after completion, it has
           ; the default type or cdecl. Passing the this pointer via the stack
           ; allows us to think that the second assumption is correct.

           xor     eax, eax
           pop     esi
           retn
main               endp
```

Default arguments. To simplify calling functions that have a "crowd" of arguments, the C++ language provides the capability of specifying default arguments. Two questions arise: Does calling functions with default arguments differ from calling other functions? Who initializes the omitted arguments — the called function, or the calling one?

If functions with default arguments are called, the compiler adds the missing arguments on its own. Therefore, the calls of such functions don't differ from the calls of other functions.

Let's prove this in the following example.

Listing 100. Passing Default Arguments

```
#include <stdio.h>

MyFunc(int a=1, int b=2, int c=3)
{
        printf("%x %x %x\n", a, b, c);
}

main()
{
        MyFunc();
}
```

The result of disassembling the example is shown in the following listing. (Only the calling function is given.)

Listing 101. The Disassembled Code for Passing Default Arguments

```
main            proc near       ; CODE XREF: start+AF↓p
        push    ebp
        mov     ebp, esp

        push    3
        push    2
        push    1
        ; Apparently, all omitted arguments have been passed
        ; to the function by the compiler on its own.

        call    MyFunc

        add     esp, 0Ch
        pop     ebp
        retn
main                            endp
```

Analyzing how an unknown compiler passes arguments. The diversity of existing compilers, and the continual emergence of new ones, doesn't allow me to give a comprehensive table for the features of each compiler. What should you do if you come across a program compiled by a compiler not covered in this book?

If you can identify the compiler (for example, using IDA or the text strings contained in the file), you need to get a copy of it. Then, you should run a series of test examples on it, passing arguments of various types to an "experimental" function. You also might want to study the compiler's documentation; all mechanisms that pass arguments and are supported by the compiler could be described briefly.

If you can't identify the compiler or get a copy of it, you'll have to investigate carefully and thoroughly the interaction of the called and calling functions.

Values Returned by Functions

The value returned by a function is traditionally a value returned by the `return` operator. However, this statement is only the tip of the iceberg, and doesn't give a complete picture of the functions' interactions. The following example, taken from real program code, illustrates this.

Listing 102. Returning a Value via an Argument Passed by Reference

```
int xdiv(int a, int b, int *c=0)
{
        if (!b) return -1;
        if (c) c[0]=a % b;
        return a / b;
}
```

The `xdiv` function returns the result of integer division of the `a` argument by the `b` argument, but it also assigns the remainder to the `c` variable, passed to the function by reference. How many values has the function returned? Why is it worse or less permissible to return a result by reference than by the classical `return`?

Popular editions tend to simplify the problem of identifying the value returned by a function, considering one case that uses the `return` operator. In particular, Matt Pietrek, in his book "*Windows 95 System Programming Secrets*," follows this approach, leaving all other options out of the frame. Nevertheless, we will consider the following mechanisms:

❑ Returning values using the `return` operator (via a register or coprocessor stack)
❑ Returning values via arguments passed by reference
❑ Returning values via the heap
❑ Returning values via global variables
❑ Returning values via CPU flags

"Returning values via the disk drive and memory-mapped files" could be included in this list, but that's beyond the topic of discussion. (However, if you consider a function as a "black box" with an input and an output, the result of the function's work written into a file is actually the value returned by the function.)

Returning values using the `return` operator. According to convention, the value returned by the `return` operator is placed into the EAX register (AX in 16-bit mode). If the result exceeds the register's bit capacity, the higher 32 bits of an operand are loaded to EDX. (In 16-bit mode, the higher word is loaded to DX.)

In most cases, `float` results are returned via the coprocessor stack. They also may be returned via the EDX:EAX registers (DX:AX in 16-bit mode).

If a function returns a structure that consists of hundreds of bytes, or an object of similar size, then neither the registers nor the coprocessor stack will be sufficient. This is true for results larger than 8 bytes.

Table 11. The Mechanisms for Returning Values Using the `Return` Operator (16-Bit Compilers)

Type (Length)	Returned via		
1 byte	AL	*or*	AX
2 bytes	AX		
4 bytes	DX:AX		
Real	DX:BX:AX		
Float	DX:AX	*or*	Coprocessor stack
Double	Coprocessor stack		
Near pointer	AX		
Far pointer	DX:AX		
More than 4 bytes	Implicit argument by reference		

Table 12. The Mechanisms for Returning Values Using the Return **Operator (32-Bit Compilers)**

Type (Length)	Returned via				
1 byte	AL	*or*	AX	*or*	EAX
2 bytes	AX		*or*		EAX
4 bytes	EAX				
8 bytes	EDX:EAX				
Float	Coprocessor stack		*or*		EAX
Double	Coprocessor stack		*or*		EDX:EAX
Near pointer	EAX				
More than 8 bytes	Implicit argument by reference				

If there is no room for the return value in the registers, then the compiler, without telling the programmer, passes an implicit argument (the reference to the local variable storing the return result) to the function. Thus, the functions struct mystruct MyFunc (int a, int b) and void MyFunc (struct mystruct *my, int a, int b) are compiled in nearly identical code, and it is impossible to extract the original prototype from the machine code.

Microsoft Visual C++ is the only one that gives a clue. In this case, it returns the pointer to the variable being returned; the reconstructed prototype looks like struct mystruct* MyFunc (struct mystruct* my, int a, int b). It seems strange that the programmer, despite having just passed the argument to the function, would return the pointer to the argument. In this situation, Borland C++ returns a void result, erasing the distinction between an argument returned by value and an argument returned by reference. However, the "original prototype" asserts that a function returns a value, when it actually returns a reference — rather like seeing a cat and calling it a mouse.

A few words about identifying the returned value are necessary. If a function explicitly stores a value in the EAX or EDX register (AX or DX in 16-bit mode) and terminates its execution, the value's type can be determined roughly by Tables 11 and 12. If the registers are left undefined, the most likely result is a void-type value (i.e., nothing will be returned). An analysis of the calling function will produce more accurate information about how the called function accesses the EAX [EDX] registers (AX [DX] in 16-bit mode). For example, char types typically address the lower half of the EAX [AX] register (i.e., the AL register), or zero the higher bytes of the EAX register using the logical AND operation. It would seem that, if the calling function doesn't use the value left by the called function in the EAX [EDX] registers, its type is void. However, this assumption is incorrect. Programmers often ignore the returned value, confusing code diggers.

The next example shows the mechanism used to return the main value types.

Listing 103. Returning the Main Value Types

```c
#include <stdio.h>
#include <malloc.h>


// A demonstration of returning a value of a char-type variable
// by the return operator
char char_func (char a, char b)

{
        return a+b;
}


// A demonstration of returning an int-type variable
// by the return operator
int int_func(int a, int b)
{
        return a+b;
}

// A demonstration of returning an int64-type variable
// by the return operator
__int64 int64_func(__int64 a, __int64 b)
{
        return a+b;
}

// A demonstration of returning a pointer to int
// by the return operator
int* near_func(int* a, int* b)
```

```
{
      int *c;
      c=(int *)malloc(sizeof(int));
      c[0]=a[0]+b[0];
      return c;
}

main()
{
      int a;
      int b;

      a=0x666;
      b=0x777;

      printf("%x\n",
      char_func(0x1,0x2)+
      int_func(0x3,0x4)+
      int64_func(0x5,0x6)+
      near_func(&a,&b)[0]);
}
```

The disassembled code of this example, compiled using Microsoft Visual C++ 6.0 with default settings, will give the following result:

Listing 104. The Disassembled Code for Returning the Main Value Types Complied Using Visual C++

```
char_func       proc near              ; CODE XREF: main+1A↓p

arg_0           = byte ptr  8
arg_4           = byte ptr  0Ch

      push    ebp
      mov     ebp, esp
      ; The stack frame is opened.

      movsx   eax, [ebp+arg_0]
```

```
; The arg_0 argument, of the signed char type, is loaded into EAX
; and, incidentally, extended to int.

movsx   ecx, [ebp+arg_4]
; The arg_4 argument, of the signed char type, is loaded into ECX
; and, incidentally, extended to int.

add     eax, ecx
; The arg_0 and arg_4 arguments, extended to int, are added
; and saved in the EAX register, producing the value to be
; returned by the function. Unfortunately, its type is impossible
; to determine precisely. It could be int or char.
; Of the two options, int is more probable: The sum
; of two char arguments should be placed into int
; for safety reasons; otherwise, an overflow is possible.

        pop     ebp
        retn
char_func       endp

int_func        proc near           ; CODE XREF: main+29↓p

arg_0           = dword ptr 8
arg_4           = dword ptr 0Ch

        push    ebp
        mov     ebp, esp
; The stack frame is opened.

        mov     eax, [ebp+arg_0]
; The value of the arg_0 argument is loaded into EAX.

        add     eax, [ebp+arg_4]
; The arg_0 and arg_4 arguments are added, and the result
; is left in the EAX register. This is the value returned
; by the function. Its type probably is int.

        pop     ebp
        retn
```

```
int_func        endp

int64_func      proc near               ; CODE XREF: main+40↓p

arg_0           = dword ptr  8
arg_4           = dword ptr  0Ch
arg_8           = dword ptr  10h
arg_C           = dword ptr  14h

        push    ebp
        mov     ebp, esp
        ; The stack frame is opened.

        mov     eax, [ebp+arg_0]
        ; The value of the arg_0 argument is loaded into EAX.

        add     eax, [ebp+arg_8]
        ; The arg_0 and arg_8 arguments are added.

        mov     edx, [ebp+arg_4]
        ; The value of the arg_4 argument is loaded into EDX.

        adc     edx, [ebp+arg_C]
        ; The arg_4 and arg_C arguments are added, taking into account
        ; the carry, which remained after the addition of arg_0 and
        ; arg_8. Hence, arg_0 and arg_4, as well as arg_8 and arg_C,
        ; are the halves of two arguments of the __int64 type that
        ; will be summed. Therefore, the result of computation is
        ; returned via the EDX:EAX registers.

        pop     ebp
        retn
int64_func      endp

near_func       proc near               ; CODE XREF: main+54↓p

var_4           = dword ptr  -4
arg_0           = dword ptr  8
arg_4           = dword ptr  0Ch
```

```
push    ebp
mov     ebp, esp
; The stack frame is opened.

push    ecx
; ECX is saved.

push    4                       ; size_t
call    _malloc
add     esp, 4
; Four bytes are allocated on the heap.

mov     [ebp+var_4], eax
; The pointer to the memory just allocated
; is placed into the var_4 variable.

mov     eax, [ebp+arg_0]
; The value of the arg_0 argument is loaded into EAX.

mov     ecx, [eax]
; The int value referenced by the ECX register
; is loaded into ECX. Hence, the arg_0 argument is an int * type.

mov     edx, [ebp+arg_4]
; The value of the arg_4 argument is loaded into EDX.

add     ecx, [edx]
; The int value of the memory cell pointed to by the EDX register
; is added to *arg_0. Hence, the arg_4 argument is a int * type.

mov     eax, [ebp+var_4]
; The pointer to the memory block allocated on the heap
; is loaded into EAX.

mov     [eax], ecx
; The sum of *arg_0 and *arg_4 is copied onto the heap.

mov     eax, [ebp+var_4]
; The pointer to the memory block allocated on the heap is loaded
; into EAX. This is the value to be returned by the function.
```

```
        ; Its prototype might look as follows: int* MyFunc(int *a, int *b)

    mov     esp, ebp
    pop     ebp
    retn
near_func       endp

main            proc near           ; CODE XREF: start+AF↓p

var_8           = dword ptr -8
var_4           = dword ptr -4

    push    ebp
    mov     ebp, esp
    ; The stack frame is opened.

    sub     esp, 8
    ; Space is allocated for local variables.

    push    esi
    push    edi
    ; Registers are saved on the stack.

    mov     [ebp+var_4], 666h
    ; The 0x666 value is placed into var_4, an int local variable.

    mov     [ebp+var_8], 777h
    ; The 0x777 value is placed into var_8, an int local variable.

    push    2
    push    1
    call    char_func
    add     esp, 8
    ; The char_func(1,2) function is called. As previously
    ; mentioned, it is impossible to know the type
    ; of the value it returns. It could return int or char.

    movsx   esi, al
    ; The value returned by the function is extended to signed int.
```

```
; Hence, it has returned signed char.

push    4
push    3
call    int_func
add     esp, 8
; The int_func(3,4) function is called. It returns the int value.

add     eax, esi
; The contents of ESI are added to the value returned by
; the function.

cdq
; The double word in the EAX register is converted to
; a quadruple word, then placed into the EDX:EAX register.
; This proves that the value returned by the function
; from int was converted into int64, although the purpose
; of this action is, as yet, unclear.

mov     esi, eax
mov     edi, edx
; The extended quadruple word is copied to the EDI:ESI registers.

push    0
push    6
push    0
push    5
call    int64_func
add     esp, 10h
; The int64_func(5,6) function is called. It returns a value
; of the __int64 type. Now, the purpose of the extension
; of the previous result becomes clear.

add     esi, eax
adc     edi, edx
; The result returned by the int64_func is added
; to the quadruple word in the EDI:ESI registers.

lea     eax, [ebp+var_8]
; The pointer to the var_8 variable is loaded into EAX.

push    eax
```

```
; The var_8 pointer is passed as an argument to near_func.

lea        ecx, [ebp+var_4]
; The pointer to the var_4 variable is loaded into ECX.

push       ecx
; The var_4 pointer is passed as an argument to near_func.

call       near_func
add        esp, 8
; The near_func function is called.

mov        eax, [eax]
; As previously mentioned, the function has returned the pointer
; to an int variable into the EAX register. Now, the value
; of this variable is loaded into the EAX register.

cdq
; EAX is extended to a quadruple word.

add        esi, eax
adc        edi, edx
; Two quadruple words are added.

push       edi
push       esi
; The result of addition is passed to the printf function.

push       offset unk_406030
; The pointer is passed to the format-specification string.

call       _printf
add        esp, 0Ch

pop        edi
pop        esi
mov        esp, ebp
pop        ebp
retn
main       endp
```

As you can see, identifying the type of value returned by the `return` operator is rather straightforward. However, consider the following example. Try to predict what will be returned, and in which registers.

Listing 105. Returning a Structure by Value

```
#include <stdio.h>
#include <string.h>

struct XT
{
        char s0[4];
        int  x;
};

struct XT MyFunc(char *a, int b)
// The function returns a value of the XT structure by value.
{
        struct XT xt;
        strcpy(&xt.s0[0], a);
        xt.x = b;
        return xt;
}

main()
{
        struct XT xt;
        xt=MyFunc("Hello, Sailor!", 0x666);
        printf("%s %x\n", &xt.s0[0], xt.x);
}
```

The disassembled listing of the compiled code is as follows:

Listing 106. The Disassembled Code for Returning a Structure by Value

---

```
MyFunc          proc near                ; CODE XREF: sub_401026+10↓p


var_8           = dword ptr -8
var_4           = dword ptr -4
; These local variables are the elements of the "split"
```

```
; XT structure. As mentioned in the section
; "Objects, Structures, and Arrays," the compiler always tends
; to access the elements of a structure by their actual addresses,
; not via the base pointer. Therefore, distinguishing
; a structure from independent variables
; is not an easy task; sometimes it is an impossible one.

arg_0           = dword ptr  8
arg_4           = dword ptr  0Ch
; The function takes two arguments.

        push    ebp
        mov     ebp, esp
        ; The stack frame is opened.

        sub     esp, 8
        ; Space is allocated for local variables.

        mov     eax, [ebp+arg_0]
        ; The arg_0 argument is loaded into EAX.
        push    eax
        ; The arg_0 argument is passed to the strcpy function;
        ; hence, arg_0 is a pointer to a string.

        lea     ecx, [ebp+var_8]
        ; The pointer to the var_8 local variable is loaded into ECX.

        push    ecx
        ; This pointer is passed to the strcpy function.
        ; Therefore, var_8 is a string buffer with a size of 4 bytes.

        call    strcpy
        add     esp, 8
        ; The string passed via arg_0 to var_8 is copied.

        mov     edx, [ebp+arg_4]
        ; The value of the arg_4 argument is loaded into the EDX register.

        mov     [ebp+var_4], edx
```

```
        ; The arg_4 argument is copied to the var_4 local variable.

        mov     eax, [ebp+var_8]
        ; The contents of (not the pointer to) the string buffer
        ; are loaded.

        mov     edx, [ebp+var_4]
        ; The value of var_4 is loaded into EDX. Loading
        ; the EDX:EAX registers before exiting the function indicates
        ; var_4 has the value returned by the function. Unexpectedly,
        ; the function returns two variables of different types
        ; into EDX and EAX, and not __int64, which might seem logical
        ; after a cursory analysis of the program. The second surprise is
        ; that the char[4] type is returned via the register,
        ; not via the pointer or the reference. This is fortunate: If the
        ; structure were declared as struct XT {short int a, char b, char c},
        ; as many as three variables of two types
        ; would be returned into the EAX.

        mov     esp, ebp
        pop     ebp
        retn
MyFunc          endp

main    proc near                   ; CODE XREF: start+AF↓p

var_8           = dword ptr -8
var_4           = dword ptr -4
; These are two local variables of the int type.
; Their type has been determined by calculating their respective sizes.

        push    ebp
        mov     ebp, esp
        ; The stack frame is opened.

        sub     esp, 8
        ; Eight bytes are allocated for local variables.

        push    666h
```

```
; An int argument is passed to the MyFunc function.
; Therefore, arg_4 is of the int type, which wasn't obvious
; from the called function's code — arg_4 easily could
; be the pointer. Hence, the function returns
; an int type into the EDX register.

push    offset aHelloSailor ; "Hello, Sailor!"
; A pointer to the string is passed to MyFunc.
; Caution! The string occupies more than 4 bytes; therefore,
; I don't recommend making this example "live."

call    MyFunc
add     esp, 8
; The MyFunc function is called. Somehow, it modifies
; the EDX and EAX registers. The returned value types
; are already known, so it only remains to make sure
; that the calling function uses them "correctly."

mov     [ebp+var_8], eax
; The contents of the EAX register are placed
; into the var_8 local variable.

mov     [ebp+var_4], edx
; The contents of the EDX register are placed
; into the var_4 local variable.
; It seems that the function will return __int64.

mov     eax, [ebp+var_4]
; The contents of var_4 are loaded to EAX (i.e., this is loading
; the contents of the EDX returned by the MyFunc function) and...

push    eax
; ...passed to the printf function.
; According to the format-specification string,
; var_4 is of the int type.
; Hence, the function has returned int,
```

```
                 ; or at least its higher part, into EDX.

                 lea      ecx, [ebp+var_8]
                 ; The pointer to the var_8 variable is loaded into ECX.
                 ; This pointer stores the value returned by the function
                 ; via the EAX register. The format-specification string
                 ; indicates it's a pointer to a string. Thus, the values
                 ; returned via the EDX:EAX registers are of different types.
                 ; With a little thought, it is possible
                 ; to reconstruct the original prototype:
                 ; struct X{char a[4]; int b} MyFunc(char* c, int d);

                 push     ecx
                 push     offset aSX          ; "%s %x\n"
                 call     _printf
                 add      esp, 0Ch

                 mov      esp, ebp
                 pop      ebp
                 ; The stack frame is closed.

retn
main     endp
```

Now, let's modify the XT structure slightly, replacing char s0[4] with char* s0[10] (which won't fit into the EDX:AAX registers), then see how the code changes.

Listing 107. The Disassembled Code of the Modified and Compiled Version for Returning a Structure by Value

```
main          proc near           ; CODE XREF: start+AF↓p

var_20        = byte ptr -20h
var_10        = dword       ptr -10h
var_C         = dword       ptr -0Ch
var_8         = dword       ptr -8
```

```
var_4           = dword           ptr -4

        push    ebp
        mov     ebp, esp
        ; The stack frame is opened.

        sub     esp, 20h
        ; Here, 0x20 bytes are allocated for local variables.

        push    666h
        ; The rightmost int argument is passed
        ; to the MyFunc function.

        push    offset aHelloSailor ; "Hello, Sailor!"
        ; The second argument from the right (a pointer
        ; to the string) is passed to the MyFunc function.

        lea     eax, [ebp+var_20]
        ; The address of a local variable is loaded into EAX.

        push    eax
        ; A pointer is passed to the var_20 variable.
        ; This argument was not present in the function's prototype!
        ; Where has it come from? The compiler has inserted it
        ; to return the structure by value. The previous sentence
        ; could have been placed in quotation marks to accentuate
        ; its irony: The structure that will be returned by value
        ; actually is returned by reference.

        call    MyFunc
        add     esp, 0Ch
        ; The MyFunc function is called.

        mov     ecx, [eax]
        ; The function has loaded into ECX a pointer to the structure
        ; returned to it by reference. This trick is used only by
        ; Microsoft Visual C++; most compilers leave the value of EAX
        ; undefined or equal to zero. In any case, ECX will contain
        ; the first double word pointed to by the pointer placed in ECX.
```

```
; At first glance, this is an element of the int type.
; However, it is unwise to draw hasty conclusions.

mov     [ebp+var_10], ecx
; The contents of ECX are saved in the var_10 local variable.

mov     edx, [eax+4]
; EDX is loaded with the second double word pointed to
; by the EAX pointer.

mov     [ebp+var_C], edx
; It is copied to the var_C variable.
; The second element of the structure likely has the
; int type as well. A comparison with the source code of the
; program under consideration shows something is wrong.

mov     ecx, [eax+8]
; The third double word using the EAX pointer is loaded, and...

mov     [ebp+var_8], ecx
; ...it is copied to var_8. Yet another element of the int type?
; Where are they coming from? The original had one!
; And where is the string?

mov     edx, [eax+0Ch]
mov     [ebp+var_4], edx
; Yet another element of the int type is moved from the structure
; into the local variable. This is too much!

mov     eax, [ebp+var_4]
; EAX is loaded with the value of the var_4 local variable.

push    eax
; The value of var_4 is passed to the printf function.
; The format-specification string shows
; var_4 really has the int type.

lea     ecx, [ebp+var_10]
; A pointer to the var_10 is obtained, and...

push    ecx
```

```
; ...it is passed to the printf function. According to
; the format-specification string, ECX is of the char * type;
; hence, var_10 is the string we are looking for. Intuition
; suggests that var_C and var_8, located below var_10
; (i.e., at higher addresses), also contain strings. The compiler,
; instead of calling strcpy, has decided it would be faster
; to copy the structure that has caused confusion.
; Never be hasty when identifying the types of elements of
; structures! Carefully check how each byte is initialized
; and used. The operations of transfer to local variables alone
; are not informative!

        push    offset aSX          ; "%s %x\n"
        call    _printf
        add     esp, 0Ch


        mov     esp, ebp
        pop     ebp
; The stack frame is closed.

        retn
main            endp



MyFunc          proc near           ; CODE XREF: main+14↑p

var_10          = dword ptr -10h
var_C           = dword ptr -0Ch
var_8           = dword ptr -8
var_4           = dword ptr -4

arg_0           = dword ptr  8
arg_4           = dword ptr  0Ch
arg_8           = dword ptr  10h
; Note that three arguments are passed to the function,
; not two, as declared in the prototype.

        push    ebp
        mov     ebp, esp
```

```
; The stack frame is opened.

sub    esp, 10h
; Memory is allocated for local variables.

mov    eax, [ebp+arg_4]
; EAX is loaded with the second argument from the right.

push   eax
; The pointer to arg_4 is passed to the strcpy function.

lea    ecx, [ebp+var_10]
; ECX is loaded with the pointer to the var_10 local variable.

push   ecx
; The pointer to the var_10 local variable is passed
; to the strcpy variable.

call   strcpy
add    esp, 8
; The string passed to the MyFunc function,
; via the arg_4 argument, is copied.

mov    edx, [ebp+arg_8]
; EDX is loaded with the value of the rightmost argument
; passed to MyFunc.

mov    [ebp+var_4], edx
; The arg_8 argument is copied to the var_4 local variable.

mov    eax, [ebp+arg_0]
; The value of the arg_0 argument is loaded into EAX.
; As you already know, the compiler uses this argument to pass
; a pointer to the local variable without notifying the programmer.
; The function places the structure returned by value
; in this variable.

mov    ecx, [ebp+var_10]
; The contents of the var_10 local variable are loaded into ECX.
; As previously mentioned, a string has been copied to the var_10
```

```
; local variable; thus, this is likely double-word copying!

mov     [eax], ecx
mov     edx, [ebp+var_C]
mov     [eax+4], edx
mov     ecx, [ebp+var_8]
mov     [eax+8], ecx
; Exactly! The var_10 local variable is copied "manually"
; to the *arg_0 local variable, without using strcpy!
; In total, 12 bytes have been copied; hence,
; the first element of the structure looks like this:
; char s0[12]. The source code contained 'char s0[10]'.
; When the compiler aligned the elements of the structure
; by the addresses that are multiples of four, it placed
; the second element, int x, at the address base+012, creating
; a "hole" between the end of the line and the beginning of
; the second element. It is not possible to reconstruct
; the structure's actual form by analysing the disassembled
; listing. The only thing that can be stated for sure is that
; the string length s0 falls in the range of 9 to 12.

mov     edx, [ebp+var_4]
mov     [eax+0Ch], edx
; The var_4 variable, which contains the arg_8 argument,
; is copied into [EAX+0C]. The second element of the structure,
; int x, is at an offset of 12 bytes from the start.

mov     eax, [ebp+arg_0]
; The pointer to the arg_0 argument is returned to EAX. This
; argument contains the pointer to the returned structure.

mov     esp, ebp
pop     ebp
; The stack frame is closed.

retn
; The function's prototype looks like this:
; struct X {char s0[12], int a} MyFunc(struct X *x, char *y, int z)

MyFunc          endp
```

How are structures that contain hundreds or thousands of bytes returned? They are copied to the local variable, which the compiler, using the MOVS instruction, has implicitly passed by reference. This can be confirmed by replacing char s0[10] in the source code of the previous example with char s0[0x666]. The result of recompiling the example should look like this:

Listing 108. The Disassembled Code, Remodified and Recompiled, for Returning a Structure by Value

```
MyFunc          proc near               ; CODE XREF: main+1C↑p

var_66C         = byte ptr -66Ch
var_4           = dword ptr -4
arg_0           = dword ptr  8
arg_4           = dword ptr  0Ch
arg_8           = dword ptr  10h

        push    ebp
        mov     ebp, esp
        ; The stack frame is opened.

        sub     esp, 66Ch
        ; Memory is allocated for local variables.

        push    esi
        push    edi
        ; The registers are saved on the stack.

        mov     eax, [ebp+arg_4]
        push    eax
        lea     ecx, [ebp+var_66C]
        push    ecx
        call    strcpy
        add     esp, 8
        ; The string passed to the function is copied
        ; to the var_66C local variable.

        mov     edx, [ebp+arg_8]
        mov     [ebp+var_4], edx
```

```
; The arg_8 argument is copied to the var_4 local variable.

mov    ecx, 19Bh
; The 0x19B value is placed into ECX; the purpose of this is unclear.

lea    esi, [ebp+var_66C]
; ESI is set to point to the var_66C local variable.

mov    edi, [ebp+arg_0]
; The EDI register is set to point to the variable
; referenced by the pointer passed to the arg_0 argument.


repe movsd
; The ECX double words are copied from the ESI address to the EDI
; address. In bytes, this is 0x19B*4 = 0x66C.
; Thus, both the var_66C variable and the var_4 variable are copied.

mov    eax, [ebp+arg_0]
; The pointer to the returned structure
; is returned to EAX.

pop    edi
pop    esi

mov    esp, ebp
pop    ebp
; The stack frame is closed.
retn
MyFunc         endp
```

Note that many compilers (such as Watcom) use registers, rather than the stack, to pass the pointer that references the buffer allocated for the return value of the function. Furthermore, these compilers use the register intended for this purpose (Watcom, for example, uses the ESI register), rather than choosing registers from the queue of candidates in the order of preference. (See Table 7.)

Returning floating-point values. The *cdecl* and *stdcall* conventions require floating-point values (float, double, long double) to be returned via the coprocessor stack. The EAX and EDX registers may store any values when the function exits the execution. (In other words, the functions that return real values leave the EAX and EDX registers in an uncertain state.)

Theoretically, fastcall functions can return floating-point variables via registers as well. In practice, this rarely occurs. The coprocessor can't read the main processor's registers directly. They should be pushed through the RAM, which brings no benefit from the fastcall.

The following example illustrates this:

Listing 109. Returning Floating-Point Values

```
#include <stdio.h>

float MyFunc(float a, float b)
{
        return a+b;
}

main()
{
        printf("%f\n", MyFunc(6.66,7.77));
}
```

The disassembled listing of this example, compiled using Microsoft Visual C++, looks as follows:

Listing 110. The Disassembled Code for Returning Floating-Point Values Compiled with Visual C++

```
main            proc near             ; CODE XREF: start+AF↓p

var_8           = qword ptr -8

        push    ebp
        mov     ebp, esp
        ; The stack frame is opened.

        push    40F8A3D7h
        push    40D51EB8h
        ; Arguments are passed to the MyFunc function.
```

```
; Their type has yet to be determined.

call    MyFunc

fstp    [esp+8+var_8]
; The floating-point value, placed into the coprocessor
; stack by the MyFunc function, is retrieved. To determine
; the instruction's type, look at its opcode: DD 1C 24.
; According to Table 10, its type must be double. But wait!
; Is it really double? The function should return float!
; In theory, this is true. However, the type is converted
; implicitly when the argument is passed to the printf
; function, which is expecting double. Note where the return
; value of the function is placed: [esp+8-8] == [esp].
; It is allocated on the top of the stack, the
; equivalent of pushing it using the PUSH instructions.

call    _printf
add     esp, 0Ch

pop     ebp
retn
main            endp


MyFunc          proc near         ; CODE XREF: main+D↑p

arg_0           = dword ptr  8
arg_4           = dword ptr  0Ch

push    ebp
mov     ebp, esp
; The stack frame is opened.

fld     [ebp+arg_0]
; The arg_0 argument is placed on the top of the stack.
; To determine its type, let's look at the FLD instruction's opcode:
; D9 45 08. Its type must be float.

fadd    [ebp+arg_4]
; The arg_0 argument just placed on the top
```

```
; of the coprocessor stack is added to arg_4.
; The result is placed on the same stack, and...

pop     ebp
retn
; ...it is returned from the function. The result of adding
; two floats is left on the top of the coprocessor stack.
; Strangely, the same code would have been obtained
; if the function had been declared double.


MyFunc          endp
```

Returning values in Watcom C. Watcom C allows the programmer to choose manually the register or registers in which the function will return the value. This seriously complicates the analysis. Conventionally, the function should not spoil the EBX, ESI, and EDI registers (BX, SI, and DI in 16-bit mode). When you see, next to the function call, the instruction for reading the ESI register, it is tempting to conclude it was initialized before the function was called — as is typical in most cases. Watcom, however, may force the function to return the value in any general-purpose register except EBP (BP). Because of this, it is necessary to analyze both the calling and the called functions.

Table 13. The Valid Registers for Returning Function Values in Watcom C

Type	Valid registers				
1 byte	**AL**		BL	CL	DL	
	AH		BH	CH	DH	
2 bytes	**AX**	CX	BX	DX	SI	DI
4 bytes	**EAX**	EBX	ECX	EDX	ESI	EDI
8 bytes	EDX:EAX	ECX:EBX	ECX:EAX	ECX:ESI	EDX:EBX	EBX:EAX
	EDI:EAX	ECX:EDI	EDX:ESI	EDI:EBX	ESI:EAX	ECX:EDX
	EDX:EDI	EDI:ESI	ESI:EBX			

continues

Table 13 Continued

Type	Valid registers					
Near pointer	**EAX**	EBX	ECX	EDX	ESI	EDI
Far pointer	**DX:EAX**	CX:EBX	CX:EAX	CX:ESI	DX:EBX	DI:EAX
	CX:EDI	DX:ESI	DI:EBX	SI:EAX	CX:EDX	DX:EDI
	DI:ESI	SI:EBX	BX:EAX	FS:ECX	FS:EDX	FS:EDI
	FS:ESI	FS:EBX	FS:EAX	GS:ECX	GS:EDX	GS:EDI
	GS:ESI	GS:EBX	GS:EAX	DS:ECX	DS:EDX	DS:EDI
	DS:ESI	DS:EBX	DS:EAX	ES:ECX	ES:EDX	ES:EDI
	ES:ESI	ES:EBX	ES:EAX			
Float	8087	???	???	???	???	???
Double	8087	EDX:EAX	ECX:EBX	ECX:EAX	ECX:ESI	EDX:EBX
	EDI:EAX	ECX:EDI	EDX:ESI	EDI:EBX	ESI:EAX	ECX:EDX
	EDX:EDI	EDI:ESI	ESI:EBX	EBX:EAX		

The register or registers used by default are marked in bold. Note that only the size of the returned value can be determined by the register used. The type of this value cannot be determined directly. In particular, the EAX register may be used to return an int variable, as well as a structure consisting of four char variables, two char variables, or one short int variable.

What does this mean? Consider the following example:

Listing 111. Returning a Value via Any Valid Register

```
#include <stdio.h>

int MyFunc(int a, int b)
{
#pragma aux MyFunc value [ESI]
// The AUX pragma, along with the value keyword, allows us
// to define manually the register via which
```

```
// the result will be returned.
// In this case, the result will be returned via ESI.

        return a+b;
}

main()
{
        printf("%x\n", MyFunc(0x666, 0x777));
}
```

The disassembled code of the compiled version of this the example should look as follows:

Listing 112. The Disassembled Code for Returning a Value via Any Valid Register

```
main_           proc near               ; CODE XREF: __CMain+40↓p
        push    14h
        call    __CHK
        ; This is a check for stack overflow.

        push    edx
        push    esi
        ; ESI and EDX are saved.
        ; This is evidence that the given compiler obeyed the convention
        ; on saving ESI. There's no instruction for saving ESI, however.
        ; This register isn't modified by this particular function;
        ; therefore, there's no need to save it.

        mov     edx, 777h
        mov     eax, 666h
        ; Two arguments of the int type are passed to the MyFunc function.

        call    MyFunc
        ; The MyFunc function is called. By convention, after exiting
        ; the function, EAX, EDX, and, sometimes, ECX may contain
        ; values that are uncertain or returned by the function.
        ; Generally, the remaining registers must be retained.

        push    esi
```

```
        ; The value of the ESI register is passed to the printf function.
        ; It is impossible to know whether it contains the value
        ; returned by the function, or it was initialized
        ; prior to calling the function.

        push    offset asc_420004 ; "%x\n"
        call    printf_
        add     esp, 8

        pop     esi
        pop     edx

        retn
main_           endp

MyFunc          proc near               ; CODE XREF: main_+16↑p
        push    4
        call    __CHK
        ; The stack overflow is checked.

        lea     esi, [eax+edx]
        ; Here is a familiar, artful trick with addition.
        ; The pointer to EAX+EBX is loaded into ESI.
        ; However, the pointer to EAX+EBX also is
        ; the sum of them (i.e., this instruction is equivalent to
        ; ADD EAX, EDX/MOV ESI, EAX). This is the value returned
        ; by the function as ESI was modified, not saved!
        ; As required, the calling function passed
        ; the sum of 0x666 and 0x777 to printf, using
        ; the PUSH ESI instruction.

        retn
MyFunc          endp
```

Returning values by inline assembler functions. The creator of the assembly function is free to return values in any register. However, because the calling functions of a high-level language expect to see the computation result in strictly defined registers, the creator must observe certain conventions. Internal assembly functions are another matter — they may not follow any rules, as shown in the following example:

Listing 113. Returning Values by Inline Assembler Functions

```
#include <stdio.h>

// This is a naked function that has no prototype;
// the programmer should take care of everything!
__declspec( naked ) int MyFunc()
{
__asm{
        lea ebp, [eax+ecx]  ; The sum of EAX and ECX is returned into EBP.
                            ; Such a trick can be used only if
                            ; the function to be called from the assembly
                            ; function knows which registers
                            ; will be used to pass arguments,
                            ; and into which registers
                            ; the computation result will be returned.

        ret
        }
}

main()
{
        int a=0x666;
        int b=0x777;
        int c;
   __asm{
        push ebp
        push edi

        mov eax,[a];
        mov ecx,[b];
        lea edi,c

        call MyFunc;
        ; The MyFunc function is called from the assembler function.
        ; The arguments are passed to it
```

```
            ; via whatever registers it "wants."

mov [edi],ebp
; The value returned is received into EBP and saved
; in a local variable.

pop edi
pop ebp
}

            printf("%x\n", c);
}
```

The disassembled code of this example, compiled using Microsoft Visual C++ (other compilers will fail to compile it because they don't support the `naked` keyword), looks as follows:

Listing 114. The Disassembled Code for Returning Values by Inline Assembler Functions

```
MyFunc          proc near              ; CODE XREF: main+25↓p

        lea     ebp, [eax+ecx]
        ; Arguments are received via the EAX and ECX registers.
        ; Their sum is returned via EBP.
        ; This example is artificial,
        ; but illustrative.

        retn
MyFunc          endp

main            proc near              ; CODE XREF: start+AF↓p

var_C           = dword ptr -0Ch
var_8           = dword ptr -8
var_4           = dword ptr -4

        push    ebp
        mov     ebp, esp
```

```
; The stack frame is opened.

sub    esp, 0Ch
; Memory is allocated for local variables.

push   ebx
push   esi
push   edi
; The modified registers are saved.

mov    [ebp+var_4], 666h
mov    [ebp+var_8], 777h
; The var_4 and var_8 variables are initialized.

push   ebp
push   edi
; Are the registers saved, or passed to the function?
; This question cannot be answered yet.

mov    eax, [ebp+var_4]
mov    ecx, [ebp+var_8]
; The value of the var_4 variable is loaded into EAX,
; and the value of var_8 is loaded into ECX.

lea    edi, [ebp+var_C]
; The pointer to the var_C variable is loaded into EDI.

call   MyFunc
; The MyFunc function is called. It's unclear from the analysis
; of the calling function how the arguments are passed to it:
; via the stack, or via registers.
; Only an analysis of the code of MyFunc confirms that the latter
; assumption is true. Yes, the arguments are passed via registers!

mov    [edi], ebp
; What does this mean? An analysis of the calling function
; can't give an exhaustive answer.
; Only an analysis of the called function suggests
; that it returns the computation result via EBP.

pop    edi
```

```
pop     ebp
; The modified registers are restored.
; This is evidence that the registers were saved previously on
; the stack; they were not passed to the function as arguments.

mov     eax, [ebp+var_C]
; The contents of the var_C variable are loaded into EAX.

push    eax
push    offset unk_406030
call    _printf
add     esp, 8
; Calling printf

pop     edi
pop     esi
pop     ebx
; The registers are restored.

mov     esp, ebp
pop     ebp
; The stack frame is closed.

retn
main            endp
```

Returning values via arguments passed by reference. The identification of values returned via arguments passed by reference is linked closely with identification of the arguments themselves. (See the "*Function Arguments*" section.) Let's detect pointers among the arguments passed to the function and include them on the list of candidates for returned values.

Now, let's see whether there are any pointers to uninitialized variables among them; obviously, they're initialized by the called function itself. However, pointers to initialized variables, especially those equal to zero, should not be discounted; they also may return values. An analysis of the called function can clarify the situation: All operations that modify the variables passed by reference will be of interest, and should not be confused with modification of the variables passed by value. These automatically cease when function execution is completed (or, more precisely, when the arguments are eliminated from the stack). They are local variables of the function, which may change them as it sees fit.

Listing 115. Returning Values via Variables Passed by Reference

```
#include <stdio.h>
#include <string.h>

void Reverse(char *dst, const char *src)
{
        strcpy(dst,src);
        _strrev( dst);

}
// The src string is reversed and written
// into the dst string.

void Reverse(char *s){
        _strrev( s );
}
// The s string is reversed.
// (The result is written into the same s string.)

int sum(int a,int b)
//This function returns the sum of two arguments.

{
        a+=b;   return a;
}
// The arguments passed by value can be modified
// and treated as standard local variables.

main()
{
        char s0[]="Hello, Sailor!";
        char s1[100];

        Reverse(&s1[0], &s0[0]);
        printf("%s\n", &s1[0]);
        // The s0 string is reversed and written into s1.

        Reverse(&s1[0]);
        printf("%s\n", &s1[0]);
```

```
// The s1 string is rewritten and, therefore, reversed.

printf("%x\n", sum(0x666, 0x777));
// The sum of two numbers is printed.
}
```

The disassembled code of the compiled version of the previous example should look as follows:

Listing 116. The Disassembled Code for Returning Values via Variables Passed by Reference

```
main            proc near           ; CODE XREF: start+AF↓p

var_74          = byte ptr -74h
var_10          = dword ptr -10h
var_C           = dword ptr -0Ch
var_8           = dword ptr -8
var_4           = word ptr -4

        push    ebp
        mov     ebp, esp
        ; The stack frame is opened.

        sub     esp, 74h
        ; Memory is allocated for local variables.

        mov     eax, dword ptr aHelloSailor ; "Hello, Sailor!"
        ; The first 4 bytes of the string "Hello, Sailor!" are placed
        ; into EAX. The compiler probably copies the string
        ; into a local variable.

        mov     [ebp+var_10], eax
        mov     ecx, dword ptr aHelloSailor+4
        mov     [ebp+var_C], ecx
        mov     edx, dword ptr aHelloSailor+8
        mov     [ebp+var_8], edx
        mov     ax, word ptr aHelloSailor+0Ch
        mov     [ebp+var_4], ax
```

```
; The string "Hello, Sailor!" is copied to the var_10
; local variable of char s[0x10] type as expected.
; The 0x10 has been obtained by counting the number
; of bytes copied — 4 iterations with 4 bytes
; in each make a total of 16!

lea     ecx, [ebp+var_10]
; The pointer to the var_10 local variable, which contains
; the "Hello, Sailor!" string, is loaded into ECX.

push    ecx                    ; int
; The pointer to the "Hello, Sailor!" string is passed
; to the Reverse_1 function. IDA has determined
; the type incorrectly: What kind of int has char *?
; However, recalling how the string was copied
; clarifies why IDA made a mistake.

lea     edx, [ebp+var_74]
; The pointer to the uninitialized var_74 local variable
; is loaded into ECX.

push    edx                    ; char *
; The pointer to the uninitialized char variable s1[100]
; is passed to the Reverse_1 function. The value 100 was obtained
; by subtracting the offset of the var_74 variable from the offset
; of the var_10 variable, which is next to it and contains
; the "Hello, Sailor!" string: 0x74 - 0x10 = 0x64, which is 100
; in decimal representation. Passing a pointer to the unassigned
; variable suggests that the function will return
; some value in it — something that should be noted.

call    Reverse_1
add     esp, 8
; The Reverse_1 function is called.

lea     eax, [ebp+var_74]
; The pointer to the var_74 variable is loaded into EAX.

push    eax
```

; The pointer to the *var_74* variable is passed to the *printf*
; function. Because the calling function has not initialized this
; variable, it can be assumed that the called function has returned
; its value via the variable. The *Reverse_1* function might modify
; the *var_10* variable as well, but it is impossible to be certain
; about this before the function's code is studied.

```
push    offset unk_406040
call    _printf
add     esp, 8
```
; The *printf* function is called for the string output.

```
lea     ecx, [ebp+var_74]
```
; *ECX* is loaded with the pointer to the *var_74* variable, which
; apparently contains the value returned by the *Reverse_1* function.

```
push    ecx                     ; char *
```
; The pointer to the *var_74* variable is passed to the *Reverse_2*
; function. *Reverse_2* also may return its value into the *var_74*
; variable, may modify the variable, or may not return any value!
; Analyzing the code of the called function will clarify this.

```
call    Reverse_2
add     esp, 4
```
; The *Reverse_2* function is called.

```
lea     edx, [ebp+var_74]
```
; The pointer to the *var_74* variable is loaded into *EDX*.

```
push    edx
```
; The pointer to the *var_74* variable is passed to the *printf* function.
; Since the value returned by the function via the *EDX:EAX*
; registers isn't used, the function may return
; it into the *var_74* variable, rather than via
; the registers. However, this is only an assumption.

```
push    offset unk_406044
call    _printf
add     esp, 8
```

```
                ; The printf function is called.

                push    777h
                ; The 0x777 value of the int type is passed to the Sum function.

                push    666h
                ; The 0x666 value of the int type is passed to the Sum function.

                call    Sum
                add     esp, 8
                ; The Sum function is called.

                push    eax
                ; The EAX register contains the value returned by the Sum function.
                ; It is passed to the printf function as an argument.

                push    offset unk_406048
                call    _printf
                add     esp, 8
                ; The printf function is called.

                mov     esp, ebp
                pop     ebp
                ; The stack frame is closed.

                retn
main            endp

; int __cdecl Reverse_1(char *,int)
; Note that the the function's prototype is defined incorrectly!
; Actually, as already inferred from the analysis of the calling
; function, it looks like this: Reverse(char *dst, char *src).
; The names of arguments are based on the fact that the left
; argument is a pointer to an uninitialized buffer,
; and is probably used as a destination;
; the right argument is a source in such a case.

Reverse_1       proc near           ; CODE XREF: main+32↑p

arg_0           = dword ptr  8
```

```
arg_4           = dword ptr   0Ch

        push    ebp
        mov     ebp, esp
        ; The stack frame is opened.

        mov     eax, [ebp+arg_4]
        ; The arg_4 argument is loaded into EAX.

        push    eax
        ; The arg_4 argument is passed to the strcpy function.

        mov     ecx, [ebp+arg_0]
        ; The value of the arg_0 argument is loaded into ECX.

        push    ecx
        ; The arg_0 argument is passed to the strcpy function.

        call    strcpy
        add     esp, 8
        ; The contents of the string pointed to by arg_4
        ; are copied to the buffer pointed to by arg_0.

        mov     edx, [ebp+arg_0]
        ; EDX is loaded with the contents of the arg_0 argument, which
        ; points to the buffer that contains the string just copied.

        push    edx                     ; char *
        ; The arg_0 argument is passed to the __strrev function.

        call    __strrev
        add     esp, 4
        ; The strrev function reverses the string pointed to
        ; by arg_0. Therefore, the Reverse_1 function returns
        ; its value via the arg_0 argument passed by reference.
        ; The string pointed to by arg_4 remains unchanged.
        ; Therefore, the prototype of the Reverse_1 function
        ; looks like this: void Reverse_1 (char *dst, const char *src).
        ; The const qualifier should never be neglected: It presents
```

```
        ; clear evidence that the given pointer references
        ; a read-only variable. This considerably facilitates work with a
        ; disassembler listing, especially if you return to it after some
        ; time and have forgotten the algorithm of the analyzed program.


        pop     ebp
        ; The stack frame is closed.


        retn
Reverse_1        endp

; int __cdecl Reverse_2(char *)
; This time, the function's prototype is defined correctly
; (apart for the returned type being void, not int).


Reverse_2       proc near              ; CODE XREF: main+4F↑p

arg_0           = dword ptr  8

        push    ebp
        mov     ebp, esp
        ; The stack frame is opened.

        mov     eax, [ebp+arg_0]
        ; The contents of the arg_0 argument are loaded into EAX.

        push    eax                    ; char *
        ; The arg_0 argument is passed to the strrev function.

        call    __strrev
        add     esp, 4
        ; The string is reversed. The result is placed at the same location.
        ; Therefore, the Reverse_2 function returns the value
        ; via arg_0, and our hypothesis proves to be correct.

        pop     ebp
        ; The stack frame is closed.

        retn
        ; According to the last investigation, the prototype of
```

```
             ; the Reverse_2 function looks like this: void Reverse_2(char *s).

Reverse_2       endp

Sum             proc near          ; CODE XREF: main+72↑p

arg_0           = dword ptr  8
arg_4           = dword ptr  0Ch

        push    ebp
        mov     ebp, esp
        ; The stack frame is opened.

        mov     eax, [ebp+arg_0]
        ; The value of the arg_0 argument is loaded into EAX.
        add     eax, [ebp+arg_4]
        ; The arg_0 and arg_4 arguments are added.
        ; The result is placed into EAX.

        mov     [ebp+arg_0], eax
        ; The sum of arg_0 and arg_4 is copied back into arg_0.
        ; Inexperienced hackers may think that this is the return of
        ; values via an argument. However, this assumption is incorrect.
        ; The arguments passed to the function are popped off the stack.
        ; They "die" after this action is completed.
        ; An important point to remember:
        ; The arguments passed by value behave as local variables do.

        mov     eax, [ebp+arg_0]
        ; Now, the returned value really is copied to the EAX register.
        ; Therefore, the prototype of the function looks like this:
        ; int Sum(int a, int b);

        pop     ebp
        ; The stack frame is closed.

        retn
Sum             endp
```

Returning values via the heap. Returning values via an argument passed by reference barely decorates the function prototype. Such an argument is not intuitive; it demands detailed explanations such as, "You don't need to pass anything with this argument; on the contrary, be ready to receive something from it." (Who said that being a programmer is easy?) Clarity and aesthetics aside, there is a more serious problem. The size of the returned data is unknown beforehand in some cases; it often is figured out only at the run time of the called function. Should the buffer be allocated a surplus? This is an ugly and inexpedient solution; even in systems with virtual memory, size is limited. It would be much simpler if the called function were able to allocate itself as much memory as it needed, then return a pointer to it. This is, actually, very easy. Many novice programmers make the mistake of trying to return pointers to local variables; unfortunately, these variables "die" as soon as the function is completed, and the pointers end up pointing at nothing. The correct solution to this problem is to allocate memory on the heap (dynamic memory) — for example, by calling the `malloc` or `new` functions. Memory thus allocated "survives" until it is released forcefully by the `free` or `delete` function.

This memory-allocation mechanism is not essential for analyzing the program; the main role is played by the type of the returned value. It is easy to distinguish a pointer from other types: Only a pointer can be used in an address expression.

Let's consider the following example:

Listing 117. Returning a Value via the Heap

```c
#include <stdio.h>
#include <malloc.h>
#include <stdlib.h>

char* MyFunc(int a)
{
        char *x;
        x = (char *) malloc(100);

        _ltoa(a, x, 16);
        return x;
}

main()
{
        char *x;
```

```
    x=MyFunc(0x666);
    printf("0x%s\n", x);
    free(x);
}
```

The disassembled code of the compiled version of the previous example looks
as follows:

Listing 118. The Disassembled Code for Returning a Value via the Heap

```
main        proc near           ; CODE XREF: start+AF↓p

var_4       = dword ptr -4

    push    ebp
    mov     ebp, esp
    ; The stack frame is opened.

    push    ecx
    ; Four bytes of memory are allocated
    ; for a local variable. (See var_4.)

    push    666h
    ; The 666 value of the int type is passed to the MyFunc function.

    call    MyFunc
    add     esp, 4
    ; The MyFunc function is called. Note that no argument
    ; has been passed to the function by reference!

    mov     [ebp+var_4], eax
    ; The value returned by the function is copied to var_4.

    mov     eax, [ebp+var_4]
    ; Outstanding! The value returned by the function
    ; is loaded back into EAX!

    push    eax
    ; The value returned by the function is passed to the printf
```

```
; function. The qualifier indicates that the returned value is
; of the char * type. Since none of the arguments were passed
; to MyFunc function by reference, it allocated memory
; on its own, then wrote the received string to that memory.
; What if one or more arguments had been passed by
; reference to the MyFunc function? The function
; could have modified, then returned, one of these arguments.
; However, modification could not occur.
; For example, pointers to two strings could be passed
; to the function, which could return the pointer to
; the shorter string, or to the string that contained more vowels.
; Therefore, not every case of returning the pointer
; is a sign of modification.

push    offset a0xS         ; "0x%s\n"
call    _printf
add     esp, 8
; The printf function is called; the string returned
; by the MyFunc function is printed.

mov     ecx, [ebp+var_4]
; ECX is loaded with the value of the pointer returned
; by the MyFunc function.

push    ecx                     ; void *
; The pointer returned by MyFunc is passed to the free function.
; This means that MyFunc allocated memory by
; calling malloc.

call    _free
add     esp, 4
; Memory allocated by MyFunc
; to return the value is released.

mov     esp, ebp
pop     ebp
; The stack frame is closed.

retn
; Thus, the prototype of MyFunc looks like this:
```

```
        ; char* MyFunc(int a)

main            endp


MyFunc          proc near           ; CODE XREF: main+9↑p

var_4           = dword ptr -4
arg_0           = dword ptr  8

        push    ebp
        mov     ebp, esp
        ; The stack frame is opened.

        push    ecx
        ; Memory is allocated for local variables.

        push    64h                 ; size_t
        call    _malloc
        add     esp, 4
        ; On the heap, 0x64 bytes are allocated, either for the needs
        ; of the function, or for returning the result. Because
        ; the analysis of the calling function's code has shown
        ; that MyFunc returns a pointer, malloc likely
        ; allocates memory for this purpose.
        ; However, there might be several calls of malloc,
        ; and the pointer might be returned only by one of them.

        mov     [ebp+var_4], eax
        ; The pointer is saved in the var_4 local variable.

        push    10h                 ; int
        ; The rightmost argument, 0x10, is passed to the __ltoa function, and
        ; the scale of notation for converting the number is specified.

        mov     eax, [ebp+var_4]
        ; EAX is loaded with the contents of the pointer to memory
        ; allocated on the heap.

        push    eax                 ; char *
        ; The pointer to the buffer is passed to the ltoa function
```

```
                ; for returning the result.

        mov     ecx, [ebp+arg_0]
        ; The value of the arg_0 argument is loaded into EAX.

        push    ecx                     ; __int32
        ; The int argument, arg_0, is passed to
        ; the ltoa function.

        call    __ltoa
        add     esp, 0Ch
        ; The ltoa function converts the number into the string and
        ; writes it into the buffer referenced by the returned pointer.

        mov     eax, [ebp+var_4]
        ; The pointer is returned to memory area
        ; that has been allocated by MyFunc on the heap
        ; and that contains the result of work of ltoa.

        mov     esp, ebp
        pop     ebp
        ; The stack frame is closed.

        retn
MyFunc          endp
```

Returning values via global variables. In general, the use of global variables is bad style. Such a programming style is indicative mainly of programmers whose minds have been irreversibly crippled by the ideology of BASIC, with its poor mechanism for calling subroutines.

The identification of global variables is considered in more detail in the "*Global Variables*" section of this chapter. Here, you'll learn the mechanisms of returning values via global variables.

All global variables can be implicit arguments of each called function and, at the same time, returned values. Any function may arbitrarily read and modify them. Neither passing nor returning global variables can be revealed by an analysis of the code of the calling function; instead, a careful investigation of the code of the called function is required. In particular, it is necessary to determine if the called function manipulates global variables, and which ones are modified. The problem can be approached from the other side: By reviewing the data segment, it may be possible to find all the global variables and their offsets, then, via a context search on the whole file, to reveal the functions that reference them. (See the "*Global Variables*" section for more details.)

Besides global variables, there are *static* ones. These also reside in the data segment, but they are directly accessible only to the function that has declared them. This limitation is not imposed on the variables, but rather on their names. To give other functions access to their own static variables, it is enough to pass a pointer. Fortunately, this trick doesn't create any problems for hackers (although some spoilsports call it "a hole in the protection"). The absence of immediate access to the static variables of "another," and the necessity for cooperation with the function owner via a predictable interface (a returned pointer), allows a program to be divided into independent units that may be analyzed separately. The following example provides an illustration of this:

Listing 119. Returning Values via Global and Static Variables

```
#include <stdio.h>

char* MyFunc(int a)
{
        static char x[7][16]={"Monday", "Tuesday", "Wednesday",\
        ⮑"Thursday", "Friday", "Saturday", "Sunday"};
        return &x[a-1][0];
}


main()
{
        printf("%s\n", MyFunc(6));
}
```

The disassembled code of this example, compiled using Microsoft Visual C++ 6.0 with default settings, looks as follows:

Listing 120. The Disassembled Code for Returning Values via Global and Static Variables

```
MyFunc          proc near          ; CODE XREF: main+5↓p

arg_0           = dword ptr  8
```

```
        push    ebp
        mov     ebp, esp
        ; The stack frame is opened.

        mov     eax, [ebp+arg_0]
        ; The value of the arg_0 argument is loaded into EAX.

        sub     eax, 1
        ; EAX is decremented by one. This is indirect evidence that arg_0
        ; is not a pointer, although mathematical operations over
        ; pointers are allowed and used actively in C language.

        shl     eax, 4
        ; Here, (arg_0 -1) is multiplied by 16.
        ; A shift of 4 bits to the right is the equivalent of
        ; raising 2 to the 4th power, or 16.

        add     eax, offset aMonday; "Monday"
        ; The obtained value is added to the base pointer that references
        ; the table of strings in the data segment. The data segment
        ; contains either static or global variables. Since the value
        ; of the arg_0 argument is multiplied by some value
        ; (in this case, by 16), you can assume this is
        ; a two-dimensional array of fixed length strings.
        ; Thus, EAX contains a pointer to the string that has
        ; the index arg_0 -1, or arg_0, if the count starts from one.

        pop     ebp
        ; The stack frame is closed, and the pointer is returned to
        ; the corresponding element of the array via the EAX register.
        ; As you can see, there is no basic difference between returning
        ; the pointer to the memory area allocated on the heap
        ; and returning the pointer to the static variables
        ; allocated in the data segment.

        retn
MyFunc          endp


main            proc near           ; CODE XREF: start+AF↓p
```

```
        push    ebp
        mov     ebp, esp
        ; The stack frame is opened.

        push    6
        ; This value of the int type is passed to the MyFunc function.
        ; (The sixth day is Saturday.)

        call    MyFunc
        add     esp, 4
        ; The MyFunc function is called.

        push    eax
        ; The value returned by MyFunc is passed to the printf function.
        ; The format-specification string indicates that
        ; this is a pointer to the string.

        push    offset aS          ; "%s\n"
        call    _printf
        add     esp, 8

        pop     ebp
        ; The stack frame is closed.

        retn
main            endp


aMonday         db 'Monday',0,0,0,0,0 ; DATA XREF: MyFunc+C↑o
; The presence of a cross-reference to one function suggests
; that this variable is of the static type.

aTuesday        db 'Tuesday',0,0,0,0,0,0,0,0,0
aWednesday      db 'Wednesday',0,0,0,0,0,0,0,0,0,0,0
aThursday       db 'Thursday',0,0,0,0,0,0,0,0,0
aFriday         db 'Friday',0,0,0,0,0,0,0,0,0
aSaturday       db 'Saturday',0,0,0,0,0,0,0,0,0
aSunday         db 'Sunday',0,0,0,0,0
aS              db '%s',0Ah,0               ; DATA XREF: main+E↑o
```

Compare that example with one that uses true global variables.

Listing 121. Returning a Value via a Global Variable

```c
#include <stdio.h>

int a;
int b;
int c;

MyFunc()
{
    c=a+b;
}

main()
{
    a=0x666;
    b=0x777;
    MyFunc();
    printf("%x\n", c);
}
```

The disassembled code of the compiled version of the previous example looks as follows:

Listing 122. The Disassembled Code Returning a Value via a Global Variable

---

```
main        proc near          ; CODE XREF: start+AF↓p
        push    ebp
        mov     ebp, esp
        ; The stack frame is opened.

        call    MyFunc
        ; The MyFunc function is called. Note that nothing is passed
        ; to the function, and nothing is returned. Therefore,
        ; the preliminary conclusion is that its prototype
        ; looks like this: void MyFunc()

        call    Sum
        ; The Sum function is called. This function doesn't receive
```

```
; or return any values. Its preliminary prototype
; looks like this: void Sum()

mov    eax, c
; The value of the c global variable is loaded into EAX.
; Now, examine the data segment. The c local variable
; equals zero. However, this value should be questioned
; because previously called functions could have changed it.
; The assumption about modification is strengthened by a pair of
; cross-references, one of which points to the Sum function.
; The w suffix that ends the cross-reference indicates that Sum
; assigns some value to the c variable, which can be worked out
; by analyzing the code of the Sum function.

push   eax
; The value returned by the Sum function is passed
; to the printf function via the c global variable.
; The format-specification string indicates that
; the argument is of the int type.

push   offset asc_406030 ; "%x\n"
call   _printf
add    esp, 8
; The result returned by Sum is printed.

pop    ebp
; The stack frame is closed.

       retn
main           endp



Sum            proc near          ; CODE XREF: main+8↑p
; The Sum function doesn't receive any arguments via the stack!

       push   ebp
       mov    ebp, esp
; The stack frame is opened.
```

```
        mov     eax, a
        ; The value of the a global variable is loaded into EAX.
        ; Now, find a in the data segment. A cross-reference
        ; to MyFunc assigns something to the a variable.
        ; Since MyFunc was called prior to the call of Sum,
        ; MyFunc presumably has returned some value into a.

        add     eax, b
        ; EAX (which stores the value of the a global variable) is added
        ; to the contents of the b global variable.

        mov     c, eax
        ; The result of a + b is assigned to the c variable.
        ; As you already know (from the analysis of the main function),
        ; the Sum function uses the c variable to return its results;
        ; now, it is clear which results.

        pop     ebp
        ; The stack frame is closed.

        retn
Sum             endp

MyFunc          proc near          ; CODE XREF: main+3↑p
        push    ebp
        mov     ebp, esp
        ; The stack frame is opened.

        mov     a, 666h
        ; The 0x666 value is assigned to the a global variable.

        mov     b, 777h
        ; The 0x777 value is assigned to the b global variable.
        ; As you discovered by analyzing the two previous functions,
        ; the MyFunc function returns its computation result into
        ; the a and b variables. Now, the result in question has been
        ; clarified. You also know how these three functions interact.
        ; First, main() calls MyFunc(), which initializes the a and b
        ; global variables. Then, main() calls Sum(), placing
```

```
        ; the sum of a and b into the c global variable. Finally,
        ; main() takes c and passes it via the stack to printf.
        ; Even an elementary example of three functions creates a knotty
        ; problem! What can be said about a real program that
        ; incorporates thousands of such functions, whose calling
        ; order and behavior are far from obvious?


        pop     ebp



        retn
MyFunc          endp


a               dd 0                    ; DATA XREF: MyFunc+3w    Sum+3↑r
b               dd 0                    ; DATA XREF: MyFunc+Dw    Sum+8↑r
c               dd 0                    ; DATA XREF: Sum+Ew main+D↑r
; The cross-references indicate that all three variables are global;
; each can be accessed by more than one function.
```

Returning values via processor flags. Assembly functions typically use the CPU flags register to return the result (success or failure) of the function execution. By convention, the carry flag (CF) indicates an error. The zero flag (ZF) is the next most popular one. Other flags practically are not used.

The carry flag is set by the STC instruction, or by any mathematical operation that results in a carry (for example, CMP a, b, where a < b). This flag is reset by the CLC instruction, or by any appropriate mathematical operation.

The carry flag is usually checked by the JC xxx and JNC xxx jump instructions, executed, respectively, depending on whether the carry is present or not. The JB xxx and JNB xxx branches are their syntactic synonyms, which give identical code after assembling.

Listing 123. Returning Values via Processor Flags

```c
#include <stdio.h>

Err(){ printf("-ERR: DIV by Zero\n");}
// This function gives a division-error message.

Ok(int a){printf("%x\n", a);}
```

```
// The result of division is printed.

__declspec(naked) MyFunc()
{
// This assembler function implements division.
// It divides EAX by EBX, then returns
// the result into EAX and the remainder into EDX.
// An attempt to divide by zero causes the function to set
// the carry flag.

        __asm{
        xor edx, edx    ; EDX is zeroed. That is, the div instruction
                        ; expects the dividend to be in EDX:EAX.
        test ebx, ebx   ; The divisor is checked for zero.
        jz _err         ; If the divisor is equal to zero,
                        ; jump to _err.

        div ebx         ; EDX:EAX is divided by EBX.
                        ; (EBX is not equal to zero.)

        ret             ; Upon exiting, the quotient is returned into EAX
                        ; and the remainder is returned into EDX.

        _err:           ; This code takes control
                        ; when an attempt is made to divide by zero.
        stc             ; The carry flag is set, which signals
                        ; the error and...
        ret             ; ...quits.
        }
}

// This is a wrapper for MyFunc.
// Two arguments — the dividend and the divisor —
// are received via the stack. The result of division
// (or the error message) is displayed on the screen.
__declspec(naked) MyFunc_2(int a, int b)
{
__asm{
        mov eax, [esp+4]   ; The contents of the a argument
                           ; are loaded into EAX.
```

```
        mov ebx, [esp+8]    ; The contents of the b argument
                            ; are loaded into EDX.

        call MyFunc         ; This is an attempt to divide a by b.
        jnc _ok             ; If the carry flag is reset,
                            ; the result is displayed; otherwise,...

        call Err            ; ...the error message is displayed.

        ret                 ; Returning
_ok:
        push eax            ; The result of division is passed and
        call Ok             ; displayed on the screen.
        add esp, 4          ; The stack is cleared.

        ret                 ; Returning
        }
}

main(){MyFunc_2(4,0);}
```

Local Stack Variables

Local variables are placed onto the *stack* (also known as *automatic memory*), then removed when the function completes execution. First, any arguments passed to the function are placed onto the stack. The CALL instruction that calls this function places the return address on top of the arguments. Upon gaining control, the function *opens the stack frame* (i.e., saves the previous value of the EBP register and sets it equal to the ESP register, which points to the top of the stack). The free stack area is above EBP (i.e., at a lower address); the service data (the stored value of EBP and the return address), as well as the arguments, are below it.

The stack area above the stack-top pointer (the ESP register) can be erased or distorted. For example, it can be used by hardware-interrupt handlers called at unpredictable places in the program and at unpredictable times. If the function uses the stack (to save registers or pass arguments), stack corruption will result. The way to avoid this is to move the stack pointer upward until it occupies this area of the stack.

The integrity of the memory "below" ESP *is guaranteed* (against unintentional distortions): The next call of the PUSH instruction will place the data on top of the stack without erasing local variables.

At the end of execution, the function is obliged to return the ESP value to its former place. If it does not return this value, the RET function will be unable to read the return address off the stack; rather, it will read the value of the "uppermost" local variable, and will pass control nowhere.

▶ *Note*

The left part of Fig. 15 shows the stack at the moment the function is called. The function opens the stack frame, saving the old value of the EBP register and setting it equal to ESP. The right part of Fig. 15 represents the allocation of 0x14 bytes of the stack memory for local variables. This is done by moving the ESP register upward — into the area of lower addresses. Local variables are allocated in the stack as if they were pushed there by the PUSH instruction. After execution, the function increases the value of the ESP register and returns the value to its former position, releasing memory occupied by local variables. Then, the function restores the EBP value from the stack, closing the stack frame.

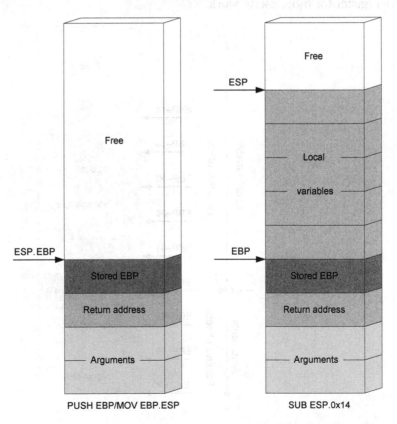

Fig. 15. The mechanism for allocating local variables in the stack

Addressing local variables. Local variables and stack arguments are addressed similarly. (See the "*Function Arguments*" section.) The only difference is arguments are located "below" EBP, and local variables reside "above" it. In other words, arguments have a positive offset relative to EBP, and local variables have a negative offset. Therefore, they can easily be distinguished. For example, [EBP+xxx] is an argument, and [EBP-xxx] is a local variable.

The register that points at the stack frame serves as a barrier: The function's arguments are on one side of it, and the local variables are on the other (Fig. 16). It's clear why ESP is copied to EBP when the stack frame is opened: If copying didn't occur, the addressing of local variables and arguments would be complicated considerably. Compiler developers are humans (strange as it may seem), and they don't want to complicate their lives unnecessarily. However, optimizing compilers are capable of addressing local variables and arguments directly via ESP, freeing the EBP register for more useful work.

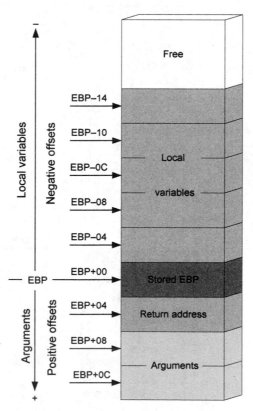

Fig. 16. Addressing local variables

Implementation details. There are plenty of ways to allocate and clear memory for local variables. For example, SUB ESP, xxx can be used at the input, and ADD ESP,xxx can be used at the output. Striving, perhaps, to be distinguished, Borland C++ and some other compilers allocate memory by increasing ESP, not decreasing it... by a negative number! By default, most disassemblers interpret this as a large positive number. When allocating a small amount of memory, optimizing compilers replace SUB reg with PUSH reg, which is shorter by a few bytes. This creates identification problems: Is this saving registers on the stack, passing arguments, or allocating memory for local variables?

The algorithm for clearing memory is also ambiguous. In addition to encountering an increase in the register of the stack-top pointer due to the ADD ESP, xxx instruction (or a decrease in it due to a negative number, as previously mentioned), you may find the construction MOV ESP, EBP. (When the stack frame was opened, ESP was copied to EBP, but EBP was not modified during the execution of the function.) Finally, memory may be released by the POP instruction, which pops out local variables one by one into any unused register. (Such a method is justified only when the number of local variables is small.)

Table 14. Allocating and Clearing Memory for Local Variables

Action	Implementation variants		
Allocating memory	SUB ESP, xxx	ADD ESP,- xxx	PUSH reg
Releasing memory	ADD ESP, xxx	SUB ESP,- xxx	POP reg
	MOV ESP, EBP		

Identifying the mechanism that allocates memory. Using the SUB and ADD instructions, memory allocation is consistent and interpreted unequivocally. If memory is allocated using the PUSH instruction and is cleared by POP, this construction becomes indistinguishable from simple allocation and deallocation of registers on and from the stack. As a complication, the function also contains instructions for allocating registers, mingled with memory-allocation instructions. Is it possible to ascertain how many bytes are allocated for local variables, or whether any bytes have been allocated? (The function may not contain local variables.)

The search for references to the memory locations "above" the EBP register (i.e., with a negative relative offset) might be helpful. Let's consider two examples.

Listing 124. Identifying the Memory-Allocation Mechanism

push ebp	push ebp
push ecx	push ecx
xxx	xxx
xxx	**mov [ebp-4], 0x666**
xxx	xxx
pop ecx	pop ecx
pop ebp	pop ebp
ret	ret

In the left-hand example, there is no reference to local variables; in the right-hand code, the MOV [EBP-4], 0x666 construction copies the 0x666 value to the var_4 local variable. If there's a local variable, memory must have been allocated for it. As there are no instructions such as SUB ESP, xxx or ADD ESP, xxx in the body of the function, the memory must have been allocated by PUSH ECX. (The contents of the ECX register are stored on the stack 4 bytes "above" EBP.) Only one instruction, PUSH ECX, can be cited, because PUSH EBP is not fit for the role of "allocator." What can be done if there are several "suspects?"

The amount of allocated memory can be determined by the offset of the "highest" local variable in the body of the function. In other words, of all the [EBP-xxx] expressions, the greatest xxx offset generally is equal to the number of bytes of memory allocated for local variables. However, local variables can be declared and not used. Memory is allocated for them (although optimizing compilers remove such variables as superfluous), but no reference occurs to them. In this case, the algorithm for calculating the amount of allocated memory produces a result that is too low. However, this error has no effect on the results of analyzing the program.

Initializing local variables. There are two ways to initialize local variables: Assign the necessary value by the MOV instruction (such as MOV [EBP-04], 0x666), or directly push the values onto the stack using the PUSH instruction (such as PUSH 0x777). This allows the allocation of memory for local variables to be favorably combined with their initialization (if there are only a few of these variables).

In most cases, popular compilers perform initialization using MOV; perverse assemblers are more likely to use PUSH, sometimes in protection aimed at misleading hackers (although any hacker led astray by such a trick must be a beginner).

Allocating structures and arrays. Structures and arrays (i. e., their elements) are placed consecutively on the stack in adjacent memory locations. *The smaller index of an array is at the smaller address, but it is addressed by a larger offset* relative to the pointer-register of the stack frame. This is no surprise; because local variables are addressed by a negative offset, [EBP-0x4] > [EBP-0x10].

The mess grows because IDA omits the minus sign when it gives names to local variables. For example, of the variables var_4 and var_10, the latter occupies the smaller address, the index of which *is larger*. If var_4 and var_10 are two ends of an array, instinct would place var_4 at the head of an array, and var_10 at the end, although they belong in the opposite locations.

Alignment in the stack. In some cases, elements of a structure, an array, or even particular variables must be aligned by addresses that are multiples of a specific power of 2. However, the stack-top pointer value is not defined beforehand. How can the compiler, which does not know the index value, fulfill this requirement? It simply discards the lower bits of ESP.

The lower bit of even numbers is zero. To ensure that the value of the stack-top pointer is divisible by two without a remainder, simply force its lower bit to zero. If two lower bits are set to zero, the resulting value will be a multiple of four; if three lower bits are set to zero, the resulting value will be a multiple of eight; and so on.

In most cases, bits are reset using the AND instruction. For example, AND ESP, FFFFFF0 makes ESP a multiple of 16. How do we obtain this? Let's convert 0xFFFFFFF0 to a binary form, which will give the following: 11111111 11111111 11110000. The four trailing zeroes mean that four lower bits of any number will be masked. The number will be divisible by 2 to the power of 4, which equals 16.

How IDA identifies local variables. Although local variables have been used in the previous listings, an example of how they are identified may be helpful.

Listing 125. Identifying Local Variables

```
#include <stdio.h>
#include <stdlib.h>

int MyFunc(int a, int b)
{
        int c;          // A local variable of the int type.
        char x[50]      // An array (shows the method of
                        // allocating arrays in memory)

        c = a + b;              // The sum of a + b is placed into c.

        ltoa(c, &x[0], 0x10) ;  // The sum of a + b is converted into
```

```
                                        // a string.

        printf("%x == %s == ", c, &x[0]);  // The string is displayed.
        return c;
}

main()
{
        int a = 0x666;    // The a and b local variables are declared,
        int b = 0x777;    // demonstrating the mechanism by which
                          // the compiler initializes them.

        int c[1];         // Tricks like this are necessary
                          // to prevent the optimizing compiler from placing
                          // the local variable into the register. (See the
                          // "Register and Temporary Variables" section.)
                          // Because the pointer to c is passed to the printf
                          // function, and a pointer to the register can't be
                          // passed, the compiler has to leave the variable
                          // in memory.

        c[0] = MyFunc(a, b);
        printf("%x\n", &c[0]);

        return 0;
}
```

The disassembled code of this example, compiled using Microsoft Visual C++
6.0 with default settings, should look as follows:

**Listing 126. The Disassembled Code for Identifying Local Variables Compiled
Using Visual C++ 6.0**

```
MyFunc         proc near            ; CODE XREF: main+1C↓p

var_38         = byte ptr -38h
var_4          = dword ptr -4
; Local variables are allocated at the negative offset, relative to
; EBP; function arguments are allocated at the positive offset.
; Note that the "higher" the variable's location,
```

```
; the larger the absolute value of its offset.

arg_0           = dword ptr  8
arg_4           = dword ptr  0Ch

        push    ebp
        mov     ebp, esp
        ; The stack frame is opened.

        sub     esp, 38h
        ; The ESP value by is decreased 0x38, and 0x38 bytes
        ; are allocated for local variables.

        mov     eax, [ebp+arg_0]
        ; The value of the arg_0 argument is loaded into EAX.
        ; This clearly is an argument, as shown by
        ; its positive offset relative to the EBP register.

        add     eax, [ebp+arg_4]
        ; The value of the arg_0 argument is added to EAX.
        mov     [ebp+var_4], eax
        ; Here is the first local variable.
        ; It is just a local variable, as shown by its negative
        ; offset relative to the EBP register. Why is it negative?
        ; Look how IDA has determined var_4. It would be better
        ; if the negative offsets of local variables were marked clearly.

        push    10h                     ; int
        ; The 0x10 value (the radix of the numeration system)
        ; is passed to the ltoa function.

        lea     ecx, [ebp+var_38]
        ; The pointer to the var_38 local variable is loaded into ECX.
        ; What kind of a variable is this? Let's scroll
        ; the disassembler screen upward to find the description
        ; of local variables that IDA has recognized:
        ; var_38 = byte ptr -38h
        ; var_4 = dword ptr -4
        ;
        ; The nearest lower local variable has an offset equal to −4.
```

```
; The var_38 variable has an offset equal to -38. Subtracting
; the latter from the former gives the size of var_38.
; It is easy to calculate that the size is equal to 0x34.
; Nevertheless, the ltoa function is expecting the pointer
; to char*. Thus, it is possible to write the following comment
; to var_38: "char s[0x34]". This is done as follows:
; Open the Edit menu, then open the Functions submenu.
; Select Stack variables, or press the <Ctrl>+<K>
; key combination. A window will open that lists all
; recognized local variables. Bring the cursor to var_34,
; press <;> to enter a recurring comment, and write
; "char s[0x34]". Now, hit the <Ctrl>+<Enter> key combination
; to finish input. Then, hit the <Esc> key to close
; the local-variables window. Now, each reference to var_34
; will be accompanied by the "char s[0x34]" comment.


push    ecx       ; char *
; The pointer to the local buffer for var_38
; is passed to the ltoa function.

mov     edx, [ebp+var_4]
; The value of the var_4 local variable is loaded into EDX.

push    edx       ; __int32
; The value of the var_38 local variable is passed
; to the ltoa function. Using the prototype of this function,
; IDA already has determined that the variable type is int.
; Press the <Ctrl>+<K> key combination, and comment var_4.

call    __ltoa
add     esp, 0Ch
; The contents of var_4 are converted to a hexadecimal number
; represented as a string. The result is placed
; in the local buffer for var_38.

lea     eax, [ebp+var_38]    ; char s[0x34]
; The pointer to the local buffer for var_34 is loaded into EAX.

push    eax
```

```
      ; The pointer to var_34 is passed to the printf function,
      ; which displays the contents on the screen.

      mov     ecx, [ebp+var_4]
      ; The value of the var_4 local variable is loaded into ECX.

      push    ecx
      ; The value of the var_4 local variable is passed to printf.

      push    offset aXS    ; "%x == %s == "
      call    _printf
      add     esp, 0Ch

      mov     eax, [ebp+var_4]
      ; The value of the var_4 local variable is returned into EAX.

      mov     esp, ebp
      ; Memory occupied by local variables is released.

      pop     ebp
      ; The former value of EBP is restored.

      retn
MyFunc          endp


main            proc near            ; CODE XREF: start+AF↓p

var_C           = dword ptr -0Ch
var_8           = dword ptr -8
var_4           = dword ptr -4

      push    ebp
      mov     ebp, esp
      ; The stack frame is opened.

      sub     esp, 0Ch
      ; The local variables are allocated 0xC bytes of memory.

      mov     [ebp+var_4], 666h
```

```
; The var_4 local variable is initialized and assigned the value 0x666.


mov     [ebp+var_8], 777h
; The var_8 local variable is initialized and assigned the value 0x777.
; Note that the order of local variables in the memory
; is the reverse of the order in which they were referenced -
; not declared. The variables are not always
; allocated in this order; this depends on the compiler,
; which is why it should never be relied on.


mov     eax, [ebp+var_8]
; The value of var_8 is copied to the EAX register.


push    eax
; The value of var_8 is passed to the MyFunc function.


mov     ecx, [ebp+var_4]
; The value of var_4 is copied to the ECX register.


push    ecx
; The value of var_4 is passed to the MyFunc function.


call    MyFunc
add     esp, 8
; The MyFunc function is called.


mov     [ebp+var_C], eax
; The returned value is copied to the var_C local variable.


lea     edx, [ebp+var_C]
; The pointer to the var_C local variable is loaded into EDX.


push    edx
; The pointer to var_C is passed to the printf function.


push    offset asc_406040 ; "%x\n"
call    _printf
add     esp, 8


xor     eax, eax
```

```
                ; Zero is returned.

        mov     esp, ebp
                ; Memory occupied by local variables is released.


        pop     ebp
                ; The stack frame is closed.


        retn
main            endp
```

That was rather easy, wasn't it? The disassembled code of this example compiled using Borland C++ 5.0 will be more difficult.

Listing 127. The Disassembled Code for Identifying Local Variables Compiled Using Borland C++ 5.0

```
MyFunc          proc near           ; CODE XREF: _main+14↓p

var_34          = byte ptr -34h
; Note that there is one local variable, although as many as three
; were declared! Where are the others? This compiler
; has placed them into the registers, rather than onto the stack,
; to speed up the process of addressing them.
; (See the "Register
; and Temporary Variables" section for more details.)

        push    ebp
        mov     ebp, esp
                ; The stack frame is opened.

        add     esp, 0FFFFFFCC
                ; After this allocation, press <-> in IDA to convert the number
                ; into the signed one, which gives -34. Therefore, 0x34 bytes
                ; were allocated for local variables. Note that memory
                ; was allocated using ADD, not SUB!

        push    ebx
                ; Does this store EBX on the stack, or does it allocate memory
```

```
; for local variables? Because memory previously was allocated
; using ADD, PUSH must save the register onto the stack.

lea    ebx, [edx+eax]
; This tricky addition gives the sum of EDX and EAX.
; Because EDX and EAX were not initialized explicitly,
; the arguments were passed via them.
; (See the "Function Arguments" section.)

push   10h
; A radix of the choosen numeration system
; is passed to the ltoa function.

lea    eax, [ebp+var_34]
; The pointer to the local buffer for var_34 is loaded into EAX.

push   eax
; The pointer to the buffer for writing the result
; is passed to the ltoa function.

push   ebx
; The sum of two arguments (not the pointer)
; is passed to the MyFunc function.

call   _ltoa
add    esp, 0Ch

lea    edx, [ebp+var_34]
; The pointer to the local buffer for var_34 is loaded into EDX.

push   edx
; The pointer to the local buffer for var_34,
; which contains the sum of MyFunc's arguments converted
; into a string, is passed to the printf function.

push   ebx
; The sum of the arguments is passed to the MyFunc function.

push   offset aXS          ; format
```

```
        call    _printf
        add     esp, 0Ch

        mov     eax, ebx
        ; The sum of the arguments is returned into EAX.

        pop     ebx
        ; EBX is popped off the stack, restoring its former state.

        mov     esp, ebp
        ; Memory occupied by local variables is released.

        pop     ebp
        ; The stack frame is closed.

        retn
MyFunc          endp

; int __cdecl main(int argc, const char **argv, const char *envp)
_main           proc near         ; DATA XREF: DATA:00407044↓o

var_4           = dword ptr -4
; IDA has recognized at least one local variable,
; which should be noted.

argc            = dword ptr 8
argv            = dword ptr 0Ch
envp            = dword ptr 10h

        push    ebp
        mov     ebp, esp
        ; The stack frame is opened.

        push    ecx
        push    ebx
        push    esi
        ; The registers are saved on the stack.

        mov     esi, 777h
```

```asm
; The value 0x777 is placed into the ESI register.

mov     ebx, 666h
; The value 0x666 is placed into the EBX register.
mov     edx, esi
mov     eax, ebx
; The arguments are passed to MyFunc via the registers.
call    MyFunc

; The MyFunc function is called.

mov     [ebp+var_4], eax
; The result returned by MyFunc is copied to the var_4 local
; variable. Wait! Which local variable? How has memory
; been allocated for it? Only one of the PUSH instructions
; could have done this. But which one? Look at the offset
; of the variable: It resides 4 bytes higher than EBP,
; and its memory area is occupied by the contents of
; the register saved by the first PUSH instruction, which
; came after the stack frame was opened. (The second PUSH places
; the value of the register at an offset of -8, and so on.)
; The first instruction was PUSH ECX. Therefore, this
; does not save the register on the stack; it allocates
; memory for a local variable. Since the var_8 and var_C
; local variables do not seem to have been accessed,
; the PUSH EBX and PUSH ESI instructions likely
; save the registers.

lea     ecx, [ebp+var_4]
; The pointer to the var_4 local variable is loaded into ECX.

push    ecx
; The pointer to var_4 is passed to the printf function.

push    offset asc_407081 ; format
call    _printf
add     esp, 8

xor     eax, eax
```

```
            ; Zero is returned into EAX.

            pop    esi
            pop    ebx
            ; The values of the ESI and EBX registers are restored.

            pop    ecx
            ; Memory allocated for the var_4 local variable is released.

            pop    ebp
            ; The stack frame is closed.

            retn

_main       endp
```

Frame Pointer Omission (FPO). The EBP register traditionally is used to address local variables. As there are only *seven* general-purpose registers, it is undesirable to designate one of them permanently for addressing local variables. Is there another, more elegant solution?

Consideration of this problem leads to the conclusion that a dedicated register for addressing local variables is not necessary; this goal can be reached (with some tricks) by using one ESP — the stack-pointer register.

The only problem is the *floating stack frame*. After allocating memory for local variables, ESP may point to the top of the allocated area. In this case, the buff variable (Fig. 17) will appear at the ESP+0xC address. As soon as something is placed onto the stack (an argument of the calling function, or the register contents for temporary storage), the frame will "move," and buff will appear at the ESP+0x10 address, not at ESP+0xC!

Contemporary compilers are capable of addressing local variables via ESP, and dynamically tracing the ESP value (unless tricky assembler inserts in the function's body unpredictably modify the ESP value).

This complicates an analysis of the code. After pointing to any part of the code, it is impossible to determine which local variable is being addressed; the whole function must be thoroughly worked out, and the ESP value must be watched closely. (Often, massive errors will nullify all preceding work.) Fortunately, the IDA disassembler knows how to treat such variables. Nevertheless, hackers never rely entirely on automatics; rather, they try to understand how things work.

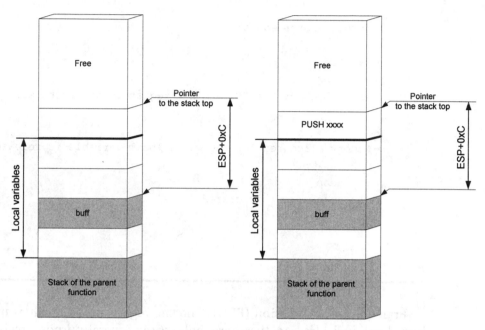

Fig. 17. Addressing local variables via the ESP register
forms a floating stack frame

Let's turn to our good old file `simple.c` and compile it with the `/O2` key, which optimizes performance by having the compiler use all registers and address local variables via `ESP`.

```
>cl sample.c /O2
    00401000: 83 EC 64            sub         esp,64h
```

Memory is allocated for local variables. Note that there are no instructions such as PUSH EBP or MOV EBP, ESP!

```
    00401003: A0 00 69 40 00      mov         al, [00406900] ; mov al,0
    00401008: 53                  push        ebx
    00401009: 55                  push        ebp
    0040100A: 56                  push        esi
    0040100B: 57                  push        edi
```

The registers are saved.

```
    0040100C: 88 44 24 10         mov         byte ptr [esp+10h],al
```

The zero value is placed into the [ESP+0x10] variable. (Let's call it `buff`.)

```
    00401010: B9 18 00 00 00      mov         ecx, 18h
```

```
00401015: 33 C0              xor        eax, eax
00401017: 8D 7C 24 11        lea        edi, [esp+11h]
```

EDI is set to point to the local variable [ESP+0x11] (an uninitialized tail of `buff`).

```
0040101B: 68 60 60 40 00     push       406060h ; "Enter password"
```

The offset of the "Enter password" string is placed onto the stack. Note that the ESP register creeps 4 bytes upward.

```
00401020: F3 AB              rep stos   dword ptr [edi]
00401022: 66 AB              stos       word ptr [edi]
00401024: 33 ED              xor        ebp, ebp
00401026: AA                 stos       byte ptr [edi]
```

The buffer is zeroed.

```
00401027: E8 F4 01 00 00     call       00401220
```

The "Enter password" string is displayed on the screen. Note that the arguments have not been popped off the stack!

```
0040102C: 68 70 60 40 00     push       406070h
```

The offset of the pointer to the stdin pointer is placed onto the stack. Note that ESP creeps another 4 bytes upward.

```
00401031: 8D 4C 24 18        lea        ecx, [esp+18h]
```

The pointer to the [ESP+0x18] variable is loaded into ECX. Is this just another buffer? No; this is the [ESP+0x10] variable, which has changed its appearance because ESP has been modified. Subtracting 8 bytes (which ESP crept upward) from 0x18 gives 0x10, our old acquaintance [ESP+0x10]. (Should old acquaintance be forgot?)

Analyzing a procedure that contains a dozen lines is fairly straightforward, but a program of a million lines would be enough to drive anyone mad. The alternative is to use IDA. Consider the following example:

```
.text:00401000 main           proc near        ; CODE XREF: start+AF↓p
.text:00401000
.text:00401000 var_64        = byte ptr -64h
.text:00401000 var_63        = byte ptr -63h
```

IDA revealed two local variables located at the offsets 63 and 64, relative to the stack frame; that's why they were given the names var_63 and var_64.

```
.text:00401000                sub        esp, 64h
.text:00401003                mov        al, byte_0_406900
```

```
.text:00401008                     push    ebx
.text:00401009                     push    ebp
.text:0040100A                     push    esi
.text:0040100B                     push    edi
.text:0040100C                     mov     [esp+74h+var_64], al
```

IDA automatically combined the local variable name and its offset in the stack frame.

```
.text:00401010                     mov     ecx, 18h
.text:00401015                     xor     eax, eax
.text:00401017                     lea     edi, [esp+74h+var_63]
```

IDA failed to recognize the initialization of the first byte of the buffer and mistook it for a separate variable. Only a human can figure out how many variables are used here.

```
.text:0040101B                     push    offset aEnterPassword ; "Enter password:"
.text:00401020                     repe    stosd
.text:00401022                     stosw
.text:00401024                     xor     ebp, ebp
.text:00401026                     stosb
.text:00401027                     call    sub_0_401220
.text:0040102C                     push    offset off_0_406070
.text:00401031                     lea     ecx, [esp+7Ch+var_64]
```

Note that IDA correctly recognized that the var_64 variable was accessed, even though its offset, 0x7C, differs from 0x64.

Register and Temporary Variables

In an attempt to minimize the number of memory access operations, optimizing compilers place the most intensively used local variables into general-purpose registers, saving them on the stack only in extreme cases (and, ideally, never).

What kind of difficulties does this create during analysis? First, it introduces a *context dependence* into the code. In an instruction such as MOV EAX, [EBP+var_10], the contents of the var_10 variable are being copied to the EAX register. The variable type can be found by searching the function body for every occurrence of var_10, which may indicate the purpose of the variable.

This trick, however, will not work with register variables. Suppose that we encountered the MOV EAX, ESI instruction and want to trace all references to the variable of the ESI register. Searching the function body for the substring "ESI" gives nothing or, even worse, produces a set of false hits. What can be done?

One register — in this case, ESI — may be used to store many *different* variables temporarily. There are only seven general-purpose registers; EBP is assigned to the stack frame, and EAX and EDX are used for the returned value of the function. Therefore, only four registers are available to store local variables. There are even fewer free registers when programs written in C are executed — one of these four registers is used as the pointer to the virtual table, and another is the pointer to an instance of this. Pressing ahead with just two registers is not really possible; there are dozens of local variables in a typical function. This is why the compiler uses registers as a cache. Cases of each local variable residing in a register are exceptional; variables often are scattered chaotically around the registers, sometimes stored on the stack, and frequently popped off into a different register (rather than the one in which the contents were stored).

No contemporary disassembler (including IDA) is capable of tracing the "migration" of register variables; this operation has to be done manually. It is simple, although tiresome, to determine the contents of a particular register at any point in the program: Just work through the program mentally from startup to the point in question, tracing all the passing operations. It is more difficult to find out *how many* local variables are stored in a particular register. When a large number of variables are mapped on a small number of registers, it becomes impossible to reconstruct the map unambiguously. For example, the programmer declares the a variable, and the compiler places it into the x register. Later, the programmer declares the b variable. If the a variable is no longer used (as is often the case), the compiler may place the b variable into the x register without worrying about saving the value of a. As a result, one variable is lost. At first glance, there are no problems; losing one variable is not a disaster. But if a was sufficient, why has the programmer introduced b? If the a and b variables are of the same type, no problems arise; if they are different, the analysis of the program becomes extremely complicated.

Let's look at techniques for identifying register variables. Many hacker manuals assert that register variables differ from other variables in that they never deal with memory. This is incorrect. Register variables can be stored on the stack temporarily by the PUSH instruction and restored by the POP instruction. In some ways, a variable of this sort ceases to be a register variable; nevertheless, it does not become a stack variable. To avoid defining hundreds of variable classes, let's agree that the register variable is a variable contained in the general-purpose register that may be stored on the stack, but always at its *top*; it can never be stored in the stack frame. In other words, register variables are never addressed via EBP. If the variable is addressed via EBP, it "lives" in the stack frame and is a stack variable. Is this correct? No; If the value of the b stack variable is assigned to the a register variable, the compiler will generate code similar to the following: MOV REG, [EBP-xxx]. Accordingly, the assignment of the value of the register variable to the stack variable will look like this: MOV [EBP-xxx],

REG. Despite reference to the stack frame, the REG variable remains a register variable. Consider the following code:

Listing 128. Distinguishing Register Variables from Temporary Variables

```
...
mov [ebp-0x4], 0x666
mov esi, [ebp-0x4]
mov [ebp-0x8], esi
mov esi, 0x777
sub esi, [ebp-0x8]
mov [ebp-0xc], esi
...
```

This code can be interpreted in two ways: Either there is an ESI register variable (the source code shown in the left part of Listing 129), or the ESI register[i] is being used as a temporary variable for passing data (the source code shown in the right part of Listing 129).

Listing 129. The Source Code When ESI Is a Register Variable (Left) and a Temporary Variable (Right)

```
int var_4=0x66;            int var_4=0x666;
int var_8=var_4;           register ESI = var_4;
int vac_C=0x777 — var_8    int var_8=ESI;
                           ESI=0x777-var_8;
                           int var_C = ESI
```

Although the algorithms of the listings are identical, the code on the left is substantially more illustrative than the code on the right. The main objective of disassembling is to reconstruct the *algorithm* of a program, not to reproduce the source

---

[i] In the C/C++ languages, the register keyword is intended for compulsory allocation of variables in registers. However, most compilers ignore the recommendations of programmers and allocate variables where it seems convenient to the compiler. Compiler developers argue that the compiler knows how to construct the most effective code, so programmers don't need help it. This reminds me of a passenger who says: "I need to go to the airport," and the taxi driver who ignores this instructions and heads to another place.

Programmers should work on a compiler, but we should not to fight it! The compiler's unwillingness to allocate a variable in the register is understandable, but the compiler should at least stop the compilation process and send a warning.

code of a program. It does not matter whether ESI represents a register or a temporary variable. The main thing is that everything works smoothly. In general, you should choose the most understandable interpretation if there are several versions.

Before examining temporary variables in detail, let's summarize our knowledge of register variables by analyzing the following example:

Listing 130. Identifying Register Variables

```
main()
{
        int a=0x666;
        int b=0x777;
        int c;
        c=a+b;
        printf("%x + %x = %x\n", a, b, c);
        c = b - a;
        printf("%x — %x = %x\n", a, b, c);
}
```

The disassembled code of this example, compiled using Borland C++ 5.x, gives the following result:

Listing 131. The Disassembled Code for Identifying Register Variables

```
; int __cdecl main(int argc, const char **argv, const char *envp)
_main           proc near               ; DATA XREF: DATA:00407044↓o

argc            = dword ptr 8
argv            = dword ptr 0Ch
envp            = dword ptr 10h
; Note that no stack variable has been recognized by IDA,
; although several were declared in the program. It seems likely
; that the compiler has allocated them in registers.

        push    ebp
        mov     ebp, esp
        ; The stack frame is opened.
```

```
push    ebx
push    esi
; What happened here? Were the registers saved
; on the stack, or was memory allocated for the stack
; variables? Since no stack has been recognized by IDA,
; this code likely saved the registers.

mov     ebx, 666h
; The register is initialized. Compare this with Listing 126
; (in the "Local Stack Variables" section),
; which contained the following line:
; mov [ebp+var_4], 666h
; Hence, EBX is likely a register variable.
; The variable's existence can be proven: Had the
; value 0x666 been passed directly to the function — for example,
; printf("%x %x %x\n", 0x666) — the compiler would have placed
; the PUSH 0x666 instruction into the code.
; This did not occur; therefore, the value 0x666 is passed via
; the variable. Thus, the reconstructed source code should contain:
; 1. int a=0x666

mov     esi, 777h
; Similarly, ESI likely represents a register variable:
; 2. int b=0x777

lea     eax, [esi+ebx]
; The sum of ESI and EBX is loaded into EAX.
; EAX is not a pointer; this is just a tricky addition.

push    eax
; The sum of the ESI and EBX register variables is passed to the
; printf function. However, the contents of EAX are interesting:
; They could be an independent variable, or the sum
; of the a and b variables, which is passed
; to the printf function directly.
; For better readability, let's choose the latter:
```

```
; 3. printf (,,,, a+b)

push    esi
; The register variable ESI, denoted as b
; in the preceding code, is passed to the printf function.
; 3. printf(,,, b, a+b)

push    ebx
; The register variable EBX, denoted as a
; in the preceding code, is passed to the printf function.
; 3. printf(,, a, b, a+b)

push    offset aXXX          ; "%x + %x = %x"
; The pointer to the format-specification string
; is passed to the printf function. This string indicates
; that all three variables are of the int type.
; 3. printf("%x + %x = %x", a, b, a+b)

call    _printf
add     esp, 10h

mov     eax, esi
; The register variable, previously denoted as b,
; is copied to EAX.
; 4. int c=b

sub     eax, ebx
; The value of the variable contained in EBX (a) is subtracted
; from the variable contained in the EAX register (c).
; 5. c=c-a

push    eax
; The difference between the variables contained
; in EAX and EBX is passed to the printf function.
; Because this difference between the b and a values was passed
; directly, it is clear that the c variable is unnecessary.
; Line 5 can be omitted (and, thus, a rollback can be peformed).
; Instead of line 4, the following can be inserted:
; 4. printf(,,,, b-a)

push    esi
```

```
; The value of the variable in the ESI register (b)
; is passed to the printf function.
; 4. printf(,,, b, b-a)

push    ebx
; The value of the variable in the EBX register (a)
; is passed to the printf function.
; 4. printf(,, a, b, b-a)

push    offset aXXX_0        ; "%x + %x = %x"
; The pointer to the format-specification string is passed to
; the printf function. This string indicates that all three
; variables are of the int type.
; 4. printf("%x + %x = %x", a, b, b-a)

call    _printf
add     esp, 10h

xor     eax, eax
; The zero value is returned into the EAX register.
; return 0

pop     esi
pop     ebx
; The registers are restored.

pop     ebp
; The stack frame is closed.

retn
; The reconstructed code should look as follows:
; 1. int a=0x666
; 2. int b=0x777
; 3. printf("%x + %x = %x", a, b, a + b)
; 4. printf("%x + %x = %x", a, b, b — a)
;
; Comparing the result with the original soure code shows that
; removing the c variable introduced a slight mistake.
; This did not ruined the work. On the contrary,
; it improved the order of the listing, making it easier
```

```
; to understand. To stick more closely to the assembler code,
; the c variable can be reintroduced. Doing this
; has the benefit of removing the rollback (i.e.,
; already reconstructed lines need not be rewritten
; to remove a superfluous variable).


_main          endp
```

Temporary variables. Here, temporary variables will be defined as variables embedded into the code of a program by the compiler. Why are they necessary? Consider the following example: int b=a. If a and b are stack variables, assigning a value directly to them is impossible because the "memory-memory" addressing mode is not available in 80x86 microprocessors. Therefore, the operation must be carried out in two stages: memory to register, followed by register to memory. Actually, the compiler generates the following code:

```
register int tmp=a;          mov eax, [ebp+var_4]
int b=tmp;                   mov [ebp+var_8], eax
```

Here, tmp is a temporary variable created to execute the operation b=a, then eliminated as superfluous.

Compilers (especially optimizing ones) tend to allocate temporary variables in registers; they only push temporary variables onto the stack in extreme cases. Mechanisms for allocating memory and the techniques for reading and writing temporary variables vary.

Typically, compilers react to an acute lack of registers by saving variables on the stack. Most often, integer variables are showered on the top of the stack by the PUSH instruction, then pulled from there by the POP instruction. It is possible to assert with confidence that an integer temporary variable is being dealt with if a program's code contains this sort of "push-pop" situation – not, however, saving the contents of the initialized register in a function's stack argument. (See the "*Function Arguments*" section.) In most cases, the allocation of memory for floating-point variables and the initialization of these variables occur separately. This is because an instruction that allows the compiler to transfer data from the top of the coprocessor stack to the top of the CPU stack doesn't exist; the operation must be carried out manually. First, the stack-top pointer (in the ESP register) is "lifted" slightly (usually by the SUB ESP, xxx instruction). Then, the floating-point value is written in the allocated memory (usually, FSTP [ESP]). Finally, when the temporary variable becomes unnecessary, it is deleted from the stack by the ADD ESP, xxx instruction or something similar (such as SUB, ESP, -xxx).

Advanced compilers (such as Microsoft Visual C++) are capable of allocating variables in the arguments that remain on the top of the stack after the most recently called function completes execution. This trick applies to cdecl functions, but not to stdcall functions; the latter clear arguments from the stack independently. (See the "*Function Arguments*" section for more details.) This type of trick appeared during the analysis of the mechanism of returning values by functions (in the "*Values Returned by Functions*" section).

Temporary variables larger than 8 bytes (strings, arrays, structures, objects) almost always are allocated on the stack. They are distinguished from other types by their initialization mechanism: Instead of the traditional MOV, one of the cyclic move instructions, such as MOVSx, is used. If necessary, it is preceded by the REP recurrence prefix (Microsoft Visual C++, Borland C++). Alternatively, several MOVSx instructions can be used consecutively (Watcom C).

The mechanism of allocating memory for temporary variables is almost identical to the mechanism of allocating memory for stack local variables. Nevertheless, correct identification is not a problem. First, memory is allocated for stack variables immediately after the stack frame is opened. For temporary variables, memory allocation takes place at any point of the function. Second, temporary variables are addressed not via the stack-frame pointer, but via the pointer to the stack top.

Table 15. The Basic Mechanisms for Handling Temporary Variables

Action	Methods		
	1st	2nd	3rd
Allocating memory	PUSH	SUB ESP, xxx	Use stack arguments[i]
Releasing memory	POP	ADD ESP, xxx	
Writing a variable	PUSH	MOV [ESP+xxx],	Move instruction
Reading a variable	POP	MOV, [ESP+xxx]	Pass to the called function

[i] for cdecl only.

Different compilers create temporary variables in different instances. However, it is possible to identify two instances in which the creation of temporary variables is unavoidable: *when performing assignment, addition, or multiplication operations*, and *when an argument of a function or a part of an expression is another function*. Let's consider each case in more detail.

Creating temporary variables when moving data or computing expressions. As previously mentioned, 80x86 microprocessors do not support the direct transfer of data from memory to memory. Therefore, assigning one variable's value to another variable requires a temporary register variable (if there are no other register variables).

Computing expressions (especially complex ones) requires temporary variables to store intermediate results. How many temporary variables are required to compute the following expression?

```
int a=0x1; int b=0x2;
int c = 1/((1-a)/(1-b));
```

Let's begin from the parentheses, and rewrite the expression in the following way: `int tmp_d = 1; tmp_d = tmp_d-a;` and `int tmp_e = 1; tmp_e=tmp_e-b;` then `int tmp_f = tmp_d/tmp_e;` and, finally, `tmp_j = 1; c = tmp_j/tmp_f.` It turns out that there are four temporary variables. This seems a little excessive; is it possible to write it in a shorter way?

```
int tmp_d = 1; tmp_d=tmp_d-a;   // (1-a);
int tmp_e=1; tmp_e=tmp_e-b;     // (1-b);
tmp_d=tmp_d/tmp_e;     // (1-a)/(1-b);
tmp_e=1; tmp_e=tmp_e/tmp_d;
```

We can manage with two temporary variables. What if the expression were more complex, employing ten pairs of parentheses, rather than three: How many temporary variables would that require?

There is no need to count: No matter how complex the expression is, two temporary variables are sufficient. If the parentheses are removed, we can manage with one variable, although excessive computation will be required. (This question will be considered in more detail in the "*Mathematical Operators*" section.) Now, let's see the results of compilation.

Listing 132. The Disassembled Code for Computing Complex Expressions

---

```
    mov     [ebp+var_4], 1
    mov     [ebp+var_8], 2
    mov     [ebp+var_C], 3
    ; The local variables are initialized.

    mov     eax, 1
    ; Here, the first variable is introduced.
    ; An intermediate value is placed into it, since the SUB
    ; instruction always places the result of computation
    ; at the location of the minuend because of architectural
```

```
; peculiarities of the 80x86 microprocessors.
; The minuend cannot be a direct value;
; therefore, a temporary variable must be introduced.

sub    eax, [ebp+var_4]
; tEAX := 1 — var_4
; The computed value (1-a).

mov    ecx, 1
; Yet another temporary variable is introduced
; because EAX is already occupied.

sub    ecx, [ebp+var_8]
; tECX := 1 - var_8
; The computed value (1-b) is stored in the ECX register.

cdq
; The double word that resides in EAX is converted into
; a quad word and placed into EDX:EAX.
; (The idiv machine instruction always expects to see the
; dividend in these registers.)

idiv   ecx
; The computed value (1-a) is divided by (1-b), and the quotient
; is placed into tEAX. Inevitably, the old value of the temporary
; variable has been overwritten. This does not create a problem,
; because it is not needed for further computation.

mov    ecx, eax
; The value (1-a)/(1-b) is copied to the ECX register.
; This is a new temporary variable, t2ECX, located in the same
; register. (The old contents of ECX are no longer needed.)
; The 2 index is given after the t prefix to show
; that t2ECX is not the same as tECX, even though
; these temporary variables are stored in the same register.

mov    eax, 1
; The immediate value 1 is placed into EAX.
; This is yet another temporary variable: t2EAX.
```

```
cdq
; EDX is zeroed.


idiv    ecx
; The value 1 is divided by ((1-a)/(1-b)).
; The quotient is placed into EAX.


mov     [ebp+var_10], eax
; c := 1 / ((1-a) / (1-b))
; Thus, only four temporary variables and two general-purpose
; registers were required to compute this expression.
```

Creating temporary variables to store a value returned by a function and the results of computing expressions. Most high-level languages (including C/C++) allow functions and expressions to be used as immediate arguments, such as myfunc (a + b, myfunc_2 (c)). Prior to calling myfunc, the compiler should compute the value of the expression a + b. This is straightforward, but there is a problem: Where should the result of addition be written? Let's see how the compiler solves this.

Listing 133. The Disassembled Code Illustrating How the Complier Stores the Results of Computing Expressions and Values Returned by Functions

```
mov     eax, [ebp+var_C]
; A temporary variable, tEAX, is created. The value
; of the var_C local variable is copied into it.


push    eax
; The tEAX temporary variable is stored on the stack.
; The value of the var_C local variable is passed as an argument
; to the myfunc function. (Theoretically, the var_C local
; variable could be passed directly to the PUSH [ebp+var_4]
; function without using temporary variables.)


call    myfunc
add     esp, 4
; The value of the myfunc function is returned into the EAX register.
```

```
; This can be regarded as a kind of temporary variable.

push    eax
; The results returned by the myfunc function
; are passed to the myfunc_2 function.

mov     ecx, [ebp+var_4]
; The value of the var_4 local variable is copied into ECX.
; ECX is yet another temporary variable. However, it is
; unclear why the compiler did not use the EAX register.
; The previous temporary variable is no longer needed;
; therefore, the EAX register that it occupied has become free.

add     ecx, [ebp+var_8]
; ECX := var_4 + var_8

push    ecx
; The sum of the two local variables
; is passed to the myfunc_2 function.

call    _myfunc_2
```

The scope of temporary variables. Temporary variables are, to a certain extent, *local variables.* In most cases, their scope is limited to several lines of code; outside of this context, temporary variables are meaningless. In general, a temporary variable only obscures the code (myfunc(a+b) is much shorter and more intelligible than int tmp=a+b; myfunc (tmp)). Therefore, to avoid cluttering the disassembler listing, temporary variables should not be used in comments; it is better to substitute actual values for them. It is a good idea to denote temporary variables with a prefix, for example tmp_ (or t, for those who love brevity).

Listing 134. An Example of Good Comment Style

```
mov eax, [ebp+var_4]        ; var_8 := var_4
                            ; ^ tEAX := var_4
add eax, [ebp+var_8],       ; ^ tEAX += var_8

push eax                    ; MyFunc(var_4 + var_8)
call MyFunc
```

Global Variables

Tackling a program stuffed with global variables is probably the worst task for hackers. Instead of a tree with a strict hierarchy, the program components are interlaced. To solve one algorithm, the entire listing must be combed out and searched for cross-references. No disassembler, not even IDA, is capable of reconstructing cross-references perfectly.

Identifying global variables is much easier than identifying any other construction in high-level languages. Global variables give themselves away immediately by addressing memory directly. In other words, references to them look like MOV EAX, **[401066]**, where 0x401066 is just the address of the global variable.

It is more difficult to understand the purpose of this variable and its content at a certain moment. Unlike local variables, global variables are *context dependent*. Each local variable is initialized by its parent function; it is not dependent on the functions called before it. On the contrary, a global variable can be modified by anyone — its value is not defined at any point of the program. To work it out, it is necessary to analyze all the functions that handle it and to reconstruct the order in which they were called. This question will be considered in more detail further on; now, let's examine how to reconstruct cross-references.

Reconstructing cross-references. In most cases, IDA copes well with cross-reference reconstruction, and manual reconstruction becomes unnecessary. However, even IDA makes mistakes occasionally, and not everyone has this disassembler at hand. Therefore, you should learn to deal with global variables manually.

Tracking references to global variables by searching for their offsets in the code (data) segment. Addressing global variables directly facilitates the search for the machine instructions that handle them. Consider the construction MOV EAX, **[0x41B904]**. Assembling it gives A1 **04 B9 41 00**. The offset of a global variable is written "as is" (while observing the reverse byte order: A higher byte is placed at a greater address, and a lower one is set at a smaller address).

A simple context search will reveal all references to the global variable of interest. You can find its offset, rewrite it from right to left and... get a load of garbage along with the useful information. Every number that coincides with the offset of a global variable is not a pointer to it. In addition, 04 B9 41 00 returns the following:

```
83EC04            sub        esp,004
B941000000        mov        ecx,000000041
```

The mistake is obvious: The value that we have found is not an operand of the instruction. Moreover, it spans two instructions! Rejecting all occurrences that cross instruction boundaries immediately removes a significant part of the garbage. The problem is how to determine the instruction boundaries; it is impossible to say anything about the instruction if you only have a part of it.

Consider the following construction: 8D **81 04 B9** 41 00 00. Ignoring the trailing zero, this sequence can be interpreted as LEA EAX, [ECX+0x41B904]. If, however, 0x8D belongs to the "tail" of the previous instruction, the following instruction will be ADD D, [ECX][EDI]*4, 000000041. There even may be several instructions here.

The most reliable way to determine the boundaries of machine instructions is to disassemble with tracing; unfortunately, this operation demands lots of resources, and not every disassembler is capable of tracing the code. Therefore, another method is required.

Machine code can be represented figuratively as typewritten text printed without spaces. An attempt to read from a random position likely will start in the middle of a word, and won't produce anything intelligible. The first several syllables may form an intelligent word (or even two), but continuous nonsense will appear further on.

The differences between constants and pointers, or salvaging the remaining garbage. At last, we have removed all the false hits. The heap of garbage has diminished appreciably, but artifacts such as PUSH 0x401010 keep turning up. What is 0x401010 — a constant or an offset? It could be either; it is impossible to tell until we reach the code that handles it. If 0x401010 is addressed by the handling code as a value, it is a constant; if it is addressed by reference, it is a pointer. (Here, it is an offset.)

This problem will be discussed in detail in the "*Constants and Offsets*" section. For now, I would like to note — with great relief — that the minimal address for loading a file in Windows 9*x* is 0x400000, and there are few constants expressed by such a large number.

▶ *Note*

The minimal address for loading a file in Windows NT is 0x10000. However, for a program to work successfully under both Windows NT and Windows 9*x*, loading should start from an address no lower than 0x400000.

The trials and tribulations of 16-bit mode. It is not as simple to distinguish a constant from a pointer in 16-bit mode as it is in 32-bit mode. In 16-bit mode, one or more segments of 0x10000 bytes are allocated for data. Admissible values of offsets are confined to a narrow range — 0x0 to 0xFFFF — and most variables have offsets that are very small and visually indistinguishable from constants.

Another problem is that one segment often cannot accommodate all the data; therefore, several segments must be initialized. Two segments are tolerable: One is addressed via the DS register, the other is addressed via ES, and no difficulties arise in determining which variable points to which segment. For example, if all references to the x global variable, located in the base segment at the 0x666 offset, are of interest, all instructions such as MOV AX, ES: [0x666] can be rejected at once. In this case, the base segment is addressed via DS (by default), and this segment refers to ES. However, addressing also may occur in two stages, such as MOV BX, 0x666/xxx---xxx/MOV AX,ES:[BX]. Having seen MOV BX, 0x666, it will be impossible to determine a segment, and even to tell whether this is an offset. Nevertheless, this does not overcomplicate the analysis.

The situation becomes worse if there are a dozen data segments in a program. (It is conceivable that 640 KB of static memory could be required.) No number of segment registers will be sufficient for this; they will have to be reassigned many times. To figure out which segment is being addressed, the value of the segment register must be determined. The simplest way to do this is to scroll the disassembler screen slightly upward and look for the initialization of the segment register in question. Bear in mind that initialization often is done by POP, rather than by the MOV segREG, REG instruction. Note that PUSH ES/POP DS is equivalent to MOV DS, ES. Unfortunately, there is no equivalent of the MOV segREG, segREG instruction in the language of the 80x86 microprocessors. There is no MOV segREG, CONST instruction either, which is why it must be emulated manually, or as follows: MOV AX, 0x666/MOV ES, AX. Another possible method is the following: PUSH 0x666/POP ES.

Thankfully, 16-bit mode almost has become a thing of the past, and its problems have been buried by the sands of time. Programmers and hackers breathed a sigh of relief after the transition to 32-bit mode.

Addressing global variables indirectly. Often, a claim is made that global variables are *always* addressed directly. However, the programmer may address a variable as desired in the inserts written in the assembler language. The situation is far from simple. If a global variable is passed by reference to a function (there is no reason by which a programmer cannot pass a global variable by reference), it will be addressed indirectly, via a pointer. At this point, an objection may be raised: Why should a global variable be passed explicitly to a function? Surely, any function can address a global variable without passing it. This is true, but only if the function knows about this beforehand. Suppose that the xchg function swaps its arguments, and two global variables urgently need to be swapped. The xchg function can access all global variables, but it does not know which of them to change, or whether doing so is necessary. This is why global variables sometimes must be explicitly passed as arguments to functions. This also means that it is impossible to find all the references to global variables by using a simple context search. IDA Pro will not find them either; to do so, it would need a full-featured processor emulator, or at least one capable of emulating its basic instructions — as can be seen in the following example.

Listing 135. Passing Global Variables Explicitly

```
#include <stdio.h>

int a; int b;  // Global variables a and b

xchg(int *a, int *b)
// The function that swaps the values of the arguments
{
        int c; c=*a; *b=*a; *b=c;
        // The arguments are addressed indirectly,
        // using a pointer. If the arguments
        // of the function are global variables,
        // they will be addressed indirectly.
}

main()
{

        a=0x666; b=0x777; // The global variables are addressed directly.

        xchg(&a, &b);    // The global variables are passed by reference.
}
```

The disassembled code of this example, compiled using Microsoft Visual C++, will look as follows:

Listing 136. The Disassembled Code for Passing Global Variables Explicitly

```
main            proc near           ; CODE XREF: start+AF↓p
        push    ebp
        mov     ebp, esp
```

```
        ; The stack frame is opened.

        mov     dword_405428, 666h
        ; The dword_405428 global variable is initialized.
        ; The indirect addressing indicates that this is
        ; a global variable.

        mov     dword_40542C, 777h
        ; The dword_40542C global variable is initialized.

        push    offset dword_40542C
        ; Note that this passes the offset of the dword_40542C global
        ; variable to the function as an argument (i.e., it is passed
        ; by reference). This means that the function will address the
        ; variable indirectly — via the pointer — in the same way as
        ; it addresses local variables.

        push    offset dword_405428
        ; The offset of the dword_405428 global variable
        ; is passed to the function.

        call    xchg
        add     esp, 8

        pop     ebp
        retn
main            endp

xchg            proc near          ; CODE XREF: main+21↑p

var_4           = dword ptr -4
arg_0           = dword ptr  8
arg_4           = dword ptr  0Ch

        push    ebp
        mov     ebp, esp
        ; The stack frame is opened.

        push    ecx
```

```
        ; Memory is allocated for the var_4 local variable.

        mov     eax, [ebp+arg_0]
        ; The contents of the arg_0 argument are loaded into EAX.

        mov     ecx, [eax]
        ; A global variable is addressed indirectly. Now you can see
        ; that, in contrast to common opinion, this can happen.
        ; Only analysis of the code of the calling function can reveal
        ; that a global variable was addressed (and which one).

        mov     [ebp+var_4], ecx
        ; The *arg_0 value is copied into the var_4 local variable.

        mov     edx, [ebp+arg_4]
        ; The contents of the arg_4 argument are loaded into EDX.

        mov     eax, [ebp+arg_0]
        ; The contents of the arg_0 argument are loaded into EAX.

        mov     ecx, [eax]
        ; The *arg_0 argument is copied into ECX.

        mov     [edx], ecx
        ; The arg_0[0] value is copied into [arg_4].

        mov     edx, [ebp+arg_4]
        ; The arg_4 value is loaded into EDX.

        mov     eax, [ebp+var_4]
        ; The value of the var_4 local variable is loaded into EAX
        ; (stores *arg_0).

        mov     [edx], eax
        ; The *arg_0 value is loaded into *arg_4.

        mov     esp, ebp
        pop     ebp
        retn
xchg            endp

dword_405428   dd 0                    ; DATA XREF: main+3↑w main+1C↑o
```

```
dword_40542C   dd 0                    ; DATA XREF: main+D↑w main+17↑o
; IDA has found all the references to both global variables.
; The first two, main+3↑w and main+D↑w, reference
; the initialization code. (The w character
; stands for "write," which refers to addressing for writing.)
: The second two are main+1C↑o and main+17↑o.
; (The o stands for "offset," which refers to obtaining an offset
; to a global variable.)
```

If there are references with the offset-designating suffix "o" — analogous to the offset assembler instruction — among the cross-references to global variables, these should be noted immediately. An offset means that the global variable has been passed by reference. Passing by reference signifies indirect addressing, which entails tiresome manual analysis, and no advances tools will be helpful.

Static variables. Static variables are similar to global variables, but they have a limited scope: They are accessible only from the function in which they were declared. In all other respects, static and global variables are nearly identical: Both are placed in the data segment, both are addressed directly (except when addressed by reference), and so on.

There is only one essential difference: Any function may address a global variable, but only one function may address a static one. But what type of global variable is used by one function? This exposes a flaw in the program's source code: If a variable is used by one function, it does not need to be declared as global.

A memory location addressed directly is a global variable (although there are exceptions), but not all global variables are addressed directly.

Constants and Offsets

The 80x86 microprocessor family supports three types of operands: *immediate, register,* and *memory.* An operand's type is specified in a special field of the computer instruction, called mod; therefore, it is not difficult to identify operand types.

You likely know what a register looks like: Conventionally, a pointer to the memory location is enclosed in square brackets, and an immediate operand is written outside them. For example:

```
mov ecx, eax        ; Register operand
mov ecx, 0x666      ; The left operand is register. The right operand
                    ; is immediate.
```

```
mov [0x401020], eax    ; The left operand is a pointer. The right
                       ; operand is register.
```

In addition, 80x86 microprocessors support two memory-addressing modes: *direct* and *register indirect*. If the operand is immediate, addressing is direct. If the operand is a pointer stored in a register, the addressing is register indirect. For example:

```
mov ecx,[0x401020]     ; Direct addressing mode
mov ecx, [EAX]         ; Register indirect addressing mode
```

To initialize the register pointer, microprocessor developers introduced a special command, LEA REG, [addr], that computes the value of the addr address expression and writes it into the REG register. For example:

```
lea eax, [0x401020]    ; The value 0x401020 is written into the EAX
                       ; register.
mov ecx, [EAX]         ; Indirect addressing: The double word
                       ; at the offset 0x401020 is loaded into ECX.
```

The right operand of the LEA instruction always represents a near pointer (except when LEA is used to sum the constants). Everything would be fine, except an internal representation of the near pointer is equal to a constant of the same value. Hence, LEA EAX, [0x401020] is the equivalent of MOV EAX, 0x401020. For certain reasons, MOV has surpassed LEA in popularity, and has knocked it almost completely out of use.

The expulsion of LEA has given rise to a fundamental problem of assembling — the *offset problem*. It is impossible to distinguish the syntax of constants and offsets (near pointers). A construction such as MOV EAX, 0x401020 may load EAX either with the constant 0x401020 (an example of the corresponding C code would be a=0x401020), or with the pointer to the memory location at the offset 0x401020 (an example of the corresponding C code would be a=&x). Obviously, a=0x401020 is different from a=&x. What would happen if the x variable in the newly assembled program appears at another offset, not at 0x401020? The program would fail, because the a pointer still points to the memory location 0x401020, which contains a different variable.

Why may a variable change its offset? There are two principal reasons. First, the assembler language is ambiguous and allows interpretation. For example, the ADD EAX, 0x66 construction may be represented by two machine instructions — 83 C0 66 and 05 66 00 00 00 — of 3 and 5 bytes. The compiler may choose either instruction, which may not be the one in the initial program (before it was disassembled). If the compiler picks the wrong-size instruction, then all other instructions, as well as data, will float away. Second, modifying the program — really changing it, not just substituting JNZ for JZ — will inevitably cause the pointers to float away. The offset instruction may help return the program to a functioning state. If MOV EAX, 0x401020 loads a pointer into EAX, not a constant, then a *label* such as loc_401020 needs to be created at the offset 0x401020, and MOV EAX, 0x401020 needs to be replaced with MOV EAX, **offset** loc_401020. Now, the EAX pointer is not bound to the fixed offset; rather, it is bound to the label.

What happens if the offset instruction is put before a constant that has been misidentified as a pointer? The program will fail, or it will work incorrectly. Imagine that the number 0x401020 represents the volume of water in a pool that has an inlet pipe and an outlet pipe. Replacing the constant with the pointer makes the volume of the pool equal the offset of the label in the newly assembled program, and computation becomes impossible.

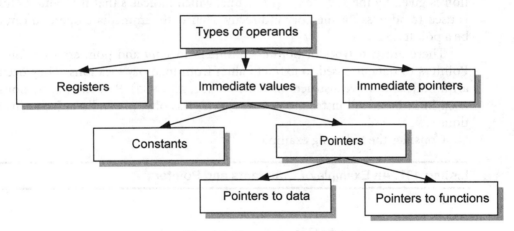

Fig. 18. Types of operands

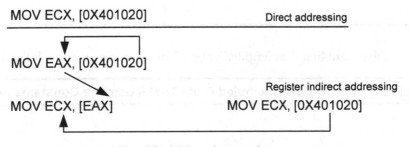

Fig. 19. Addressing modes

Thus, it is important to determine every immediate operand's type, and even more important to determine it *correctly*. One mistake can kill a program's operability, and a typical program contains thousands or tens of thousands of operands. Two questions arise: How are operand types determined? Is it possible to determine them automatically, or at least semiautomatically?

Determining the type of an immediate operand. An immediate operand of the LEA instruction is a pointer. (However, to mislead hackers, some forms of protection use LEA to load a constant.)

Immediate operands of the MOV and PUSH instructions may be either constants or pointers. To determine the type of an immediate operand, it is necessary to analyze how its value is used in the program. If it is used for addressing memory operands, it is a pointer; otherwise, it is a constant.

Suppose that the MOV EAX, 0x401020 instruction turns up in the code of a program (Fig. 19). What is it — a constant or a pointer? The answer to this question is given by the MOV ECX, [EAX] line, which indicates that the value 0x401020 is used to address the memory indirectly. Hence, the immediate operand can only be a pointer.

There are two types of pointers: pointers to *data* and pointers to a *function*. Pointers to data are used to extract values from memory locations. They occur in arithmetic and move instructions (such as MOV, ADD, SUB). Pointers to functions are used in indirect call instructions (CALL) and, less often, in indirect jump instructions (JMP).

Consider the following example:

Listing 137. An Example of Constants and Pointers

```
main()
{
        static int a=0x777;
        int *b = &a;
        int c=b[0];
}
```

Disassembling the compiled code of this example gives the following:

Listing 138. The Disassembled Code That Illustrates Constants and Pointers

---

```
main            proc near

var_8           = dword ptr -8
```

```
var_4              = dword ptr -4

        push    ebp
        mov     ebp, esp
        sub     esp, 8
        ; The stack frame is opened.

        mov     [ebp+var_4], 410000h
        ; The value 0x410000 is loaded into the var_4 local variable.
        ; As yet, it is not possible to say
        ; whether it is a constant or a pointer.

        mov     eax, [ebp+var_4]
        ; The contents of the var_4 local variable
        ; are loaded into the EAX register.

        mov     ecx, [eax]
        ; ECX is loaded with the contents of the memory location pointed
        ; to by the EAX pointer. This means that EAX is a pointer.
        ; Therefore, the var_4 local variable from which it was loaded
        ; is also a pointer, and the immediate operand 0x410000
        ; is a pointer, not a constant. To preserve the program's
        ; operability, the loc_410000 label must be created at the offset
        ; 0x410000. The label will convert the memory location at this
        ; address into a double word. In addition,
        ; the MOV [ebp+var_4], 410000h instruction must be replaced with
        ; MOV [ebp+var_4], offset loc_410000.

        mov     [ebp+var_8], ecx
        ; The value of *var_4 (offset loc_41000)
        ; is assigned to the var_8 local variable.

        mov     esp, ebp
        pop     ebp
        ; The stack frame is closed.

        retn
main            endp
```

The following example calls a procedure indirectly:

Listing 139. An Indirect Call of a Procedure

```
func(int a, int b)
{
      return a+b;
};

main()
{
      int (*zzz) (int a, int b) = func;

      // The function is called indirectly using the zzz pointer.
      zzz(0x666,0x777);
}
```

The disassembled code of the compiled example looks as follows:

Listing 140. The Disassembled Code That Illustrates Indirect Procedure Calls

---

```
.text:0040100B main     proc near          ; CODE XREF: start+AF↓p
.text:0040100B
.text:0040100B var_4    dword ptr -4
.text:0040100B
.text:0040100B          push    ebp
.text:0040100C          mov     ebp, esp
.text:0040100C          ; The stack frame is opened.
.text:0040100C
.text:0040100E          push    ecx
.text:0040100E          ; Memory is allocated for
.text:0040100E          ; the var_4 local variable.
.text:0040100E
.text:0040100F          mov     [ebp+var_4], 401000h
.text:0040100F          ; The value 0x401000 is assigned to
.text:0040100F          ; the local variable.
.text:0040100F          ; It is not yet possible to say
.text:0040100F          ; whether it is a constant or an offset.
.text:0040100F
.text:00401016          push    777h
```

```
.text:00401016              ; The value 0x777 is placed onto the stack.
.text:00401016              ; Is it a constant, or a pointer?
.text:00401016              ; This cannot be determined
.text:00401016              ; before the called function is analyzed.
.text:00401016
.text:0040101B      push    666h
.text:0040101B              ; The immediate value 0x666 is placed
.text:0040101B              ; onto the stack.
.text:0040101B
.text:00401020      call    [ebp+var_4]
.text:00401020              ; The function is called indirectly.
.text:00401020              ; Hence, the var_4 variable is a pointer.
.text:00401020              ; Therefore, the immediate value
.text:00401020              ; assigned to it, 0x401000, is also a pointer.
.text:00401020              ; In addition, 0x401000 is the address
.text:00401020              ; where the called function is located.
.text:00401020              ; Let's name it MyFunc,
.text:00401020              ; and replace mov [ebp+var_4], 401000h with
.text:00401020              ; mov [ebp+var_4], offset MyFunc.
.text:00401020              ; Now, the program can be modified
.text:00401020              ; without any fear of collapse.
.text:00401020
.text:00401023      add     esp, 8
.text:00401023
.text:00401026      mov     esp, ebp
.text:00401028      pop     ebp
.text:00401028              ; The stack frame is closed.
.text:00401028
.text:00401029              retn
.text:00401029 main         endp


.text:00401000 MyFunc       proc near
.text:00401000 ; Here is the indirectly called MyFunc function.
.text:00401000 ; Let's examine it to determine type of the
.text:00401000 ; immediate values passed to it.
.text:00401000
.text:00401000 arg_0         = dword ptr 8
.text:00401000 arg_4         = dword ptr 0Ch
.text:00401000 ; Here are the arguments.
.text:00401000
```

```
.text:00401000              push    ebp
.text:00401001              mov     ebp, esp
.text:00401001              ; The stack frame is opened.
.text:00401001
.text:00401003              mov     eax, [ebp+arg_0]
.text:00401003              ; The value of the arg_0 argument is loaded into EAX.
.text:00401003
.text:00401006              add     eax, [ebp+arg_4]
.text:00401006              ; The value of the arg_0 argument is added to
.text:00401006              ; EAX (arg_0). This operation indicates that
.text:00401006              ; at least one of the two arguments is not
.text:00401006              ; a pointer; adding two pointers is senseless.
.text:00401006
.text:00401009              pop     ebp
.text:00401009              ; The stack frame is closed.
.text:00401009
.text:0040100A              retn
.text:0040100A              ; The sum of the two arguments
.text:0040100A              ; is returned into EAX. The immediate
.text:0040100A              ; values 0x666 and 0x777 were used neither here
.text:0040100A              ; nor in the calling function for addressing
.text:0040100A              ; memory, which means that they are constants.
.text:0040100A
.text:0040100A MyFunc              endp
.text:0040100A
```

Complex cases of addressing, or arithmetic operations over pointers. C/C++ and some other programming languages allow arithmetic operations over pointers that complicate the identification of the direct operand type. If such operations on pointers were forbidden, the occurrence of any arithmetic instruction that handles an immediate operand would indicate a constant-type operand.

Fortunately, even in languages that allow arithmetic operations over pointers, only a limited number of such operations are carried out. For example, it makes no sense to add two pointers — and even less to multiply or divide them. Subtraction is another matter. The compiler allocates functions in memory in the order they were declared in the program; therefore, it is possible to calculate the size of a function by subtracting the pointer to the function from the pointer to the next function (Fig. 20). Such a trick sometimes is used in packers (unpackers) of executable files and protection with self-modifying code, but it is rarely used in application programs.

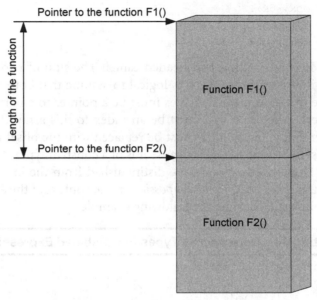

Fig. 20. Subtracting pointers to calculate the size of a function
(a data structure)

A pointer also may be combined with a constant. These combinations are so popular that 80x86 microprocessors have a special addressing mode for the purpose. Suppose that we have a pointer to an array and the index of a certain element of the array. To obtain the value of the element, the index, multiplied by the size of the element, must be added to the pointer. Subtraction of a constant from the pointer is used rarely; it is required by a smaller scope of calculations, it often results in serious problems. The following technique is popular among beginners: To get an array whose index begins with one, they declare a standard array, obtain a pointer to it, and decrease the pointer by one. This appears to be an elegant solution. Nevertheless, consider what happens if the pointer to the array is equal to zero. In this situation, "the snake will bite itself by the tail," and the index will become a large positive number. Generally, under Windows NT/9x, an array cannot be allocated at an offset of zero. However, it is unwise to get used to the tricks that work on one platform and not on others.

"Normal" programming languages forbid the mixing of different types. Such mixing can result in a mishmash and a fundamental problem of disassembling — *determining types in combined expressions*. Consider the following example:

```
mov eax, 0x...
mov ebx, 0x...
add eax, ebx
mov ecx, [eax]
```

It seems to be a two-headed camel! The sum of two immediate values is used for indirect addressing. It is logical to assume that both values cannot be pointers. One of the immediate values must be a pointer to an array (a data structure or an object); the other one must be an index to this array. To preserve the program's operability, the pointer must be replaced with the offset to the label, and the index must be left unchanged because it is of a constant type.

How can the pointer be distinguished from the index? Unfortunately, there is no universal answer; *it is impossible* in the context of the above example.

Instead, consider the following example:

Listing 141. Determining Types in Combined Expressions

```
MyFunc(char *a, int i)
{
      a[i]='\n';
      a[i+1]=0;
}

main()
{
      static char buff[]="Hello, Sailor!";
      MyFunc(&buff[0], 5);
}
```

The disassembled code of this example, compiled using Microsoft Visual C++, gives the following:

Listing 142. The Disassembled Code for Determining Types in Combined Expressions Compiled Using Visual C++

```
main            proc near               ; CODE XREF: start+AF↓p
        push    ebp
        mov     ebp, esp
```

```
          ; The stack frame is opened.

          push   5
          ; The immediate value 0x5 is passed to MyFunc.

          push   405030h
          ; The immediate value 0x405030 is passed to MyFunc.

          call   MyFunc
          add    esp, 8
          ; The MyFunc(0x405030, 0x5) function is called.

          pop    ebp
          ; The stack frame is closed.

          retn
main            endp

MyFunc          proc near          ; CODE XREF: main+A↑p

arg_0           = dword ptr  8
arg_4           = dword ptr  0Ch

          push   ebp
          mov    ebp, esp
          ; The stack frame is opened.

          mov    eax, [ebp+arg_0]
          ; The value of the arg_0 argument is loaded into EAX.
          ; (The arg_0 argument contains the immediate value 0x405030.)

          add    eax, [ebp+arg_4]
          ; The value of the arg_4 argument is added to EAX.
          ; (The arg_4 argument contains the value 0x5.)
          ; This operation indicates that one argument is a constant,
          ; and the other is either a constant or a pointer.

          mov    byte ptr [eax], 0Ah
          ; The sum of immediate values is used to indirectly address
          ; the memory, meaning that this is a case of a constant and a pointer.
          ; But which is which? To answer this question, it is necessary
```

```
; to understand the sense of the program code: What did
; the programmer want to achieve by adding pointers?
; Assume that the value 0x5 is a pointer. Is this logical?
; Not quite; if this is a pointer, then where does it point?
; The first 64 KB of the address space of Windows NT
; are reserved for "catching" uninitialized and null pointers.
; It is clear that a pointer cannot be equal to five in any case,
; unless the programmer has used some cunning trick.
; And if 0x401000 is a pointer? It looks like a fair
; and legal offset. But what is coming up now?
; 00401000 db 'Hello,Sailor!',0
;
; Now everything matches — a pointer to the "Hello, Sailor!" string
; (value 0x401000) and the index of a character of this string
; (value 0x5) are passed to the function; the function has added
; the index to the pointer, and has written the \n character into
; the memory location thus obtained.

mov     ecx, [ebp+arg_0]
; The value of the arg_0 argument is placed into ECX
; (a pointer, as was established previously).

add     ecx, [ebp+arg_4]
; The arg_0 and arg_4 arguments are added.
; (The arg_4 argument is an index, as was established previously.)

mov     byte ptr [ecx+1], 0
; This is the sum stored in ECX to indirectly address the memory
; (or, to be more exact, for the indirect-based addressing,
; because 1 is added to the sum of the pointer and index, and 0 is
; placed into this memory location). As suspected, the pointer to
; the string and the index of the first character of the string
; being cut off are passed to the function. Therefore, to
; preserve the program's operability, a loc_s0 label needs to be
; created at the offset 0x401000. In addition, PUSH 0x401000 must
; be replaced in the calling function with PUSH offset loc_s0.

        pop     ebp
        retn
MyFunc          endp
```

Now let's compile the same example in Borland C++ 5.0, and see the difference compared to the code obtained from Microsoft Visual C++. To save space, the code of only one function, `MyFunc`, is presented; the `main` function is almost identical to the one in the previous listing.

Listing 143. The Disassembled Code for Determining Types in Combined Expressions Compiled Using Borland C++ 5.0

```
MyFunc          proc near              ; CODE XREF: _main+D↑p
        push    ebp
        ; The empty stack frame is opened; there are no local variables.

        mov     byte ptr [eax+edx], 0Ah
        ; Borland C++ has immediately summed the pointer and the constant
        ; right in the address expression! Which register stores
        ; the constant, and which stores the pointer? As in
        ; the previous listing, this needs an analysis of their values.

        mov     byte ptr [eax+edx+1], 0

        mov     ebp, esp
        pop     ebp
        ; The stack frame is closed.

        retn
MyFunc          endp
```

The order of indexes and pointers. A little secret: When summing an index with a constant, most compilers put a pointer in the first position and a constant in the second, regardless of their order in the program. In other words, the expressions a[i], (a+i)[0], *(a+i), and *(i+a) are compiled into the same code. Even if (0)[i+a] is used, the compiler will put a in the first place. Why? The answer is ridiculously simple: The addition of a pointer to a constant gives a pointer. Therefore, the result of computation is always written into a pointer-type variable.

Let's return to the previous listing and apply this new rule in the analysis.

Listing 144. The Result of Adding the Constant to the Pointer Is Written into the Pointer-Type Variable

---

```
        mov     eax, [ebp+arg_0]
        ; The value of the arg_0 argument is loaded into EAX.
```

```
;  (The arg_0 argument contains the immediate value 0x405030.)

add    eax, [ebp+arg_4]
; The value of the arg_4 argument (containing
; the value 0x5) is added to EAX. This operation
; indicates that one argument is a constant,
; while the other is either a constant or a pointer.

mov    byte ptr [eax], 0Ah
; The sum of immediate values is used to address
; the memory indirectly, hence it is either a constant or
; a pointer. But which one? EAX is most likely to be
; a pointer because it is positioned in the first place,
; and var_4 is likely an index because it comes second.
```

Using LEA to sum constants. The LEA instruction is widely used by compilers not only to initialize indexes, but also to sum constants. Because the internal representation of constants and indexes is identical, the result of adding two indexes is the same as the sum of the constants that match them (i.e., LEA EBX, [EBX+0x666] == ADD EBX, 0x666). However, the functionality of LEA considerably outperforms ADD. Consider LEA ESI, **[EAX*4+EBP-0x20]**. Try to feed the same to the ADD instruction.

After you encounter the LEA instruction in the code of a program, do not hurry to stick the tag "pointer" on it; the instruction may be a constant. If the "suspect" is never used to address expressions indirectly, it is not a pointer; rather, it is a true constant.

Identifying the constants and pointers "visually." Here are some hints that may help you distinguish pointers from constants:

❏ In 32-bit Windows programs, pointers can accept a limited range of values. The region of address space accessible to processors begins with the offset 0x1.00.00 and stretches to the offset 0x80.00.00.00; in Windows 9x/ME, the accessible space is even smaller — from 0x40.00.00 to 0x80.00.00.00. Therefore, all immediate values smaller than 0x1.00.00 and larger than 0x80.00.00 represent constants, rather than pointers. There is one exception: the number 0, which designates the null pointer[i].

---

[i] Protective mechanisms directly address the code of the operating system located above the *0x80.00.00* address.

❏ If an immediate value looks like an index, check where it points. If a function prolog or a meaningful text string is located at this offset, it is likely that this is a pointer, although this may be coincidence only.

❏ Look at the table of relocatable elements. (See "*Step Four: Getting Acquainted with the Debugger.*") If the address of the "suspected" immediate value is present in the table, it is a pointer. However, most executable files are not relocatable. Such an approach can be used only to examine DLLs, since these are relocatable by definition.

Incidentally, the IDA Pro disassembler uses all three methods just described to identify the pointers automatically.

Literals and Strings

At first glance, identifying strings would seem to present few difficulties: If the object referred to by a pointer (see "*Constants and Offsets*") looks like a string, it certainly is a string. Moreover, in most cases, strings are revealed and identified simply by looking through the dump of a program (if it is not encrypted; encryption is a theme for a separate discussion). This is all true, but there are some complications.

The first task is automatic detection of strings in the program — megabyte-size dumps cannot be examined manually. There is a set of algorithms for identifying strings. The simplest, although not the most reliable, is based on the following two ideas:

❏ *The string consists of a limited set of characters.* As a rough approximation, the characters are digits and letters of the alphabet (including blanks), punctuation marks, and control characters, such as tabulation or carriage-return characters.

❏ *The string should consist of at least several characters.*

Let's agree that if the minimal length of the string is N bytes, it is enough to find all sequences of N or more valid string characters. If N is small (about 3 or 4 bytes, for example), the search will generate plenty of false hits. If N is large (about 6 or 8 bytes, for example), the number of false hits will be close to zero and can be ignored, but all short strings (such as "OK", "YES", or "NO") will not be recognized. In addition to digits and letters, strings may contain pseudo-graphic elements (an especially frequent feature in console applications), faces, arrows, marks — almost everything that the ASCII table contains. Is there, therefore, any difference between a string and a random sequence of bytes? Frequency analysis is useless here; for normal work, it needs at least 100 bytes of text, not strings of just two or three characters. The problem can be approached from the other side as well: If a string is present in a program, there must be a reference to it. It is possible to search among immediate values for the pointer to the recognized string. If it is found, then the chances that it is a string, and not just a random sequence of bytes, increase sharply.

However, it is not quite that easy. Consider the following example:

Listing 145. A Text String within a Program

```
BEGIN
WriteLn('Hello, Sailor!');
END
```

Compile this example using any suitable Pascal compiler (Delphi or Free Pascal, for example). After loading the compiled file into the disassembler, walk through the data segment. Soon, the following will appear:

Listing 146. The Contents of the Data Segment of the Compiled Example

---

```
.data:00404040 unk_404040    db 0Eh ;
.data:00404041               db 48h ; H
.data:00404042               db 65h ; e
.data:00404043               db 6Ch ; l
.data:00404044               db 6Ch ; l
.data:00404045               db 6Fh ; o
.data:00404046               db 2Ch ; ,
.data:00404047               db 20h ;
.data:00404048               db 53h ; S
.data:00404049               db 61h ; a
.data:0040404A               db 69h ; i
.data:0040404B               db 6Ch ; l
.data:0040404C               db 6Fh ; o
.data:0040404D               db 72h ; r
.data:0040404E               db 21h ; !
.data:0040404F               db  0 ;
.data:00404050 word_404050   dw 1332h
```

This is the sought string, and there is no doubt that it is a string. Now, let's try to work out how it was referred to. In IDA Pro, this is done by using the <ALT>+<I> key combination and entering the offset of the beginning of the string — 0x404041 — into the search field.

"Search Failed?" How can that be? What is passed to the WriteLn function in that case? Has IDA become faulty? Looking through the disassembled code also fails to return a result.

It fails because in Pascal, there is a byte at the beginning of strings that contains the length of the string. The value 0xE (14 in the decimal system) is contained in the dump at the offset 0x404040. And how many characters are there in the string "Hello, Sailor!"? Fourteen. Pressing the <ALT>+<I> combination again and searching for the immediate operand equal to 0x404040 returns the following:

Listing 147. The Result of Searching for the Immediate Operand

```
.text:00401033        push    404040h
.text:00401038        push    [ebp+var_4]
.text:0040103B        push    0
.text:0040103D        call    FPC_WRITE_TEXT_SHORTSTR
.text:00401042        push    [ebp+var_4]
.text:00401045        call    FPC_WRITELN_END
.text:0040104A        push    offset loc_40102A
.text:0040104F        call    FPC_IOCHECK
.text:00401054        call    FPC_DO_EXIT
.text:00401059        leave
.text:0040105A        retn
```

Identifying a string appears to be insufficient; in addition, at least its boundaries must be determined.

The following types of strings are most popular: *C strings*, ending in zero; *DOS strings*, ending in $; and *Pascal strings*, beginning with a one-, two-, or four-byte field that contains the string length. Let's consider each of these types in more detail.

C strings. Also called ASCIIZ strings (*Z* means *Zero* at the end), C strings are widely used in operating systems of the Windows and Unix families. The character "\0" (not to be confused with "0") has a special task, and is interpreted in a special way — as a *string terminator*. The length of ASCIIZ strings is limited only by the size of the address space allocated for the process, or by the size of the segment.

Accordingly, the maximum size of an ASCIIZ string is only a little less than *2 GB* in Windows NT/9*x*, and it is about *64K* in Windows 3.1 and MS-DOS. The ASCIIZ string is only 1 byte longer than the initial ASCII string. Despite these advantages, ASCIIZ strings have certain drawbacks. First, an ASCIIZ string cannot contain zero bytes; therefore, it is not suitable for processing binary data. Second, performing copying, comparison, and concatenation over C strings incurs significant overhead. Working with single bytes is not the best variant for modern processors; it is better for them to deal with double words. Unfortunately, the length of ASCIIZ strings is unknown beforehand; it must be computed "on the fly," checking *each byte* to see whether or not it is a string terminator. However, certain compilers use a trick: They terminate the string *with seven zeros*, making it possible to work with double words, thus increasing the speed noticeably. Initially, it seems strange to add seven trailing zeros rather than four, as a double word contains 4 bytes. However, if the last significant character of the string falls on the first byte of the double word, its end will be taken up with three 0 bytes, but the double word will not equal zero any more because of the intervention of the first character. Therefore, the following double word should be given four more 0 bytes, in which case it certainly will equal zero. However, seven auxiliary bytes for each string is too much.

DOS strings. In MS-DOS, the function that outputs lines reads the "$" character as the end-of-line character, which is why programmers call them DOS strings. The term is not absolutely correct — all other MS-DOS functions work exclusively with ASCIIZ strings. This strange terminator character was chosen when there was no graphic interface in sight, and console terminal was considered a rather advanced system for interaction with the user. <Enter> could not be used to end the line, since it was sometimes necessary to enter several lines into the program at once. Combinations like <Ctrl>+<Z> or <Alt>+<000> were also unsuitable since many keyboards at that time did not contain the <Ctrl> and <Alt> keys. Computers were mainly used to solve engineering tasks, not accounting ones, and the dollar sign was the least-used character. Therefore, it was used to signal that the user had finished entering the line — in other words, as a string terminator. (Yes, the string terminator was entered by the user; it was not added by the program, as is the case with ASCIIZ strings). Now, DOS strings are encountered very rarely.

Pascal strings. Pascal strings have no terminator character; instead, they are preceded by a special field containing the string length. The advantages of this approach are the possibility of storing any characters in the string (including 0 bytes), and the high speed of processing the string variables. Instead of constantly checking each byte to find a terminator, memory is addressed only once — when the string length is read. If the string length is known, then it is possible to work with double words that are the native data type for 32-bit processors, not with single bytes. The only question is how many bytes to allocate for the size field. Allocating only 1 byte is economical, but the maximum length of the string will be limited to 255 characters, an insufficient amount in many cases. This type of string is used by practically all Pascal compilers (Borland Turbo Pascal and Free Pascal, for example); therefore, such strings are called Pascal strings, or, more exactly, *short Pascal strings*.

Delphi strings. Realizing the absurdity of restricting the length of Pascal strings to 255 characters, the Delphi developers expanded the size field to 2 bytes, thus increasing the greatest possible length to 65,535 characters. Although such strings are supported by other compilers (Free Pascal, for example), they are traditionally called *Delphi strings* or *two-byte Pascal strings*.

The restriction to more than 60K can hardly be called a restriction. Most strings are much shorter, and the heap (dynamic memory), as well as a number of specialized functions, can be used to process large data files (text files, for example). The overhead (two auxiliary bytes for each string variable) is not substantial enough to be taken into account. Therefore, Delphi strings, which combine the best features of C and Pascal strings (practically unlimited length and high processing speed, respectively), seem to be the most convenient and practical type.

Wide Pascal strings. Wide Pascal strings have as many as 4 bytes for the size field, thus "limiting" the length to 4,294,967,295 characters, or 4 GB, even more than the amount of memory that Windows NT/9x allocates for "personal use" by an application process. However, this luxury comes at a high price, as each string has four extra bytes, three of which will remain empty in most cases. The overhead incurred by using Wide Pascal strings becomes rather substantial; therefore, this type is rarely used.

Combined types. Certain compilers use a combined C-Pascal type. On one hand, the combined C-Pascal type allows you to process strings at a high speed and store any characters in such strings. On the other hand, it provides compatibility with a huge quantity of C libraries that work with ASCIIZ strings. Each combined string is forcefully terminated with zero, but this zero does not appear in the string. Regular libraries (operators) of the language work with it, as with a Pascal string. When calling functions of C libraries, the compiler passes a pointer to the first character of the string, not to its true beginning.

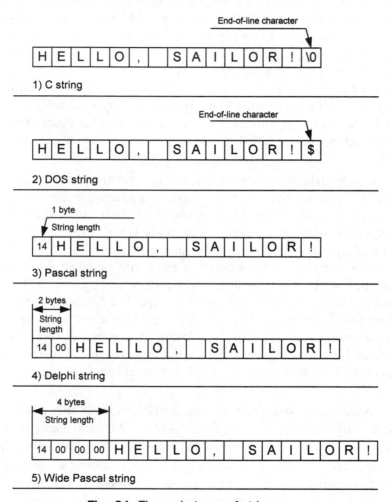

Fig. 21. The main types of strings

Determining string types. It is rather difficult to determine the type of a string by its appearance. The presence of zero terminators at the end of a string is not a sufficient reason to label it an ASCIIZ string: Pascal compilers often add one or several zeroes to the end of a string to align data on boundaries that are multiples of power-of-2 values.

The string type can be determined roughly by the type of compiler (C or Pascal), and precisely by the processing algorithm (i.e., by an analysis of the code that handles it). Consider the following example.

Listing 148. Identifying Strings

```
VAR
      s0, s1 : String;


BEGIN
      s0 :='Hello, Sailor!';
      s1 :='Hello, World!';
      IF s0=s1 THEN WriteLN('OK') ELSE Writeln('Woozl');
END.
```

After compiling this using Free Pascal, look in the data segment, where the following line can be found:

```
.data:00404050 aHelloWorld db 0Dh,'Hello, World!',0 ; DATA XREF:_main+2B↑o
```

Isn't it reminiscent of an ASCIIZ string? Even if the compiler has yet to be identified, no one would think that 0xD is the length field rather than the carriage-return character. To test the hypothesis concerning type, proceed according to the cross-reference found by IDA Pro, or find the immediate operand 0x404050 (the offset of the string) in the disassembled code manually.

```
push offset _S1                 ; A pointer is passed
                                ; to the string destination.
push offset aHelloWorld         ;"\rHello, World!" A pointer is passed
                                ; to the string source.
push 0FFh                       ; This is the maximum length
                                ; of the string.
call FPC_SHORTSTR_COPY
```

The pointer to the string was passed to the FPC_SHORTSTR_COPY function. From the documentation supplied with Free Pascal, it is clear that this function works with short Pascal strings. Therefore, the 0xD byte is not a carriage-return character, but the string length. How would it be possible to discover this without the Free Pascal documentation? It is hardly possible to get documentation for every compiler. Incidentally, the regular delivery of IDA Pro, including version 4.17, does not contain the signatures of FPP libraries, which have to be created manually.

When the string function is unidentified or does not have a description, the only way out is to investigate the code to find its operation algorithm. This is shown in the following example.

Listing 149. The Code of the FPC_SHORTSTR_COPY Function

```
FPC_SHORTSTR_COPY      proc near      ; CODE XREF: sub_401018+21↑p

arg_0           = dword ptr 8         ; Maximum length of the string
arg_4           = dword ptr 0Ch       ; A source string
arg_8           = dword ptr 10h       ; A destination string

        push    ebp
        mov     ebp, esp
        ; The stack frame is opened.

        push    eax
        push    ecx
        ; Registers are saved.

        cld
        ; The direction flag is reset (i.e.,
        ; the LODS, STOS, and MOVS instructions are forced to increment
        ; the register pointer).

        mov     edi, [ebp+arg_8]
        ; The value of the arg_8 argument is loaded into the EDI register
        ; (the offset of the destination buffer).

        mov     esi, [ebp+arg_4]
        ; The value of the arg_4 argument is loaded into the ESI register
        ; (the offset of the source string).

        xor     eax, eax
        ; The EAX register is forced to be zero.

        mov     ecx, [ebp+arg_0]
        ; The value of the arg_0 argument is loaded into ECX
        ; (the maximum allowable length).

        lodsb
        ; The first byte of the source-string pointer is loaded
        ; to the ESI register, and ESI is incremented by one.
```

```
cmp     eax, ecx
; The first byte of the string is compared with the maximum string
; length. It is already clear that the first character of the
; string is the length. However, let's pretend the purpose
; of the arg_0 argument was unclear, and continue the analysis.

jbe     short loc_401168
; if (ESI[0] <= arg_0) goto loc_401168


mov     eax, ecx
; The ECX value is copied to EAX.


loc_401168:                           ; CODE XREF: sub_401150+14↑j
        stosb
; The first byte of the source string is written into the
; destination buffer, and EDI is incremented by one.

cmp     eax, 7
; The string length is compared with the 0x7 constant.

jl      short loc_401183
; Is the string length less than 7 bytes?
; Then it is being copied byte by byte!

mov     ecx, edi
; ECX is loaded with the pointer to the destination buffer,
; which was incremented by one. (It was incremented
; by the STOSB instruction when a byte was written.)

neg     ecx
; ECX is complemented to zero, NEG(0xFFFF) = 1;
; ECX :=1

and     ecx, 3
; The three least significant bits are left in ECX,
; and the others are reset. ECX :=1

sub     eax, ecx
; The "castrated" ECX is subtracted from EAX (which contains
; the first byte of the string).
```

```
repe    movsb
; ECX bytes are copied from the source string
; into the destination buffer. In this case, 1 byte is copied.

mov     ecx, eax
; Now, ECX contains the value of the first byte of the string,
; which is decremented by one.

and     eax, 3
; The three least-significant bits are left in EAX.
; The others are reset.

shr     ecx, 2
; Using the cyclic shift instruction,
; ECX is divided by four (2 to the second power is 4).

repe    movsd
; ECX double bytes are copied from ESI to EDI.
; It becomes clear that ECX contains the string length.
; Since the value of the first byte of the string is loaded
; into ECX, it is possible to state confidently
; that the first byte of the string (just
; the byte, not the word) contains the length of this string.
; Therefore, it is a short Pascal string.

loc_401183:                         ; CODE XREF: sub_401150+1C↑j
        mov     ecx, eax
        ; If the string length is less than 7 bytes, then EAX contains
        ; the string length for its byte-by-byte copying (see the branch
        ; jbe short loc_401168). Otherwise, EAX contains the remainder of
        ; the string's "tail," which could not fill the last double word
        ; with itself. In one way or another, ECX is loaded
        ; with the number of bytes to be copied.

        repe    movsb
        ; ECX bytes are copied from ESI to EDI.

        pop     ecx
```

```
    pop     eax
    ; The registers are restored.

    leave
    ; The stack frame is closed.

    retn    0Ch
FPC_SHORTSTR_COPY                    endp
```

The next example will be helpful in the identification of C strings.

Listing 150. Identifying C Strings

```c
#include <stdio.h>
#include <string.h>

main()
{
    char s0[]="Hello, World!";
    char s1[]="Hello, Sailor!";
    if (strcmp(&s0[0], &s1[0])) printf("Woozl\n"); else printf("OK\n");
}
```

Compile this example using any suitable C compiler, such as Borland C++ 5.0. Microsoft C++ does not fit in the case. Then, look for the strings in the data segment. It should not take long to find them.

```
DATA:00407074 aHelloWorld    db 'Hello, World!',0  ; DATA XREF: _main+16↑o

DATA:00407082 aHelloSailor   db 'Hello, Sailor!',0  ; DATA XREF: _main+22↑o

DATA:00407091 aWoozl     db 'Woozl',0Ah,0   ; DATA XREF: _main+4F↑o

DATA:00407098 aOk        db 'OK',0Ah,0      ; DATA XREF: _main+5C↑o
```

Note that the strings follow one another, each ends in a "0" character, and the value of the first byte of the string does not match its length. These are indubitably ASCIIZ strings. However, analyzing the code that handles them will not hurt.

Listing 151. An Analysis of the Code That Handles ASCIIZ Strings

---

```
_main           proc near                ; DATA XREF: DATA:00407044↓o

var_20          = byte ptr -20h
var_10          = byte ptr -10h

        push    ebp
        mov     ebp, esp
        ; The stack frame is opened.

        add     esp, 0FFFFFFE0h
        ; Space is allocated for local variables.

        mov     ecx, 3
        ; The value 0x3 is placed into the ECX register.

        lea     eax, [ebp+var_10]
        ; EAX is loaded with the pointer to the var_10 local buffer.

        lea     edx, [ebp+var_20]
        ; EDX is loaded with the pointer to the var_20 local buffer.

        push    esi
        ; The ESI register is saved —
        ; not passed to the function,
        ; since ESI has not been initialized yet!

        push    edi
        ; The EDI register is saved.

        lea     edi, [ebp+var_10]
        ; EDI is loaded with the pointer to the var_10 local buffer.

        mov     esi, offset aHelloWorld ; "Hello, World!"
        ; IDA has recognized the immediate operand as an offset
        ; of the "Hello, World!" string. If it had not, it would be
        ; possible to do it manually, given that
        ; the immediate operand coincides with the offset of the string,
```

```
; and that the next instruction uses ESI
; to address memory indirectly.
; Hence, a pointer is loaded into ESI.

repe   movsd
; ECX double words are copied from ESI to EDI.
; What does ECX equal? It equals 0x3.
; To convert double words into bytes, multiply 0x3 by 0x4.
; This obtains 0xC, which is one byte shorter than the copied
; "Hello, World!" string, pointed to by ESI.

movsw
; The last byte of the "Hello, World!" string
; is copied, with the terminating zero.

lea    edi, [ebp+var_20]
; EDI is loaded with the pointer to the var_20 local buffer.

mov    esi, offset aHelloSailor ; "Hello, Sailor!"

; The ESI register is loaded with the pointer to the
; "Hello, Sailor!" string.

mov    ecx, 3
; ECX is loaded with the number of complete double words contained
; in the "Hello, Sailor!" string.

repe   movsd
; The 0x3 double words are copied.

movsw
; A word is copied.

movsb
; The last byte is copied.

; A function for comparing the strings.
loc_4010AD:                          ; CODE XREF: _main+4B↓j
       mov   cl, [eax]
```

```
; The contents of the next byte of the
; "Hello, World!" string are loaded.

cmp    cl, [edx]
; Is CL equal to the contents of the next byte of the
; "Hello, Sailor!" string?

jnz    short loc_4010C9
; If the characters of both strings do not match, jump
; to the loc_4010C9 label.

test   cl, cl
jz     short loc_4010D8
; Is the CL register equal to zero? (In other words, has
; the "0" character been seen in the string?).
; If so, jump to loc_4010D8.
; Now the string type can be determined.
; The first byte of the string contains the first character
; of the string, not the string length. In addition, each byte of
; the string is checked for being a "0" character. Hence, these are
; ASCIIZ strings!

mov    cl, [eax+1]
; The next character of the "Hello, World!" string is loaded into CL.

cmp    cl, [edx+1]
; It is compared with the next character of "Hello, Sailor!".

jnz    short loc_4010C9
; If the characters do not match, the comparison finishes.

add    eax, 2
; The pointer of the "Hello, World!" string is moved ahead
; by two characters.

add    edx, 2
; The pointer of the "Hello, Sailor!" string is moved ahead
; by two characters.
```

```
        test    cl, cl
        jnz     short loc_4010AD
        ; Repeat matching until the terminating character of the string
        ; is reached.

loc_4010C9:                              ; CODE XREF: _main+35↑j _main+41↓j
        jz      short loc_4010D8
        ; See the "Conditional IF—THEN—ELSE Statements" section.

        ; Outputting the string "Woozl"
        push    offset aWoozl        ; format
        call    _printf
        pop     ecx
        jmp     short loc_4010E3

loc_4010D8:                              ; CODE XREF: _main+39↑j _main+4D↓j
        ; Outputting the string "OK"
        push    offset aOk           ; format
        call    _printf
        pop     ecx

loc_4010E3:                              ; CODE XREF: _main+5A↑j
        xor     eax, eax
        ; The function returns zero.

        pop     edi
        pop     esi
        ; The registers are restored.

        mov     esp, ebp
        pop     ebp
        ; The stack frame is closed.

        retn
_main           endp
```

Turbo-initialization of string variables. Distinguishing strings is not always simple. To illustrate this, it is enough to compile the previous example in the Microsoft Visual C++ and, using any suitable disassembler (IDA Pro, for example), open the file obtained.

It will take you an eternity to scroll through the data section. There is no trace of strings like `"Hello, Sailor!"` and `"Hello, World!"`. The striking feature, however, is a strange bulk of double words:

```
.data:00406030 dword_406030  dd 6C6C6548h
.data:00406034 dword_406034  dd 57202C6Fh
.data:00406038 dword_406038  dd 646C726Fh
.data:0040603C word_40603C   dw 21h
.data:0040603E              align 4
.data:00406040 dword_406040  dd 6C6C6548h
.data:00406044 dword_406044  dd 53202C6Fh
.data:00406048 dword_406048  dd 6F6C6961h
.data:0040604C word_40604C   dw 2172h
.data:0040604E byte_40604E   db 0
```

What can they be? They are not pointers, since they do not point anywhere. Nor are they `int`-type variables, since none were declared in the program. Pressing the <F4> key to move into hex mode reveals the strings:

```
.data:00406030 48 65 6C 6C 6F 2C 20 57-6F 72 6C 64 21 00 00 00 "Hello, World!..."
.data:00406040 48 65 6C 6C 6F 2C 20 53-61 69 6C 6F 72 21 00 00 "Hello, Sailor!.."
.data:00406050 57 6F 6F 7A 6C 0A 00 00-4F 4B 0A 00 00 00 00 00 "Woozl...OK....."
```

So why has IDA Pro treated them like double words? Analyzing the code that handles the string will help to answer this. Before doing so, let's convert these double words into normal ASCIIZ strings. (The <U> key converts double words into a chain of typeless bytes, and the <A> key converts them into strings.) Bring the cursor to the first cross-reference and press the <Enter> key.

Listing 152. An Analysis of the Code That Manipulates Strings

```
main    proc near                     ; CODE XREF: start+AF↓p

var_20          = byte ptr -20h
var_1C          = dword ptr -1Ch
var_18          = dword ptr -18h
var_14          = word ptr -14h
var_12          = byte ptr -12h
var_10          = byte ptr -10h
```

```
var_C           = dword ptr -0Ch
var_8           = dword ptr -8
var_4           = word ptr -4
; Where have so many variables come from?

        push    ebp
        mov     ebp, esp
        ; The stack frame is opened.

        sub     esp, 20h
        ; Memory is allocated for local variables.

        mov     eax, dword ptr aHelloWorld ; "Hello, World!"
        ; EAX is loaded — not with a pointer to the string
        ; "Hello, World!", but with the first 4 bytes of this string.
        ; Now it is obvious why IDA Pro has made a mistake —
        ; the original code (before it was converted into the string)
        ; looked like this:
        ; mov  eax, dword_406030
        ; This is illustrative: If it were someone else's program under
        ; examination, this disassembler trick would be confusing.

        mov     dword ptr [ebp+var_10], eax
        ; The first 4 bytes of the string are copied
        ; into the var_10 local variable.

        mov     ecx, dword ptr aHelloWorld+4
        ; The 4th through 8th bytes of the string "Hello, World!"
        ; are loaded into ECX.

        mov     [ebp+var_C], ecx
        ; These bytes are copied into the var_C local variable.
        ; However, we already know that this is not a var_C variable,
        ; but a part of the string buffer.

        mov     edx, dword ptr aHelloWorld+8
        ; The 8th through 12th bytes of the string "Hello, World!"
        ; are loaded into EDX.

        mov     [ebp+var_8], edx
```

```
; These bytes are copied into the var_8 local variable or,
; to be more accurate, into the string buffer.

mov    ax, word ptr aHelloWorld+0Ch
; The remaining two-byte tail of the string is loaded into AX.

mov    [ebp+var_4], ax
; The tail is written into the var_4 local variable. Thus,
; fragments of the string are copied into the following local
; variables: int var_10; int var_0C; int var_8; short int var_4.
; Hence, this is actually one local variable:
; char var_10[14].

mov    ecx, dword ptr aHelloSailor ; "Hello, Sailor!"
; The same copy operation is performed on the
; "Hello, Sailor!" string.

mov    dword ptr [ebp+var_20], ecx
mov    edx, dword ptr aHelloSailor+4
mov    [ebp+var_1C], edx
mov    eax, dword ptr aHelloSailor+8
mov    [ebp+var_18], eax
mov    cx, word ptr aHelloSailor+0Ch
mov    [ebp+var_14], cx
mov    dl, byte_40604E
mov    [ebp+var_12], dl
; The "Hello, Sailor!" string is copied
; into the char var_20[14] local variable.

lea    eax, [ebp+var_20]
; The register is loaded with the pointer to the var_20 local
; variable, which contains the "Hello, Sailor!" string.

push   eax                 ; const   char *
; It is passed to the strcmp function.
; From this, it can be inferred that var_20 actually stores
```

```
                ; a string, not a value of the int type.

                lea     ecx, [ebp+var_10]
                ; The pointer to the var_10 local variable, which
                ; stores the "Hello, World!" string, is loaded into ECX.

                push    ecx                ; const char *
                ; It is passed to the strcmp function.

                call    _strcmp
                add     esp, 8
                ; strcmp("Hello, World!", "Hello, Sailor!")

                test    eax, eax
                jz      short loc_40107B
                ; Are the strings equal?

                ; Displaying the "Woozl" string
                push    offset aWoozl      ; "Woozl\n"
                call    _printf
                add     esp, 4
                jmp     short loc_401088

                ; Displaying the "OK" string
loc_40107B:                                ; CODE XREF: sub_401000+6A↑j
                push    offset aOk         ; "OK\n"
                call    _printf
                add     esp, 4

loc_401088:                                ; CODE XREF: sub_401000+79↑j
                mov     esp, ebp
                pop     ebp
                ; The stack frame is closed.

                retn
main            endp
```

Conditional IF–THEN–ELSE *Statements*

There are two kinds of algorithms, *unconditional* and *conditional*. The order of performing operations in unconditional algorithms is always invariable and does not depend on the input data — for example: a = b + c. The order of operations in conditional algorithms, on the contrary, depends on the input data. For example: **IF** c is not zero **THEN** a = b/c, **ELSE** send an error message.

Take note of the keywords **IF**, **THEN**, and **ELSE** marked in bold. These are called *branches*. No program can manage without them. (Simple examples like "Hello, World!" do not count.) Branches are the heart of any programming language. Therefore, it is extremely important to identify them correctly.

Without going into syntactic details of particular programming languages, branch statements can be schematically represented in this general form:

IF (*condition*) **THEN** {*statement₁; statementₙ;*} **ELSE** {*statement1₁; statement1ₘ;*}

The task of the compiler is to translate this statement into a sequence of machine instructions that execute statement₁ and statementₙ if condition is true and, respectively, statement1₁ and statement1ₘ if it is false. Microprocessors of the 80x86 family, however, support rather modest set of conditional statements limited to conditional jumps. Programmers who are familiar only with PCs based on the 80x86 family will not consider such a limitation unnatural. However, there are plenty of processors supporting a *prefix of conditional instruction execution*: Instead of writing TEST ECX, ECX/JNZ xxx/MOV EAX, 0x666, it is possible to write TEST ECX, ECX/IFZ MOV EAX, 0x666. The IFZ is just the prefix of conditional execution; it allows the execution of the following instruction only if the zero flag is set.

In this sense, 80x86 microprocessors can be compared with the early dialects of BASIC, which did not admit any statement except GOTO into branches. Compare the following listings.

Listing 153. The New (Left) and Old (Right) BASIC Dialects

IF A=B THEN PRINT "A=B"	10 IF A=B THEN GOTO 30
	20 GOTO 40
	30 PRINT "A=B"
	40 ... // The rest of code

Anyone familiar with old dialects of BASIC will probably remember that it is better to execute GOTO if the condition is false, and to continue the normal execution of the program otherwise. (Contrary to popular opinion, knowledge of BASIC programming is not entirely useless, especially in disassembling.)

Most compilers (even nonoptimizing ones) invert the value of the condition, converting the statement IF *(condition)* **THEN** *{statement₁; statementₙ;}* into the following pseudo-code:

Listing 154. The Pseudo-Code Produced from the IF-THEN Branch

```
IF (NOT condition) THEN continue
     statement₁;
     ...
     statementₙ;
continue:
...
```

Hence, to reconstruct the source code of the program, the condition must be inverted, and the block of statements *{statement₁; statementₙ;}* must be stuck to the THEN keyword. Suppose the compiled code looked like this:

Listing 155. A Reconstruction of the Source Code of a Program

```
10 IF A<>B THEN 30
20 PRINT "A=B"
30 ...// The rest of the code
```

In this case, the source code must have contained the following lines: IF A=B THEN PRINT "A=B". However, could the programmer check the variables A and B for an inequality (i.e., IF A<>B THEN PRINT "A<>B")? The compiler would invert the value of the condition and generate the following code:

Listing 156. The Complier Inverts the Condition

```
10 IF A=B THEN 30
20 PRINT "A<>B"
30 ...// The rest of the code
```

Certainly, you might encounter compilers that suffer from verbosity. They are easy to recognize by the unconditional jump that immediately follows the branch.

Listing 157. A Verbose Complier Is Recognized by the Unconditional Jump

```
IF (condition) THEN do
GOTO continue
do:
        statement₁;
        ...
        statementₙ;
continue:
```

In cases like this, the conditional value does not need to be inverted. However, nothing terrible will happen if it is inverted; the code of the program merely may become less understandable.

Now let's consider how the complete statement IF (condition) THEN {statement₁; statementₙ;} ELSE {statement1₁; statement1ₘ;} may be converted. Some compilers act like this:

Listing 158. The Result of Converting the Complete IF-THEN-ELSE Statement

```
IF (condition) THEN do_it
// The ELSE branch is executed.
statement1₁;
...
statement1ₙ;
GOTO continue

do_it:
// The IF branch is executed.
statement₁;
...
statementₘ;
continue:
```

Others convert it like this:

Listing 159. An Alternate Result of Converting the IF-THEN-ELSE Statement

```
IF (NOT condition) THEN else
// The IF branch is executed.
```

```
statement₁;
...
statementₘ;
GOTO continue

else:
// The ELSE branch is executed.
statement1₁;
...
statement1ₘ;
continue:
```

The latter inverts the condition value; the former does not. Therefore, without knowing the compiler's preferences, it will be impossible to figure out what the original code of the program looked like. However, this does not create any problems, since it is always possible to write the condition in a convenient form. For example, if you don't like the statement IF (c<>0) THEN a=b/c ELSE PRINT "Error!", you can write IF (c==0) THEN PRINT "Error!" ELSE a=b/c.

Types of conditions. Conditions can be *simple* (elementary) or *complex* (compound). An example of the former is if (a==b)...; an example of the latter is if ((a==b) && (a!=0)).... Thus, *any complex conditional expression can be decomposed into several simple conditional expressions.* Let's start with simple conditions.

There are two types of elementary conditions: *relational conditions* (with the operators "less," "equal," "less than or equal," "not equal," "greater than," and "greater than or equal," designated as <, ==, >, <=, !=, and >=, respectively) and *logical conditions* (with the operators AND, OR, NOT, and exclusive OR, designated in C notation as &, |, !, and ^, respectively). Well-known hacking authority Matt Pietrek adds testing the bits in here as well. In this book, we will cover this topic separately.

A true expression returns the Boolean value TRUE; a false one returns FALSE. The internal (physical) representation of the Boolean variables can vary, depending on a particular implementation. Generally, FALSE *is represented by zero*, and TRUE *is represented by a nonzero value.* TRUE is often represented by 1 or −1, but this is not always the case. For example, IF ((a>b)!=0)... is correct, and IF ((a>b)==1)... is bound to a particular implementation, which is undesirable.

Note that IF ((a>b)!=0)... does not check the a and b variables for an inequality to zero; rather, it checks the result of their comparison. Consider the following example: IF ((666==777)==0) printf("Woozl!"). What will be displayed on the screen by launching this example? "Woozl!", of course.

Neither 666 nor 777 is equal to zero, but 666!=777. Therefore, the condition (666==777) is false and equal to zero. Incidentally, writing IF ((a=b)==0)... would give a different result: The value of the variable b would be assigned to the variable a, and then checked for equality to zero.

Logical conditions mostly are used to bind two or more elementary relational conditions into a compound condition (for example, IF ((a==b) && (a!=0)) ...). When compiling the program, the compiler always resolves compound conditions into simple ones (in this example, as IF a==b THEN IF a=0 THEN...). At the second stage, the conditional statements are replaced by GOTO.

Listing 160. The Complier Resolves Compound Conditions into Simple Ones

```
IF a!=b THEN continue
IF a==0 THEN continue
...// The code of the condition
:continue
...// The rest of code
```

The order of computing the elementary conditions in a complex expression is at the compiler's discretion. The only guarantee is that the conditions bound by the logical AND will be tested from left to right in the order they appear in the program. If the first condition is false, the next one *will not be computed*, which allows us to write code like if ((filename) and (f=fopen(&filename[0],"rw")))... If the filename pointer points to nonallocated memory area (i.e., contains zero, a logical FALSE), the fopen function is not called and the crash does not occur. These types of computations have been called *fast Boolean operations*.

Now, let's proceed to the problem of identifying logical conditions and analyzing complex expressions. Let's take the following expression: if ((a==b) && (a!=0))... and see what happens when it is compiled.

Listing 161. The Result of Compiling the `if ((a==b) && (a!=0))` Expression

```
IF a!=b THEN continue ———————————
IF a==0 THEN continue ———————————
...// This code is executed
// if at least one of the
  // above conditions is false.
:continue ◄—————————————————— ◄——
// The rest of the code follows.
```

Obviously, this code gives itself away with a series of conditional jumps to the same label. Note that each elementary condition is tested for being true or false, and the label is located *after* the code that immediately follows the branch statements.

Identifying the logical OR operation is more difficult because of the ambiguity of its translation. Let's consider this on the example of the `if ((a==b) || (a!=0))...` statement. It can be broken into elementary statements in this way:

Listing 162. Breaking `if ((a==b) || (a!=0))` into Elementary Statements

```
IF a==b THEN do_it
IF a!=0 THEN do_it
goto continue
:do_it
...// The code is executed
   // if at least one of the
   // above conditions is true.
:continue
...// The rest of the code follows.
```

It can also be broken down as follows:

Listing 163. An Alternate Breakdown of `if ((a==b) || (a!=0))`

```
IF a==b THEN do_it
IF a==0 THEN continue
:do_it
...// The code is executed
   // if at least one of the
   // above conditions is true.
:continue
...// The rest of the code follows.
```

The first variant is rather distinctive, comprising a series of tests (without inverting the condition), which pass control to the label preceding the code that is executed if the condition is true, with an unconditional jump at the end of the series, which passes control to the label that follows this code.

However, optimizing compilers eliminate the unconditional-jump instruction by inverting the test of the last condition in the chain and changing the jump address. Beginners often take this construction for a mix of OR and AND. Consider

address. Beginners often take this construction for a mix of OR and AND. Consider the result of compiling the if ((a==b) || (a==c) && a(!=0))... statement.

Listing 164. A Compilation of the if ((a==b) || (a==c) && a(!=0)) Statement

---

```
IF a==b THEN check_null
IF a!=c THEN continue
check_null:
IF a==0 THEN continue
...// The code is executed if at least one of the
   // conditions in the last two IF statements is true.
continue:
...// The rest of the code follows.
```

How can a single, readable compound condition be obtained from the impenetrable jungle of elementary conditions? Let's start from the beginning (i.e., from the first comparison operation). If the a==b condition happens to be true, it makes the a!=c condition "quit the game." Such a construction is typical for the OR operation (i.e., if one of two conditions is true, it is enough for the code to work). Keeping if ((a==b) || ...) in mind, let's move on. If the (a!=c) condition is true, all further tests cease and control is passed to the label, located after the code, pertaining to conditions. It is reasonable to assume that this is the last OR operation in a chain of comparisons, which is typical behavior. Therefore, let's invert the expression of the condition and continue to write: if ((a==b) || (a==c)...). The last stage tests the a==0 condition. It will be impossible to execute code pertaining to conditions if the a==0 condition is bypassed. Hence, it is not OR; it is AND. But AND always inverts the condition. Consequently, the original code should look like this: if ((a==b) || (a==c) && (a!=0)).

Do not be deluded: This example is elementary. In reality, optimizing compilers can have you troubled.

Representing complex conditions as a tree. A statement consisting of three or four elementary conditions can be analyzed mentally. However, patterns of five or more conditions form a labyrinth that is difficult to comprehend immediately. The ambiguity of translating complex conditions brings about an ambiguity of interpretation. This results in varying analyses, and progressively more information must be remembered with each step. It would be easy to go mad in such a case, or to get confused and obtain incorrect results.

The way out is to use a two-level system of translation. At the first stage, the elementary conditions are converted into an intermediate form that clearly and consistently represents the interrelation of the elementary operations. Then, the final translation is put into any suitable notation (for example, C, BASIC, or Pascal).

The only problem is how to choose the successful intermediate form. There are many options, but to save paper, let's consider just one: *trees.*

Let's represent each elementary condition as a *node* with two branches going to the appropriate states: *the condition is true* and *the condition is false.* For clarity, let's designate "false" as a triangle and "true" as a square. Let's agree always to place "false" on the left and "true" on the right. We will call the obtained design a *nest.*

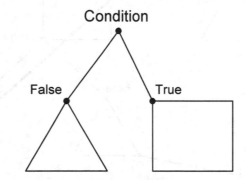

Fig. 22. A schematic representation of the nest

Nests may be joined into trees. Each node can join only one nest, but each nest can join several nodes. Let's consider this in more detail.

Let's join two elementary conditions by a logical AND operation, taking the example ((a==b) && (a!=0)). Let's take the first condition from the left, (a==b), and place it in a nest with two branches, the left one corresponding to a!=b (i.e., the condition a==b is false), and the right one corresponding to the opposite case. Then, let's do the same with the second condition, (a!=0). This gives two nests; the only thing that remains is to join them with the logical AND operation. As you know, AND tests the second condition only when the first condition is true. Hence, the (a!=0) nest should be hitched to the right branch of (a==b). The right branch (a!=0) will correspond to the ((a==b) && (a!=0)) expression being true, and both left branches will correspond to this expression being false. Let's designate the first case with the do_it label, and the second case with the continue label. As a result, the tree should look like the one shown in Fig. 23.

For better presentation, let's mark the route from top of the tree to the label do_it with a thick arrow. It is only possible to get to do_it by one route. Graphically, the AND operation looks like this:

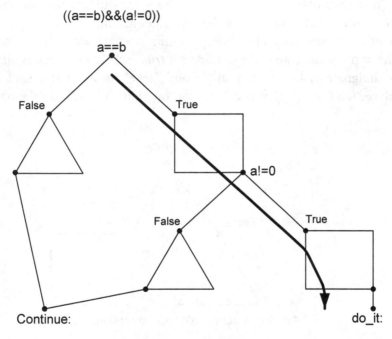

Fig. 23. A graphical representation of the AND operation as a binary tree (which shows only one way to get into the do_it point)

Let's proceed to the logical OR operation and consider the following expression: ((a==b) || (a!=0)). If the (a==b) condition is true, the entire expression is also true. Hence, the right branch of the (a==b) nest is connected to the do_it label. If the (a==b) condition is false, the next condition is tested. This means that the left branch of (a == b) is connected to the (a!=b) nest. If the (a!=b) condition is true, the entire ((a==b) || (a!=0)) expression is also true; if the (a!=b) condition is false, the entire expression is also false, since the (a!=b) condition is tested only when the (a==b) condition is false. It can be concluded that the left branch of the (a!=b) nest is connected to the continue label, and the right one to do_it. Note that it is possible to get to do_it by two different routes. The OR operation graphically looks like it is shown in Fig. 24.

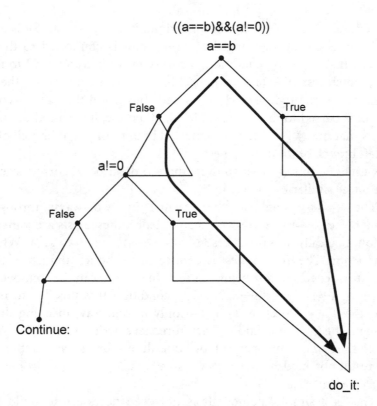

Fig. 24. A graphical representation of the OR operation as a binary tree
(which shows two ways to get to the do_it point)

So far, logical operations have been represented by trees. However, trees were meant for just the opposite purpose — to convert the sequence of elementary conditions into intuitively clear representation. Let's try this with the following code:

Listing 165. Converting a Sequence of Elementary Conditions

```
IF a==b THEN check_null
IF a!=c THEN continue
check_null:
IF a==0 THEN continue
...// This is code pertaining to the condition.
continue:
...// The rest of the code follows.
```

Let's take the (a==b) condition and put it into the nest. If it is false, the (a!=c) condition is tested, meaning the (a!=c) nest is connected to the left branch of (a==b). If the (a==b) condition is true, control is transferred to the check_null label, which tests the (a==0) condition for being true; hence, the (a==0) nest is connected to the right branch of (a==b). In turn, if the (a!=c) condition is true, control is passed to the continue label; otherwise, it is passed to check_null. This means that the (a!=0) nest is connected both to the right branch of (a==b) and to the left branch of the (a!=c) nest.

Certainly, this is easier to draw than to describe. A correct sketch should produce a tree similar to the one in Fig. 25.

The (a==0) nest can be reached in two ways: through (a==b), or through the (a==b) → (a!=c) chain. Hence, these nests are joined by the OR operation. Logically, this produces if ((a==b) || !(a!=c)...). Where has this NOT come from? The (a==0) nest is connected to the left branch of the (a!=c) nest (i.e., it is checked for being true). Now, NOT can be removed by inverting the if ((a==b) || (a==c)...)... condition It is possible to move further — from the (a==0) nest to do_it — only in one way, meaning this is a junction through the AND operation. Therefore, let's write if (((a==b) || (a==c)) && !(a==0))... and get rid of superfluous brackets and the NOT operation. The result obtained is ((a==b) || (a==c) && (a!=0)) {// *The code pertaining to the condition*}.

This is a simple method. It is not even necessary to build trees manually, as a program can be written to do the work.

Analyzing specific implementations. Before translating the IF (*a complex condition*) THEN {*statement₁:statementₙ*} ELSE statement into a machine language, remember that the IF–THEN–ELSE statement can be represented through IF–THEN, the THEN {*statement₁:statementₙ*} aggregate expression can be represented by THEN GOTO do_it, and any complex condition can be reduced to a sequence of elementary relational conditions. Therefore, at a basic level, the operation can be reduced to statements of the type IF (*a simple relational condition*) THEN GOTO do_it, which then can be used like building blocks to produce the necessary combination.

Let's consider *relational conditions*, or the *results of comparing two numbers*. In Intel 80x86 microprocessors, integer values are compared using the CMP instruction, and floating-point values are compared using the coprocessor instructions such as FCOM, FCOMP, FCOMPP, FCOMI, FCOMIP, FUCOMI, and FUCOMIP. You should be familiar with assembler, so these instructions will be considered only briefly.

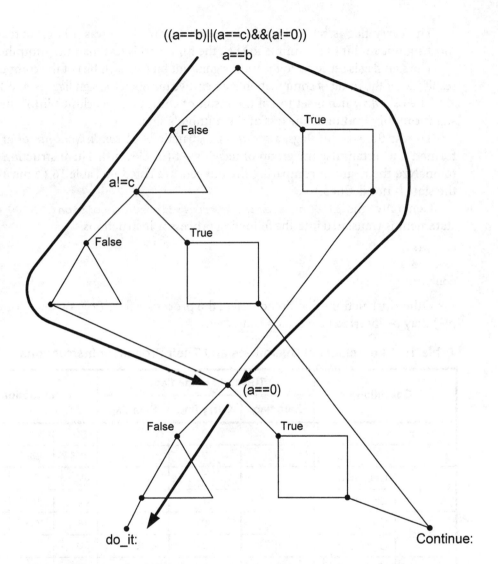

Fig. 25. A graphical representation of a complex expression

The CMP instruction. This is equivalent to the SUB integer subtraction operation with one exception — unlike SUB, CMP does not modify the operands. It only affects the flags of the main processor: the *zero flag*, the *carry flag*, the *sign flag*, and the *overflow flag*.

The zero flag is set to 1 if the result of subtraction is zero (i.e., if the operands are equal).

The carry flag is set to 1 if, during subtraction, there was a borrow from the most significant bit of the minuend (i.e., the minuend is less than the subtrahend).

The sign flag is set equal to the most significant bit (the sign bit) of the computation result (i.e., if the result of computation is a negative number, the sign flag is set to 1).

The overflow flag is set to 1 if the result of computation "climbs into" the most significant bit, leading to the loss of the number's sign.

To test the state of flags, a group of instructions of *conditional jumps* are performed if a certain flag (or group of flags) is set (or cleared). The instructions used to analyze the result of comparing the integers are listed in Table 16 (? means that the state is not defined.)

Generally, the IF (*an elementary relational condition*) THEN do_it statement is translated into the following processor instructions:

```
cmp a, b
jxx do_it
continue:
```

Other instructions that do not affect the processor flags (MOV or LEA, for example) may be inserted between CMP and Jxx.

Table 16. The Relational Operations and Their Processor Instructions

Condition		The state of the flags			Instruction		
		Zero flag	Carry flag	Sign flag			
a == b		1	?	?	JZ	JE	
a != b		0	?	?	JNZ	JNE	
a < b	Unsigned	?	1	?	JC	JB	JNAE
	Signed	?	?	!=OF	JL	JNGE	
a > b	Unsigned	0	0	?	JA	JNBE	
	Signed	0	?	==OF	JG	JNLE	
a >=b	Unsigned	?	0	?	JAE	JNB	JNC
	Signed	?	?	==OF	JGE	JNL	
a <=b	Unsigned	(ZF == 1) || (CF == 1)		?	JBE	JNA	
	Signed	1		? !=OF	JLE	JNG	

Comparing floating-point numbers. The FCOMxx instructions that compare floating-point numbers (see Table 18), in contrast to instructions that compare integers, affect the coprocessor registers, rather than the main-processor registers. At first glance, this seems reasonable. However, there are no conditional-jump instructions controlled by the coprocessor flags. Additionally, the coprocessor flags are not accessible directly — to read their status, the SW coprocessor status register must be loaded into memory or into a general-purpose register of the main processor.

Analyzing the flags manually is worse. When comparing integers, the flags controlling the conditional jump are not taken into account — producing, for example, CMP A,B; JGE do_it (jump IF A is greater OR equal to B). Here, the trick will not work. However, it is possible to cheat and copy the coprocessor flags to the flag register of the main processor, then use native conditional-jump instructions of Jxx type.

The coprocessor flags cannot be copied to the main processor directly. This operation should be carried out in two stages: The FPU flags have to be loaded into memory or into any general-purpose register available, then pushed into the CPU flags register. Only one instruction, POPF, is capable of directly modifying the CPU flags register. All that remains is to figure out which coprocessor flags correspond to which processor flags. Surprisingly, flags 8, 10, and 14 of the coprocessor coincide with flags 0, 2, and 6 of the main processor — with CF, PF, and ZF, respectively (see Table 17). Therefore, the most significant byte of the coprocessor flags register can be pushed into the least significant byte of the main-processor flags register without any conversion. However, bits 1, 3, and 5 of the CPU flags register, which are not used in current versions of the processor, but are reserved for the future use, will be distorted. The values of the reserved bits must never be changed. Who can guarantee that, tomorrow, one of them will not be responsible for the self-destruction of the processor? This is a joke, of course, but many a true word is spoken in jest.

Fortunately, no complex manipulations are necessary. The processor developers have provided a special instruction, SAHF, that copies bits 8, 10, 12, 14, and 15 of the AX. From Table 17, it is possible to work out that bit 7 of the CPU flags register contains the sign flag, and the corresponding bit of the coprocessor flags register contains the FPU busy flag!

Therefore, *it is not possible to use signed conditional jumps* (JL, JG, JLE, JNL, JNLE, JGE, and JNGE) to analyze the result of comparing the floating-point numbers. These jumps work with the sign and overflow flags. If, instead of the sign flag, these instructions receive the FPU busy flag, and the overflow flag is left in a suspended state, the conditional jump will not work as desired. Unsigned jump instructions (JE, JB, JA, etc. — see Table 16) should be used instead.

This does not mean that it is impossible to compare the signed floating-point numbers — it is possible. But, for the analysis of the comparison results, only unsigned conditional jumps should be used.

Table 17. The Correspondence of the CPU and FPU Flags

CPU	7	6	5	4	3	2	1	0
	SF	ZF	--	AF	--	PC	--	CF
FPU	15	14	13	12	11	10	9	8
	Busy!	C3(ZF)	TOP			C2(PF)	C1	C0(CF)

Thus, the floating-point statement IF (*an elementary relational condition*) THEN do_it can be translated into one of the two following sequences of the processor instructions:

Listing 166. Two Variants of the Processor Instructions

```
fld          [a]              fld          [a]
fcomp        [b]              fcomp        [b]
fnstsw ax                     fnstsw ax
sahf                          test         ah, bit_mask
jxx          do_it            jnz          do_it
```

The first variant is more illustrative, but the second one works faster. However, only Microsoft Visual C++ may be capable of generating this code. Borland C++ and Watcom C have an inclination for the instruction SAHF, which slightly slows but drastically simplifies the code analysis. An instruction like JNA would tell even a half-asleep hacker that the jump is being carried out when a<=b. Checking the bit mask such as TEST AH, 0x41/JNZ do_it would make us take a pause for thought, or mechanically consult a reference manual. (See Table 16.)

In this sense, the instructions of the FUCOMIxx family are more convenient: They return the result of comparison directly into registers of the main processor. Unfortunately, only Pentium Pro understands them; they are lacking in earlier microprocessors. Therefore, you will rarely encounter them in real programs. Pages 3–112 of Intel's "*Instruction Set Reference*" describe these instructions in detail.

Table 18. The Instructions for Comparing Floating-Point Values

Instruction	Purpose	Result
FCOM	Compares the floating-point value located on top of the coprocessor stack with the operand located in memory or on the FPU stack	The FPU flags
FCOMP	Same as FCOM, but pops the floating-point value off the top of the stack	
FCOMPP	Compares two floating-point values located on top of the coprocessor stack, then pops them off the stack	
FCOMI	Compares the floating-point value located on top of the coprocessor stack with another floating-point value located on the FPU stack	The CPU flags
FCOMIP	Compares the floating-point value located on top of the coprocessor stack with the floating-point value located on the FPU stack, then pops it off the stack	
FUCOMI	Makes an unordered comparison of the floating-point value located on top of the coprocessor stack with the floating-point value located on the FPU stack	
FUCOMIP	Makes an unordered comparison of the floating-point value located on top of the coprocessor stack with the floating-point value located on the FPU stack, then pops the value off top of the stack	

Table 19. The Coprocessor Flags

FPU flags	Purpose	Bit mask
OE	Overflow flag	#0x0008
C0	Carry flag	#0x0100
C1	---	#0x0200
C2	Parity flag	#0x0400
C3	Zero flag	#0x4000

Table 20. The State-Of-Flag Registers for Relational Operations

Relation	The state of the FPU flags		SAHF instruction	Bit mask
a<b*	C0 == 1		JB	#0x0100 == 1
a>b	C0 == 0	C3 == 0	JNBE	#0x4100 == 0
a==b	C3 == 1		JZ	#0x4000 == 1
a!=b	C3 == 0		JNZ	#0x4000 == 0
a>=b	C0 == 0		JNB	#0x0100 == 0
a<=b	C0 == 1	C3 === 1	JNA	#0x4100 == 1

* The left operand of the instruction that compares floating-point values is a; the right operand is b.

Table 21. The Behavior of Compilers

Compiler	The algorithm that analyzes the FPU flags...
Borland C++	...copies the coprocessor flags to the flags register of the main processor.
Microsoft Visual C++	...tests the bit mask.
Watcom C	...copies the coprocessor flags to the flags register of the main processor.
Free Pascal	...copies the coprocessor flags to the flags register of the main processor.

Boolean set-on-condition instructions. Starting with 80386 chips, the language of Intel microprocessors was enriched with the instruction for setting a byte on condition, SETxx. This instruction sets its single operand to 1 (Boolean TRUE) if the condition xx is true, and clears it to 0 (Boolean FALSE) if the condition xx is false.

The SETxx instruction is widely used by optimizing compilers to eliminate the branches (i.e., to remove conditional jumps), since branches clear the processor pipeline, seriously reducing the program performance.

Table 22. The Boolean Set-On-Condition Instructions

Instruction			Relationship		Condition
SETA	SETNBE		a>b	Unsigned	CF == 0 && ZF == 0
SETG	SETNLE			Signed	ZF == 0 && SF == OF
SETAE	SETNC	SETNB	a>=b	Unsigned	CF == 0
SETGE	SETNL			Signed	SF == OF
SETB	SETC	SETNAE	a<b	Unsigned	CF == 1
SETL	SETNGE			Signed	SF != OF
SETBE	SETNA		a<=b	Unsigned	CF == 1 || ZF == 1
SETLE	SETNG			Signed	ZF == 1 || SF != OF
SETE	SETZ		a==b	————	ZF == 1
SETNE	SETNZ		a!=0	————	ZF == 0

Other conditional instructions. 80x86 family of microprocessors supports a set of the conditional instructions that generally do not involve the relational operation. Therefore, these instructions are rarely used by compilers. However, they are used frequently in assembler inserts. They deserve to be mentioned at least briefly.

Conditional-jump instructions. In addition to those described in Table 16, there are eight conditional-jump instructions: JCXZ, JECXZ, JO, JNO, JP (also known as JPE), JNP (also known as JPO), JS, and JNS. Of these, only JCXZ and JECXZ have a direct relationship to the comparison operations. Optimizing compilers occasionally replace the CMP [E]CX, 0\JZ do_it construction with the shorter equivalent J[E]CXZ do_it.

The JO and JNS conditional jumps are mainly used in mathematical libraries to process the long numbers (1024-bit integers, for example).

Besides basic applicability, the JS and JNS conditional jumps are frequently used to quickly test the value of the most significant bit.

The JP and JNP conditional jumps are used only in exotic assembler inserts.

Table 23. The Auxiliary Conditional Jumps

Instruction	Jump if...	Flags
JCXZ	...the CX register equals zero.	CX == 0
JECXZ	...the ECX register equals zero.	ECX == 0
JO	...there is an overflow.	OF == 1
JNO	...there is no overflow.	OF == 0
JP/JPE	...parity of the least significant byte of the result is even.	PF == 1
JNP/JPO	...parity of the least significant byte of the result is odd.	PF == 0
JS	...the sign bit is set.	SF == 1
JNS	...the sign bit is cleared.	SF == 0

Conditional-move instructions. The processors of the Pentium family starting from Pentium Pro, Pentium II, Celeron support the conditional-move instruction CMOVxx, which sends a value from the source to the destination if the condition xx is satisfied. This leads to more effective code that does not contain branches and fits into a smaller number of instructions.

Let's consider the IF a<b THEN a=b statement. Compare how it is translated using conditional-jump (left) and conditional-move (right) instructions.

Listing 167. Comparing a Conditional Jump and a Conditional Move

```
cmp a, b            cmp a, b
jae continue:       cmovb a, b
mov a, b
continue:
```

Unfortunately, at the time of writing, no compiler seemed to use CMOVxx when generating code. However, the benefits are so obvious that advanced optimizing compilers should emerge in the near future. Table 24 presents a brief description sufficient for disassembling the programs. See pages 3–59 of the "*Instruction Set Reference*" guide from Intel for more detailed explanations.

Table 24. The Main Conditional-Move Instructions

Instruction			Relationship		Condition
CMOVA	CMOVNBE		a>b	Unsigned	CF == 0 && ZF == 0
CMOVG	CMOVNLE			Signed	ZF == 0 && SF == OF
CMOVAE	CMOVNC	CMOVNB	a>=b	Unsigned	CF == 0
CMOVGE	CMOVNL			Signed	SF == OF
CMOVB	CMOVC	CMOVNAE	a<b	Unsigned	CF == 1
CMOVL	CMOVNGE			Signed	SF != OF
CMOVBE	CMOVNA		a<=b	Unsigned	CF == 1 || ZF == 1
CMOVLE	CMOVNG			Signed	ZF == 1 || SF != OF
CMOVE	CMOVZ		a==b	——	ZF == 1
CMOVNE	CMOVNZ		a!=0	——	ZF == 0

Boolean comparisons. The logical FALSE corresponds to the zero value, and the logical TRUE to any nonzero value. Thus, Boolean relationships are reduced to comparing the value of a variable with zero. The IF (a) THEN do_it statement is translated into IF (a!=0) THEN do_it.

Practically all compilers replace the CMP A, 0 instruction with the shorter instructions such as TEST A, A or OR A, A. In all cases, if A==0, the zero flag is set; if A!=0, the zero flag is cleared.

Therefore, code like TEST EAX, EAX\JZ do_it in the disassembler listing indicates a Boolean comparison.

Identifying the "(condition)?do_it:continue" construction. In C, the statement such as a=(condition)?do_it:continue generally is converted into IF (condition) THEN a=do_it ELSE a=continue. However, the results of compiling these statements are not always the same.

For a variety of reasons, the ? operator is more amenable to optimization than the IF–THEN–ELSE branch, as the following example demonstrates.

Listing 168. Identifying the Conditional Operator

```
main()
{
int a;        // The variable is not initialized on purpose.
```

```
int b;          // Therefore, the compiler does not replace
                // it with a constant.

a=(a>0)?1:-1;  // A conditional operator

if (b>0)        // A branch
        b=1;
else
        b=-1;

return a+b;
}
```

If we disassemble this example compiled using Microsoft Visual C++, we will get the following result:

Listing 169. The Disassembled Code of the Test Example Compiled Using Visual C++

```
        push    ebp
        mov     ebp, esp
        ; The stack frame is opened.

        sub     esp, 8
        ; The space is allocated for local variables.

        ; This is the beginning of the ? conditional operator.
        xor     eax, eax
        ; EAX is zeroed.

        cmp     [ebp+var_a], 0
        ; The variable is compared with zero.

        setle   al
        ; The value 0x1 is placed into al if var_a <= 0.
        ; The value 0 is placed into al if var_a > 0.

        dec     eax
        ; EAX is decremented by 1.
```

```
; Now, if var_a > 0, then EAX := -1,
; and if var_a <=0, then EAX := 0.

and      eax, 2
; All bits are cleared except for the second bit from the left.
; Now, if var_a > 0, then EAX := 2,
; and if var_a <=0, then EAX := 0.

add      eax, 0FFFFFFFFh
; 0x1 is subtracted from EAX.
; Now, if var_a > 0, then EAX := 1,
; and if var_a <=0, then EAX := -1.

mov      [ebp+var_a], eax
; The result is assigned to the var_a variable.
; This is the end of the ? operator.
; Note that not a single conditional jump was needed
; to translate the conditional operator —
; the compiler has managed to do without branches.

; This is the beginning of the IF—THEN—ELSE branch.
cmp      [ebp+var_b], 0
; The var_b variable is compared with zero.

jle      short else
; Jump if var_b <= 0.

; The var_b > 0 branch
mov      [ebp+var_b], 1
; The value 1 is assigned to var_b.

jmp      short continue
; Jump to the continue label.

; The var_b > 0 branch
else:                                  ; CODE XREF: _main+1D↑j
         mov      [ebp+var_b], 0FFFFFFFFh
; The value -1 is written into the var_b variable.

continue:                              ; CODE XREF: _main+26↑j
```

```
; This is the end of the IF-THEN-ELSE branch.
; Note that the implementation of the IF-THEN-ELSE statement
; is more compact than that of ?. However, it contains conditional
; jumps that considerably degrade the program performance.

mov    eax, [ebp+var_a]
; The value of the var_a variable is loaded into EAX.

add    eax, [ebp+var_b]
; The value of the var_a variable is added to the value
; of the var_b variable. The result is placed into EAX.

mov    esp, ebp
pop    ebp
; The stack frame is closed.
retn
```

Thus, it is impossible to assert that the result of translating the ? conditional operator is always the same as the result of translating the IF-THEN-ELSE statement. However, in aggressive optimization mode, Microsoft Visual C++ generates identical code in both cases.

Listing 170. Compiling the Program Using Aggressive Optimization

```
_main      proc near
      push   ecx
      ; Memory is allocated for a and b local variables.
      ; Since they are never used together, but only individually,
      ; the compiler places them into one memory cell.

      mov    edx, [esp+0]        ; Instruction #1 of the ? operator
      ; The value of the a variable is loaded into EDX.

      xor    eax, eax            ; Instruction #2 of the ? operator
      ; EAX is zeroed.
      ; Since the setle al instruction only modifies the content
      ; of the AL register (and does not affect the rest of the
      ; register), it must be cleared manually.

      test   edx, edx            ; Instruction #3 of the ? operator
```

```
; The a variable is tested for equality to zero.

mov     edx, [esp+0]        ; Instruction #1 of the IF branch
; The value of the b variable is loaded into EDX.

setle  al                   ; Instruction #4 of the ? operator
; The value 0x1 is placed into al if a <= 0.
; The value 0 is placed into al if a > 0.

dec     eax                 ; Instruction #5 of the ? operator
; EAX is decremented by 1.
; Now, if a > 0, then EAX := -1,
; and if a <=0, then EAX := 0.

xor     ecx, ecx            ; Instruction #2 of the IF branch
; Zeroing ECX

and     eax, 2              ; Instruction #6 of the ? operator
; All bits are cleared except the second bit from
; the left, counting from 1.
; Now, if a > 0, then EAX := 2,
; and if a <=0, then EAX := 0.

dec     eax                 ; Instruction #7 of the ? operator
; EAX is decremented by 1.
; Now, if a > 0, then EAX := 1,
; and if a <=0, then EAX := -1.

test    edx, edx            ; Instruction #3 of the IF branch
; The b variable is tested for equality to zero.

setle  cl                   ; Instruction #4 of the IF branch
; The value 0x1 is placed into cl if b <= 0.
; The value 0 is placed into cl if b > 0.

dec     ecx                 ; Instruction #5 of the IF branch
; ECX is decremented by 1.
```

```
        ; Now, if b > 0, then ECX := -1,
        ; and if b <=0, then ECX := 0.

        and     ecx, 2                  ; Instruction #6 of the IF branch
        ; All bits are cleared except the second bit from the left,
        ; counting from 1.
        ; Now if b > 0, then ECX := 2;
        ; and if b <=0, then ECX := 0.

        dec     ecx                     ; Instruction #7 of the IF branch
        ; ECX is decremented by 1.
        ; Now, if b > 0, then ECX := -1,
        ; and if b <=0, then ECX := 0.

        add     eax, ecx
        ; The b variable is added to the a variable.

        pop     ecx
        ; The stack frame is closed.
        retn
_main           endp
```

The compiler has mixed the instructions relevant to the ? conditional operator with the IF-THEN-ELSE branch statements. However, comparing them shows that the implementations of both constructions are identical.

From a language point of view, however, the ? conditional operator favorably differs from a branch. For example, it can be used directly in expressions.

Listing 171. Using the ? Conditional Operator Directly in an Expression

```
main()
{
        int a;
        printf("Hello, %s\n", (a > 0) ? "Sailor" : "World!");
}
```

This could be implemented so compactly using branches! However, this convenience is superficial; the compiler translates this example as follows:

Listing 172. The Compilation of the Example with the ? Conditional Operator

```
main()
{
        int a;
        char *p;
        static char s0[]="Sailor";
        static char s1[]="World";
        if (a>0) p=s0; else p=s1;

        printf("Hello, %s\n", p);
}
```

Compile both listings, then disassemble the files obtained — they should be identical. Thus, when decompiling C/C++ programs, it generally is impossible to say whether a branch or a conditional operator was used in them. In certain cases, a few hooks can help determine the appearance of the source code.

For example, it seems improbable that the programmer could build the listing shown in the last example. Why should the programmer introduce static variables and manipulate a pointer in a complex way, when it's easier to use a conditional operator, rather than a branch?

Thus, if the conditional operator smoothly fits into the program being decompiled, and branching does not, then a conditional operator, not a branch, was used in the source code.

Identifying the types. Conditional instructions are a key for identifying the types. Since the result of comparing signed and unsigned variables is analyzed by different groups of instructions, signed int can be distinguished from unsigned int.

However, the identification of types is a theme for a separate discussion.

16-bit mode. One unpleasant feature of 16-bit mode is the limited scope of conditional-jump instructions. In an attempt to make the code highly compact, the microprocessor developers allotted only 1 byte for the destination address, limiting the jump length to an interval of 255 bytes. This *short jump* is defined by the relative signed offsets, counted from the beginning of the instruction next to the jump instruction (see Fig. 26). Such addressing restricts the length of the "forward" jump (i.e., the "downward" jump) to just 128 bytes. The "backward" jump is even shorter: 127 bytes! (The backward jump is shorter because it needs to "jump over" the jump instruction itself.) These restrictions are not relevant to the *near* unconditional jump, which uses 2 bytes for addressing and works within the limits of the entire segment.

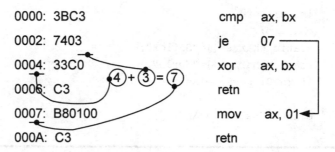

Fig. 26. An internal representation of a short jump

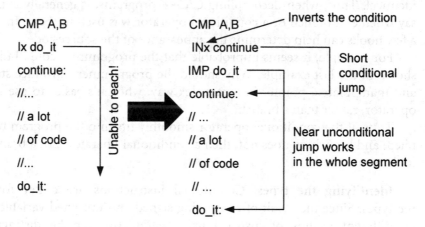

Fig. 27. Translating short jumps

Short jumps complicate the translation of branches: Not all the destination addresses are within the 128-byte limit. There are many ways to bypass this restriction. The following is most popular: If the compiler sees that the destination address falls outside the limits reached by the conditional jump, it inverts the condition of the IF statement and performs a short jump to the continue label. Alternatively, it uses a near jump, which works within the limits of one segment, to pass control to the do_it label (see Fig. 27).

A similar approach can be used when the destination address is located in a different segment. It is enough to replace the near unconditional jump with the far one. To the great pleasure of compiler developers — and of hackers who disassemble programs — in 32-bit mode, the conditional jump "strikes" within the limits of the entire 4 GB address space, and all these problems disappear.

Listings of examples. To better understand the points made in this section, let's consider several examples using various compilers. Let's begin with analysis of elementary integer relationships.

Listing 173. Elementary Integer Relationships

```c
#include <stdio.h>

main()
{
        int a; int b;
        if (a<b) printf("a<b");
        if (a>b) printf("a>b");
        if (a==b) printf("a==b");
        if (a!=b) printf("a!=b");
        if (a>=b) printf("a>=b");
        if (a<=b) printf("a<=b");
}
```

Disassembled code of this example compiled using Microsoft Visual C++ looks as follows:

Listing 174. Compiling Elementary Integer Relationships Using Visual C++

```asm
main            proc near               ; CODE XREF: start+AF↑p

var_b           = dword ptr -8
var_a           = dword ptr -4

        push    ebp
        mov     ebp, esp
        ; The stack frame is opened.

        sub     esp, 8
```

```
; Memory is allocated for the var_a and var_b local variables.

mov    eax, [ebp+var_a]
; The value of the var_a local variable is loaded into EAX.

cmp    eax, [ebp+var_b]
; The value of the var_a local variable is compared
; to the value of the var_b variable.

jge    short loc_40101B
; If var_a >= var_b, jump to continue; otherwise,
; print the strings.
; Note that the original code looked like this:
; if (a < b) printf("a < b");
; In other words, the relational condition has been inverted
; by the compiler.
; The JGE instruction is signed; therefore,
; the var_a and var_b variables
; are also signed.

; The DO_IT branch
push   offset aAB_4 ; "a < b"
call   _printf
add    esp, 4
; Printing the strings "a < b".

; // The CONTINUE branch
loc_40101B:                          ; CODE XREF: main+C↑j
mov    ecx, [ebp+var_a]
; The value of the var_a variable is loaded into ECX.

cmp    ecx, [ebp+var_b]
; The value of the var_a variable is compared with the var_b variable.

jle    short loc_401030
; Jump if var_a <= var_b; otherwise, print the strings.
; Hence, the strings are printed if !(var_a <= var_b), or
; if var_a > var_b. Therefore, the original code of the program
; looked as follows.
```

```
; if (a > b) printf("a > b");

push    offset aAB_3 ; "a>b"
call    _printf
add     esp, 4
;


loc_401030:                         ; CODE XREF: main+21↑j
        mov     edx, [ebp+var_a]
        ; The value of the var_a variable is loaded into EDX.

        cmp     edx, [ebp+var_b]
        ; The value of the var_a variable is compared
        ; with the var_b variable.

        jnz     short loc_401045
        ; Jump if var_a!=var_b; otherwise, print the strings.
        ; Hence, the original code of the program looked like this:
        ; if (a==b) printf("a==b");

        push    offset aAB ; "a==b"
        call    _printf
        add     esp, 4

loc_401045:                         ; CODE XREF: main+36↑j
        mov     eax, [ebp+var_a]
        ; The value of the var_a variable is loaded into EAX.

        cmp     eax, [ebp+var_b]
        ; The value of the var_a variable is compared
        ; with the value of the var_b variable.

        jz      short loc_40105A
        ; Jump if var_a==var_b; otherwise, print the strings.
        ; Hence, the original code of the program looked like this:
        ; if (a!==b) printf("a!=b");

        push    offset aAB_0 ; "a!=b"
        call    _printf
```

```
        add     esp, 4

loc_40105A:                              ; CODE XREF: main+4B↑j
        mov     ecx, [ebp+var_a]
        ; The value of the var_a variable is loaded into ECX.

        cmp     ecx, [ebp+var_b]
        ; The value of the var_a variable is compared
        ; with the var_b variable.

        jl      short loc_40106F
        ; Jump if var_a < var_b; otherwise, print the strings.
        ; Hence, the original code of the program looked like this:
        ; if (a>=b) printf("a>=b");

        push    offset aAB_1 ; "a>=b"
        call    _printf
        add     esp, 4

loc_40106F:                              ; CODE XREF: main+60↑j
        mov     edx, [ebp+var_a]
        ; The value of the var_a variable is loaded into EDX.

        cmp     edx, [ebp+var_b]
        ; The value of the var_a variable is compared
        ; with the var_b variable.

        jg      short loc_401084
        ; Jump if var_a>var_b; otherwise, print the strings.
        ; Hence, the original code of the program looked like this:
        ; if (a<=b) printf("a<=b");

        push    offset aAB_2 ; "a<=b"
        call    _printf
        add     esp, 4

loc_401084:                              ; CODE XREF: main+75↑j
        mov     esp, ebp
        pop     ebp
```

```
        ; The stack frame is closed.

        retn
main            endp
```

Now let's compare this 32-bit code with the 16-bit code generated by Microsoft C++ 7.0. (To save space, only a fragment is given.)

Listing 175. The Disassembled Code of Elementary Integer Relationships Compiled by Microsoft C++ 7.0

```
        mov     ax, [bp+var_a]
        ; The value of the var_a variable is loaded into AX.

        cmp     [bp+var_b], ax
        ; The value of the var_a variable is compared
        ; with the value of the var_b variable.

        jl      loc_10046
        ; Jump to the code that prints the string if var_a < var_b.

        jmp     loc_10050
        ; An unconditional jump is made to continue.
        ; Note that the compiler, being unsure that the scope
        ; of the short jump will be sufficient to reach the
        ; continue label, has jumped to the do_it label,
        ; located within the scope.
        ; The unconditional jump has taken control.
        ; Thus, the conversion of the
        ; comparison condition has occurred twice: once when the
        ; relational condition was parsed, and once when the
        ; code was generated. Therefore, NOT falls on NOT and can be
        ; canceled. Hence, the original code to the program looked like this:
        ; if (a<b) printf("a<b");

loc_10046:                              ; CODE XREF: _main+11↑j
        mov     ax, offset aAB ; "a<b"
        push    ax
        call    _printf
        add     sp, 2

loc_10050:                              ; CODE XREF: _main+13↑j
        ; // The rest of the code follows.
```

Now let's change type of variables being compared from int to float, and see how this affects the resulting code. The disassembled code of the example compiled using Microsoft Visual C++ should be the following. (Only a fragment is given.)

Listing 176. The Disassembled Code of Elementary Floating-Point Relationships Compiled by Visual C++

```
fld     [ebp+var_a]
; The value of the var_a floating-point variable is loaded
; on top of the coprocessor stack.

fcomp   [ebp+var_b]
; The value of the var_a variable is compared
; with the var_b variable.
; The result of comparison is saved in the coprocessor flags.

fnstsw ax
; The coprocessor flags register is copied into the AX register.

test    ah, 1
; Is bit 0 of the AH register set?
; Is bit 8 of the coprocessor flags register set?
; And what is in the eighth bit?
; The eighth bit contains the carry flag.

jz      short loc_20
; Jump if the carry flag is cleared (i.e., this is the
; equivalent of the JNC construction when integer values are
; compared). Let's look in Table 16 — the JNB instruction
; is a synonym for JNC. Hence, the original code looked like this:
; if (a < b) printf("a < b");

push    offset $SG339 ; "a<b"
call    _printf
add     esp, 4
loc_20:                          ; CODE XREF: _main+11↑j
```

The code generated by Borland C++ or Watcom C is much clearer.

Listing 177. The Disassembled Code of Elementary Floating-Point Relationships Compiled by Borland C++ or Watcom C

```
        fld     [ebp+var_a]
        ; The value of the var_a floating-point variable is loaded
        ; on top of the coprocessor stack.

        fcomp   [ebp+var_b]
        ; The value of the var_a variable is compared with the var_b variable,
        ; and the result is saved in the coprocessor flags.

        fnstsw ax
        ; The coprocessor flags register is copied to the AX register.

        sahf
        ; The corresponding bits of the AH register are copied
        ; to the flags of the main processor.

        jnb     short loc_1003C
        ; Jump if !(a<b); otherwise, print the strings printf("a<b").
        ; Now, without digging in any reference tables,
        ; the original code can be reconstructed:
        ; if (a < b) printf("a < b");

        push    offset unk_100B0 ; format
        call    _printf
        pop     ecx
loc_1003C:                                  ; CODE XREF: _main+F↑j
```

Now, with some experience identifying elementary conditions, let's proceed to more complex operations. Consider the following example:

Listing 178. Identifying Complex Operations

```c
#include <stdio.h>

main()
{
        unsigned int a; unsigned int b; int c; int d;
```

```c
       if (d) printf("TRUE");
       else
       if (((a>b) && (a!=0)) || ((a==c) && (c!=0))) printf("OK\n");
       if (c==d) printf("+++\n");
}
```

Disassembling the compiled code of this example should give roughly the following:

Listing 179. The Disassembled Code with Complex Operations

```asm
_main           proc near

var_d           = dword ptr -10h
var_C           = dword ptr -0Ch
var_b           = dword ptr -8
var_a           = dword ptr -4

       push    ebp
       mov     ebp, esp
       ; The stack frame is opened.

       sub     esp, 10h
       ; Memory is allocated for local variables.

       cmp     [ebp+var_d], 0
       ; The value of the var_d variable is compared with zero.

       jz      short loc_1B
       ; If the var_d variable is equal to zero, jump to
       ; the loc_1B label; otherwise, print the "TRUE" string.
       ; This can be represented schematically as follows:
       ;                      var_d == 0
       ;                     /          \
       ;         loc_1B                   printf("TRUE")
       push    offset $SG341 ; "TRUE"
       call    _printf
       add     esp, 4
       jmp     short loc_44
       ;
       ; This is a dead giveaway. Let's include this jump
```

```
        ; into the existing tree.
        ;
        ;               var_d == 0
        ;            /              \
        ;      loc_1B            printf("TRUE")
        ;                               |
        ;                            loc_44
        ;

loc_1B:                                 ; CODE XREF: _main+A↑j
        mov     eax, [ebp+var_a]
        ; The value of the var_a variable is loaded into EAX.

        cmp     eax, [ebp+var_b]
        ; The var_a variable is compared with the var_b variable.

        jbe     short loc_29
        ; If var_a is less or equal to var_b, jump to loc_29.
        ; Let's graft a new nest, keeping in mind
        ; that var_a and var_b are unsigned variables!
        ;
        ;                      var_d == 0
        ;                    /            \
        ;          loc_1B            printf("TRUE")
        ;             |                      |
        ;      var_a <= var_b             loc_44
        ;      /          \
        ; continue      loc_29
        ;

        cmp     [ebp+var_a], 0
        ; The value of the var_a variable is compared with zero.

        jnz     short loc_37
        ; Jump to loc_37 if var_a is not equal to zero.
        ;
        ;                         var_d == 0
        ;                       /            \
        ;            loc_1B            printf("TRUE")
        ;               |                      |
        ;        var_a <= var_b             loc_44
        ;        /          \
        ;  var_a !=0      loc_29
        ;  /      \
        ; continue    loc_37
```

```
        ;
loc_29:                                          ; CODE XREF: _main+21↑j
        ; The loc_29 label is already present. Let's correct
        ; the tree.
        ;
        ;
        ;                                 var_d == 0
        ;                     loc_1B                    printf("TRUE")
        ;
        ;                   var_a <= var_b                  loc_44
        ;
        ;         var_a !=0              loc_29
        ;                    loc_37
        ;
        ;

mov     ecx, [ebp+var_a]
; The value of the var_a variable is loaded into ECX.

cmp     ecx, [ebp+var_C]
; The value of the var_a variable is compared with the var_C variable.

jnz     short loc_44
; Jump if var_a != var_C.
        ;
        ;
        ;                                 var_d == 0
        ;                     loc_1B                    printf("TRUE")
        ;
        ;                   var_a <= var_b                  loc_44
        ;
        ;         var_a !=0              loc_29
        ;                    loc_37
        ;
        ;
        ;                     var_a != var_C
        ;              continue                loc_44
        ;
        ;
```

```
cmp     [ebp+var_C], 0
; The value of the var_C variable is compared with zero.

jz      short loc_44
; Jump to the loc_44 label if var_C == 0.
;
;                                          var_d == 0
;                              loc_1B              printf("TRUE")
;
;                                  var_a <= var_b           loc_44
;
;                       var_a !=0          loc_29
;
;                              loc_37
;
;
;
;                           var_a != var_C
;
;                    var_C == 0            loc_44
; continue
;
```

```
loc_37:                                      ; CODE XREF: _main+27↑j
; The loc_37 label is already present in the tree.
; Let's graft it!
;                                      var_d == 0
;                           loc_1B            printf("TRUE")
;
;                               var_a <= var_b        loc_44
;
;                     var_a !=0          loc_29
;
;
;
;
;                           var_a != var_C
;
;                    var_C == 0
;
;
;
;                                  loc_44        loc_37
;
;                                          printf("OK")
;
```

```
        ;
        ;
        push    offset $SG346 ; "OK\n"
        call    _printf
        add     esp, 4


loc_44:                                 ; CODE XREF: _main+19↑j  _main+2F↑j ...
        ; The loc_44 and loc_37 branches close up.
        ;
        ;                           var_d == 0
        ;                   loc_1B              printf("TRUE")
        ;
        ;               var_a <= var_b          loc_44
        ;
        ;           var_a !=0           loc_29
        ;
        ;
        ;
        ;
        ;           var_a != var_C
        ;
        ;       var_C == 0
        ;
        ;
        ;
        ;
        ;                       loc_44      loc_37
        ;
        ;                           printf("OK")
        ;
        ;
        ;


        mov     edx, [ebp+var_C]
        ; The value of the var_C variable is loaded into EDX.

        cmp     edx, [ebp+var_d]
        ; The value of the var_C variable is compared
        ; with the value of the var_D variable.

        jnz     short loc_59
        ; Jump if var_C != var_D.
```

```
push    offset $SG348 ; "+++\n"
call    _printf
add     esp, 4
;
;
;                            var_d == 0
;               loc_1B                  printf("TRUE")
;
;               var_a <= var_b               loc_44
;
;        var_a !=0              loc_29
;
;
;
;
;               var_a != var_C
;
;     var_C == 0
;
;
;
;                    loc_44        loc_37
;
;
;                          printf("OK")
;
;
;
;                    var_C != var_D
;
;        printf("+++")              finish
;
;
;
loc_59:                                    ; CODE XREF: _main+4A↑j
        mov     esp, ebp
        pop     ebp
        retn
_main   endp
```

As a result, a huge tree with many branches has grown. At first glance, it seems impossible to figure out. However, a little pruning will yield results. Let's optimize the tree, remove the "twisted" branches by inverting the condition in the nest, and eliminate all labels — now that the skeleton of the tree is ready, they are unnecessary. If everything is done correctly, the tree should look like this:

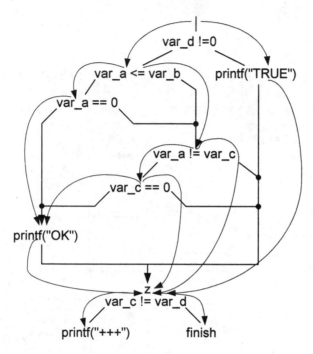

Fig. 28. The logical tree

It is striking that all routes pass through the point Z (see Fig. 28), which joins all branches. This means that there are two separate trees, each represented by its own IF statement. Wonderful! This considerably simplifies the analysis — if the trees are independent, they can be analyzed independently! Let's begin from the upper one.

Two branches grow from the var_d!=0: nest: the right one leading to printf("TRUE") and, further, to the end of the IF–THEN[-ELSE] statement; and the left one passing through a crowd of nests before it reaches Z. The situation looks like this: *If the var_d variable is not equal to zero, print "OK" and finish the job; otherwise, carry out additional tests.* In other words, IF (var_d !=0) THEN printf("OK") ELSE..., and the left branch of the nest (var_d != 0) is the ELSE branch. Let's analyze it.

From the (var_a <= var_b) nest to the printf("OK") nest, there are two routes: !(var_a <= var_b) → !(var_a == 0) and !(var_a != var_c) → !(var_c == 0). If there is an alternative, there must always be an OR operation:

either the first way, or the second. At the same time, the nests of both ways are connected serially; they are joined by an AND operation. Therefore, this branch should look like this: IF ((var_a > var_b) && (var_0 != 0)) || (var_a == var_c) && (var_c != 0)) printf("OK"). Putting ELSE into the first IF statement gives: IF (var_d !=0) THEN printf("OK") ELSE IF ((var_a > var_b) && (var_0 != 0)) || (var_a == var_c) && (var_c != 0)) printf("OK").

The analysis of the second tree is trivial: IF (var_c==var_d) printf "+++"). The source code of the program being disassembled looked like the following:

Listing 180. The Source Code of the Program Being Disassembled

```
u_int a; u_int b; ?_int c; ?_int d;
if (d) printf("TRUE");
else
 if (((a>b) && (a!=0)) || ((a==c) && (c!=0))) printf("OK\n");


if (c==d) printf("+++\n");
```

Therefore, the a and b variables are unsigned int, since the result of comparison was analyzed using the JNB unsigned relational instruction. Unfortunately, the c and d variables are impossible to determine. Nevertheless, we were able to reconstruct a complex condition using trees, in which it would be easy to get lost.

Optimizing the branches. Let's examine a tangled code. (The SETGE instruction sets the destination operand to 1 if the SF and OF status flags are equal (i.e., SF == OF); otherwise, the destination operand is set to zero.)

Listing 181. A Tangled Code Produced by an Optimizing Compiler

```
        mov     eax, [var_A]
        xor     ecx, ecx
        cmp     eax, 0x666
        setge   cl
        dec     ecx
        and     ecx, 0xFFFFFC00
        add     ecx, 0x300
        mov     [var_zzz], ecx
```

At first glance, this fragment seems to have been borrowed from a crafty protection mechanism. In fact, it is the result of compiling the following trivial statement: if (a<0x666) zzz=0x200 else zzz=0x300, whose nonoptimized form looks as follows:

Listing 182. The Nonoptimized Form of the Tangled Code

```
        mov eax,[var_A]
        cmp eax,0x666
        jge Label_1
        mov ecx, 0x100
        jmp Label_2
Label_1:
        mov ecx, 0x300
Label_2:
        mov [var_zzz],ecx
```

Why did the compiler reject this variant? The variant is shorter, but it contains *branches* (i.e., unplanned changes of the normal flow of the program's execution). Branches negatively affect performance — they clear the pipeline, which in contemporary processors is very long and cannot be refilled quickly. Therefore, removing branches by using mathematical calculations is entirely justified and warmly greeted. In addition, it complicates the analysis of the program, protecting it from hackers.

Let's execute the program step by step.

Listing 183. A Step-by-Step Execution of the Tangled Code

```
mov eax, [var_A]
        ; eax == var_A


xor ecx, ecx
        ; ecx=0;


cmp eax, 0x666
        ; if eax<0x666 { SF=1; OF=0} else {SF=0; OF=0}

setge cl
```

```
      ; if eax<0x666 (i.e. SF==1, OF ==0) cl=0 else cl=1

dec ecx
      ; if eax<0x666 ecx=-1 else ecx=0

and ecx, 0xFFFFFC00
      ; if eax<0x666 (i.e., ecx==-1) ecx=0xFFFFFC00 (-0x400) else ecx=0;

add ecx, 0x300
      ; if eax<0x666 (i.e., ecx=-0x400) ecx=0x100 else ecx=0x300;

mov [esp+0x66],ecx
```

The algorithm has been cleared up and reversed. It is a rather simple example —
in real life, the code will be much more complicated — but the basic idea is appar-
ent: Encountering the SETxx instruction makes it likely that a conditional jump is
near. In elementary cases, SETxx may be replaced with SBB (subtraction with a borrow). Knowing this, let us solve the second problem.

Listing 184. Another Example of Code That Looks Like a Puzzle

```
sub ebx, eax
sbb ecx, ecx
and ecx, ebx
add eax, ecx
```

What does this code do? Does it perform some complex arithmetic operation?

Listing 185. A Step-by-Step Execution of the Puzzle-Like Code

```
sub ebx, eax
      ; if (EBX<EAX) SF=1 else SF=0

sbb ecx, ecx
      ; if (EBX<EAX) ECX=-1 else ECX=0

and ecx, ebx
      ; if (EBX<EAX) ECX=EBX else ECX=0

add eax, ecx
      ; if (EBX<EAX) EAX=EAX+(EBX-EAX) else EAX=EAX
```

Removing the brackets from the last expression (while remembering that EAX has been subtracted from EBX) gives if (EBX<EAX) EAX=EBX. Therefore, it is a classical algorithm for finding a smallest of two signed numbers. One more example:

Listing 186. Another Example That Looks Complicated but Is Rather Simple

```
cmp eax, 1
sbb eax, eax
and ecx, eax
xor eax, -1
and eax, ebx
or eax, ecx
```

Try to solve the example manually, then look at the answer.

Listing 187. The Step-by-Step Execution of the Seemingly Complex Code

```
cmp eax, 1
        ; if (EAX!=0) SF=0 else SF=1

sbb eax, eax
        ; if (EAX!=0) EAX=-1 else EAX=0
and ecx, eax
        ; if (EAX!=0) ECX=ECX else ECX=0

xor eax, -1
        ; if (EAX!=0) EAX=0 else EAX=-1

and eax, ebx
        ; if (EAX!=0) EAX=0 else EAX=EBX

or eax, ecx
        ; if (EAX!=0) EAX=ECX else EAX=EBX
```

After all these exercises, readers could be excused for dreaming in Boolean terms. However, such is the cost of civilization. Incidentally, most compilers deal with conditional jumps well enough, and do not tend to expel them completely. Therefore, analyzing optimized code is not a great strain. Although, manual optimization is not included, as professional developers eliminate conditional jumps first of all.

The **switch–case–break** *Statements*

To improve the readability of programs, the switch statement was introduced in the C language. In Pascal, the case statement is more flexible than its C analogue and is used for solving the same task. These distinctions will be considered further on.

It is easy to show that switch is equivalent to the following statement: IF (a == x₁) THEN statement₁ ELSE IF (a == x₂) THEN statement₂ ELSE IF (a == x₃) THEN statement₃ ELSE IF (a == x₄) THEN statement₄ ELSE... a default statement. Representing this branch as a logical tree gives a structure that resembles a braid (Fig. 29).

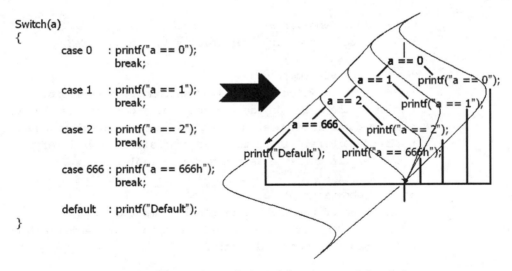

```
Switch(a)
{
        case 0    : printf("a == 0");
                    break;

        case 1    : printf("a == 1");
                    break;

        case 2    : printf("a == 2");
                    break;

        case 666 : printf("a == 666h");
                    break;

        default   : printf("Default");
}
```

Fig. 29. A general translation of the switch statement

It might seem that identifying switch is an easy task: Even without constructing a tree, we cannot overlook a long chain of nests that test an expression against a set of immediate values for equality (since switch cannot compare a variable against another variable).

In reality, however, matters stand differently. Compilers translate switch into a real mess stuffed from top to bottom with various relational operations. Let's compile the above example in Microsoft Visual C++ and see the result.

Listing 188. The Disassembled Code of the `switch` Statement Compiled by Visual C++

```
main            proc near               ; CODE XREF: start+AF↓p

var_tmp         = dword ptr -8
var_a           = dword ptr -4

        push    ebp
        mov     ebp, esp
        ; The stack frame is opened.

        sub     esp, 8
        ; Space is allocated for local variables.

        mov     eax, [ebp+var_a]
        ; The value of the var_a variable is loaded into EAX.

        mov     [ebp+var_tmp], eax
        ; Notice that switch creates its own temporary variable.
        ; Even if the value of the variable being compared is changed
        ; in some branch of case, the result of executing switch will not be
        ; affected! Hereinafter, to avoid confusion, we will refer to
        ; the var_tmp variable as the var_a variable.

        cmp     [ebp+var_tmp], 2
        ; The value of the var_a variable is compared to 2.
        ; Hm... In the source code, case began with 0, and ended with 0x666.
        ; What has this got to do with 2?

        jg      short loc_401026
        ; A jump is made if var_a > 2.
        ; Note that there was no such operation in the source code!
        ; This jump does not lead to calling the printf function
        ; (i.e., this code fragment is obtained not
        ; by directly translating some case branch, but in some other way.)

        cmp     [ebp+var_tmp], 2
        ; The value of var_a is compared to 2.
        ; It is an obvious flaw of the compiler; we perfomed
```

```
; this operation just a moment ago and have not changed any
; flags since then.

jz      short loc_40104F
; A jump is made to the call of printf("a == 2") if var_a == 2.
; This code is obtained by translating the branch
; case 2: printf("a == 2").

cmp     [ebp+var_tmp], 0
; The value of var_a is compared to 0.

jz      short loc_401031
; A jump is made to the call of printf("a == 0") if var_a == 0.
; This code is obtained by translating the branch
; case 0: printf("a == 0").

cmp     [ebp+var_tmp], 1
; The value of var_a is compared to 1.

jz      short loc_401040
; A jump is made to the call of printf("a == 1") if var_a == 1.
; This code is obtained by translating the branch
; case 1: printf("a == 1").

jmp     short loc_40106D
; A jump is made to the call of printf("Default").
; This code is obtained by translating the branch
; default: printf("a == 0").

loc_401026:                         ; CODE XREF: main+10↑j
        ; This branch gains control if var_a > 2.
        cmp     [ebp+var_tmp], 666h
        ; The value of var_a is compared to the value 0x666.

jz      short loc_40105E
; A jump is made to the call of printf("a == 666h")
; if var_a == 0x666. This code is obtained by translating
; the branch case 0x666: printf("a == 666h").
```

```
jmp     short loc_40106D
; A jump is made to the call of printf("Default").
; This code is obtained by translating the branch
; default: printf("a == 0").


loc_401031:                         ; CODE XREF: main+1C↑j
        ; printf("A == 0")
        push    offset aA0 ; "A == 0"
        call    _printf
        add     esp, 4
        jmp     short loc_40107A
; Here is the first break statement, which passes control
; outside the switch statement. If there were no break statement,
; the rest of the branches of case would be executed
; irrespective of the var_a value to which they correspond!


loc_401040:                         ; CODE XREF: main+22↑j
        ; printf("A == 1")
        push    offset aA1 ; "A == 1"
        call    _printf
        add     esp, 4
        jmp     short loc_40107A


loc_40104F:                         ; CODE XREF: main+16↑j
        ; printf("A == 2")
        push    offset aA2 ; "A == 2"
        call    _printf
        add     esp, 4
        jmp     short loc_40107A


loc_40105E:                         ; CODE XREF: main+2D↑j
        ; printf("A == 666h")
        push    offset aA666h ; "A == 666h"
        call    _printf
        add     esp, 4
        jmp     short loc_40107A


loc_40106D:                         ; CODE XREF: main+24↑j main+2F↑j
```

```
        ; printf("Default")
        push    offset aDefault      ; "Default"
        call    _printf
        add     esp, 4


loc_40107A:                          ; CODE XREF: main+3E↑j main+4D↑j ...
        ; The end of switch
        mov     esp, ebp
        pop     ebp
        ; The stack frame is closed.

        retnm
main            endp
```

By constructing a logical tree (see the "*Conditional IF–THEN–ELSE Statements*" section), the following picture will be obtained (Fig. 30). First, notice the a > 2 condition, which was not present in the source code. Then, notice the changes to the order of processing the cases. The calls of the printf function still follow one after another, according to the order in which they were declared. Why does the compiler behave in such a way?

The purpose of the (a > 2) nest can be easily explained: Consecutive processing of all cases of the switch statement is extremely unproductive. Such processing is fine if there are only four or five cases, but what if the programmer stuffs the switch statement with a hundred or so of them? The processor will become exhausted from testing each of them. (Especially since the sought case "likes" to appear at the end). Therefore, the compiler "compresses" the tree to reduce its height. Instead of one branch (in Fig. 30) in the given case, the compiler has constructed two of them. It placed the numbers that are less than two into the left branch, and the rest of the numbers into the right branch. As a result, the branch 666h appeared to be relocated from the end of the tree to its beginning. This method of optimizing the search for values is called a *fork algorithm*.

The compiler has the right to change the order in which it processes the cases: The standard does not say anything about it, and each implementation is free to act as it considers appropriate. The case routines (i.e., the code to which case passes control if the condition is true) are another matter. They must be ordered just as they were declared in the program because, in the absence of the terminating break statement, they should be executed strictly in the order suggested by the programmer. However, this opportunity of the C language is rarely used.

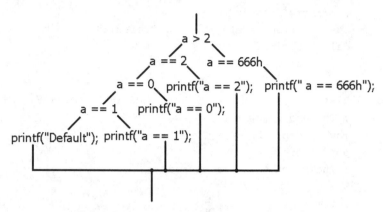

Fig. 30. Translating the `switch` statement
using Microsoft Visual C++

Thus, we can identify the `switch` statement by applying this statement: *After removing the central nest and grafting the right branch to the left one (or vice versa), if we obtain an equivalent tree that forms a structure like a braid, we are dealing with a `switch` statement or its analogue.*

Do we have the right to delete nests, and would this operation impair the tree's structure? Note that the left branch of the node's nest contains the `(a == 2)`, `(a == 0)`, and `(a == 1)` nests; the right one contains `(a == 0x666)`. Obviously, if `a == 0x666`, then `a != 0` and `a != 1`. Hence, it is safe to graft the right branch to the left one. After such a transformation, the tree becomes typical for the `switch` construction (Fig. 31).

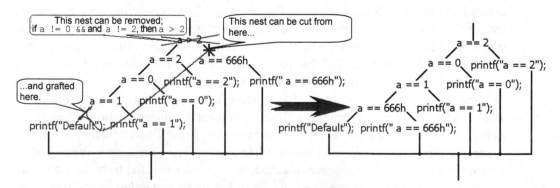

Fig. 31. Pruning the logical tree

However, such simple identification tricks do not always work. Particular compilers may create such a mess that your hair will stand on end. Compiling this example in Borland C++ 5.0 results in the following:

Listing 189. The Disassembled Code of the `switch` Statement Compiled by Borland C++

```
; int __cdecl main(int argc, const char **argv, const char *envp)
_main          proc near           ; DATA XREF: DATA:00407044↓o

       push   ebp
       mov    ebp, esp
       ; The stack frame is opened.
       ; The compiler places the variable into the EAX register.
       ; Since it was not initialized, making note of it is not easy!

       sub    eax, 1
       ; Now, EAX is decremented by 1. What might it mean?
       ; There was no subtraction in the program.

       jb     short loc_401092
       ; If EAX < 1, a jump is made to the call of printf("a == 0").
       ; As already mentioned, CMP is the SUB instruction, except
       ; it does not change the operands.
       ; Therefore, this code is generated as a result of translating
       ; the branch case 0: printf("a == 0").
       ; Think! What values can EAX take to satisfy
       ; the condition of this relation? At first glance,
       ; EAX < 1 (in particular, 0, -1, -2, ...) STOP!
       ; You know that JB is an unsigned instruction of comparison,
       ; and -0x1 appears as 0xFFFFFFFF in an unsigned form.
       ; 0xFFFFFFFF is much greater than 1;
       ; therefore, the only suitable value is 0.
       ; Thus, this construction is simply a veiled test of EAX
       ; for equality to zero.

       jz     short loc_40109F
       ; A jump is made if the zero flag is set.
       ; It will be set if EAX == 1.
       ; Indeed, the jump is performed to printf("a == 1").
```

```
        dec    eax
        ; EAX is decremented by 1.


        jz     short loc_4010AC
        ; A jump is made if the zero flag is set. The flag is set if,
        ; after 1 is subtracted by the SUB instruction, 1 is left in EAX.
        ; In other words, the original value of EAX should have been 2.
        ; Control is passed to the branch that calls printf("a == 2").


        sub    eax, 664h
        ; The value 0x664 is subtracted from EAX.


        jz     short loc_4010B9
        ; A jump is made if the zero flag is set.
        ; After decrementing EAX twice, it becomes equal to 0x664,
        ; hence the original value is 0x666.


        jmp    short loc_4010C6
        ; A jump is made to the call of printf("Default").
        ; Hence, this is the end of the switch statement.

loc_401092:                              ; CODE XREF: _main+6↑j
; printf("a==0");
        push   offset aA0 ; "a == 0"
        call   _printf
        pop    ecx
        jmp    short loc_4010D1

loc_40109F:                              ; CODE XREF: _main+8↑j
; printf("a==1");
        push   offset aA1; "a == 1"
        call   _printf
        pop    ecx
        jmp    short loc_4010D1

loc_4010AC:                              ; CODE XREF: _main+B↑j
; printf("a==2");
```

```
        push    offset aA2 ; "a == 2"
        call    _printf
        pop     ecx
        jmp     short loc_4010D1


loc_4010B9:                          ; CODE XREF: _main+12↑j
; printf("a==666");
        push    offset aA666h ; "a == 666h"
        call    _printf
        pop     ecx
        jmp     short loc_4010D1


loc_4010C6:                          ; CODE XREF: _main+14↑j
; printf("Default");
        push    offset aDefault    ; "Default"
        call    _printf
        pop     ecx


loc_4010D1:                          ; CODE XREF: _main+21↑j  _main+2E↑j ...
        xor     eax, eax
        pop     ebp
        retn
_main           endp
```

The code generated by the compiler modifies the variable being compared. The optimizer decided that DEC EAX is shorter and works faster than the instruction for comparison with a constant. However, hackers are none the better for it! The direct retranslation of the code (see "*Conditional IF–THEN–ELSE Statements*") gives a code like this: IF (a-- == 0) printf("a == 0"); ELSE IF (a==0) printf("a == 1"); ELSE IF (--a == 0) printf("a == 2"); ELSE IF ((a-=0x664)==0) printf("a == 666h); ELSE printf("Default"). The switch statement does not seem to be visible in it. However, it is still visible: The switch must be near the long chain IF-THEN-ELSE-IF-THEN-ELSE. It will be easier to recognize the switch statement if we represent it as a tree; note the typical braid (Fig. 32).

There is another distinctive feature — case routines or, to be more precise, the break statements that traditionally terminate them. They form the right half of the "braid" and converge to the point Z. However, many programmers prefer case routines that have a size of two or three screens and that include loops, branches, and even nested switch statements! As a result, the right part of the "braid" turns into an impassable jungle. The left part of the "braid" remains recognizable.

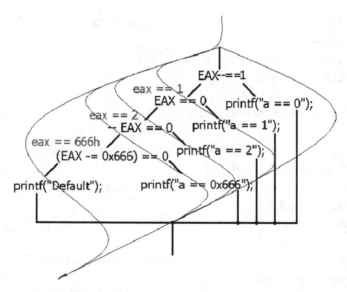

Fig. 32. Constructing a logical tree with nests that modify
the variable being compared

The last compiler to be considered regarding this topic is Watcom C. As one would expect, we should watch for specific subtleties and "delicacies" here. The compiled code of the previous example looks like the following:

Listing 190. The Disassembled Code of the switch Statement Compiled by Watcom C

```
main_           proc near           ; CODE XREF: __CMain+40↓p
        push    8
        call    __CHK
        ; The stack is tested for overflow.

        cmp     eax, 1
        ; The value 1 is compared with the register variable
        ; containing the a variable.
```

```
jb      short loc_41002F
; If EAX == 0, a jump is made to the branch
; that contains additional tests.

jbe     short loc_41003A
; If EAX == 1 (i.e., the condition EAX < 1 has been tested already),
; a jump is made to the branch that calls printf("a == 1").

cmp     eax, 2
; EAX is compared to 2.

jbe     short loc_410041
; If EAX == 2 (the condition EAX < 2 has been tested already),
; a jump is made to the branch that calls printf("a == 2").

cmp     eax, 666h
; EAX is compared to the value 0x666.

jz      short loc_410048
; If EAX == 0x666, a jump is made to the branch that calls
; printf("a == 666h").

jmp     short loc_41004F
; None of the conditions is satisfied and a jump
; to the branch "Default" must be performed.

loc_41002F:                     ; CODE XREF: main_+D↑j
; // printf("a == 0");
test    eax, eax
jnz     short loc_41004F
; There is no reason for this additional test.

push    offset aA0 ; "A == 0"
; Watcom has managed to do with only one call of printf.
; The case routines just pass the necessary argument to printf.
; That is indeed an optimization!
jmp     short loc_410054

loc_41003A:                     ; CODE XREF: main_+F↑j
; printf("a == 1");
```

```
        push    offset aA1 ; "A == 1"
        jmp     short loc_410054


loc_410041:                             ; CODE XREF: main_+14↑j
; printf("a == 2");
        push    offset aA2 ; "A == 2"
        jmp     short loc_410054


loc_410048:                             ; CODE XREF: main_+1B↑j
; printf("a == 666h");
        push    offset aA666h ; "A == 666h"
        jmp     short loc_410054


loc_41004F:                             ; CODE XREF: main_+1D↑j  main_+21↑j
; printf("Default");
        push    offset aDefault    ; "Default"


loc_410054:                             ; CODE XREF: main_+28↑j  main_+2F↑j ...
        call    printf_
        ; Here, printf is receiving arguments from the case routines.

        add     esp, 4
        ; The stack frame is closed.


        retn
main_           endp
```

Strangely enough, Watcom generates an illustrative and readable code.

Distinguishing switch from the case statement of the Pascal language.
The case statement of Pascal is practically identical to its C rival —
the switch statement. However, they are not twins: The Pascal case statement favorably differs in that it supports *sets* and *ranges of values*. Sets can be processed using switch, although not as elegantly as in Pascal. (See Listing 189.) However, testing to discover if a value falls into a range in C exclusively uses the
IF—THEN—ELSE statement. In Pascal, each case body is terminated by the
implicit break, and the C programmer is free to use it or not at his or her own
discretion.

Listing 191. Distinguishing the `switch` Statement from the `case` Statement

```
CASE a OF                                    switch(a)
begin                                        {
        1       : WriteLn('a == 1');             case 1 : printf("a == 1");
                                                          break;
        2,4,7   : WriteLn('a == 2|4|7');         case 2 :
                                                 case 4 :
                                                 case 7 : printf("a == 2|4|7");
                                                          break;
        9       : WriteLn('a == 9');             case 9 : printf("a == 9");
                                                          break;
end;
```

Both languages impose a restriction on the variable being tested: It must belong to one of the integer types. In addition, all sets (ranges) of values must be constants or constant expressions computed at compile time. Variables or function calls should not be used.

It is interesting to see how Pascal translates the tests of ranges and how this differs in the C compilers. Let's consider the following example:

Listing 192. Translating Tests of Ranges in Pascal

```
VAR
        a : LongInt;
BEGIN

        CASE a OF
                2         :         WriteLn('a == 2');
                4, 6      :         WriteLn('a == 4 | 6 ');
                10..100   :         WriteLn('a == [10,100]');
        END;
END.
```

Compiling this example in Free Pascal should give the following result. (To save space, only the left part of the "braid" is shown.)

Listing 193. The Disassembled Code of the Range-Test Translation Using Free Pascal

```
mov     eax, ds:_A
; The value of the variable being compared is loaded into EAX.
```

```
cmp     eax, 2
; EAX is compared to the value 0x2.


jl      loc_CA                  ; This is the end of CASE.
; If EAX < 2, a jump is made to the end of case.


sub     eax, 2
; The value 0x2 is subtracted from EAX.


jz      loc_9E                  ; WriteLn('a == 2');
; A jump is made to the call of WriteLn('a == 2') if EAX == 2.


sub     eax, 2
; The value 0x2 is subtracted from EAX.


jz      short loc_72            ; WriteLn('a == 4|6');
; A jump is made to the call of WriteLn('a == 4|6') if EAX == 2
; (or a == 4, respectively).


sub     eax, 2
; The value 0x2 is subtracted from EAX.


jz      short loc_72            ; WriteLn('a == 4|6');
; A jump is made to the call of WriteLn('a == 4|6') if EAX == 2
; (or a == 6).


sub     eax, 4
; The value 0x4 is subtracted from EAX.


jl      loc_CA                  ; This is the end of CASE.
; A jump is made to the end of case if EAX < 4 (or a < 10).


sub     eax, 90
; The value 90 is subtracted from EAX.


jle     short loc_46            ; WriteLn('a = [10..100]');
; A jump is made to the call of WriteLn('a = [10..100]')
```

```
; if EAX <= 90 (or a <= 100).
; Since the case of a > 10 has been processed above,
; this branch works if a>=10 && a<=100.

jmp     loc_CA                      ; This is the end of CASE.
; A jump is made to the end of case;
; none of the conditions had been satisfied.
```

Apparently, Free Pascal generates practically the same code as Borland C++ 5.x does; therefore, no complexities should arise during analysis.

Balancing tall trees. In rare cases, the switch statements contain hundreds or even thousands of sets of values. A straightforward solution to such a comparison task will produce a logical tree of enormous height. Passing through such a logical tree will take a long time, negatively affecting the program's performance.

However, we should think about what the switch statement is engaged in. Let's digress from the commonly accepted maxim: "*The* switch *statement provides a special means for choosing one of many variants, and consists of testing the coincidence of the value of a given expression with one of the given constants and in the corresponding branch.*" Instead, we can say that switch is a statement for finding an appropriate value. In such a case, the initial switch tree is a trivial algorithm of sequential search — the most inefficient searching algorithm.

Suppose that the source code of a program is the following:

Listing 194. An Example of the Source Code of a Program

```
switch (a)
{
        case 98 : ...;
        case 4  : ...;
        case 3  : ...;
        case 9  : ...;
        case 22 : ...;
        case 0  : ...;
        case 11 : ...;
        case 666: ...;
        case 096: ...;
        case 777: ...;
        case 7  : ...;
}
```

An appropriate nonoptimized logic tree will appear to be 11 nests high (Fig. 33, at the left). The left branch of the root nest will appear to contain as many as 10 other nests, but the right branch will appear to contain none (only a corresponding case routine).

The "skew" can be corrected by splitting one branch into two parts, and grafting the resultant halves into a new nest, containing a condition that determines which branch should be sought for the variable being compared. The left branch, for example, may contain nests with even values, while the right branch may hold the odd ones. However, this is a bad criterion: The number of even and odd values is rarely split fifty-fifty, and the skew arises again. The following method is much more reliable: Take the smallest value and throw it into the heap A, then take the greatest value and throw it into the heap B. Repeat this procedure until all available values have been sorted.

A unique value is required for the switch statement (i.e., each number only may occur once in the set, or range, of values). Therefore, it is easy to show that the heaps will contain equal quantities of numbers (in the worst case, one heap may contain one more number). In addition, each number on the A heap will be less than the smallest number on the B heap. Hence, we can make one comparison to determine in which heap we should look for the values being compared.

The height of the new tree will be equal to $(N + 1)/2 + 1$, where N is the number of nests of the old tree. Really, the branch of the tree is split into two parts, and a new nest added, creating $N/2$ and $+1$. Then, $(N+1)$ is needed to round off the division result to the upper value. For example, if the height of the nonoptimized tree reached 100 nests, it now decreases to 51. You think 51 is a large number, too? What prevents us from again splitting each branch into two parts? This will reduce the height of the tree to 27 nests. Subsequent compaction will give $16 \rightarrow 12 \rightarrow 11 \rightarrow 9 \rightarrow 8$ — this is all. Further compaction of the tree is impossible (think — or construct the tree — to figure out why). Still, 8 nests are not as unmanageable as 100 nests. Passing through the entire optimized tree will require less than nine comparisons.

Practically all compilers, even nonoptimizing ones, are capable of compacting logical trees of the switch statement! Compaction boosts performance, but it complicates analysis of compiled programs. Look at Fig. 33 again: The left, unbalanced tree is illustrative and intuitively clear; the right, balanced tree is difficult to understand.

Fortunately, the tree's balance admits an effective rollback. But before we begin climbing trees, let's introduce the concept of a *balancing node*. A balancing node does not change the operation logic of a binary tree; it is an optional node, whose only function is to truncate the branches. The balancing node of a tree may be replaced by any of the branches without losing the functionality. Each branch of a balancing node should contain more than one nest.

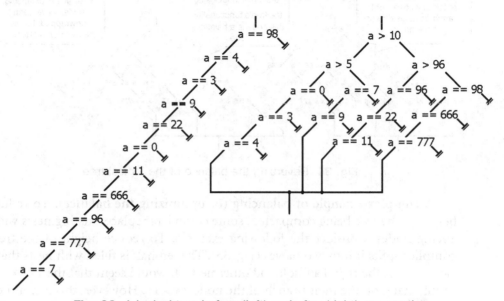

Fig. 33. A logical tree before (left) and after (right) compaction

If all nodes of a logic tree, the right branch of which contains one or more nests, can be replaced by this right branch without losing of the tree's functionality, then the given construction represents a `switch` statement. Why just the right branch? The `switch` statement, in its unwrapped condition, represents a chain of nests. These are interconnected by left branches and contain `case` routines on the right branches. Therefore, we try to hook all the right nests on the left branch. If we succeed, we are dealing with the `switch` statement; if not, we have encountered something different.

Consider the reconstruction of the balance in the following example (Fig. 34, at the left). Starting from the lower-left branch, we shall climb the tree until we encounter a node that has one or more nests on its right branch. In this case, this is the (a > 5) node. If we replace this node with its nests — (a == 7) and (a == 9), the tree's functionality will not be disturbed (as shown in the middle of Fig. 34). Similarly, the (a > 10) node can be replaced by the (a > 96), (a == 96), (a == 22), and (a == 11) nests without any serious consequences. Then, the (a > 96) node can be replaced by the (a == 98), (a == 666), and (a == 777) nests. A `switch` tree, in which the multiple-selection statement can easily be recognized, is formed.

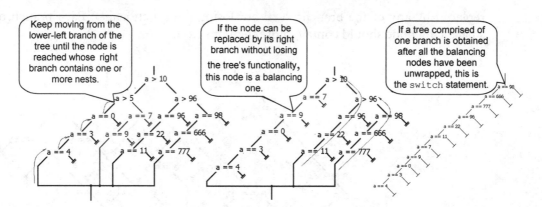

Fig. 34. Reversing the balance of the logical tree

A complex example of balancing (or optimizing the balance). To reduce the height of the tree being compacted, some compilers replace existing nests with balancing nodes. Consider the following example: To reduce height of the tree, the compiler splits it into two halves (Fig. 35). The left half is filled with nests that have values <= 1; the right half holds all other nests. It would seem that the (a == 2) nest should hang on the right branch of the node (a > 1). However, this is not the case. The (a > 2) node and the case routine :2 are hooked to the left branch. This is quite logical: if (a > 1) and !(a > 2), then a == 2.

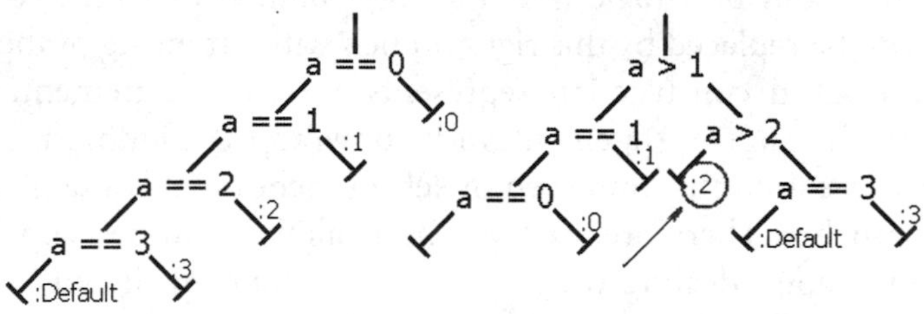

Fig. 35. An intricate example of balancing

The (a > 2) node is rigidly connected to and works with the (a > 1) node. It is impossible to throw out one of them without impairing the functionality of the other. It also is impossible to use the algorithm described above to reconstruct the balance of a tree without impairing the tree's functionality! It might seem that we are not dealing with the switch statement, but with something different.

To dispel this delusion, several additional steps need to be taken. First, case routines are always on the right branch of the switch tree. Is it possible to transform the tree so that the case routines appear on the left branch of the balancing node? Yes, this can be done by replacing (a > 2) with (a < 3) and swapping the locations of the branches (in other words, by performing an *inversion*). Second, all nests of the switch tree comprise equality conditions. Can the (a < 3) inequality be replaced by a corresponding equality? It certainly can: (a == 2).

After these transformations, the tree's balance can be easily reversed.

Branches in case routines. In reality, case routines teem with a variety of branches, loops, and conditional jumps. As a consequence, the logical tree resembles a thistle thicket, not the switch statement. It should be clear that, after identifying the case routines, this problem can be solved. But how can we identify the case routines?

Except for rare, unusual instances, case routines do not contain branches relative to the variable being compared. Statements such as switch(a)... case 666 : if (a == 666)... or switch(a)... case 666 : if (a > 666)... are pointless. Thus, we may safely remove from the logical tree all the nests containing conditions that involve the variable being compared (the variable of the root nest).

What if the programmer puts into case routines a branch relative to the variable being compared? This does not complicate the analysis: The inserted branches are easily recognized as superfluous or as nonexecuting, and they simply can be pruned off. For example, if (a > 0) is hooked to the right branch of the (a == 3) nest, it can be removed; it does not carry any information. If (a == 2) is hooked to the right branch of the same nest, it can be removed; it never executes, since if a == 3, then a != 2.

Loops

Loops are the only constructions (except the offensive GOTO) in the high-level languages that have a backward reference (i.e., to the area of lower addresses). All other kinds of branches — be it the IF—THEN—ELSE or switch statement — are directed "downward" (i.e., to the area of higher addresses). Consequently, the logical tree representing a loop is so typical that it can be identified at first glance.

There are three basic types of loops: *loops with a condition at the beginning* (Fig. 36, *a*), *loops with a condition at the end* (Fig. 36, *b*), and *loops with a condition in the middle* (Fig. 36, *c*). Combined loops can have several conditions in different places, such as at the beginning and at the end simultaneously.

In turn, conditions can be of two types: *conditions of the loop termination* and *conditions of the loop continuation*. In the first case — if the loop termination is *true* — a jump is made to the end of the loop; otherwise, the execution of the loop is continued. In the second case — if the loop continuation condition is *false* — again, a jump is made to the end of the loop; otherwise, the execution of the loop is continued. Conditions of the loop continuation represent the inverted conditions of the loop termination. Thus, it is enough for the compiler to support the conditions of only one type. The `while`, `do`, and `for` statements of the C language work only with conditions of the loop continuation. The Pascal `while` statement also works with the condition of the loop continuation; the only exception is `repeat-until`, which expects the loop termination condition.

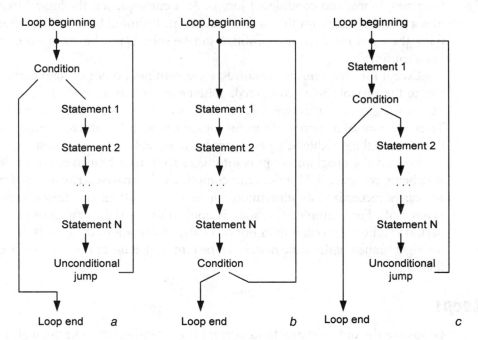

Fig. 36. The logical tree of a loop with the condition at the beginning (*a*), at the end (*b*), and in the middle (*c*)

Loops with conditions at the beginning (or loops with the precondition). In the C and Pascal languages, support for loops with the precondition is provided by the statement `while (expression)`, where `expression` is a loop continuation condition. For example, the `while (a < 10) a ++;` loop will execute as long as the condition `(a < 10)` remains true. However, the compiler may invert the loop continuation condition into the loop termination condition. If the Intel 80x86 platform is used, such a trick saves one or two machine instructions. In Listing 195, a loop with the termination condition is at the left, and one with the continuation condition is at the right. The loop with the termination condition is shorter by one instruction! Therefore, practically all compilers generate the left variant. However, some of them are capable of transforming loops with the precondition into more efficient loops with the postcondition.

Listing 195. The Same Loop with a Termination and a Continuation Condition

```
while:                                      while:
        cmp a, 10                                   cmp a, 10
        jae end                                     jb continue
        inc A                                       jmp end
        jmp while                           continue:
end:                                                inc a
                                                    jmp while
                                            end:
```

The loop with the termination condition cannot be directly represented by the `while` statement. This is frequently overlooked by beginners: They make this mistake by writing what they see: `while (a >= 10) a++`. The loop with such a condition will never be executed. How can we invert the condition and avoid mistakes? If this seems to be an easy task, ask a novice hacker to name the inverse operation of "more than." The most probable answer will be "less than." However, this answer would be incorrect — "less than or equal" is correct. The complete list of inverse relational operations is given in Table 25.

Table 25. The Relational Operators

Logical operators	Inverse logical operators
==	!=
!=	==
>	<=
<	>=
<=	>
>=	<

Loops with the condition at the end (also known as loops with the postcondition). In the C language, support for loops with the postcondition is provided by the statement pair `do-while`. In Pascal, support comes from the pair `repeat\until`. Loops with the postcondition are directly translated from a high-level language into computer code without any problems (as opposed to loops with a precondition, with which inverting the condition does not occur).

For example, do a ++; while (a < 10) is generally compiled into the following code. (Note that the relational operation in the original loop is also used in the jump. This looks beautiful, and no errors occur when it is decompiled.)

Listing 196. A Compilation of a Loop with a Postcondition

```
repeat:
        inc a
        cmp a, 10
        jl repeat
end:
```

Compare the code of the loop with a postcondition with the previous code of the loop with a precondition (shown in Listing 195). The loop with the condition at the end is more compact and faster, isn't it? Certain compilers (Microsoft Visual C++, for example) are capable of translating loops with a precondition into loops with a postcondition. At first glance, it is an inadmissible initiative on the part of the compiler — if the programmer wishes to test the condition at the beginning, should the compiler be able to put it at the end? Actually, the difference between "at the beginning" and "at the end" is not important. If the compiler is sure that the loop is executed at least once, it can test the condition whenever it sees fit. Certainly, the condition being tested should be slightly corrected: while (a<b) is not equivalent to do ... while (a<b), since, in the first case, the loop is already terminated if (a == b), and, in the second case, one more iteration is performed before exiting the loop. However, this is easy to resolve: Increase a by one (making it do ... while ((a+1)<b)), or subtract one from b (making it do ... while (a<(b-1))). Everything will work.

Why do we the need all these tricks, which considerably inflate the code? The static branch-prediction unit of Pentium processors is optimized for jumps directed backward (i.e., into the area of lower addresses). Therefore, loops with a postcondition should execute a little faster than similar loops with a precondition.

Loops with a counter. Loops with a counter (for) are not independent types; they only represent a syntactic version of loops with a precondition. As a first approximation, for (a = 0; a < 10; a ++) is the same as a = 0; while (a < 10) {...;a++;}. However, the results of compiling these statements may not be identical.

Optimizing compilers (as well as a significant part of nonoptimizing ones) pass control to the statement that tests the condition of the loop termination after initializing the variable counter. The resulting statement is evident at once when the program is analyzed. In addition, it cannot be translated directly into a `while` loop of a high-level language. Consider this listing:

Listing 197. An Example of a Loop with a Counter

```
mov a, xxx
; The variable of the "counter" is initialized.


jmp conditional
; A jump is made to the testing of the loop continuation condition.


repeat:
; The beginning of the loop is reached.


    ...                           ; The loop's
    ...                           ; body follows.


add a, xxx [sub a, xxx]
; The counter is modified.


conditional:
cmp a, xxx
; The loop continuation condition is tested.


jxx repeat
; A jump is made to the loop's beginning if the condition is true.
```

The immediate jump downward may result from compiling the `for` loop or the GOTO statement. The latter is out of fashion and is seldom used; however, without it, the IF-THEN conditional jump statement cannot jump directly into the middle of the `while` loop. Of all "candidates," only the `for` loop remains.

Certain advanced compilers (such as Microsoft Visual C++ and Borland C++, but not Watcom C) try to determine at compile time whether the given loop is executed at least once. If such an action occurs, they convert `for` into a typical loop with the postcondition.

Listing 198. An Example of the Conversion of a Counter

```
mov a, xxx
; The variable of the "counter" is initialized.

repeat:
; This is the beginning of the loop.

    ...                          ; The loop's
    ...                          ; body follows.

add a, xxx [sub a, xxx]
; The counter is modified.

cmp a, xxx
; The loop continuation condition is tested.

jxx repeat
; A jump is made to the loop's beginning if the condition is true.
```

The most advanced compilers (only Microsoft Visual C++ 6.0 comes to mind) are capable of translating loops with an increment into loops with a decrement — provided that the loop parameter is not used by the loop statements and only allows the loop to execute a certain number of times. Why does the compiler need this? Loops with a decrement appear to be much shorter: The DEC 1-byte instruction not only decrements the operand, but also sets the zero flag when zero is achieved. As a result, the CMP A, xxx instruction becomes unnecessary.

Listing 199. Changing a Loop with an Increment for a Loop with a Decrement

```
mov a, xxx          ; The variable of the "counter" is initialized.

repeat:             ; This is the beginning of the loop.

    ...             ; The loop's
    ...             ; body follows.

dec a               ; The counter is decremented.

jnz repeat          ; This is repeated while A != 0.
```

Thus, depending on the configuration and nature of the compiler, the for loops can be translated either into the loops with the precondition, or into the loops with the postcondition that start to execute from the testing of the loop continuation condition. The continuation condition may be converted into the termination condition, and the loop with an increment may turn into the loop with a decrement.

Such ambiguity complicates the identification of for loops. Only the loops that begin with testing the postcondition are reliably identified (since they cannot be represented using do without GOTO). In all other cases, it is impossible to give strict recommendations about how to recognize for.

My advice is the following: If the logic of the loop being analyzed is easier to represent syntactically through the for statement, use for! Otherwise, use while or do (repeat\until) to represent loops with a precondition or a postcondition.

Finally, a few words about the "castrated" for loops: The C language allows the initialization of the loop variable, the termination condition, and the decrement statement to be omitted separately or altogether. Thus, for degenerates to while and becomes practically indistinguishable from it.

Loops with the condition in the middle. Popular high-level languages do not directly support loops with a condition in the middle, despite the frequency of the need for such loops. Therefore, programmers implement them on the basis of available loops: while (while\do), and the break statement for quitting the loop.

Listing 200. Implementing a Loop with the Condition in the Middle

```
while(1)                          repeat:
{                                     ...
    ...                               cmp xxx
    if (condition) break;         jxx end
    ...                               ...
}                                     jmp repeat
                                  end:
```

The compiler usually unwraps an infinite loop into the unconditional jump JMP directed, naturally, backward (although some compilers generate code like this: MOV EAX, 1\CMP EAX, 1\JZ repeat). The unconditional jump directed backward is rather specific: Except in an infinite loop, it can originate only from the GOTO statement. However, GOTO, as previously mentioned, is out of fashion. The condition of termination for an infinite loop may only be in the middle of this loop (not considering complex cases of multithread protection, which modify an unconditional jump into NOP). All that remains is to look up the loop's body and find this condition.

This is easy — the break statement is translated into the jump to the instruction next to JMP repeat, and break itself gains control from the IF(condition)–THEN-[ELSE] branch. The condition of the statement also is required for the loop termination.

Loops with multiple termination conditions. The break statement allows the loop termination to be organized in any place the programmer considers fit; therefore, many termination conditions may be scattered throughout the body of any loop. This complicates the analysis of the program being disassembled; we risk "missing" one of the loop termination conditions and, consequently, misunderstanding the program's logic.

Identifying the loop termination conditions is easy: They always are directed "downward" (i.e., to the area of the higher addresses), and they point to the instruction next to the instruction of the conditional (unconditional) jump directed "upward" (i.e., to the area of lower addresses).

Loops with several counters. The support of comma-separated lists in the C language allows multiple initialization and update counters of the for loop to be carried out, such as for (a = 0, b = 10; a != b; a++, b--). But what about several termination conditions? The "old and new testaments" (the first and the second edition of K&R, respectively); the ANSI C standard; and manuals applied to the Microsoft Visual C++, Borland C, and Watcom C compilers keep silent on this point.

If you try to compile the code for (a = 0, b = 10; a > 0, b < 10; a++, b--), it will be "swallowed" by practically all compilers. However, none of them will compile the given example correctly. The $(a_1, a_2, a_3, \ldots, a_n)$ logical expression is senseless, and compilers will reject everything except the rightmost expression, a_n. This expression will exclusively define the loop continuation condition. Only Watcom grumbles in this instance: "**Warning! W111: Meaningless use of an expression**: *the line contains an expression that does nothing useful. In the example "i = (1,5);", the expression "1", is meaningless. This message is also generated for a comparison that is useless.*"

If the loop continuation condition depends on several variables, their comparisons should be combined into one expression using the logical operations OR, AND, etc. For example, using for (a = 0, b = 10; (a > 0 && b < 10); a++, b--), the loop will be terminated as soon as one of two conditions becomes false; using for (a = 0, b = 10; (a > 0 || b < 10); a++, b--), the loop will be continued while at least one of the conditions is true.

Loops with several counters are translated similarly to loops with one counter, except that several variables, not one, are initialized and modified simultaneously.

Identifying the continue statement. The continue statement causes control to pass immediately to the code that tests the loop continuation (termination) conditions. Generally, in loops with a precondition, this is translated into an unconditional jump directed upward, and in loops with a postcondition, into one directed downward. The code that follows continue does not gain control; therefore, continue is practically always used in conditional statements.

For example, while (a++ < 10) if (a == 2) continue; ... is compiled into code like this one:

Listing 201. The Result of Compilating Code with a continue Statement

```
repeat:
; This is the beginning of while.

inc a           ; a++
cmp a, 10
; The loop termination condition is tested.

jae end
; End if a >= 10.

cmp a,2
; If (a == 2),...

jnz woo
; This is a jump to the case "else" if a != 2.

jmp repeat
woo:            ; The loop's
    ...         ; body follows.

jmp repeat
; A jump is made to the loop's beginning.
```

Complex conditions. Until now, while discussing loop termination and continuation conditions, we only considered elementary relational conditions. Practically all high-level languages use compound conditions. However, compound conditions can be schematically represented as an abstract "black box," which has an input, an output, and, inside it, a logical binary tree. Constructing and reconstructing logical trees is considered in detail in the "*Conditional IF–THEN–ELSE Statements*" section. Now, our primary interest is the organization of loops, not conditions.

The nested loops. Loops may be nested. No problems would seem to arise. The beginning of each loop is reliably determined from the cross-reference directed downward. The conditional or unconditional jump to the loop's beginning is the loop's end. Each loop has only one beginning and only one end (although there may be any amount of termination conditions). Loops cannot cross each other — if the beginning of one loop lies inside another loop, this loop is nested.

However, not everything is that simple. Two stumbling blocks are *the continue statement in loops with a precondition* and *complex continuation conditions in loops with a postcondition.* Let's consider them in more detail.

In loops with a precondition, the continue statement is translated into an unconditional jump directed "upward." This statement becomes practically indistinguishable from the end of the loop. Consider this:

```
while(condition1)
{
        ...
        if (condition2) continue;
        ...
}
```

translated into:

```
NOT condition1 of the loop termination
...
if NOT condition2 GOTO continue
unconditional jump to the beginning
continue:
...
unconditional jump to the beginning
the end of the entire loop
```

The two ends and two beginnings are likely to belong to two loops, one of which is enclosed into another. However, the beginnings of both loops coincide. May a loop with a precondition be enclosed into a loop with a postcondition?

At first glance, yes. But `condition1` of the loop termination is behind the second end. If it were the precondition of the enclosed loop, it would be behind the first end. If `condition1` were the precondition of the parent loop, the end of the enclosed loop would not be able to pass control to the parent loop. It turns out that we have one loop, not two. The first "end" is just the result of translating the `continue` statement.

The things are easier with the analysis of complex conditions of continuation of the loop with a postcondition. Let's consider the example:

```
do
{
    ...
} while(condition1 || condition2);
```

In general, translating this example results in:

```
...
continuation condition1
continuation condition2
```

This is the same, isn't it?

```
do
{
        do
        {
            ...
        }while(condition1)
}while(condition2)
```

The offered case is logically correct, but syntactically ugly. The parent loop runs only one enclosed loop in its body and does not contain any other statements. So why is it necessary? Let's combine it with the enclosed loop!

Disassembler listings of examples. To illustrate the previous discussions, let's consider several examples.

Let's begin with the simplest one: the `while\do` loops.

Listing 202. Identifying `while\do` Loops

```
#include <stdio.h>

main()
{
```

```
int a=0;
while(a++<10) printf("The while loop\n");

do {
        printf("The do loop\n");
} while(--a >0);
}
```

Compiling this example in Microsoft Visual C++ 6.0, with the default settings, should give the following:

Listing 203. The Disassembled Code of Identifying a `while\do` Loop Using Visual C++ 6.0

```
main    proc near               ; CODE XREF: start+AF↓p

var_a       = dword         ptr -4

    push    ebp
    mov     ebp, esp
    ; The stack frame is opened.

    push    ecx
    ; Memory is allocated for one local variable.

    mov     [ebp+var_a], 0
    ; The value 0x0 is assigned to the var_a variable.

loc_40100B:                     ; CODE XREF: main_401000+29↓j
    ; The cross-reference directed downward indicates
    ; that this is the beginning of the loop.
    ; Naturally, if the cross-reference is directed downward,
    ; the jump that refers this address will be directed upward.

    mov     eax, [ebp+var_a]
    ; The value of the var_a variable is loaded into EAX.

    mov     ecx, [ebp+var_a]
    ; The value of the var_a variable is loaded into ECX.
    ; (This might be achieved in a shorter way: MOV ECX, EAX).
```

```
add     ecx, 1
; ECX is incremented by 1.

mov     [ebp+var_a], ecx
; The var_a variable is updated.

cmp     eax, 0Ah
; The value of the var_a variable
; before it was updated is compared to the value 0xA.

jge     short loc_40102B
; If var_a >= 0xA, a "forward" jump is made, just behind the instruction
; of the unconditional jump that is directed "backward."
; Therefore, this is a loop. Since the loop termination condition
; is tested in the loop's beginning, this is a loop with
; a precondition. To represent it as the while loop,
; we need to replace the loop termination condition with
; the continuation condition (i.e., to replace >= with <).
; Having done this, we obtain:
; while (var_a++ < 0xA)

; Here is the beginning of the loop's body.
push    offset aOperatorOfWloop ; "The operator of the while loop\n"
call    _printf
add     esp, 4
; printf("The while loop\n")

jmp     short loc_40100B
; An unconditional jump is directed backward to the loc_40100B label.
; There is only one loop termination condition — jge short loc_40102B —
; between loc_40100B and jmp short loc_40100B. Therefore, the original
; loop was: while (var_a++ < 0xA) printf("The while loop\n")

loc_40102B:                           ; CODE XREF: main_401000+1A↓j
; main_401000+45_j
; This is the beginning of the loop with a postcondition.
; However, we cannot be sure of this yet.
; We may only guess this based on the presence of the
```

```
; cross-reference directed downward.

; There is no condition in the loop's beginning; therefore,
; this is a loop with a condition at the end or in the middle.
push    offset aOperatorOfLoopD ; "The operator of the do loop\n"
call    _printf
add     esp, 4
; printf("The do loop\n")
; The loop's body follows.

mov     edx, [ebp+var_a]
; The value of the var_a variable is loaded into EDX.

sub     edx, 1
; EDX is decremented by 1.

mov     [ebp+var_a], edx
; The var_a variable is updated.

cmp     [ebp+var_a], 0
; The var_a variable is compared to zero.

jg      short loc_40102B
; If var_a > 0, a jump is made to the loop's beginning. Since this
; condition is at the end of the loop's body, the following is a do loop:
; do printf("The operator of the do loop\n"); while (--a > 0)
; To improve the readability of the disassembled text, it is
; recommended that you replace the loc_ prefixes at the loop's
; beginning with while and do (repeat) in the loops with
; a precondition and a postcondition, respectively.

mov     esp, ebp
pop     ebp
; The stack frame is closed.
retn
main    endp
```

The result will be different if optimization is enabled. Let's compile the same example with the /Ox key (the aggressive optimization).

Listing 204. The Disassembled Code of the `while\do` Loop with Aggressive Optimization

---

```
main          proc near          ; CODE XREF: start+AF↓p
      push    esi
      push    edi
      ; The registers are saved on the stack.

      mov     esi, 1
      ; The value 0x1 is assigned to ESI.
      ; Attention! Look at the original code;
      ; none of the variables had such a value.

      mov     edi, 0Ah
      ; The value 0xA is assigned to EDI. This is a constant for testing
      ; the loop termination condition.

loc_40100C:                        ; CODE XREF: main+1D↓j
      ; Judging from the cross-reference directed downward, this is a loop!

      push    offset aOperatorOfWLoop ; "The while loop\n"
      call    _printf
      add     esp, 4
      ; printf("The while loop\n")
      ; Is this a body of the while loop?
      ; If so, where is the precondition?

      dec     edi
      ; EDI is decremented by 1.

      inc     esi
      ; ESI is incremented by 1.

      test    edi, edi
      ; EDI is tested for being zero.

      ja      short loc_40100C
```

```
; A jump is made to the loop's beginning while EDI != 0.
; In a burst of optimization, the compiler transformed an inefficient
; loop with a precondition into a more compact and faster loop with
; a postcondition. Does the compiler have the right to do this?
; Why not?! After analyzing the code, the compiler has understood that
; this loop is executing at least once. Therefore, after the continuation
; condition has been corrected, it can be moved to the end of the loop.
; That is why the initial value of the loop's variable is 1, not 0.
; The compiler has replaced while ((int a = 0) < 10) with:
; do ... while (((int a = 0)+1) < 10) ==
; do ... while ((int a=1) < 10)
;
; Interestingly, the compiler did not compare the loop's variable
; to a constant. Instead, it placed the constant into the register,
; and decremented it until it became zero. Why? To make the loop
; shorter and work faster! This is fine, but how can the loop
; be decompiled?
; A direct representation in the C language gives the following:
; var_ESI = 1; var_EDI = 0xA;
; do {
;       printf("The while loop\n"); var_EDI--; var_ESI++;
; } while(var_EDI > 0)
;
; This is clumsy and intricate, isn't it? Let's try to remove
; one of two variables. This is possible, since the varaibles are
; modified simultaneously, and var_EDI = 0xB — var_ESI.
; Let's use the substitution:
; var_ESI = 1; var_EDI = 0xB — var_ESI ; (== 0xA;)
; do {
;       printf("The while loop\n"); var_EDI--; var_ESI++;
;
; Let's cancel var_EDI, since it is already represented
; through var_ESI.
; } while((0xB — var_ESI) > 0); (== var_ESI > 0xB)
;
; We likely will obtain something sensible, such as:
; var_ESI = 1; var_EDI == 0xA;
; do {
;       printf("The while loop\n"); var_ESI++;
```

```
;  } while(var_ESI > 0xB)
;
; We may stop here or go further, having transformed the loop
; with a postcondition into a more illustative loop with a
; precondition, that is, var_ESI = 1; var_EDI == 0xA;
;
; Now, var_EDI is not used and can be canceled.
; while (var_ESI <= 0xA) {
;       printf("The while loop\n"); var_ESI++;
; }
;
; This is not the limit of expressiveness, since
; var_ESI <= 0xA is equivalent to var_EDI < 0xB. In addition,
; since the var_ESI variable is used only as a counter,
; its initial value can be set to zero,
; and the increment statement can be brought into the loop:
; var_ ESI = 0;
; while (var_ESI++ < 0xA) ; subtracting 1 from the left and right half
; printf("The while loop\n");
;
; This is wonderful, isn't it? Compare this variant with
; the previous one and see how much simpler and clearer it has become.


loc_40101F:                             ; CODE XREF: main+2F↓j
    ; The downward cross-reference indicates that
    ; this is the loop's beginning.

    ; There is no precondition; hence, this is the do loop.

    push    offset aOperatorOfDLoop ; "The operator of the do loop\n"
    call    _printf
    add     esp, 4
    ; printf("The do loop\n");

    dec     esi
    ; The var_ESI variable is decremented.

    test    esi, esi
    ; ESI is tested for zero.
```

```
        jg      short loc_40101F
        ; The loop is continued while var_ESI > 0.
        ; This loop is easily represented in the C language:
        ; do printf("The do loop\n"); while (--var_ESI > 0 )

        pop     edi
        pop     esi
        ; The saved registers are restored.


        retn
main            endp
```

Borland C++ 5.x optimizes loops somewhat differently. Look at this example:

Listing 205. The Disassembled Code of a `while\do` Loop Optimized Using Borland C++

```
_main           proc near               ; DATA XREF: DATA:00407044↓o

        push    ebp
        mov     ebp, esp
        ; The stack frame is opened.

        push    ebx
        ; EBX is saved on the stack.

        xor     ebx, ebx
        ; The 0 value is assigned to the EBX register variable.
        ; It is easy to guess that EBX is a.

        jmp     short loc_40108F
        ; A downward unconditional jump is made. This is like the for loop.

loc_401084:                             ; CODE XREF: _main+19↓j
        ; This is the cross-reference directed downward;
        ; therefore, this is the beginning of some loop.

        push    offset aOperatorOfWLoop ; "The operator of the while loop\n"
        call    _printf
```

```
        pop     ecx
        ; printf("The while loop\n")


loc_40108F:                             ; CODE XREF: _main+6↓j
        ; The first jump is targeted here. Let's see what this is.

        mov     eax, ebx
        ; EBX is copied to EAX.


        inc     ebx
        ; EBX is incremented.


        cmp     eax, 0Ah
        ; EAX is compared to the value 0xA.


        jl      short loc_401084
        ; A jump is made to the loop's beginning if EAX < 0xA.
        ; This is how Borland optimized the code: It placed the condition
        ; at the end of the loop. To avoid translating the loop
        ; with a precondition into the loop with a postcondition,
        ; it simply began executing the loop with this same condition!
        ;
        ; Representing this loop in the C language gives the following:
        ; for (int a=0; a < 10; a++) printf("The while loop\n")
        ;
        ; Even though the original loop did not look like this,
        ; our variant is no worse. (It is probably better,
        ; since it is more illustrative.)


loc_401097:                             ; CODE XREF: _main+29↓j
        ; Here is the loop's beginning! There is no condition;
        ; hence, this is a loop with a precondition.

        push    offset aOperatorOfDLoop ; "The operator of the do loop\n"
        call    _printf
        pop     ecx
        ; printf("The do loop\n")


        dec     ebx
```

```
; The var_EBX variable is decremented.

test    ebx, ebx
jg      short loc_401097
; The loop is continued while var_EBX > 0.
; do printf("The do loop\n"); while (--var_EBX > 0)

xor     eax, eax
pop     ebx
pop     ebp
; The saved registers are restored.

retn
_main           endp
```

Other compilers generate similar or even more primitive and obvious code. Therefore, we shall describe the translation methods they use only briefly.

Free Pascal 1.x behaves similarly to Borland C++ 5.0, always placing the condition at the loop's end and starting the execution of the while loops from it.

Watcom C is not capable of transforming loops with a precondition into loops with a postcondition. Therefore, it places the loop termination condition at the beginning of while loops and inserts an unconditional jump into their ends.

The GCC compiler does not optimize loops with a precondition, generating the most nonoptimal code. Look at this example:

Listing 206. The Disassembled Code of a Loop with a Precondition Generated by the GCC Compiler

```
mov     [ebp+var_a], 0
; The value 0 is assigned to the a variable.

mov     esi, esi

loc_401250:                              ; CODE XREF: sub_40123C+34↓j
; The loop's beginning is reached.

mov     eax, [ebp+var_a]
; The value of the var_a variable is loaded into EAX.
```

```
        inc     [ebp+var_a]
        ; The var_a variable is incremented by 1.


        cmp     eax, 9
        ; EAX is compared to the value 0x9.


        jle     short loc_401260
        ; A jump is made if EAX <= 0x9 (EAX < 0xA).


        jmp     short loc_401272
        ; An unconditional jump is made to the loop's end.
        ; Hence, the previous conditional jump is a jump to the loop's
        ; continuation. What a nonoptimal code this is! Nevertheless,
        ; there is no inversion of the loop continuation condition,
        ; which simplifies disassembling.


        align 4
        ; Aligning the jump on addresses that are multiples of four
        ; makes code faster, but it increases the size significantly
        ; (especially if there are many jumps).

loc_401260:                              ; CODE XREF: sub_40123C+1D↑j
        add     esp, 0FFFFFFF4h
        ; Now, 12 (0xC) is subtracted from ESP.


        push    offset aOperatorOfWLoop ; "The operator of the while loop\n"
        call    printf
        add     esp, 10h
        ; The stack (0xC + 0x4) == 0x10 is restored.


        jmp     short loc_401250
        ; A jump is made to the beginning of the loop.

loc_401272:
        ; The end of the loop is reached.
```

Now that we have cleared up while\do, let's look at the for loops in the following example.

Listing 207. Identifying `for` Loops

```c
#include <stdio.h>

main()
{
    int a;
    for (a = 0; a < 10; a ++)  printf("The for loop\n");
}
```

Compiling this example in Microsoft Visual C++ 6.0, with the default settings, should give the following result:

Listing 208. The Disassembled Code of a `for` Loop Compiled by Visual C++ 6.0

```
main            proc near              ; CODE XREF: start+AF↓p

var_a        = dword ptr -4

     push    ebp
     mov     ebp, esp
     ; The stack frame is opened.

     push    ecx
     ; Memory is allocated for the local variable.

     mov     [ebp+var_a], 0
     ; The value 0 is assigned to the var_a local variable.

     jmp     short loc_401016
     ; An immediate jump is made to the code that tests the loop
     ; continuation condition, an indication that this is a for loop.

loc_40100D:                            ; CODE XREF: main+29↓j
     ; The cross-reference directed downward indicates that
     ; this is the beginning of the loop.

     mov     eax, [ebp+var_a]
     ; The var_a variable is loaded into EAX.
```

```
        add     eax, 1
        ; Now, 1 is added to EAX.

        mov     [ebp+var_a], eax
        ; EAX is updated.
        ; Hence, the original code was this:
        ; ++a

loc_401016:                              ; CODE XREF: main+B↓j
        cmp     [ebp+var_a], 0Ah
        ; The var_a variable is compared to the value 0xA.

        jge     short loc_40102B
        ; The loop is quit if var_a >= 0xA.

        push    offset aOperatorOfFLoop ; "The operator of the for loop\n"
        call    _printf
        add     esp, 4
        ; printf("The for loop\n")

        jmp     short loc_40100D
        ; An unconditional jump is made to the loop's beginning.
        ; Thus, we:
        ; Initialize the variable var_a
        ; Jump to the loop termination condition  ─────────────┐
        ; Increment the variable var_a    ◄──────────────────┐ │
        ; Test the condition relative to var_a  ◄───────────┐│ │
        ; Jump to the loop termination if the condition is true ─┤
        ; Call printf                                        ││ │
        ; Jump to the loop's beginning  ─────────────────────┘│
        ; Reach the end of the loop  ◄────────────────────────┘
        ;
        ; The test at the loop's beginning for loop termination indicates
        ; that this is a loop with a precondition.
        ; However, representing it as a while loop is not possible —
        ; we're hindered by the unconditional jump to the middle of the loop,
        ; which bypasses the code that increments the var_a variable.
        ; However, this loop is easily represented with the for loop:
```

```
; for (a = 0; a < 0xA; a++) printf("The operator of the for loop\n")
;
; The for loop initializes the variable counter,
; tests the loop continuation condition (optimized into the
; termination condition by the compiler), and executes the loop's
; body. Then, it modifies the counter, tests the condition, and so on.


loc_40102B:                            ; CODE XREF: main+1A↑j
        mov     esp, ebp
        pop     ebp
; The stack frame is closed.


        retn
main            endp
```

Now, let's put the optimization into action and see how the loop changes.

Listing 209. The Disassembled Code of the `for` Loop Using Optimization

```
main            proc near         ; CODE XREF: start+AF↓p
        push    esi
        mov     esi, 0Ah
; The variable counter is initialized.
; Caution! In the source code, the initial value of the counter was zero.


loc_401006:                       ; CODE XREF: main+14↓j
        push    offset aOperatorOfFLoop ; "The operator of the for loop\n"
        call    _printf
        add     esp, 4
; printf("The for loop\n")
; The loop's body is executed without any tests.
; By analyzing the code, the compiler has figured out that
; the loop is executing at least once!

        dec     esi
; The counter is decremented, although it was incremented
; in the source code. This is reasonable; dec \ jnz is much shorter
```

```
; than INC\ CMP reg, const\ jnz xxx. The compiler seems to complicate
; matters unnecessarily. The reason is simple: It has found out
; the loop's parameter used only as a counter. It doesn't make any
; difference if it is incremented or decremented with each iteration!

jnz        short loc_401006
; A jump is made to the loop's beginning if ESI > 0.
; But in its appearance, it is typical:
; a = 0xa; do printf("The for loop\n"); while (--a);
;
; If the readability of this statement is convenient for you,
; leave it as it is. If not, then:
; for (a = 0; a < 10; a++) The for loop\n");
;
; But wait! On what basis has the author carried out
; such a transformation? On the same basis that the compiler has:
; If the loop's parameter is used only as a counter, any statement
; that executes the loop exactly 10 times is correct. It only remains
; to choose the most convenient one (from an aesthetic point of
; view): for (a = 10; a > 0; a--) or for (a = 0; a < 10; a++).

pop        esi
retn
main       endp
```

How will Borland C++ 5.0 deal with this? Let's compile and see.

Listing 210. The Disassembled Code of the `for` Loop Optimized by Borland C++

```
_main          proc near              ; DATA XREF: DATA:00407044↓o

push    ebp
mov     ebp, esp
; The stack frame is opened.

push    ebx
; EBX is saved on the stack.

xor     ebx, ebx
```

```
        ; The value 0 is assigned to the EBX variable.

loc_401082:                             ; CODE XREF: _main+15↓j
        ; The loop's beginning is reached.

        push    offset aOperatorOfFLoop ; format
        call    _printf
        pop     ecx
        ; The loop is begun with the execution of its body.
        ; Borland has understood that the loop is executed at least once.

        inc     ebx
        ; The loop's parameter is incremented.

        cmp     ebx, 0Ah
        ; EBX is compared to the value 0xA.

        jl      short loc_401082
        ; A jump is made to the loop's beginning while EBX < 0xA.

        xor     eax, eax
        pop     ebx
        pop     ebp
        retn
_main           endp
```

Borland C++ 5.0 could not compete with Microsoft Visual C++ 6.0; it understood that the loop was executed only once, but it didn't prove to be smart enough to invert the counter. Most compilers — in particular, Watcom C — behave in a similar manner.

Next are the loops with a condition in the middle, or the loops terminated manually by the break statement. Let's consider the following example:

Listing 211. Identifying a break Statement

```
#include <stdio.h>

main()
{
```

```c
        int a=0;
        while(1)
        {
                printf("1st statement\n");
                if (++a > 10) break;
                printf("2nd statement\n");
        }

do
{
        printf("1st statement\n");
        if (--a < 0) break;
        printf("2nd statement\n");
        }while(1);
}
```

Compiling this example in Microsoft Visual C++ 6.0, with default settings, should give the following:

Listing 212. The Disassembled Code of the `break` Statement Compiled by Visual C++ 6.0

```asm
main            proc near           ; CODE XREF: start+AF↓p

var_a           = dword         ptr -4

        push    ebp
        mov     ebp, esp
        ; The stack frame is opened.

        push    ecx
        ; Memory is allocated for the local variable.

        mov     [ebp+var_a], 0
        ; The value 0x0 is assigned to the var_a variable.

loc_40100B:                             ; CODE XREF: main+3F↓j
        ; The cross-reference is directed downward — we have a loop.
```

```
mov     eax, 1
test    eax, eax
jz      short loc_401041
; Note: When the optimization is disabled, the compiler translates
; the unconditional loop "too literally" — it assigns the value 1 (TRUE)
; to EAX, and then tests it for zero. Should TRUE ever become FALSE,
; the loop will be terminated. In other words, these three instructions
; are silly and useless code of the while (1) loop.

push    offset a1iOperator ; "1st statement\n"
call    _printf
add     esp, 4
; printf("1st statement\n")

mov     ecx, [ebp+var_a]
; The value of the var_a variable is loaded into ECX.

add     ecx, 1
; Now, 1 is added to ECX.

mov     [ebp+var_a], ecx
; The var_a variable is updated.

cmp     [ebp+var_a], 0Ah
; The var_a variable is compared to the value 0xA.

jle     short loc_401032
; A jump is made if var_a <= 0xA.
; But to where does it jump? First, the jump is directed downward
; (i.e., this is not a jump to the loop's beginning).
; Therefore, the condition is not a loop condition;
; it's the result of compiling the IF—THEN statement.
; Second, it is a jump to the first instruction that follows the
; unconditional jump loc_401041. This, in turn, passes control to
; the instruction that follows jmp short loc_401075 — an unconditional
; jump directed upward to the loop's beginning.
; Hence, jmp short loc_401041 terminates the loop, and
; jle short loc_401032 continues executing it.
```

```
        jmp     short loc_401041
        ; This is a jump to the loop termination. What terminates the loop?
        ; Certainly, break does!
        ; Therefore, the final decompilation should look as this:
        ; if (++var_a > 0xA) break
        ; We have inverted <= into >,
        ; since JLE passes control to the loop continuation code,
        ; and the THEN branch passes control to break, in this case.

loc_401032:                             ; CODE XREF: main+2E↑j
        ; The cross-reference is directed upward;
        ; this is not the loop's beginning.

        push    offset a2iOperator  ; "2nd statement\n"
        call    _printf
        add     esp, 4
        ; printf("2nd statement\n")

        jmp     short loc_40100B
        ; A jump is made to the loop's beginning.
        ; Therefore, we have reached the loop's end,
        ; restoring the source code:
        ; while(1)
        ; {
        ;       printf("1st statement\n");
        ;       if (++var_a > 0xA) break;
        ;       printf("2nd statement\n");
        ; }

loc_401041:                             ; CODE XREF: main+12↑j main+30↓j ...
        ; The cross-reference directed downward indicates that
        ; this is the loop's beginning.

        push    offset a1iOperator_0 ; "1st statement\n"
        call    _printf
        add     esp, 4
        ; printf("1st statement\n")

        mov     edx, [ebp+var_a]
        ; The value of the var_a variable is loaded into EDX.
```

```
        sub     edx, 1
        ; EDX is decremented by 1.

        mov     [ebp+var_a], edx
        ; The var_a variable is updated.

        cmp     [ebp+var_a], 0
        ; The var_a variable is compared to the value 0x0.

        jge     short loc_40105F
        ; A downward jump is made if var_a >= 0.
        ; Note: The break statement of the do loop
        ; does not differ from break of the while loop!
        ; Therefore, we shall decompile it right away
        ; without speaking at length.
        ; if (var_a < 0)...

        jmp     short loc_401075
        ; ...break

loc_40105F:                             ; CODE XREF: main+5B↑j
        push    offset a2iOperator_0 ; "2nd statement\n"
        call    _printf
        add     esp, 4
        ; printf("2nd statement\n")

        mov     eax, 1
        test    eax, eax
        jnz     short loc_401041
        ; This tests the loop continuation.

loc_401075:                             ; CODE XREF: main+5D↑j
        mov     esp, ebp
        pop     ebp
        ; The stack frame is closed.

        retn
main            endp
```

The break statement is identical in both loops. It is easily recognized (not at first glance, but when several jumps are traced). The nonoptimizing compiler has inadequately translated infinite loops into the code that tests the obviously true condition. How would an optimizing compiler behave?

Let's compile the same example in Microsoft Visual C++ 6.0, with the /Ox key, and see the result.

Listing 213. The Disassembled Code of the break Compiled by C++ with Aggressive Optimization

---

```
main            proc near            ; CODE XREF: start+AF↓p
        push    esi
        ; ESI is saved on the stack.

        xor     esi, esi
        ; The zero value is assigned to ESI.
        ; var_ESI = 0;


loc_401003:                          ; CODE XREF: main+23↓j
        ; A cross-reference is directed forward.
        ; This is the loop's beginning.

        push    offset aliOperator ; "1st statement\n"
        call    _printf
        add     esp, 4
        ; printf("1st statement\n")
        ;
        ; This is no test; therefore, this is a loop with a
        ; postcondition (or with a condition in the middle).

        inc     esi
        ; ++var_ESI

        cmp     esi, 0Ah
        ; The var_ESI variable is compared to the value 0xA.

        jg      short loc_401025
        ; The loop is terminated if var_ESI > 0xA.
        ; Since this instruction is not the last one in the loop's body,
```

```
; this loop has a condition in the middle:
; if (var_ESI > 0xA) break

        push    offset a2iOperator ; "2nd statement\n"
        call    _printf
        add     esp, 4
; printf("2nd statement\n")


        jmp     short loc_401003
; An unconditional jump is made to the loop's beginning.
; Obviously, the optimizing compiler has eliminated
; the unnecessary test of the condition,
; making the code simpler and more comprehensible.
; Therefore:
; var_ESI = 0
; for (;;)
; {
; printf("1st statement\n");
; ++var_ESI;
; if (var_ESI > 0xA) break;
;printf("2nd statement\n");
; }
;
; The degenerated for is an infinite loop.

loc_401025:                        ; CODE XREF: main+14↑j
; This is not the loop's beginning.

        push    offset a1iOperator_0 ; "1st statement\n"
        call    _printf
        add     esp, 4
; printf("1st statement\n")
; Is this the loop's beginning? It is likely.

        dec     esi
; The var_ESI variable is decremented.

        js      short loc_401050
; The loop is terminated if var_ESI < 0.
```

```
      inc    esi
      ; The var_ESI variable is incremented by 1.


loc_401036:                              ; CODE XREF: main+4E↑j
; Here is the loop's beginning!

      push   offset a2iOperator_0 ; "2nd statement\n"
      call   _printf
      ; printf("2nd statement\n")
      ; Oddly enough, the loop's beginning is in its center.

      push   offset a1iOperator_0 ; "1st statement\n"
      call   _printf
      add    esp, 8
      ; printf("1st statement\n")
      ; Strange things are going on. We already encountered
      ; the call of the first statement of the loop above,
      ; and it is improbable that the middle of the loop
      ; would be followed by its beginning.

      dec    esi
      ; The var_ESI variable is decremented.

      jnz    short loc_401036
      ; The execution of the loop is continued while var_ESI != 0.


loc_401050:                              ; CODE XREF: main+33↑j
      ; The end of the loop is reached.
      ; Well, there is much to think over. The compiler processed
      ; crossed over the first line of the loop normally:
      ; printf("1st statement\n")
      ;
      ; then "ran into" the branch:
      ; if (--a<0) break
      ;
      ; Microsofties know that branches are as unappealing
      ; to high-pipelined processors (such as the Pentium chips) as
      ; thistles are to Tigger. In addition, the C compilers for the
```

```
; CONVEX family of processors refuse to compile the loops with branches.
; Thus, the compiler has to correct programmer's mistakes.
; In general, it is not obliged to do this. We should be thankful!
; It is as though the compiler is "circling" the loop
; and "dazzling" the calls of the printf functions,
; bringing out branches to the end.
; Think of the execution of the code as a racetrack and the
; processor as a racer. The longer the straightaway,
; the quicker the racer will speed down the racetrack!
; The compiler can move the condition from the middle
; of the loop to its end — branching is performed relative to
; a variable modified neither by printf, nor by any other function.
; So, does it make any difference where it is tested?
; It certainly does. When the (--a < 10) condition
; becomes true, only the execution of the first printf is
; completed, and the second printf has no chance to gain control.
; That is why the compiler placed the code for testing
; the condition immediately after the first call of the printf function,
; and then it changed the order of calling printf in the loop's body.
; Because the first printf occurs twice, it executed one time more
; than the second printf did when the loop terminated.
; One point is left to clear up: What does incrementing var_ESI mean?
; Let's think about what would happen if we threw out the instruction
; inc ESI. Since the loop's counter is decremented twice
; during the first iteration, the loop will be executed one
; fewer times. To keep this from happening,
; var_ESI is incremented by 1, using the inc ESI instruction.
; Solving this puzzle was a tough task.
; Think about the ease of implementing a compiler
; that knows how to carry out such tricks.
; Surprisingly, some people criticize automatic optimization.
; Certainly, manual optimization may give a better result
; (especially when you understand the sense of the code), but it could
; easily drive you insane! The compiler, even when constrained by
; a programmer's crooked code, manages it in a fraction of a second.

        pop     esi
        retn
main            endp
```

When translating infinite loops, Borland C++ and Watcom replace code that tests the loop continuation condition with an unconditional jump. However, they do not know how to optimize branches by moving them to the end of the loop, as Microsoft Visual C++ 6.0 does.

Now that we have considered break, let's see how compilers translate the continue statement. Consider the following example:

Listing 214. Identifying the continue Statement

```c
#include <stdio.h>

main()
{
        int a = 0;
        while (a++<10)
        {
                if (a == 2) continue;
                printf("%x\n", a);
        }

        do
        {
                if (a == 2) continue;
                printf("%x\n", a);
        } while (--a>0);
}
```

Compiling this example in Microsoft Visual C++ 6.0 with default settings should give the following:

Listing 215. The Disassembled Code of the continue Statement Compiled by Visual C++ 6.0

```
main            proc near               ; CODE XREF: start+AF↑p

var_a           = dword                 ptr -4

        push    ebp
        mov     ebp, esp
        ; The stack frame is opened.
```

```
push    ecx
; Memory is allocated for the local variable.

mov     [ebp+var_a], 0
; The value 0 is assigned to the var_a local variable.

loc_40100B:                         ; CODE XREF: main+22↑j; main+35↓j
        ; Two cross-references directed forward indicate that this is either
        ; the beginning of two loops (one of which is nested), or this is
        ; a jump to the beginning of the loop with the continue statement.

mov     eax, [ebp+var_a]
; The value of var_a is loaded into EAX.

mov     ecx, [ebp+var_a]
; The value of var_a is loaded into ECX.

add     ecx, 1
; The value 1 is added to ECX.

mov     [ebp+var_a], ecx
; The var_a variable is updated.

cmp     eax, 0Ah
; The value of the var_a variable, before it is increased,
; is compared to the value 0xA.

jge     short loc_401037
; The loop is terminated if var_a >= 0xA.
; (A jump is made to the instruction
; next to the one directed upward — to the loop's beginning.)

cmp     [ebp+var_a], 2
; The var_a variable is compared to the value 0x2.

jnz     short loc_401024
; If var_a != 2, then jump to the instruction that is next to
; the instruction of the unconditional jump directed upward —
```

```
; to the loop's beginning. It is likely that this is the condition
; of the loop termination.
; However, it is unwise to draw hasty conclusions.
; We encountered two cross-references at the loop's beginning.
; The jmp short loc_40100B unconditional jump forms one of them.
; What is "responsible" for the other one?
; To answer this question, the rest of code must be analyzed.

jmp     short loc_40100B
; An unconditional jump is directed to the loop's beginning.
; This is either the loop's end, or continue.
; If this is the loop's end, what is "jge short loc_401037"?
; Is it a precondition for terminating the loop? No, this is unlikely.
; If it were a precondition for terminating the loop, the jump
; would be made to the loc_401024 label — a much "shorter" one.
; Maybe jge short loc_401037 is a precondition of one loop,
; and jnz short loc_401024 is a postcondition of another one
; nested within it. This is possible, but improbable — in such a case,
; a postcondition would be a loop continuation condition,
; not a termination condition. Therefore, it seems most likely that
; the code CMP var_a, 2 \ JNZ loc_401024 \ JMP loc_40100B
; is if (a==2) continue.


loc_401024:                              ; CODE XREF: main+20↑j
        mov     edx, [ebp+var_a]
        push    edx
        push    offset asc_406030 ; "%x\n"
        call    _printf
        add     esp, 8
        ; printf("%x\n", var_a)


        jmp     short loc_40100B
; This is the loop's end; the last reference
; to the loop's beginning is jmp short loc_40100B.
; Let's summarize what we have:
; The condition located at the loop's beginning executes the loop
; while var_a < 0xA, with the loop's parameter incremented
; before the comparison is made. One more condition follows,
; which returns control to the loop's beginning if var_a == 2.
```

```
; The printf statement closes the loop, and an unconditional jump
; is made to the loop's beginning. Therefore, we have:
;
; The loop's beginning    ◄─────────────────────────────◄─┐
; The incrementation of the variable var_a               │
; The condition for "far" exit ──────────────────────┐   │
; The condition for "near" exit ─────────────────┐   │   │
; The loop's body                                │   │   │
; The unconditional jump to the beginning ───────┼───┘   │
; The loop's end  ◄──────────────────────────────┘       │
;
; The "near" continuation condition cannot be the loop's end;
; in such a case, the "far" continuation condition
; would have to step behind the borders of the loop.
; Neither break, nor any other statement, is capable of this.
; Thus, the "near" continuation condition may only be represented
; by the continue statement. In the C language,
: the whole construction should look like this:
; while(a++<10)           // The incrementation of var_a and
;                         // the condition for the "far" exit.
; {
; if (a == 2) continue;   // The condition for the "near"
;                         // continuation.
; printf("%x\n", var_a);  // The loop's body.
; }                       // The unconditional jump to the loop's
;                         // beginning.


loc_401037:                         ; CODE XREF: main+1A↑j main+5D↓j
    ; The loop's beginning is reached.

    cmp     [ebp+var_a], 2
    ; The var_a variable is compared to the value 0x2.

    jnz     short loc_40103F
    ; The execution of the loop continues if var_a != 2.

    jmp     short loc_401050
```

```
        ; A jump is made to the code that tests the loop continuation condition.
        ; Undoubtedly, this is continue,
        ; and the entire construction looks as this:
        ; if (a==2) continue;


loc_40103F:                          ; CODE XREF: main+3B↑j
        mov     eax, [ebp+var_a]
        push    eax
        push    offset asc_406034 ; "%x\n"
        call    _printf
        add     esp, 8
        ; printf("%x\n", var_a);


loc_401050:                          ; CODE XREF: main+3D↑j
        mov     ecx, [ebp+var_a]
        sub     ecx, 1
        mov     [ebp+var_a], ecx
        ; --var_a;


        cmp     [ebp+var_a], 0
        ; The var_a variable is compared to zero.


        jg      short loc_401037
        ; The loop execution is continued while var_a > 0.
        ; This is likely to be a postcondition:
        ; do
        ; {
        ; if (a==2) continue;
        ; printf("%x\n", var_a);
        ; } while (--var_a > 0);


        mov     esp, ebp
        pop     ebp
        retn
main            endp
```

Now, let's see how optimization (the /Ox key) affects the code of the loops.

Listing 216. The Disassembled Code of the `continue` Statement Compiled with Aggressive Optimization

```
main           proc near              ; CODE XREF: start+AF↓p
       push    esi
       mov     esi, 1


loc_401006:                           ; CODE XREF: main+1F↓j
; This is the loop's beginning.


       cmp     esi, 2
       jz      short loc_401019
; A jump is made to loc_401019 if ESI == 2.


       push    esi
       push    offset asc_406030 ; "%x\n"
       call    _printf
       add     esp, 8
; printf("%x\n", ESI)
; This branch is executed only if ESI != 2.
; Hence, it can be represented as:
; if (ESI != 2) printf("%x\n", ESI)


loc_401019:                           ; CODE XREF: main+9↑j
       mov     eax, esi
       inc     esi
; ESI++;


       cmp     eax, 0Ah
       jl      short loc_401006
; The execution of the loop is continued while (ESI++ < 0xA).
; Thus:
; do
; {
; if (ESI != 2) printf("%x\n", ESI);
; } while (ESI++ < 0xA)
;
```

```
        ; Does this look worse than if (ESI == 2) continue?

loc_401021:                          ; CODE XREF: main+37↓j
        ; This is the loop's beginning.

        cmp     esi, 2
        jz      short loc_401034
        ; A jump is made to loc_401034 if ESI == 2.

        push    esi
        push    offset asc_406034 ; "%x\n"
        call    _printf
        add     esp, 8
        ; printf("%x\n", ESI);
        ; This branch is executed only if ESI != 2.

loc_401034:                          ; CODE XREF: main+24↑j
        dec     esi
        ; ESI is decremented.

        test    esi, esi
        jg      short loc_401021
        ; The loop continuation condition — iterate while ESI > 0
        ; Thus:
        ; do
        ; {
        ; if (ESI != 2)
        ; {
        ; printf("%x\n", ESI);
        ; }

        ; } while (--ESI > 0)


        pop     esi
        retn
main            endp
```

Other compilers will generate similar code. In all loops with a precondition, the `continue` statement is practically indistinguishable from the nested loop; in loops with a postcondition, `continue` is the equivalent of a simple branch.

Now, it only remains to consider the `for` loops, which work with several counters simultaneously. Let's consider the following example:

Listing 217. Identifying a `for` Loop with Several Counters

```
main()
{
        int a; int b;
        for (a = 1, b = 10; a < 10, b > 1; a++, b --)
        printf("%x %x\n", a, b);
}
```

The result of compiling this example in Microsoft Visual C++ 6.0 should be the following:

Listing 218. The Disassembled Code of a `for` Loop with Several Counters Compiled by Visual C++

```
main           proc near           ; CODE XREF: start+AF↓p

var_b          = dword ptr -8
var_a          = dword ptr -4

       push   ebp
       mov    ebp, esp
       ; The stack frame is opened.

       sub    esp, 8
       ; Memory is allocated for two local variables.

       mov    [ebp+var_a], 1
       ; The value 0x1 is assigned to the var_a variable.

       mov    [ebp+var_b], 0Ah
       ; The value 0xA is assigned to the var_b variable.

       jmp    short loc_401028
       ; A jump is made to the code that tests
```

```
; the conditions for quitting the loop.
; This is a typical feature of nonoptimized for loops.

loc_401016:                              ; CODE XREF: main+43↓j
; The cross-reference directed downward indicates that
; this is the beginning of the loop.
; We already figured out that the loop's type is for.

mov     eax, [ebp+var_a]
add     eax, 1
mov     [ebp+var_a], eax
; var_a++

mov     ecx, [ebp+var_b]
sub     ecx, 1
mov     [ebp+var_b], ecx
; var_b--

loc_401028:                              ; CODE XREF: main+14↑j
cmp     [ebp+var_b], 1
jle     short loc_401045
; The loop is terminated if var_b <= 0x1.
; Only one counter (the second one from the left) is
; checked. The compiler regards the (a1,a2,a3,...,an) expression
; as senseless and uses only an, ignoring the rest of it.
; (Of all the compilers that I know,
; only Watcom complains in such a case.)
; In this compilation, only the (b > 1) condition is tested;
; the (a < 10) condition is ignored.

mov     edx, [ebp+var_b]
push    edx
mov     eax, [ebp+var_a]
push    eax
push    offset aXX           ; "%x %x\n"
call    _printf
add     esp, 0Ch
; printf("%x %x\n", var_a, var_b)

jmp     short loc_401016
```

```
; This is the end of the loop.
; Thus, this loop can be represented as:
; while(1)
; {
; var_a++;
; var_b--;
; if (var_b <= 0x1) break;
; printf("%x %x\n", var_a, var_b)
; }
;
; For better readability, it makes sense to represent this code
; as the for loop:
; for (var_a=1, var_b=0xA; var_b>1; var_a++, var_b--)
; printf("%x %x\n", var_a, var_b);
;
loc_401045:                              ; CODE XREF: main+2C↑j
        mov     esp, ebp
        pop     ebp
        ; The stack frame is closed.

        retn
main            endp
```

We will not consider the optimized variant of the program; it will not show us anything new. Whichever compiler you choose, expressions for initializing and modifying counters will be processed correctly — in the order they have been declared in the program's code. However, none of compilers can process multiple continue expressins correctly.

Mathematical Operators

Identifying the + operator. In most cases, the + operator is translated either into the ADD machine instruction, which "grinds up" integer operands, or into the FADDx instruction, which processes floating-point values. Optimizing compilers may replace ADD xxx, 1 with a more compact instruction — INC xxx. They also may translate the c = a + b + const expression into the LEA c, [a + b + const] machine instruction. This trick allows several variables to be summed in one stroke, returning the obtained sum via any general-purpose register, not necessarily in the left summand, as required by the ADD instruction mnemonics. However, LEA cannot be directly decompiled into the + operator, because this instruction is used for more than optimized addition. In general, this is only a by-product of its activity; its primary purpose is calculating the effective offset. (See the "*Constants and Offsets*" section.)

Consider the following example:

Listing 219. Identifying the + Operator

```
main()
{
        int a, b, c;
        c = a + b;
        printf("%x\n", c);
        c=c+1;
        printf("%x\n", c);
}
```

Compiling this example using Microsoft Visual C++ 6.0 with default settings should produce the following:

Listing 220. The Disassembled Code with the + Operator in Visual C++

```
main            proc near           ; CODE XREF: start+AF↓p

var_c           = dword ptr -0Ch
var_b           = dword ptr -8
var_a           = dword ptr -4

        push    ebp
        mov     ebp, esp
        ; The stack frame is opened.

        sub     esp, 0Ch
        ; Memory is allocated for the local variables.

        mov     eax, [ebp+var_a]
        ; The value of the var_a variable is loaded into EAX.

        add     eax, [ebp+var_b]
        ; The value of the var_b variable is added to EAX, and
        ; the result is placed into EAX.
```

```
        mov     [ebp+var_c], eax
        ; The sum of var_a and var_b is copied into the var_c variable.
        ; Hence, var_c = var_a + var_b.

        mov     ecx, [ebp+var_c]
        push    ecx
        push    offset asc_406030 ; "%x\n"
        call    _printf
        add     esp, 8
        ; printf("%x\n", var_c)

        mov     edx, [ebp+var_c]
        ; The value of the var_c variable is loaded into EDX.

        add     edx, 1
        ; The 0x1 value is added to EDX, and the result is placed in EDX.

        mov     [ebp+var_c], edx
        ; The var_c variable is updated:
        ; var_c = var_c +1

        mov     eax, [ebp+var_c]
        push    eax
        push    offset asc_406034 ; "%x\n"
        call    _printf
        add     esp, 8
        ; printf("%\n", var_c)

        mov     esp, ebp
        pop     ebp
        ; The stack frame is closed.

        retn
main    endp
```

Now, let's see what the same example will look like when compiled using the /Ox key (aggressive optimization).

Listing 221. The Disassembled Code with the + Operator Compiled Using Aggressive Optimization

---

```
main        proc near              ; CODE XREF: start+AF↓p
        push  ecx
        ; Memory is allocated for one local variable.
        ; (The compiler has decided to squeeze
        ; three variables into one.)

        mov   eax, [esp+0]
        ; The value of the var_a variable is loaded into EAX.

        mov   ecx, [esp+0]
        ; The value of the var_b variable is loaded into EAX.
        ; (Because the variable is not initialized, it is possible to
        ; load from anywhere.)

        push  esi
        ; The ESI register is saved on the stack.

        lea   esi, [ecx+eax]
        ; LEA is used to add ECX and EAX quickly and
        ; to write the sum into the ESI register. Adding quickly does
        ; not mean that the instruction LEA executes faster than ADD:
        ; Each uses the same number of clock cycles,
        ; but LEA gets rid of the need to create a temporary variable
        ; to save the intermediate result of addition,
        ; and the result is placed directly into ESI. Thus, this
        ; instruction is decompiled as reg_ESI = var_a + var_b.

        push  esi
        push  offset asc_406030 ; "%x\n"
        call  _printf
        ; printf("%x\n", reg_ESI)

        inc   esi
        ; ESI is incremented by one:
        ; reg_ESI = reg_ESI + 1

        push  esi
```

```
        push    offset asc_406034 ; "%x\n"
        call    _printf
        add     esp, 10h
        ; printf("%x\n", reg_ESI)

        pop     esi
        pop     ecx
        retn
main            endp
```

Other compilers (Borland C++, Watcom C) generate almost identical code. It offers no new insights; therefore, it will not be considered here.

Identifying the – operator. The – operator generally is translated either into the SUB machine instruction (if the operands are integer values), or into the FSUBx instruction (if the operands are floating-point values). Optimizing compilers may replace SUB xxx, 1 with a more compact instruction — DEC xxx. They also may translate SUB a, const into ADD a, -const. The latter is not more compact or faster (both fit into one cycle), as the following example shows.

Listing 222. Identifying the – Operator

```
main()
{
        int a, b, c;

        c = a — b;
        printf("%x\n", c);

        c = c — 10;
        printf("%x\n", c);
}
```

The nonoptimized variant should be approximately as follows:

Listing 223. The Disassembled Code with the – Operator

```
main            proc near               ; CODE XREF: start+AF↓p

var_c           = dword ptr -0Ch
```

```
var_b          = dword ptr -8
var_a          = dword ptr -4

        push    ebp
        mov     ebp, esp
        ; The stack frame is opened.

        sub     esp, 0Ch
        ; Memory is allocated for local variables.

        mov     eax, [ebp+var_a]
        ; The value of the var_a local variable is loaded into EAX.

        sub     eax, [ebp+var_b]
        ; The value of the var_b variable is subtracted from var_a.
        ; The result is placed into EAX.

        mov     [ebp+var_c], eax
        ; The difference between var_a and var_b is placed into var_c:
        ; var_c = var_a − var_b

        mov     ecx, [ebp+var_c]
        push    ecx
        push    offset asc_406030 ; "%x\n"
        call    _printf
        add     esp, 8
        ; printf("%x\n", var_c)

        mov     edx, [ebp+var_c]
        ; The value of the var_c variable is loaded into EDX.

        sub     edx, 0Ah
        ; The 0xA value is subtracted from var_c. The result is placed in EDX.

        mov     [ebp+var_c], edx
        ; The var_c variable is updated:
        ; var_c = var_c − 0xA

        mov     eax, [ebp+var_c]
        push    eax
```

```
        push    offset asc_406034 ; "%x\n"
        call    _printf
        add     esp, 8
        ; printf("%x\n", var_c)

        mov     esp, ebp
        pop     ebp
        ; The stack frame is closed.
        retn
main            endp
```

Now, let's consider the optimized version of the same example.

Listing 224. The Disassembled Code with the – Operator Compiled Using Aggressive Optimization

```
main            proc near           ; CODE XREF: start+AFp
        push    ecx
        ; Memory is allocated for the var_a local variable.

        mov     eax, [esp+var_a]
        ; The value of the var_a local variable is loaded into EAX.

        push    esi
        ; Memory is allocated for the var_b local variable.

        mov     esi, [esp+var_b]
        ; The value of the var_b variable is loaded into ESI.

        sub     esi, eax
        ; The var_b value is subtracted from var_a.
        ; The result is placed into ESI.

        push    esi
        push    offset asc_406030 ; "%x\n"
        call    _printf
        ; printf("%x\n", var_a - var_b)

        add     esi, 0FFFFFFF6h
```

```
; The value 0xFFFFFFF6 (the difference between var_a
; and var_b) is added to ESI. Since 0xFFFFFFF6 == -0xA,
; this line of code should look as follows:
; ESI = (var_a − var_b) + (− 0xA) = (var_a − var_b) − 0xA

        push    esi
        push    offset asc_406034 ; "%x\n"
        call    _printf
        add     esp, 10h
        ; printf("%x\n", var_a − var_b − 0xA)

        pop     esi
        pop     ecx
        ; The stack frame is closed.

        retn
main            endp
```

Other compilers (Borland, Watcom) generate practically the same code. Therefore, they are not considered here.

Identifying the / operator. The / operator generally is translated into the DIV machine instruction (unsigned-integer division), IDIV (signed-integer division), or FDIVx (floating-point division). If the divider is a multiple of a power of 2, DIV is replaced with SHR a, N, a faster instruction of the bit shift to the right, where a is a dividend and N is an exponent of base 2.

The fast division of signed numbers is a little more complex. The arithmetic shift to the right is insufficient. (The SAR instruction of the arithmetic shift to the right fills in the high-order bits, taking into account the number's sign.) If the absolute value of the dividend is less than the absolute value of the divisor, the arithmetic shift to the right will remove all significant bits into a "bit bin," resulting in 0xFFFFFFFF (i.e., −1, rather than the correct value, 0). In general, using the arithmetic shift to the right to divide signed numbers rounds *up* the result. This goes against what is desired here: To round off the signed result to smaller numbers, the number 2^N-1 should be added to the dividend before shifting (N is the quantity of bits the number is shifted). This increases all shifted bits by one, and adds the carry to the most significant bit if at least one bit is not equal to zero.

It must be noted that division is a slow operation, much slower than multiplication. (Executing DIV may take more than 40 clock cycles; MUL usually fits in 4.)

Therefore, the advanced optimizing compilers replace division with multiplication. There are many formulas for similar transformations; the most popular version is as follows:

$$a/b = 2^N/b \times a/2^N$$

In this case, N is a bit capacity of the number. The distinction between multiplication and division appears to be slight, which makes their identification rather difficult. Consider the following example:

Listing 225. Identifying the / Operator

```
main()
{
     int a;
     printf("%x %x\n", a/32, a/10);
}
```

Compiling this example using Microsoft Visual C++ with default settings should give the following.

Listing 226. The Disassembled Code with the / Operator in Visual C++

```
main          proc near          ; CODE XREF: start+AF↓p

var_a         = dword ptr -4

     push    ebp
     mov     ebp, esp
     ; The stack frame is opened.

     push    ecx
     ; Memory is allocated for a local variable.

     mov     eax, [ebp+var_a]
     ; The value of the var_a variable is copied to EAX.

     cdq
     ; EAX is extended to the quadword EDX:EAX.
```

```
mov     ecx, 0Ah
; The 0xA value is placed into ECX.

idiv    ecx
; Taking into account the sign, EDX:EAX is divided by 0xA,
; and the quotient is placed into EAX.
; EAX = var_a / 0xA

push    eax
; The computation result is passed to the printf function.

mov     eax, [ebp+var_a]
; The value of var_a is loaded into EAX.

cdq
; EAX is extended to the quadword EDX:EAX.

and     edx, 1Fh
; Five low-order bits of EDX are selected.

add     eax, edx
; The number's sign for rounding off the negative values
; is added to the smaller integer numbers.

sar     eax, 5
; The arithmetic 5-bit shift to the right is equivalent
; to dividing the number by 2 to the fifth power, or 32.
; Thus, the last four instructions can be represented
; as follows: EAX = var_a / 32.
; Note that although optimization mode has been disabled,
; the compiler has optimized division.

push    eax
push    offset aXX          ; "%x %x\n"
call    _printf
add     esp, 0Ch
; printf("%x %x\n", var_a / 0xA, var_a / 32)

mov     esp, ebp
pop     ebp
```

```
; The stack frame is closed.


        retn
main        endp
```

Now, let's consider the optimized version of the same example.

Listing 227. The Disassembled Code with the / Operator Compiled by Visual C++ with Aggressive Optimization

```
main        proc near            ; CODE XREF: start+AF↓p
        push    ecx
        ; Memory is allocated for the var_a local variable.


        mov     ecx, [esp+var_a]
        ; The value of the var_a variable is loaded into ECX.


        mov     eax, 66666667h
        ; Where did this number come from?
        ; There was nothing like this in the source code.


        imul    ecx
        ; This strange number is multiplied by the value
        ; of the var_a variable.
        ; Note: multiplied, not divided.
        ; However, let's carry on as though we did not have the
        ; source code of the example, and as though there was
        ; nothing strange in using multiplication.


        sar     edx, 2
        ; All the bits of EDX are shifted two positions to the right.
        ; Our first guess may be that this is the equivalent of
        ; dividing it by 4. However, EDX contains the higher
        ; double word of the multiplication result. Therefore,
        ; the three previous instructions can be represented as follows:
        ; EDX = (66666667h * var_a) >> (32 + 2) =
        ; = (66666667h * var_a) / 0x400000000;
        ; Closely examine this code for anything strange.
        ; (66666667h * var_a) / 0x400000000 =
```

```
; = var_a * 66666667h / 0x400000000 =
; = var_a * 0,1000000000349245965480804433594
; Strictly following mathmatical rules, replace multiplication
; with division and round off the result to the smaller integer.
; The result will be as follows:
; var_a * 0.1000000000 = var_a * (1/0.1000000000) = var_a/10
;
; After the transformation, the code has become
; more comprehensible. Is it possible to recognize
; such a situation in another person's program,
; the source code of which is unknown? Actually, it is easy:
; If multiplication occurs and is followed by
; the shift to the right, the indication of division,
; any normal mathematician will abbreviate such an
; expression using the above method.

mov    eax, edx
; The obtained quotient is copied to EAX.


shr    eax, 1Fh
; EAX is shifting 31 bits to the right.


add    edx, eax
; Addition: EDX = EDX + (EAX >> 31).
; What does this mean? Obviously, after EDX is shifted 31 bits
; to the right, only the sign bit of the number will remain.
; If the number is negative, 1 is added to the division result.
; This rounds it off to the smaller number.
; Therefore, all this code
; is nothing but a simple signed-division operation:
; EDX = var_a/10
; Is this too much code for a mere division? Certainly,
; the program becomes substantially "inflated," but executing
; all this code takes only 9 cycles. The nonoptimized variant
; takes as much as 28 cycles. (The measurements
; were carried out on a Celeron processor with a P6 core;
; on other processors, the number of clock cycles may differ.)
; Thus, the optimization has provided a more-than-threefold gain.
; Bravo, Microsoft.
```

```
        mov     eax, ecx
        ; What is in ECX?
        ; Scrolling the disassembler window upward
        ; shows that the last value loaded into ECX
        ; was that of the var_a variable.

        push    edx
        ; The result of dividing var_a by 10 is passed to printf.

        cdq
        ; EAX (var_a) is extended to the quadruple word EDX:EAX.

        and     edx, 1Fh
        ; The lower 5 bits of the EDX register, containing
        ; the sign of var_a, are selected.

        add     eax, edx
        ; Rounding down

        sar     eax, 5
        ; The arithmetic shift by 5 is identical to dividing var_a by 32.

        push    eax
        push    offset aXX          ; "%x %x\n"
        call    _printf
        add     esp, 10h
        ; printf("%x %x\n", var_a/10, var_a/32)

        retn
main            endp
```

It is interesting to compare compilers and see how advanced they are in terms of optimization. Unfortunately, neither Borland nor Watcom is capable of replacing division by the faster multiplication of numbers that are not powers of 2. To demonstrate this, let's consider the result of compiling the same example in Borland C++.

**Listing 228. The Disassembled Code with the / Operator Compiled by
Borland C++**

```
_main            proc near               ; DATA XREF: DATA:00407044↓o

        push    ebp
        mov     ebp, esp
        ; The stack frame is opened.

        push    ebx
        ; EBX is saved.

        mov     eax, ecx
        ; The contents of the uninitialized ECX register
        ; variable are copied to EAX.

        mov     ebx, 0Ah
        ; The value 0xA is placed into EBX.

        cdq
        ; EAX is extended to the quadruple word EDX:EAX.

        idiv    ebx
        ; ECX is divided by 0xA (a long process of 20 cycles
        ; or more).

        push    eax
        ; The obtained value is passed to the printf function.

        test    ecx, ecx
        jns     short loc_401092
        ; If the dividend is not negative, a jump is made to loc_401092.

        add     ecx, 1Fh
        ; If the dividend is negative, 0x1F is added to it for rounding off.

loc_401092:                              ; CODE XREF: _main+11↑j
        sar     ecx, 5
        ; The number is divided by 32, by shifting it 5 bits
        ; to the right.
```

```
        push    ecx
        push    offset aXX          ; "%x %x\n"
        call    _printf
        add     esp, 0Ch
        ; printf("%x %x\n", var_a/10, var_a/32)

        xor     eax, eax
        ; Returning zero

        pop     ebx
        pop     ebp
        ; The stack frame is closed.

        retn
_main           endp
```

Identifying the % operator. The instruction set of the 80x86 microprocessor family does not include a special instruction for computing the remainder. Instead, the remainder, with the quotient, is returned by the DIV, IDIV, and FDIVx division instructions.

If the divider is a power of 2 (2^N = b), and the dividend is an unsigned number, the remainder will be equal to the number represented by N low-order bits of the dividend. If the dividend is signed, all the bits (except for the first N), must equal the sign bit to preserve the number's sign. However, if the first N bits are zeroes, all the bits of the result should be cleared, regardless of the value of the sign bit.

Thus, if the dividend is an unsigned number, the a%2^N expression is translated into AND a, (b-1); otherwise, the translation becomes ambiguous: The compiler may insert an explicit test for zero into a branch statement, or it may use cunning mathematical algorithms, the most popular of which is DEC x\ OR x, -N\ INC x. The point is that if the first N bits of the number x are zeros, all the bits of the result, except for the most significant — the sign bit — will equal 1. In addition, OR x,-N will force the most significant bit to be set to zero as well (i.e., the resulting value will be –1). As for INC-1, it will give zero. On the contrary, if at least one of N low-order bits is 1, there is no carry from the high-order bits, and INC x restores the initial value of the result.

Using complex transformations, advanced optimizing compilers may replace division with one of several faster operations. Unfortunately, there are no algorithms for the fast calculation of the remainder for all dividers, and the divider should be a multiple of $k \times 2^t$, where k and t are integers. Then the remainder can be calculated using the formula

$$a \% b = a \% k \times 2^t = a - (2^N/k + (a/2^N)(-2) - 2^k) \times k$$

This formula is complex, and identifying the optimized $\%$ operator may appear to be a tough task, especially with optimizers' tendency to change the order of instructions.

Consider the following example:

Listing 229. Identifying the $\%$ Operator

```
main()
{
     int a;
     printf("%x %x\n", a%16, a%10);
}
```

Compiling this example in Microsoft Visual C++ with default settings should give the following:

Listing 230. The Disassembled Code with the $\%$ Operator

```
main          proc near            ; CODE XREF: start+AF↓p

        var_4                     = dword ptr -4
        push    ebp
        mov     ebp, esp
        ; The stack frame is opened.

        push    ecx
        ; Memory is allocated for a local variable.

        mov     eax, [ebp+var_a]
        ; The value of the var_a variable is placed into EAX.

        cdq
        ; EAX is extended to the quadword EDX:EAX.

        mov     ecx, 0Ah
```

```
; The 0xA value is placed into ECX.

idiv    ecx
; EDX:EAX (var_a) is divided by ECX (0xA).

push    edx
; The remainder from division of var_a by 0xA is passed to the
; printf function.

mov     edx, [ebp+var_a]
; The value of the var_a variable is placed into EDX.

and     edx, 8000000Fh
; The sign bit and four low-order bits of the number are "cut out."
; Four low-order bits contain the remainder from dividing EDX by 16.

jns     short loc_401020
; If the number is not negative, a jump is made to loc_401020.

dec     edx
or      edx, 0FFFFFFF0h
inc     edx
; This sequence, as previously mentioned, is typical for the
; fast calculation of the remainder of the signed number.
; Therefore, the last six instructions can be written as follows:
; EDX = var_a % 16


loc_401020:                         ; CODE XREF: main+19↑j
        push    edx
        push    offset aXX          ; "%x %x\n"
        call    _printf
        add     esp, 0Ch
        ; printf("%x %x\n", var_a % 0xA, var_a % 16)

        mov     esp, ebp
        pop     ebp
        ; The stack frame is closed.
        retn
main            endp
```

It is curious that optimization does not influence the algorithm for calculating the remainder. Unfortunately, neither Microsoft Visual C++ nor any other compiler I know of is able to calculate the remainder using multiplication.

Identifying the * operator. The * operator is generally translated into the MUL machine instruction (unsigned-integer multiplication), IMUL (signed-integer multiplication), or FMULx (floating-point multiplication). If one of the multipliers is a multiple of a power of 2, MUL (IMUL) usually is replaced with the SHL instruction, which shifts bits to the left, or with the LEA instruction, which multiplies the contents of the registers by 2, 4, or 8. The two latter instructions require two clock cycles for execution; MUL requires between two and nine cycles, depending on the processor type. In the same clock cycle, LEA has time to add the multiplication result to the contents of the general-purpose register and/or a constant; this multiplies the register by 3, 5, or 9, simply by adding its own value to it. This may sound ideal, but LEA has a shortcoming: It may cause Address Generation Interlock (AGI), which will "eat up" the gain in performance.

Consider the following example:

Listing 231. Identifying the * Operator

```
main()
{
        int a;
        printf("%x %x %x\n", a*16, a*4+5, a*13);
}
```

Compiling this example using Microsoft Visual C++, with default settings, should give the following:

Listing 232. The Disassembled Code with the * Operator Compiled by Visual C++

```
main            proc near               ; CODE XREF: start+AF↓p

var_a           = dword ptr -4

        push    ebp
        mov     ebp, esp
        ; The stack frame is opened.
```

```
push    ecx
; Memory is allocated for the var_a local variable.

mov     eax, [ebp+var_a]
; The value of the var_a local variable is loaded into EAX.

imul    eax, 0Dh
; This multiplies var_a by 0xD, and places the result into EAX.

push    eax
; The product var_a * 0xD is passed to the printf function.

mov     ecx, [ebp+var_a]
; The value of var_a is loaded into ECX.

lea     edx, ds:5[ecx*4]
; ECX is multiplied by 4. Then, 5 is added, and the result
; is placed into EDX.
; Note that this only takes one clock cycle.

push    edx
; The value of the var_a*4 + 5 expression is passed to
; the printf function.

mov     eax, [ebp+var_a]
; The value of the var_a variable is loaded into EAX.

shl     eax, 4
; The value of the var_a variable is multiplied by 16.

push    eax
; The value of the product var_a * 16 is passed to the printf function.

push    offset aXXX         ; "%x %x %x\n"
call    _printf
add     esp, 10h
; printf("%x %x %x\n", var_a * 16, var_a * 4 + 5, var_a * 0xD)
```

```
        mov     esp, ebp
        pop     ebp
        ; The stack frame is closed.
        retn
main            endp
```

Except for calling the `printf` function and loading the `var_a` variable from memory, executing this code will take just *three* processor clock cycles. Compiling this example with the `/Ox` key will give the following:

Listing 233. The Disassembled Code with the * Operator Compiled by Visual C++ with Aggressive Optimization

```
main            proc near           ; CODE XREF: start+AF↓p
        push    ecx
        ; Memory is allocated for the var_a local variable.

        mov     eax, [esp+var_a]
        ; EAX is loaded with the value of the var_a variable.

        lea     ecx, [eax+eax*2]
        ; ECX = var_a * 2 + var_a = var_a * 3

        lea     edx, [eax+ecx*4]
        ; EDX = (var_a * 3)* 4 + var_a = var_a * 13
        ; That is how the compiler manages to multiply var_a by 13
        ; using just one clock cycle! Both LEA instructions can be
        ; paired on Pentium MMX and Pentium Pro.

        lea     ecx, ds:5[eax*4]
        ; ECX = EAX*4 + 5

        push    edx
        push    ecx
        ; Passing var_a*13 and var_a*4 + 5 to the printf function

        shl     eax, 4
        ; var_a is multiplied by 16.
```

```
        push    eax
        push    offset aXXX           ; "%x %x %x\n"
        call    _printf
        add     esp, 14h
        ; printf("%x %x %x\n", var_a*16, var_a*4 + 5, var_a*13)


        retn
main            endp
```

This code is no faster than the previous, nonoptimized version, and it takes three clock cycles. In other areas, however, the gain may be substantial.

Other compilers use LEA to multiply numbers quickly. For example, Borland C++ produces the following:

Listing 234. The Disassembled Code with the * Operator Compiled in Borland

```
_main           proc near         ; DATA XREF: DATA:00407044↓o
        lea     edx, [eax+eax*2]
        ; EDX = var_a*3


        mov     ecx, eax
        ; ECX is loaded with the uninitialized var_a register variable.


        shl     ecx, 2
        ; ECX = var_a*4.


        push    ebp
        ; EBP is saved.


        add     ecx, 5
        ; The value 5 is added to var_a*4.
        ; Borland does not use LEA for addition, which is a pity.


        lea     edx, [eax+edx*4]
        ; EDX = var_a + (var_a*3) * 4 = var_a*13
        ; In this case, Borland and Microsoft are unanimous.


        mov     ebp, esp
        ; The stack frame is opened —
```

```
; in the middle of the function.
; By the way, the "missing" push EBP instruction is above.

push    edx
; The product of var_a*13 is passed to the printf function.

shl     eax, 4
; Here, ((var_a*4) + 5) is multiplied by 16.
; What is this? It is a bug in the compiler,
; which has decided that the var_a variable should
; not necessarily be loaded
; if it was not initialized.

push    ecx
push    eax
push    offset aXXX         ; "%x %x %x\n"
call    printf
add     esp, 10h
xor     eax, eax
pop     ebp
retn
_main           endp
```

Although Borland generates less interesting code, executing it takes three processor-clock cycles as well. Watcom is another matter: It shows a disappointingly low result compared to two compilers just considered.

Listing 235. The Disassembled Code with the * Operator Compiled in Watcom

```
main            proc near
        push    ebx
; EBX is saved on the stack.

        mov     eax, ebx
; EAX is loaded with the value of the uninitialized var_a register
; variable.

        shl     eax, 2
```

```
; EAX = var_a*4
sub     eax, ebx
; EAX = var_a*4 − var_a = var_a*3
; This is how Wactom works: It multiplies with a "surplus,"
; then it subtracts the excess.

shl     eax, 2
; EAX = var_a*3 * 4 = var_a*12

add     eax, ebx
; EAX = var_a*12 + var_a = var_a*13
; Is that so? Four instructions have been used, whereas Microsoft
; Visual C++, hated by many people, manages with two instructions.

push    eax
; The var_a*13 value is passed to printf.

mov     eax, ebx
; The value of the uninitialized var_a register
; variable is loaded into EAX.

shl     eax, 2
; EAX = var_a * 4

add     eax, 5
; EAX = var_a*4 + 5
; Like Borland, Watcom doesn't know how to use LEA.

push    eax
; The var_a*4 + 5 value is passed to to printf.

shl     ebx, 4
; EBX = var_a * 16

push    ebx
; The var_a * 16 value is passed to printf.

push    offset aXXX        ; "%x %x %x\n"
call    printf_
```

```
        add     esp, 10h
        ; printf("%x %x %x\n", var_a*16, var_a*4 + 5, var_a*13)

        pop     ebx

        retn
main_           endp
```

The code generated by Watcom requires six clock cycles (i.e., twice as many as the code generated by its competitors.)

Complex operators. C/C++ differs favorably from most of its competitors in its support for complex operators: x= (x is any simple operator,) ++, and --.

Complex operators of the type a x= b are translated into a = a x b, and are identified in the same way as the simple operators mentioned previously.

The ++ and — operators. In their prefix forms, these operators can be represented as simple expressions of the type a = a + 1 and a = a - 1, which are of no interest here. Their postfix forms, however, are another matter.

Part II: Ways of Making Software Analysis Difficult

Introduction

Counteracting Debuggers

Counteracting Disassemblers

An Invitation to the Discussion,
   or New Protection Tips

Introduction

The three basic stages of cracking protection mechanisms are *locating the protection code* in hundreds of kilobytes (or megabytes) of application code, *analyzing the algorithm* of its work, and *breaking*. These stages are equally important: For example, if the second stage is not passed, it makes no sense to start cracking.

It is possible to classify protection typographically. Cryptographic protection, for example, is used at the third stage. As a rule, its algorithm is widely available, well documented, and known to the hacker. Nevertheless, this does not aid cracking greatly (unless it simplifies the writing of a program for a brute-force attack). Protection based on registration numbers, however, stresses imposing secrecy on the algorithm that generates the registration numbers and hampering the search for and analysis of the algorithm in the program code. (Once the algorithm is known, it is easy to write the key generator.)

However, even protection that employs cryptographic methods, such as by ciphering the bodies of crucial functions using a strong cipher and a long key, may be separated from the key (for example, by saving a dump of the program after deciphering). Distributing the program with an applied key is a simpler tactic commonly used by pirates. One way of thwarting such an unlawful action is to include the encoded specification data of the computer into the key, or to check the authenticity of the copy through the Internet. (It is even possible, although considered bad form, to do this without notifying the user.) But what prevents a hacker who owns a licensed copy of the program from deciphering it with his or her own key and removing any checks from the program?

Therefore, any protection should be able to effectively counteract attempts at detection and analysis, and poison the disassembler and the debugger — the main tools of the cracker — along the way. Without this, protection is no protection at all.

During the reign of MS-DOS, the computer world was governed by real-time programs that used the processor, memory, and other hardware exclusively, and that switched to protected mode or back at any moment. At that time, debuggers (still shaky, feeble, and impractical) could easily be deceived (frozen, or forced to abort execution) by simple programming tricks actively used by protection mechanisms. Disassemblers fell into a stupor upon merely seeing ciphered or self-modifying code. It was paradise for protection-mechanism developers.

Now, everything has changed. Windows applications are not allowed to show off. Pressing ahead with the protected mode is no longer possible — only prosaic, nonprivileged instructions can be used, and tricks of different kinds can be only dreamed of. A few protective measures that can function even in such a "user friendly" environment fails against wise debuggers and disassemblers.

The hardware support for debugging in 386+ processors, along with v86 mode, privileged instructions, and virtual memory, allow the creation of debuggers that are almost undetectable by the application program. Moreover, it is impossible for the application to gain control over such debuggers. There are also debugger-emulators, true-to-life virtual machines executing code independently, instead of running it on a "live" processor. The emulator always runs in supervisor mode, even in relation to the zero-ring code being debugged. Protection mechanisms have little chance of detecting the debugger or hindering it (only possible if the emulator is implemented with mistakes).

Interactive disassemblers (like IDA) also have appeared. Their close relationship with the user (i.e., the hacker), allows them to bypass traps left by the developer.

The application sets up its own vxd. (This is executed in the zero-level protection ring and can do whatever it wants.) However, this only *facilitates* the hacker's task: The interaction of protection mechanisms and vxd is only possible through a special API, which simplifies the study of the protection algorithm and the emulation of vxd for un-binding the application from the electronic key or key diskette.

Even hiding something in the zero-ring protection is a problem in Windows. To guarantee compatibility with all Windows-like operating systems, only the system's documented capabilities can be used. Building protection in Windows is like trying to get lost in a park with a million trees, all of which are laid out geometrically and hung abundantly with signs reading "Exit this way."

Thus, it is very difficult, if not impossible, to reliably thwart the study of a program. However, many techniques for counteracting debuggers and disassemblers are interesting in themselves.

Counteracting Debuggers

A Brief History

The first debugger, *debug.com*, bore slight resemblance to today's debuggers. Moreover, it came as part of a regular MS-DOS package. Today, it is probably only suitable for entertainment and for studying assembler. Few people were delighted with it when it first appeared, and new debuggers mushroomed. However, most did not make significant advances as compared with the prototype. For example, some differed from the original only in the interface.

It was the golden age for protection developers. To make it impossible to debug a program, it was enough to lock the keyboard, disable interrupts, and clear the trap flag.

The first debuggers even slightly suitable for cracking appeared only after computers equipped with the 80286 processor. Hackers may remember *AFD PRO*, presented in 1987 by AdTec GmbH; the well-known *Turbo Debugger*, created by two brothers, Chris and Rich Williams, a year later; and the first emulating debugger by Sergey Pachkovski, written much later, in 1991. Protection developers withstood the assault: Debuggers still allowed the program being debugged to gain control over them, and they hardly withstood operations on the stack, the screen, the keyboard, and so on.

The situation changed when 80386 processors appeared. Major complications in the software (and, consequently, enormous complications in debugging) demanded the presence of advanced means of debugging in the processor itself.

As a result, these appeared in 386. From that moment, protection developers began to feel uneasy.

Fuel was added to the fire by NuMega, which presented its remarkable *SoftIce* at the end of the 1980s. SoftIce gained huge popularity among hackers and, adapted for Windows 9*x*/NT/2000, remains an undisputed favorite (although not without competitors). However, it would be incorrect to consider NuMega a criminal company and SoftIce a product only used by hackers: The debugger was intended primarily for driver-developers and for legal investigations of the operating system. (Writing drivers is a tough task unless the intricacies of the OS are understood.)

Nevertheless, SoftIce gave protection programs and their developers a lot of trouble. Certainly, it was not (and is still not) a stealth debugger, completely invisible to the program being debugged, and it had (and still has) several bugs that allow the protection to detect it, freeze it, and/or to escape from its control. Nevertheless, in skilful hands, it coped successfully with all these limitations and bypassed carefully set "traps." Each new version of SoftIce became more difficult to counteract. (Old bugs were fixed faster than new ones were introduced.)

Anti-debugging tricks gradually came to nothing; they have disappeared as a result of the victorious advance of Windows. The ridiculous belief that it is impossible to stop someone working in Windows with a debugger at the application level has become common. This brings smiles to the faces of professionals who build different traps into their programs (more for fun than to combat hackers seriously).

In view of the current possibilities for analyzing applications, struggling against hackers is a useless occupation. However, another serious threat comes from yesterday's beginners, who have read a lot of different "how-to-crack-programs" FAQs. (Thank goodness they are accessible to everyone.) These beginners now are looking for something on which to test their powerful capabilities.

How the Debugger Works

Struggling against a debugger without knowing how it works would, at best, be an indication of ill manners; therefore, the basic principles underlying it must be considered. The description that follows is not exhaustive. Nevertheless, it will give the reader a general idea about the issue. Full technical details can be found in the "*Debugging and Performance Monitoring*" chapter of the technical manual "*IA-32 Intel Architecture Software Developer's Manual. Volume 3: System Programming Guide,*" distributed free of charge by Intel.

All existing debuggers can be divided into two categories: ones that use the processor's debugging capabilities, and ones that emulate the processor independently, monitoring the execution of the program being tested.

A high-quality emulating debugger cannot be detected or bypassed the code being debugged. However, there are no high-quality emulators of Pentium processors, and they are unlikely to appear in the foreseeable future.

In general, it is worth asking if it makes sense to create such emulators. Pentium microprocessors provide immense debugging opportunities, allowing the developer to monitor even privileged code. They support *step-by-step execution of the program,* control execution of an instruction at a given address, monitor references to a given memory location (or to input-output ports), signal task switching, and so on.

If the trap bit of the flags register is set, the INT 1 debug exception is generated automatically after each machine instruction is executed, and control is transferred to the debugger. The code being debugged may detect tracing by analyzing the flags register. Therefore, to stay invisible, the debugger should recognize the instructions for reading the flags register, emulate their execution, and return zero for the value of the trap flag.

One point must be noted: After executing the instruction that modifies the value of the SS register, the debug exception *is not generated.* The debugger should be able to recognize this situation, and independently set a breakpoint on the following instruction. Otherwise, the automatic tracer will not be able to enter the procedure preceded by the POP SS instruction (for example, PUSH SS; POP SS; CALL MySecretProc). Not all contemporary debuggers take this subtlety into account. Such a decision, despite its archaic nature, may appear helpful.

Four debug registers, DR0 through DR3, store the linear addresses of four checkpoints. The DR7 debug register contains a condition for each of the points. When any condition is true, the processor generates the INT 0x1 exception and control is transferred to the debugger. There are four conditions: *an instruction is executed*; *the contents of a memory location are modified*; *a memory location is read or updated, but not executed*; and *an input-output port is referenced.*

Setting a special bit enables the generation of the debug exception following any reference to debug registers, even when the privileged code tries to read or modify them. A competently designed debugger can hide its presence by not allowing the code being debugged to detect the debugger, no matter what privileges the code may have. (However, if the code under study debugs itself, involving all four breakpoints, the debugger will not be able to work.)

If the T bit in TSS of the task being debugged is set, each time this task is switched to, it will cause the debug exception *before* the first instruction of the task is executed. To prevent detection, the debugger may trace all references to TSS and return counterfeit data to the program. Note that to improve performance, Windows NT does not use TSS (to be more precise, it uses only one), rendering this debug opportunity useless.

A *software breakpoint* is the only thing that cannot be hidden without writing a full-scale processor emulator. This is the one-byte code 0xCC that, placed at the beginning of the instruction, causes the INT 0x3 exception when an attempt is made to execute it. To discover whether at least one point has been set, it is enough for the program being debugged to count its checksum. To do this, it may use MOV, MOVS, LODS, POP, CMP, CMPS, or any other instructions; no debugger is capable of tracing and emulating any of them.

Software breakpoints are recommended only when hardware capabilities are insufficient. However, by default, practically all contemporary debuggers (including SoftIce) always set software breakpoints, rather than hardware ones. This can be successfully used in protection mechanisms, examples of which are given in the "*How to Counteract Tracing*" section.

Processing Exceptions in Real and Protected Modes

When the debug exception (or any other exception) arises, the processor places the contents of the flags register and the address of the following instruction (or the current one, depending on the exception) to be executed onto the stack. Only then does it pass control to the debugger.

In real mode, the flags with the return address are placed onto the *stack of the program being debugged*, making debugging easy to detect. It is enough to keep control over the integrity of the stack contents above the stack pointer. One option is to point to the top of the stack. In this case, it will be impossible to add new data on the stack, and the debugger will be unable to work.

Another situation that arises in protected mode is that the exception handler may reside in its own address space and not use any resources (including the stack) of the application being debugged. In principle, a debugger competently designed for protected mode cannot be detected or disabled — even by the privileged code being executed in the zero ring.

This is true for Windows NT, but not for Windows 9x; the latter operating systems do not use all the advantages of protected mode, and they always litter the stack of the task, whether or not it is being debugged.

How Hackers Break Programs

Generally, revealing a protective mechanism is no problem for the hacker. What is really difficult is finding it in many megabytes of the application being cracked. Today, few people use automatic tracing for this purpose; hardware breakpoints have supplanted it.

For example, let's suppose that a protection requests a password, then checks its authenticity (for example, by comparing it with a reference value). Depending on the result of the check, the protection passes control to an appropriate branch of the program. The hacker may crack this protection without even going into the authentication algorithm. The hacker simply enters the first password that comes to mind (not necessarily the correct one), finds it in the memory, sets a breakpoint on the first character of the password string, waits for the debugger to appear that has tracked referencing the password, exits the comparison procedure, and corrects the condition of the jump so that the desired branch of the program always gains control.

The time needed to remove this sort of protection is measured in seconds! Such programs are usually cracked before they reach a legal consumer. Fortunately, this can be counteracted.

Protecting Programs

No matter where the key information comes from — a register, a file, the keyboard — a hacker can determine its location in memory and set a breakpoint on it almost instantly. Preventing this is impossible, but a mean trick can be played on the hacker: Instead of allowing the key information to be analyzed immediately after it is received, it can be passed as an argument to several functions that do something with it, then transfer it to other functions. These functions, in turn, transfer it to the following ones.

The protective mechanism may be built into everything (the file-open procedure, a program for calculating salaries, etc.). Explicit checks are not recommended: It is better if, in the case of incorrect key information, the called function returns an incorrect result but does not signal the mistake. At first glance, the broken program will work normally. The fact that it works incorrectly will be detected only later (for example, if it displays one result and prints another). To secure the legal user against the erroneous input of the password, it is enough to explicitly compute the checksum in one place; the checksum will not give the hacker any information about the true value of the password.

Thus, protection is "smeared" around the program and buffers containing key data are duplicated repeatedly. The hacker will not have enough breakpoints or the patience to analyze the huge volume of code manipulated with tracing references. It is even better if the buffers that check the key information also are used to store service data, accessed as frequently as possible. This will prevent the hacker from quickly separating the protective mechanism from other code of the application.

Since most hackers set a breakpoint on the beginning of the control buffer, it is reasonable to place the "stub" in the first four bytes of the key; the stub is either not referenced at all, or it is manipulated by a protection simulator, which keeps the hacker on the wrong track.

In such a situation, the hacker only can undertake a laborious study of *all* code that directly or indirectly manipulates key information (and that comprises many megabytes of disassembler listing). If the crucial part of code is encrypted but not decrypted completely at any moment of running the program (i.e., each function is decrypted when entered and encrypted again when exited), the hacker will be unable to obtain a dump ready for disassembling, and will be compelled to trace. This is where the second surprise will be waiting.

How to Counteract Tracing

The basic possibility of creating completely "invisible" debuggers mainly remains a possibility: Most can be detected by even nonprivileged code.

The severest criticism is caused by using the 1-byte `0xCC` code to set a breakpoint, instead of charging with the task the debug registers specially intended for this. SoftIce, Turbo Debugger, Code Viewer, and the debugger integrated in Microsoft Visual Studio all use `0xCC`. The last debugger uses breakpoints when it runs a program in step-by-step mode, placing the notorious `0xCC` byte at the beginning of the next instruction.

A trivial integrity self-check reveals breakpoints that indicate debugging. Statements like `if (CalculateMyCRC()!=MyValidCRC) {printf("Hello, Hacker!\n"); return;}` are not recommended, because it is easy to discover and neutralize them by correcting the conditional jump so it always transfers control to the necessary branch of the program. It is better to decrypt the critical data or some code using the obtained checksum value.

A simple protection mechanism may look like this:

Listing 236. A Simple Protection Mechanism

```c
int main(int argc, char* argv[])
{
// The ciphered string "Hello, Free World!"
char s0[]="\x0C\x21\x28\x28\x2B\x68\x64\x02\x36\
\x21\x21\x64\x13\x2B\x36\x28\x20\x65\x49\x4E";
    __asm
{
BeginCode:                          ; The beginning of the code
                                    ; being debugged
        pusha                       ; All general-purpose
                                    ; registers are saved.
        lea ebx, s0                 ; ebx=&s0[0]
GetNextChar:                        ; do
        xor eax, eax                ; eax = 0;
        lea esi, BeginCode          ; esi = &BeginCode
        le ecx, EndCode             ; The length of code
        sub ecx, esi                ; being debugged is computed.
        HarvestCRC:                 ; do
        lodsb                       ; The next byte is loaded into al.
        Add eax, eax                ; The checksum is computed.
        loop HarvestCRC             ; until(--cx>0)
        xor [ebx], ah               ; The next character is decrypted.
        Inc ebx                     ; A pointer to the next character
        cmp [ebx],0                 ; Until the end of the string
        jnz GetNextChar             ; Continue decryption
        popa                        ; All registers are restored.
EndCode:                            ; The end of the code being debugged
        nop                         ; A breakpoint is safe here.
}
printf(I s0);                       ; The string is diplayed.
return 0;
}
```

After starting the program normally, the line "Hello, Free World!" should appear on the screen. But when the program is run under the debugger, even with at least one breakpoint set within the limits of `BeginCode` and `EndCode`, senseless garbage like `"Jgnnm."Dpgg"Umpnf#0"` will show up on the screen. Protection can be strengthened considerably if the procedure computing the checksum is placed into a separate thread engaged in another useful process, making the protective mechanism as unobtrusive as possible.

In general, threads are great things that demand a special approach. It is difficult for a human to recognize that a program can run simultaneously in several places. Commonly used debuggers have a weak point: They debug each thread separately, never simultaneously. The following example shows how this can be used for protection.

Listing 237. The Weakness of Debugging Threads Separately

```
// This function will be executing in a separate thread.
// Its purpose is to alter imperceptibly the case of the characters
// in the string that contains the user name.
void My(void *arg)
{
        int p=1;
        // This is a pointer to the byte being encrypted.
        // Note that encryption is not carried out
        // from the first byte, since this allows the breakpoint
        // set at the beginning of the buffer to be bypassed.
        // If the line feed is not encountered, execute.
        while ( ((char *) arg)[p]!='\n')
        {
                // If the next character is not initialized, wait.
                while( ((char *) arg)[p]<0x20 );

                // The fifth bit is inverted.
                // This toggles the case of the Latin characters.
                ((char *) arg)[p] ^=0x20;

                // A pointer to the next byte being processed
                p++;
        }
}

int main(int argc, char* argv[])
{
        char name[100];
```

```
// A buffer containing the user name

char buff[100];
// A buffer containing the password

// The buffer of the user name is stuffed with zeroes.
// (Some compilers do this, but not all.)
memset(&name[0], 0, 100);

// The My routine is executed in a separate thread.
_beginthread(&My, NULL,(void *) &name[0]);

// The user name is requested.
printf("Enter name:"); fgets(&name[0], 66, stdin);

// The password is requested.
// Note: While the user enters the password, the second
// thread has enough time to alter the case of all
// characters of the user name. This is not evident
// and does not follow from the analysis of the program,
// especially if it is studied under a debugger that poorly
// shows the mutual influence of the program's components.
printf("Enter password:"); fgets(&buff[0], 66, stdin);

// The user name and the password are compared
// with the reference values.
if (!(strcmp(&buff[0], "password\n")
// Note: Since the name entered by the user has been
// transformed to strcmp(&name[0], "Kpnc\n"),
// not strcmp(&name[0], "KPNC\n"), it is compared.
// (This is not apparent at first glance.)

|| strcmp(&name[0], "KPNC\n")))
// The correct name and password
printf("USER OK\n");
      else
// Error: Wrong user name or password
printf("Wrong user or password!\n");

return 0;
}
```

Initially, the program expects to receive KPNC:password. But the true answer is Kpnc:password. As the user enters the password, the second thread processes the buffer that contains the user name, and toggles the case of all characters except the first one. When one thread is traced step by step, all other threads are functioning independently. These other threads may intervene randomly in the functioning of the thread being debugged (for example, to modify its code).

The threads can be controlled if a breakpoint is placed in each of them. However, if there are more than four threads (nothing prevents the protection developer from creating them), the quantity of debug registers will become insufficient for all threads. In this case, the necessity arises of using the 0xCC opcode, which can easily be detected by the protective mechanism.

The situation is aggravated by the poor tolerance of most debuggers, including SoftIce, for programs with *structural exception handling* (SEH). The instruction that causes the exception being processed either "defeats" the debugger, releasing itself from the debugger's control, or passes control to the library exception filter, which only passes control to the application's handler after it calls several service functions that may "drown" the hacker.

However, when compared to early SoftIce versions, this is progress. Formerly, SoftIce strictly held certain interrupts. For example, it would not allow the program to process independently division by zero.

If the following example is run under any SoftIce version through 4.05, the debugger, having reached the int c=c/(a-b) line, suddenly will abort execution, losing the control over this application. Theoretically, the situation can be corrected by presetting the breakpoint on the first instruction of the block __except. Then, the question is how to find the location of this block without looking in the source code, which the hacker would not have.

Listing 238. An Example That Employs Structural Exception Handling

```
int main(int argc, char* argv[])
{

// A protected block
__try{
        int a=1;
        int b=1;
        int c=c/(a-b);
        // This is an attempt to divide by zero.
        // Several statements are used because most compilers
```

```
        // return an error after encountering a statement like
        // int a=a/0;
        // When SoftIce executes the following instruction, it loses
        // control over the program being debugged. It "falls off" to
        // code that never gains control but may be misleading.
        // If the a and b variables are assigned values
        // returned by some functions, not immediate values,
        // their equality will not be obvious when
        // the program is disassembled. As a result, the hacker
        // may waste time analyzing useless code.
    }

    __except(EXCEPTION_EXECUTE_HANDLER)
    {
        // This code will gain control when the exception "division by
        // zero" arises, but SoftIce will not recognize this
        // situation. Instead, it will ask that a breakpoint be
        // set manually on the first instruction of the block __except.
        // To determine an address of the block __except, the hacker
        // will have to figure out exactly how SEH support is
        // implemented in a particular compiler.
    }
}
```

To cope with such protection, the hacker will have to study in depth how structural exceptions are processed, both at the operating system level and at the level of a particular compiler. Most of the existing literature bypasses this theme, probably because implementing SEH is complex and bulky. As a result, most programmers and technical writers do not know what is "under the hood."

Since SEH is implemented differently in each compiler, it is not surprising that SoftIce refuses to support it. Therefore, the previous example is highly resistant to breaking and, at the same time, is easy to implement. It works equally well under all operating systems of the Windows family, starting from Windows 95.

Counteracting Breakpoints

Breakpoints set on major system functions are powerful weapons in the hands of a hacker. Suppose that protection tries to open a key file. Under Windows, the only documented way of doing this is to call the CreateFile function (actually,

CreateFileA or CreateFileW for the ASCII or UNICODE name of the file, respectively). All other functions inherited from early Windows versions, such as OpenFile, serve as wrappers to CreateFile.

Knowing this, the hacker may set a breakpoint on the starting address of the beginning of this function (which is known to the hacker), and instantly locate the protection code by calling this function.

However, not all hackers know that the file can be opened in other ways: by calling the ZwCreateFile (or NtCreateFile) function exported by NTDLL.DLL, or by addressing the kernel directly via a call to the INT 0x2Eh interrupt. This is true not only for CreateFile, but for all functions of the kernel. Interestingly, no privileges are needed for this. Such a call can even originate from an application code.

This trick will not stop an experienced hacker for long, but it is worth preparing a small surprise by placing the call of INT 0x2E in the __try block. Control will be gained not only by the system kernel, but also by this exception's handler in the __try block. The hacker, without the source code, cannot determine quickly whether this call has any relation to the __try block. Hence, the hacker easily can be led astray — it is enough to simulate opening a file without actually opening it. Besides, nothing prevents the INT 0x2E interrupt from being used to organize the interaction of the program components; it will be difficult for the hacker to distinguish the user's call from the system's call.

Now, what can be done with functions of the USER and GDI modules (for example, GetWindowsText) that are used to read the user-entered key information (as a rule, a serial number or a password)? Fortunately, practically all these functions begin with the PUSH EBP\MOV EBP, ESP instructions. This can be executed independently by the application code: Control can be passed *not to the beginning of the function*, but *to three bytes lower*. (Since PUSH EBP modifies the stack, control must be transferred using JMP instead of CALL.) The breakpoint set at the beginning of the function will not produce any effect. Such a trick may temporarily lead even a skilled hacker astray.

Finally, if the intention is to poison the hacker's life, the system function should be copied to its own stack, and control should be transferred to it. The hacker's breakpoint will have to "retire." The greatest complexity is recognizing all instructions with relative address arguments appropriately corrected. For example, the double word after the CALL instruction represents not an address of the jump, but the difference between the target address and the address of the instruction next to the CALL instruction. Moving the CALL instruction to a new place requires a correction of its argument. This task is not as complex as it might initially seem to be.

In addition, the result justifies the means: Each time the function starts, its address can be changed randomly. Moreover, by checking the integrity of code, the software breakpoints can easily be revealed; the number of hardware points simply will not be sufficient for all calls.

Hardware breakpoints set on memory are even easier to counteract. There are only four such breakpoints, and each may control no more than a double word. Therefore, the hacker may control simultaneously no more than 16 bytes of memory. If references to the buffers containing the key information do not occur consecutively (byte-after-byte from beginning to end), but occur randomly, and if the quantity of buffers is more than four, it becomes impossible to trace all read or write operations on them.

Some debuggers can set a breakpoint on a memory range, but this feature is questionable: The only way to control the whole area is to trace the program being investigated. This is done by checking whether the next instruction addresses this area and, if it does, generating an exception.

Many instructions work with memory. It is possible to invent unexpected combinations. (For example, to point the stack pointer to the required memory location, then to call RET to read the value it contains.) The exception that will arise in this case can get rid of the debugger. (See the "*How to Counteract Tracing*" section.)

Thus, counteracting checkpoints is no problem for the protection mechanism.

As previously mentioned, the software breakpoint is a one-byte instruction, 0xCC, that generates the 0x3 exception on an attempt to execute it. The handler of INT 0x3 gains control and can do whatever it wishes with a program. However, before the interrupt handler is called, the current values of *the flags register*, *the pointer of the code segment* (the CS register), and *the instruction pointer* (the IP register) are placed onto the stack. In addition, *the interrupts are disabled* (the IF flag is cleared), and *the trap flag* is cleared. Therefore, a call of the debug interrupt does not differ from a call of any other interrupt (see Fig. 9).

To learn the point of the program in which the halt has occurred, the debugger pulls the saved values of registers off the stack, taking into account that CS:IP points to the next instruction to be executed.

Breakpoints can tentatively be divided into two categories: *breakpoints built into the program by the developer* and *dynamic breakpoints set by the debugger itself*. The first category is clear: To stop the program and pass control to the debugger at a certain place, it is necessary to write `__asm{int 0x3}`.

It is more complex to set a breakpoint in an arbitrary place of the program. The debugger should save the current value of the memory location at the specified address, then write the code 0xCC there. Before exiting the debug interrupt, the debugger should return everything to its former place, and should modify IP saved in the stack so that it points to the beginning of the restored instruction. (Otherwise, it points to its middle.)

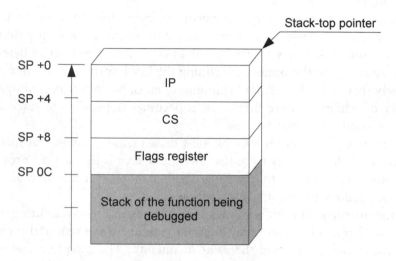

Fig. 37. The contents of the stack when the interrupt routine is entered

What are the drawbacks of the breakpoint mechanism of the 8086 processor? The most unpleasant is that the debugger must modify code directly when it sets the breakpoints.

SoftIce implicitly places the breakpoint at the beginning of each next instruction when it traces the program using **Step Over** (the <F10> key). This distorts the chesksum used by protection.

The simplest solution to this problem is instruction-by-instruction tracing. Of course, this is a joke; it is necessary to set a hardware breakpoint. In a similar situation, our ancestors (the hackers of the 1980s) usually decrypted the program manually and replaced the decrypting procedure with the NOP instructions. As a result, debugging the program did not present a problem (if there were no other traps in protection). Before IDA appeared, the decrypting procedure had to be written in C (Pascal, BASIC) as an independent program. Now this task is easier, since decrypting has become possible in the disassembler itself.

Decrypting is reduced to the reproduction of the decrypting procedure in the IDA-C language. In this case, the checksum from BeginCode to EndCode must be calculated, taking into account the sum of the bytes and using the lower byte of the checksum to load the following character. The obtained value is used to process the s0 string using the exclusive OR operation. All this can be done using the following script (assuming that the appropriate labels are already in the disassembled code):

Listing 239. Reproducing the Decrypting Mechanism in IDA-C

```
auto a; auto p; auto crc; auto ch;
for (p=LocByName("s0"); Byte(p)!=0; p++)
{
        crc = 0;

        for(a=LocByName("BeginCode"); a<(LocByName("EndCode")); a++)
        {
                ch = Byte(a);
                // Since IDA does not support the byte and word types
                // (which is a pity), it is necessary to engage in bit
                // operations. The lower byte, CRC, is cleared,
                // and then the value of CH is copied to it.

                crc = crc & 0xFFFFFF00;
                crc = crc | ch;
                crc=crc+crc;
        }
        // The high-order byte is taken from CRC.
        crc = crc & 0xFFFF;
        crc = crc / 0x100;

        // The next byte of the string is decrypted.
        PatchByte(p, Byte(p) ^ crc);
}
```

If IDA is not available, HIEW can be used to carry out this operation as follows:

```
    NoTrace.exe   ↓W      PE 00001040 a32 <Editor>    28672 ? Hiew 6.04 (c)SEN
00401003: 83EC18                      sub         esp, 018 ;"↑"
00401006: 53                          push        ebx
00401007: 56                          push        esi
00401008: 57                          push        edi
00401009: B905000000                                          000005
```

```
0040100E: BE30604000   ┌─[Byte/Forward ]════════════┐  406030 ;" @`0"
00401013: 8D7DE8        ║  1>mov   bl, al     │ AX=0061 ║p][-0018]
00401016: F3A5          ║  2 add   ebx, ebx   │ BX=44C2 ║
00401018: A4            ║  3                  │ CX=0000 ║
run from here:          ║  4                  │ DX=0000 ║
00401019: 6660          ║  5                  │ SI=0000 ║ [0FFFFFFE8]
0040101B: 8D9DE8FFFF     ║  6                  │ DI=0000 ║
00401021: 33C0          └────────────────────┴─────────┘
.0040101B: 8D9DE8FFFFFF
.00401021: 33C0                     xor     eax, eax
.00401023: 8D3519104000            lea     esi, [000401019] ; < BeginCode
.00401029: 8D0D40104000            lea     ecx, [000401040] ; < EndCode
.0040102F: 2BCE                    sub     ecx, esi
.00401031: AC                      lodsb
00401032: 03C0                     add     eax, eax
00401034: E2FB                     loop    000001031
00401036: 3023                     xor     [ebx], ah
00401038: 43                       inc     ebx
00401039: 803B00                   cmp     b, [ebx], 000 ;" "
0040103C: 75E3                     jne     000001021
0040103E: 6661                     popa
to here:
00401040: 90                       nop
00401041: 8D45E8                   lea     eax, [ebp][-0018]
00401044: 50                       push    eax
00401045: E80C000000               call    000001056
0040104A: 83C404                   add     esp, 004
1Help  2Size   3Direct 4Clear  5ClrReg 6        7Exit  8        9Store 10Load
```

At the first stage, the checksum is computed. The file is loaded in HIEW, and the necessary fragment is found. Then, the <Enter> key is pressed twice to toggle in the assembler mode, the <F8>+<F5> key combination is pressed to jump to the entry point, and the main procedure in the start code is found. Next, the <F3> key is pressed to enable editing the file. The editor of the decryptor is called using the <Ctrl>+<F7> key combination. (This combination varies from one version to another.) Finally, the following code is entered:

```
mov bl, al
add ebx, ebx
```

Another register can be used instead of EBX, apart from for EAX, since HIEW clears EAX as it reads out the next byte. Now, the cursor is brought to the 0x401019 line and the <F7> key is pressed to run the decrypt up to, but not including, the 0x401040 line. If all is done correctly, the high-order byte BX should contain the value 0x44, precisely the checksum.

In the second stage, the encrypted line is found (its offset, .406030, is loaded into ESI), and "xor-ed" by 0x44. (The <F3> key is pressed to toggle the editing mode, the <Ctrl>+<F8> key combination is used to specify the key for encrypting, 0x44, then the <F8> key is pressed to conduct the decryptor along the line.)

```
NoTrace.exe   ↓W    PE 00006040    <Editor>   28672 ? Hiew 6.04 (c)SEN
00006030:   48 65 6C 6C-6F 2C 20 46-72 65 65 20-57 6F 72 6C   Hello, Free World
00006040:   20 65 49 4E-00 00 00 00-7A 1B 40 00-01 00 00 00   eIN    z←@ ☺
```

All that is left is to patch XOR in the 0x401036 line with the NOP instructions; otherwise, when the program is started, XOR will spoil the decrypted code (by encrypting it again), and the program will not work.

After the protection is removed, the program can be debugged without serious consequences for as long as necessary. The checksum is still computed, but not used. (If a check for CRC correctness is in the protection, it must be neutralized as well. For clarity, such a check was not included in this example.)

How to Reveal Debugging Using Windows

In his book "*Windows 95 System Programming Secret*s," Matt Pietrek describes the structure of the *Thread Information Block* (*TIB*), after discussing the purpose of many undocumented fields. The double word located at the offset 0x20 from the beginning of the TIB structure is of special interest: It contains a *context of the debugger* if the given process is debugged; otherwise, it contains zero. The TIB is accessible through the selector loaded into the FS register. It can be read by application code without any problems.

If the FS:[0x20] double word is not equal to zero, the process is being debugged. This is so tempting that some programmers have included a check for this in protection code, ignoring the fact that it is undocumented. As a result, these programs cannot be executed under Windows NT; this OS stores not the context of the debugger in this field, but the process identifier, which never equals zero. The protection wrongly believes that the process is being debugged.

This issue was considered in detail by Pietrek in *Microsoft Systems Journal*, May 1996, in the paper "*Under The Hood.*" Pietrek presented the following structure:

Listing 240. Checking for `FS:[0x20]`

```
union                           // 1Ch (NT/Win95 differences)
{
struct // Win95 fields
{
        WORD    TIBFlags;          // 1Ch
        WORD    Win16MutexCount;   // 1Eh
        DWORD   DebugContext;      // 20h
        DWORD   pCurrentPriority;  // 24h
        DWORD   pvQueue;           // 28h Message Queue selector
} WIN95;

struct // WinNT fields
{
        DWORD   unknown1;          // 1Ch
        DWORD   processID;         // 20h
        DWORD   threadID;          // 24h
        DWORD   unknown2;          // 28h
} WINNT;
} TIB_UNION2;
```

This confirmed that undocumented features should never be used needlessly. As a rule, using them brings more problems than benefits.

Counteracting Disassemblers

Self-Modifying Code
in Contemporary Operating Systems

A decade or two ago, in the prime of MS-DOS, programmers often used self-modifying code. No serious protection could do without it. It also could be encountered in compilers that compiled code into memory, unpackers of executable files, polymorphic generators, and so on.

In the mid-1990s, users began a massive migration from MS-DOS to Windows 95/NT. Developers had to think about porting the gained experience and programming techniques to the new platform; the uncontrolled access to hardware, memory, and operating-system components, and smart programming tricks concerning them, had to be forgotten. In particular, directly modifying the executable code of applications became impossible, since Windows protects it from inadvertent changes. This gave birth to the ridiculous belief that, under Windows, creating self-modifying code is impossible without using VxD and the undocumented capabilities of the operating system.

Actually, at least two documented ways of changing application code work equally well under Windows starting from 95, with guest-user privileges being sufficient.

First, *kernel32.dll* exports the WriteProcessMemory function, intended, as follows from its name, for modifying the memory of a process. Second, practically all operating systems, Windows and Linux included, allow the code placed *on the stack* to be modified.

The task of creating self-modifying code can be solved just by using high-level languages (for example, C/C++, or Pascal), without employing the assembler.

The material of this section mostly focuses on the Microsoft Visual C++ compiler and on 32-bit executable code.

The Architecture of Windows Memory

Creating self-modifying code requires knowledge of certain subtleties of the Windows architecture. These subtleties are not elucidated in the documentation, but they do not yet have the status of undocumented features, because they are implemented on all Windows platforms and are used actively by Microsoft Visual C++. Hence, the company does not plan any changes; otherwise, the code generated by this compiler will not work, an unacceptable situation for Microsoft.

To address 4 GB of virtual memory allocated for a process, Windows uses two selectors. One is loaded into the CS segment register; the other is loaded into the DS, ES, and SS registers. The selectors use the same base address of memory equal to zero, and have identical limits of memory space equal to 4 GB.

 Note

Besides the segment registers listed above, Windows also uses the FS register, which it loads with the segment selector containing the Thread Information Block (*TIB*).

Actually, only *one* segment contains both code and data, as well as the stack of a process. Therefore, control of the code located in the stack is passed using the near call, or a jump. Using the SS prefix to access the contents of the stack is unnecessary. Although the value of the CS register is *not* equal to the value of the DS, ES, and SS registers, the MOV dest, CS:[src], MOV dest, DS:[src], and MOV dest, SS:[src] instructions address the same memory location.

Memory areas containing code, the stack, and data differ in the attributes of pages belonging to them. Code pages admit *reading* and *executing*, data pages admit *reading* and *writing*, and the stack admits *reading, writing*, and *executing* simultaneously.

In addition, each page has a special flag that determines the level of privilege necessary for accessing the page. Certain pages, such as those belonging to the operating system, require the rights of the administrator, granted only to the code of the zero ring. Application programs executing in ring 3 have no such rights, and any attempt to reference a protected page causes an exception.

Only the operating system or the code executing in the zero ring can manipulate page attributes or associate pages with linear addresses. There are hatches in Windows 95/98 protection that allow an application code to raise the privileges to the administrator level. However, the benefit of using them is doubtful: The user is bound to this operating system and is denied the opportunity to use the same trick on Windows NT/2000.

> ### Note
>
> A ridiculous fable circulating among novice programmers says that if someone addresses the code of a program using the instruction preceded by the DS prefix, Windows will allow modification of this code. This is incorrect. Regardless of the addressing used, the system allows the code to be addressed, not modified, since the protection works at the level of physical pages, not logical addresses.

Using the *WriteProcessMemory* Function

If the number of bytes of a process needs to be changed, the simplest method is to call the WriteProcessMemory function. This modifies the existing memory pages whose supervisor flags are not set (i.e., all pages accessible from ring 3 in which applications are running). Trying to change critical data structures of the given operating system (*page directory*, or *page table*, for example) using WriteProcessMemory is senseless, since these are accessible only from the zero ring. Therefore, this function does not represent any threat to the safety of the system, and is successfully called irrespective of the level of the user privileges. (I once heard the statement that WriteProcessMemory requires rights for debugging applications, but this is not so.)

The memory process on which the write operation is to be carried out should first be opened by the OpenProcess function, with the PROCESS_VM_OPERATION and PROCESS_VM_WRITE access attributes. Programmers often choose a shorter way, setting the PROCESS_ALL_ACCESS value to all attributes. This is admissible, although it is considered bad programming style.

A simple example of using the WriteProcessMemory function to create the self-modifying code is given in Listing 241. It replaces the instruction of the infinite loop JMP short $-2 with a conditional jump JZ $-2, which continues normal execution of the program. This is a good way of complicating the analysis of the program for the hacker, especially if the call of WriteMe is located not in the vicinity of changeable code, but in a separate thread. It is even better if the modified code looks natural and does not arouse any suspicions. In such a case, the hacker may waste a lot of time wandering along the branch of code that never gains control during the program execution.

Listing 241. Using `WriteProcessMemory` to Create Self-Modifying Code

```
int WriteMe(void *addr, int wb)
{
        HANDLE h=OpenProcess(PROCESS_VM_OPERATION|PROCESS_VM_WRITE,
        true, GetCurrentProcessId());
        return WriteProcessMemory(h, addr, &wb, 1, NULL);
}


int main(int argc, char* argv[])
{
        _asm {
                push 0x74               ; JMP --> > JZ
                push offset Here
                call WriteMe
                add esp, 8
        Here:                           JMP short here
        }
        printf("#JMP SHORT $-2 was changed to JZ $-2\n");
        return 0;
}
```

To save random-access memory, Windows shares code between processes. What will happen if the second copy of the self-modifying program is started? Will the operating system create new pages, or will it send the application to the code already being modified? The documentation on Windows NT/2000 says these systems support *copy on write* (i.e., the code pages are automatically duplicated on an attempt to update them). On the contrary, Windows 95/98 *do not support* this feature. Does this all mean that all copies of the self-modifying application will be compelled to work with the *same* code pages, which inevitably will result in conflicts and failures?

No, although copying on write is not implemented in Windows 95/98, this is taken care of by the `WriteProcessMemory` function, which creates copies of all pages belonging to different processes and being modified. Due to this, the self-modifying code works well under Windows 95/98/Me/NT/2000. However, remember that all copies of the application modified *in any other way* (the MOV instruction of the zero ring, for example) and started under Windows 95/98 will share the same pages of a code, with all consequences following from this.

Now, a few words about limitations: Using WriteProcessMemory is only reasonable in compilers that compile into memory, or in unpackers of executable files. Using it in protection is a little naive. A fairly experienced hacker will quickly find a dirty trick, having seen this function in the import table. Then, the hacker will set a breakpoint on the call of WriteProcessMemory, and will control each operation of writing to memory, which does not fit the plans of the protection developer.

Another limitation of WriteProcessMemory is its inability to create new pages; only the pages already existing are accessible to it. But what can be done, for example, if another amount of memory must be allocated for the code dynamically generated "on the fly?" Calling the heap-control functions, such as malloc, will not be helpful, since executing the code in the heap is not permitted. But the possibility of executing code in the stack is helpful.

Executing Code in the Stack

Executing code in the stack is permitted because many programs and the operating system need an executable stack to perform certain system functions. This makes it easier for compilers and compiling interpreters to generate code.

However, the potential threat of an attack increases with this. If the execution of code in the stack is permitted, under certain conditions, the implementation bugs cause control to be passed to user-entered data. This gives the hacker the opportunity to pass harmful code to the remote computer and execute it. Patches for the Solaris and Linux operating systems can be installed to prohibit the execution of code in the stack, but they have not become commonly used since they make it impossible to run several programs. Most users find it easier to resign themselves to the threat of an attack than to remain without necessary applications.

Therefore, using the stack to execute self-modifying code is admissible and independent of the system (i.e., it is universal). Besides, such a solution eliminates the following drawbacks of the WriteProcessMemory function.

First, it is extremely difficult to reveal and trace the instructions that modify an unknown memory location. The hacker will have to laboriously analyze the protection code without any hope of quick success (provided that the protective mechanism is implemented without serious bugs that facilitate the hacker's task).

Second, at any moment, the application may allocate as much memory for the stack as it sees fit, and then, when it becomes unnecessary, free that space. By default, the system allocates 1 MB of memory for the stack. If this memory appears to be insufficient to solve the task, the necessary quantity can be specified when the program is configured.

Fortunately, for programs being executed in the stack, John von Neumann's principle is fair: Program code can be considered data at one moment and executable code at another. This is just what is needed for normal functioning of all unpackers and decryptors of executable code.

However, programming code that will be executed in the stack involves several specific issues that will be covered in the following sections.

The Pitfalls of Relocatable Code

When developing the code that will be executed in the stack, you take into account that the location of the stack is different in Windows 9x, Windows NT, and Windows 2000. To retain operability after a migration is made from one system to another, the code should be indifferent to the address at which it is loaded. Such code is called *relocatable*. There is nothing complex about creating it; you only need to follow several simple conventions.

Fortunately, in microprocessors of the Intel 80x86 family, all short jumps and near calls are *relative* (i.e., they do not contain a linear target address, but rather, the difference between the target address and the address of the next instruction). This considerably simplifies the creation of relocatable code, but, at the same time, it imposes certain restrictions.

What happens if the `void Demo() {printf("Demo\n");}` function is copied to the stack, and control is passed to it? Since the `CALL` instruction that calls the `printf` function has moved to a new place, the difference between the address of the function being called and the address of the instruction next to `CALL` will change. Therefore, control could be passed to any code different from `printf`. It most likely will appear to be "garbage" and cause an exception, with the subsequent abnormal termination of the application.

In assembler programs, such a restriction can be bypassed easily with register addressing. A relocatable call of the `printf` function may look simplistic (for example, like `LEA EAX, printf\NCALL EAX`). An absolute linear address, not a relative one, will be placed in the `EAX` register (or any other general-purpose register). Irrespective of the position of the `CALL` instruction, control will be passed to the `printf` function.

However, such an approach requires knowledge of support for inline assembler inserts by the compiler, which is not very pleasant for application programmers uninterested in instructions and the structure of the microprocessor.

To solve this using a high-level language exclusively, the stack function must pass the pointers (as arguments) to the functions called by it. This is a little inconvenient, but a shorter way does not seem to exist. A simple program that shows how functions are copied to and executed in the stack is given in Listing 242.

Listing 242. How a Function Is Copied to and Executed in the Stack

```
void Demo(int (*_printf) (const char *,...) )
{
        _printf("Hello, World!\n");
        return;
}


int main(int argc, char* argv[])
{
        char buff[1000];
        int (*_printf) (const char *,...);
        int (*_main) (int, char **);
        void (*_Demo) (int (*) (const char *,...));
        _printf=printf;

        int func_len = (unsigned int) _main — (unsigned int) _Demo;
        for (int a=0; a<func_len; a++)
        buff[a]= ((char *) _Demo)[a];
        _Demo = (void (*) (int (*) (const char *,...))) &buff[0];

        _Demo(_printf);
        return 0;
}
```

The Pros and Cons of Optimizing Compilers

When using high-level languages to develop code that will be executed in the stack, the distinctions between the implementations of the compilers being used must be considered before a choice is made, and the documentation supplied with compilers must be studied in depth. In most cases, the code of a function copied to the stack will fail on the first attempt, especially if optimized compiling is enabled.

This happens because in a *pure* high-level language such as C or Pascal, it is impossible, in principle, to copy the code of a function to the stack (or elsewhere): The language standards do not specify how compiling should be carried out. The programmer may obtain the pointer to a function, but the standard does not specify how to interpret it. From the programmer's point of view, it represents a "magic number," the purpose of which is known to only the compiler.

Fortunately, most compilers use almost identical logic to generate code, allowing the application program to make some assumptions about the organization of the compiled code.

In particular, the program given in Listing 242 tacitly assumes that the pointer to the function coincides with the beginning of this function, and that the whole body of the function is located just behind the beginning. Such code (the most obvious to common sense) is generated by an overwhelming majority of compilers, but not by all of them. Microsoft Visual C++, when working in the debug mode, inserts "adapters" instead of functions, and allocates functions in a different place. As a result, the contents of the "adapter," not the body of the function, are copied to the stack. Microsoft Visual C++ can be forced to generate correct code if the **Link incrementally** checkbox is cleared. The name of this option may differ considerably in different compilers or, at worst, may be absent. If so, either self-modifying code or the compiler should be abandoned.

Another problem is how to determine reliably the length of the body of the function. C does not provide any means of doing this; the `sizeof` operator returns the size of the pointer to a function, not the size of the function itself. However, as a rule, compilers allocate functions in memory according to the order in which they are declared in the source code; hence, the length of the body of a function is equal to the difference between the pointer to the given function and the pointer to the function following it. Since Windows compilers use 32-bit integers to represent pointers, they can be converted to `unsigned int` type without any serious consequences. Then, various mathematical operations can be carried out on them. Unfortunately, optimizing compilers do not always allocate functions in such a simple order. In some cases, they even "unwrap" them, substituting the contents of a function for the `call` instruction. Therefore, the corresponding optimization options (if any) must be disabled.

Yet another insidious feature of optimizing compilers is the deletion of all variables that are not used — from their point of view. For example, in the program given in Listing 242, something is written to the `buff` buffer, but nothing is read from that place. Most compilers are unable to recognize that control was passed to the buffer (including Microsoft Visual C++); therefore, they omit the copying code. That is why control is passed to the uninitialized buffer and undesired consequences follow. If similar problems arise, try to clear the **Global optimization** checkbox, or disable the optimization totally (a bad, but necessary, step).

If the compiled program still does not work, the most likely reason is the compiler inserts the call of a routine that monitors the state of the stack into the end of each function. Microsoft Visual C++ behaves this way, placing the call of the function __chkesp into the projects being debugged. (Do not search the documentation; __chkesp is not described.) This call is relative. Unfortunately, there is no documented way of disabling it. However, in final projects, Microsoft Visual C++ does not inspect the state of the stack when exiting the function, and everything works smoothly.

Using Self-Modifying Code to Protect Applications

After successfully passing through this ordeal, the ill-starred example will be started and will victoriously display "Hello, World!". A reasonable question arises: What is the benefit of running a function in the stack? The answer is: The code of a function run in the stack can be changed "on the fly;" for example, it can be decrypted.

The encrypted code severely complicates disassembling and strengthens protection. Certainly, encrypting just the code is not a serious obstacle for a hacker equipped with a debugger or an advanced disassembler like IDA Pro. However, anti-debugging tricks (which are numerous) are a theme for a separate discussion beyond the scope of this book.

The simplest encrypting algorithm sequentially processes each element of the initial code using the exclusive OR operation (XOR). Repeated processing of the encrypted code with XOR gives the initial code again.

The following example reads the contents of the Demo function, encrypts it, and writes the result into a file.

Listing 243. How to Encrypt the Demo Function

```
void _bild()
{
        FILE *f;
        char buff[1000];
        void (*_Demo) (int (*) (const char *,...));
```

```
void (*_Bild) ();
_Demo=Demo;
_Bild=_bild;

int func_len = (unsigned int) _Bild - (unsigned int) _Demo;
f=fopen("Demo32.bin", "wb");
for (int a=0; a<func_len; a++)
fputc(((int) buff[a]) ^ 0x77, f);
fclose(f);
}
```

After its encrypted contents are placed into a string variable (but not necessarily just a string variable), the Demo function can be removed from the initial code. At the appropriate moment, it may be decrypted, copied into a local buffer, and called for execution. One of the variants of implementation is given in Listing 244.

Note how the printf function in Listing 242 displays a greeting. At first glance, there is nothing unusual, but look at *where* the line "Hello, World!" is located. It should not be in the code segment (although certain compilers from Borland place it there). Therefore, it probably is in the data segment, where it ought to be. But, if so, copying only the body of the function will be insufficient; the string constant must be copied as well — a tiresome task. However, a local buffer could be created and initialized when the program is run (for example, like this: _buf[666]; buff[0]='H'; buff[1]='e'; buff[2]='l'; buff[3]='l'; buff[4]='o', ...). This is not the shortest option, but it is commonly used because of its simplicity.

Listing 244. The Encrypted Program

```
int main(int argc, char* argv[])
{
        char buff[1000];
        int (*_printf) (const char *,...);
        void (*_Demo) (int (*) (const char *,...));
        char code[]="\x22\xFC\x9B\xF4\x9B\x67\xB1\x32\x87\
\x3F\xB1\x32\x86\x12\xB1\x32\x85\x1B\xB1\
\x32\x84\x1B\xB1\x32\x83\x18\xB1\x32\x82\
\x5B\xB1\x32\x81\x57\xB1\x32\x80\x20\xB1\
\x32\x8F\x18\xB1\x32\x8E\x05\xB1\x32\x8D\
\x1B\xB1\x32\x8C\x13\xB1\x32\x8B\x56\xB1\
```

```
\x32\x8A\x7D\xB1\x32\x89\x77\xFA\x32\x87\
\x27\x88\x22\x7F\xF4\xB3\x73\xFC\x92\x2A\
\xB4";

        _printf=printf;
        int code_size=strlen(&code[0]);
        strcpy(&buff[0], &code[0]);

        for (int a=0; a<code_size; a++)
        buff[a] = buff[a] ^ 0x77;
        _Demo = (void (*) (int (*) (const char *,...))) &buff[0];
        _Demo(_printf);
        return 0;
}
```

Now (see Listing 244), even if the source code is available, the working algorithm of the Demo function will be a puzzle. This circumstance can be used to conceal crucial information, such as procedures for generating the key or for verifying the serial number.

The verification of the serial number should be organized so that, even after the code is decrypted, its algorithm will puzzle the hacker. An example of such an algorithm is in the next listing.

Essentially, the instruction responsible for transforming bits dynamically changes as the program runs, and the result of computations changes accordingly.

When creating self-modifying code, the precise memory address at which byte is located must be known; therefore, an assembler should be used, instead of a high-level language.

One problem is connected with this. To modify a certain byte, the MOV instruction needs to be passed the absolute linear address, which is unknown beforehand. However, this can be learned in the course of running the program. The CALL $+5\POP REG\MOV [reg+relative_address], xx statement has gained the greatest popularity. Inserted as the following statement, it executes the CALL instruction, and pops the return address from the stack (or the absolute address of this instruction). This is used as a base for addressing the code of the stack function. (However, all these are probably intricacies.)

Listing 245. A Routine That Generates a Serial Number and Runs in the Stack

```
MyFunc:
        push    esi                 ; Saving the esi register on the stack
        mov     esi, [esp+8]        ; ESI = &username[0]
        push    ebx                 ; Saving other registers on the stack
        push    ecx
        push    edx
        xor     eax, eax            ; Zeroing working registers
        xor     edx, edx


RepeatString:                       ; Byte-by-byte string-processing loop

        lodsb                       ; Reading the next byte into AL
        test    al, al              ; Has the end of the string been reached?
        jz      short Exit

; The value of the counter that processes 1 byte of the string
; must be choosen so that all bits are intermixed, but parity
; (oddness) is provided for the result of transformations
; performed by the XOR operation.

        mov     ecx, 21h
        RepeatChar:
        xor     edx, eax            ; Repeatedly replacing XOR with ADC
        ror     eax, 3
        rol     edx, 5
        call    $+5                 ; EBX = EIP
        pop     ebx                 ; /
        xor     byte ptr [ebx-0Dh], 26h;
; This instruction provides for the loop.
; The XOR instruction is replaced with ADC.
        loop    RepeatChar
        jmp     short RepeatString


Exit:
        xchg    eax, edx            ; The result of work (ser.num) in EAX
```

```
pop     edx                     ; Restoring the registers
pop     ecx
pop     ebx
pop     esi
retn                            ; Returning from the function
```

This algorithm is interesting: Repeatedly calling a function and passing it the same arguments may return either the same or a completely different result. If the length of the user name is odd, XOR is replaced with ADC when the function is exited, and obvious consequences follow. If the length of the name is even, nothing similar happens.

Certainly, the resistance of this protection is insignificant. However, it may be increased. There are numerous programming tips for this purpose, including dynamic asynchronous decoding, substituting the results of comparison for factors in various expressions, and placing the crucial part of code directly in the key.

The purpose of this discussion is not to offer ready-to-use protection (which hackers could study), but to prove and show that it is possible theoretically to create self-modifying code under control of Windows 95/NT/2000. How to make use of this possibility is your task.

Summary

Many people consider the use of self-modifying code a "bad" programming style, emphasizing the lack of portability, poor compatibility with various operating systems, the necessity of using the assembler, and so on. With the introduction of Windows 95/NT, this list has been replenished with one more conclusion: "Self-modifying code is suitable only for MS-DOS, and cannot be used under normal operating systems, which serves it right."

As shown in this chapter, all these claims, to put it mildly, are incorrect. The inefficiency of existing protection (programs usually are broken before they reach legal consumers), and the huge number of people aspiring to make their livings pressing keys, testifies to the necessity of strengthening protection by any accessible means, including self-modifying code.

An Invitation to the Discussion, or New Protection Tips

In concluding this book, I would like to share my experiences from creating protection that is, in theory, impossible to break. To be more precise, I believe breaking it on the typical home computer would take thousands or even millions of years.

The analysis of code can be thwarted successfully only by encrypting the program. However, the processor cannot directly execute the encrypted code. Therefore, it must be decrypted before control is passed to the program. If the key is contained within the program, the reliability of the protection is close to zero. At best, the developer can complicate the search for and acquisition of the key by thwarting the debugging and disassembling of programs.

It is quite another matter if the key is outside the program. Then, the reliability of protection is defined by the reliability of the crypt-algorithm used (provided that the key cannot be intercepted). Many crack-proof ciphers reliably secure against the attacks of ordinary hackers have been described in detail and published.

In general, protection consists of implementing a certain mathematical model in a program that is used to generate the key. Different branches of the program are encrypted using various keys. To work out the keys, it is necessary to know the state of the model at the moment control is passed to the corresponding branch of the program. The code is dynamically decrypted at run time. To decrypt it entirely, all possible states of the model need to be tried sequentially. If there are lots of them, which is easy to achieve, the reconstruction of all code will be practically impossible.

To implement this idea, I have created a special event-oriented programming language. In this language, events represent the only means of calling a subroutine. Each event has an ID and one or more arguments. An event may have any number of handlers or none, in which case, an error is returned to the code being called.

Using the event name and the value of arguments, the event manager generates three keys: The first is based on the event name only, the second on the arguments only, and the third on the name and arguments. (See the "*Explanation*" section.) Then, using the keys obtained, the manager tries to decipher sequentially all event handlers. If decrypting is successful, the handler is ready to process the given event, and control is passed to it.

The algorithm of encrypting should be chosen so that the reverse operation is impossible. Thus, determining which event the given handler processes only is possible by trying all the variants. To prevent this, a context dependence has been added to the language that generates an additional series of keys, which take into account several previous events. This allows handlers to be installed for any sequences of user actions, such as opening the file named "my file," writing the line "my line" in it, and renaming it "not my file."

Obviously, trying the combinations of all events with all conceivable arguments will take an infinite amount of time. Reconstructing the source code of the program thus protected will not be possible before each of its branches gains control at least once. However, the frequency of calling different branches is not identical; it is very low for some of them. For example, a special handler can be installed for the word "pine" entered in the text editor. This handler may carry out some additional checks for the integrity of the program code, or for the cleanliness of the license for the software being used.

The hacker will not be able to figure out whether the program is cracked and end quickly. Careful and laborious testing will be necessary, but even carrying out this will not be helpful.

The trial periods of demo versions are limited in the same way. Engaging the real-time clock is useless, as it easily can be set back, confusing the protection. It is more reliable to base it on the creation dates of files being opened; even if the clock is set back, the files created by other users mostly have the correct creation dates. However, the hacker will be unable to figure out either the algorithm of determining the date or the expiration of the trial period of the product. In principle, the date can be found, but what does this achieve? Modification to this code can be easily prevented; it will be enough if the length of the crypted code is sensitive to any changes to the source code. In this case, the hacker will be unable to correct the "necessary" byte in the protection handler and encrypt it again. All other handlers will need to be decrypted and modified (if they monitor the offset at which they are located), but this is impossible; the keys corresponding to them are unknown beforehand.

The essential drawbacks of the solution being offered are low performance and high complexity of implementation. While the complexity of implementation can be tolerated, the performance imposes serious restrictions on the field of application. However, the algorithm can be considerably optimized, all modules crucial to performance can be left uncrypted, or each handler can be decrypted only once. Does this technique, in principle, really allow the creation of applications that cannot be investigated, or there is some mistake in the above argumentation? The opinions of colleagues specializing in information protection would be interesting.

Explanation

Three keys are necessary to avoid an explicit check for the values of arguments, which can be easily revealed by the person analyzing the code. Suppose that the event KEY (key_code) is generated each time a key is pressed on the keyboard. The handler that reads the input information should lock itself only to the code of the event (KEY), and should receive the entered symbol as an argument.

If one key (or a combination of keys) is reserved for a special purpose (for example, for using some additional functions in the program), its handler may become locked to KEY and key_code simultaneously without being disclosed. This is possible because the correct key is produced by a unique combination of KEY and key_code only, and an explicit check for the conformity of the pressed character to the secret code is not carried out.

Looking to arguments allows the sequences sought to be caught in data streams, irrespective of how these sequences were obtained. For example, an authentication procedure expecting the password "MyGoodPassword" does not care where it came from (the keyboard, a remote terminal, a file, etc.).

Such an approach considerably simplifies programming and reduces the dependence of one module on the other. The program represents a set of handlers automatically switched by arising events. There is no determinism! This is reminiscent of the interaction of a biological cell with the environment, and soon may become a promising trend.

How to...

This index will help you find the solutions to specific problems. It is often difficult to locate the information you need in a certain situation, even if this information is contained in the book.

Index